CAPRICORN

David Stirling at Salima, 1956

CAPRICORN

David Stirling's Second African Campaign

Richard Hughes

The Radcliffe Press

LONDON · NEW YORK

SIR PAUL GETTY,
DAVID STIRLING'S FRIEND,
HAS GENEROUSLY SUPPORTED THE
PUBLICATION OF THIS BOOK

Published in 2003 by The Radcliffe Press
6 Salem Road, London W2 4BU

In the United States and in Canada
distributed by Palgrave Macmillan, a division of St Martin's Press
175 Fifth Avenue, New York NY 10010

ISBN 1–86064–919–X

A full CIP record for this book is available from the British Library
A full CIP record for this book is available from the Library of Congress

Library of Congress Catalog card: available

Typeset in Sabon by Oxford Publishing Services, Oxford
Printed and bound in Great Britain by MPG Books Ltd, Bodmin

FOR ANNE
AND IN MEMORY OF HER FATHER
MERVYN HILL

Contents

List of Illustrations

Acronyms and Abbreviations

AA	Architectural Association School of Architecture
ADC	aide-de-camp
AFL-CIO	American Federation of Labor and Congress of Industrial Organizations
AGM	annual general meeting
AMREF	African Medical and Research Foundation
ANC	African National Congress
BAT	British-American Tobacco Company
BOAC	British Overseas Airways Corporation
BP	British Petroleum
CAS	Capricorn Africa Society
CBE	Commander of the Order of the British Empire
CBS	Columbia Broadcasting System
CCEA	Christian Churches Educational Association
CCK	Christian Council of Kenya
CIDA	Canadian International Development Agency
CIGS	Chief of the Imperial General Staff
CMG	Companion of the Order of St Michael and St George
CO	Colonial Office
CRO	Commonwealth Relations Office
CSS	College of Social Studies
DD	Doctor of Divinity
DL	Doctor of Laws
DOE	Department of the Environment
DS	David Stirling
DSO	(Companion of the) Distinguished Service Order
FARM	Food and Agricultural Research Mission
FBC	Finnish radio station
GCE	General Certificate of Education
GCIE	(Knight) Grand Commander of the Order of the Indian Empire
GCMG	(Knight *or* Dame) Grand Cross of the Order of St Michael and St George

GCSI	(Knight) Grand Commander of the Order of the Star of India
GCVO	(Knight *or* Dame) Grand Cross of the Royal Victorian Order
HM	His Majesty / Her Majesty
HMG	His Majesty's Government / Her Majesty's Government
ICA	International Cooperation Administration (United States)
ICFTU	International Confederation of Free Trade Unions
ICI	Imperial Chemical Industries
ISH	International Students' House
KBE	Knight Commander of the Order of the British Empire
KCB	Knight Commander of the Order of the Bath
KGB	Komitet Gosudarstvennoi Bezopasnotsti (Russian: Committee of State Security)
KFL	Kenya Federation of Labour
LSE	London School of Economics (and Political Science)
MBA	Master of Business Administration
MBE	Member of the Order of the British Empire
MC	Military Cross
MI5	Military Intelligence, section five (British counterintelligence agency)
MLC	Member of Legislative Council
MRA	Moral Rearmament
NDP	National Democratic Party
NH	N. H. Wilson
NHC	National Housing Corporation
NY	New York
OBE	Officer of the Order of the British Empire
OST	Overseas Students' Trust
OSWEP	Overseas Students' Welfare Expansion Programme
PAFMECA	Pan African Freedom Movement of East and Central Africa
PPS	Parliamentary Private Secretary
PRO	Public Record Office
RAF	Royal Air Force
RHC	Ranche House College

RNAA	Rhodesian National Affairs Association
RST	Rhodesian (later Roan) Selection Trust
SAS	Special Air Service Regiment
SoS	Secretary of State
SR	Southern Rhodesia
TANU	Tanganyika African National Union
TIE	Television International Enterprises Limited
UDI	unilateral declaration of independence
UK	United Kingdom
UNESCO	United Nations Educational, Scientific, and Cultural Organization
UNO	United Nations Organization
UoY	University of York
USSR	Union of Soviet Socialist Republics
UTP	United Tanganyika Party
VSO	Voluntary Service Overseas
WEA	Workers' Educational Association
YMCA	Young Men's Christian Association
ZAPU	Zimbabwe African Peoples Union
ZHA	Zebra Housing Association
ZNA	Zimbabwe National Archives
ZT	Zebra Trust

Acknowledgements

In books dealing with 'abroad' it is usual to establish the system adopted for identifying changes in, and spelling of, foreign names. In countries colonized by the British, spelling is not a problem, but there have been a number of changes in place names. I have used the name of a town or country that was current at the time, for instance Southern Rhodesia, which became Rhodesia and then independent Zimbabwe. Some individuals' names have also changed: Jeannine Scott became Jeannine Bartosik, Robin and Jennifer Plunket became the Lord and Lady Plunket and Charles March, then the Earl of March, is now the Duke of Richmond and Gordon. Long after the period about which I am writing, David Stirling, Michael Wood and Laurens van der Post were knighted in recognition of services in many and various fields.

After such a span of time, most of the protagonists are elderly and many are dead, so this book has been constructed from a mixture of faltering memories, fading newspaper cuttings and fragile documents, some unforgivably undated. I owe a debt of gratitude to the survivors and many others with whom I have corresponded or whom I have interviewed in Kenya, Zimbabwe and in England, including Dr M. K. Adalja; the late Petal Allen (née Erskine); Joram Amadi; Jeannine Bartosik (Scott); Nigel Boosey; Colin Campbell; Oliver Carruthers; Peter Comyns; Betty Couldrey; Robert Dick Read; John Fox; Peter Garlake; Satish Gautama; Terence Gavaghan; John Michael Gibbs; Timothy Gibbs; Richard Gray; Sir Wilfred Havelock; Christopher Hill; Alan Hoe; Elspeth and Hardwicke Holderness; J. D. F. Jones; Martin Kenyon; Jonathan Kingdon; the late Teddy Kingdon; James Lemkin; Peter Mackay; the late Peter Marrian; Christopher McAlpine; the late Philip Mason; Kenneth Mew; Robert Menzies; J. D. Otiende; the Lord and Lady Plunket; Terence Ranger; the Duke of Richmond and Gordon; James Skinner; John Sutcliffe; Edwin Townsend-Coles; Lawrence Vambe; Eric Wilkinson and Lady (Susan) Wood.

A number of books and papers have been published by, or about, some of the personalities involved, without necessarily concentrating on the Capricorn Africa Society. These have been an invaluable source of information, background and useful quotations. I am very grateful to the authors: Paul Fordham et al; Rowland Fothergill; Alan Hoe; the late Guy Hunter; J. D. F. Jones; the late Philip Mason; Kenneth Mew; the late Michael Wood and Susan Wood. Publications used for background are listed in the Bibliography. I am particularly indebted to Jeannine Bartosik, Paul Fordham, Ian Hancock, Peter Mackay and John Sutcliffe who have generously lent me their papers. The University of York provided copies of the microfilms they hold of Capricorn archives and the Zimbabwe National Archives in Harare gave me access to the Capricorn files they hold. The Colonial Office files from the period have now been released for study at the Public Record Office in Kew, which provided valuable insight into contemporary official attitudes to Capricorn and the personalities involved. The Zebra Trust generously contributed to the cost of the research but has no responsibility for its accuracy or for the conclusions I have drawn.

My greatest debt is due to my wife, Anne, without whose calm intelligence and constant support I could not have given time to Capricorn and much else, and her honest analysis of these pages has been crucial.

Foreword

General Sir Peter de la Billière, KCB, KBE, DSO, MC, DL

Ten years ago I wrote the foreword to Alan Hoe's biography of David Stirling, a man I knew as a friend and the founder of the SAS regiment, in which I served for 20 years. In that book the author described the Capricorn Africa Society as perhaps one of David's greatest undertakings, adding that it deserved a book to itself, written by someone who could bear personal witness to the determination of the small band of enthusiasts who tried to change the face of Africa. Richard Hughes, who was closely involved with Capricorn in Africa and with the successor organization in London, has now answered that challenge and written the definitive history of the Society. This book traces its early beginnings in the middle of the last century to the present time when the Zebra Trust offers friendship and help to overseas students and cash to schools in Africa. Knowing David Stirling as I did, I can understand how his enthusiasm for action sometimes led him into racing ahead of his followers, and sometimes taking a wrong turning. Richard Hughes has honestly and sympathetically traced the growth of Capricorn, recording its failings as well as its successes, of which the convention at Salima in 1956, must have been the greatest.

Among the many personalities who appear in this narrative, one couple stand out as being immensely important to David and to Capricorn: Sir Michael Wood and his wife Susan. After the Capricorn Africa Society closed down in Africa Michael Wood continued to devote his energies to developing the flying doctor service, more formally known as the African Medical Research Foundation, serving people over an increasingly wide area of east and central Africa. In 1984 Wood and a friend of mine, David Campbell, began discussing the plight of rural Africa and the decline in food production, concluding that something should be done to help. Wood was about to retire from AMREF and could contribute some of his pension and David Campbell undertook to be executive director of the organization they started – the Food and Agriculture Research Mission, known as FARM-Africa. After my retirement from the army I became increasingly involved with it and continue to offer support, now as patron, under the chairmanship of Michael's brother, Sir Martin Wood. Michael Wood died in 1987 so I never knew him, though I can appreciate his extraordinary qualities through knowing his wife and helper, Susan, and working with the organization he helped to found.

Because of my long friendship with David Stirling and my knowledge of Michael and Susan Wood through FARM-Africa I am happy to write this Foreword and recommend this fascinating story of a period in Britain's colonial history that has been little reported. It was a period that was more honourable than is generally recognized – when valiant efforts were made to solve the intractable problem of how countries in Africa were to become self-governing while continuing to offer peace and prosperity to all those who lived there, of whatever colour. This important book tells the story of one such effort and should be read by all who are interested in Africa and a continuing issue of the contemporary world.

Introduction

In the 1950s a small number of individuals believed they could change the course of history in Africa. It was a time of hope and confidence after the destruction of war, a particular moment when idealists, and some realists, made utopian plans for a future free from white imperialism and black nationalism between the equator and the tropic of Capricorn. This book is the story of that gallant and doomed attempt and about the men and women who were involved in Africa, and in Britain where enthusiasm and support helped keep the enterprise alive. They were led by an extraordinary man, David Stirling, renowned as the creator of the Special Air Service Regiment during the war in the Western Desert, whose exploits behind the German lines led General Rommel to call him the 'Phantom Major'. David was a big man in every sense and the personality clashes revealed in the archives, nominally about policy or administration, were fierce, sometimes leading to resignation and oblivion. He was a man of action and a visionary whose persuasive charm made him a natural leader of men, and of women.

To realize his hopes for Africa David started a society with a constitution and office bearers rather than a political party. The Capricorn Africa Society, when I joined it, believed that millions of Africans, hundreds of thousands of Asians and tens of thousands of Europeans could develop a system of government that would allow the varying skills and cultures of each race to contribute to the lands they shared. During the life of the society, David's philosophy and programme changed as his understanding of the situation broadened through personal contacts in Africa and in Britain.

There never was a cast of thousands, but there was a wonderfully varied collection of visionaries and opportunists, people of convinced religious faith and some equally firm agnostics, one hero and a number of hero-worshippers who, for their various reasons, came together in an attempt to solve one intractable problem: how three races, so different except for their common humanity, could live together and prosper in Africa.

Today, the legacies of the idealism that drove the members of Capricorn are the Zebra hostels for overseas students in Britain, a thriving adult education college, welfare for country women in Zimbabwe and many memories and friendships. The memories are most poignant for those of us who attended the legendary convention at Salima on the shores of Lake Nyasa in 1956. Salima was the high point in the life of many members of Capricorn, comparable to being a student on the streets of Paris in 1968. Over 200 people, black, white and brown, lived, talked, ate and drank together for a few days in the belief that Africa would be changed forever. It was an extraordinary occasion at a time when people of different races were unable to eat together in public, or live in adjacent houses, and when the possibility that a country could be governed by the African majority was thought to be generations in the future. At Salima we debated and put our names to a document, the Capricorn Contract, which set out our beliefs and detailed the means to be employed in achieving our aim of unity between the races in Africa.

We were encouraged and exhilarated by the press coverage in Britain and Africa. The historian Sir Arthur Bryant wrote: 'the philosophy and work of the Capricorn Africa Society [is] so interesting to anyone with any knowledge of our history, and so full of hope ... for the human future ... it takes its stand on the dual ground of right and expediency. It is this combination that makes it, as a portent, so much more hopeful for mankind than the narrow and selfish racialism of one section of the European minority in Africa and the equally narrow and selfish racialism which it is bound to evoke, and is evoking, among those — the vast majority of Africans — whose human dignity has been affronted by the monstrous doctrine it has proclaimed. To that doctrine the words enshrined in the Capricorn Contract are the true answer, alike for African, European and Asian.'[1]

The ideas embedded in the word 'Salima' have remained potent for many people involved with Capricorn even when they had not been there, or even lived in Africa. Some 30 years after Salima, Nigel Boosey, a Zebra trustee and the initiator of the students' hostel in Bristol, wrote with continuing optimism: 'There is something in the whole spirit of the CAS [Capricorn Africa Society] purpose which savours of the universal, or perhaps even the eternal. I know that sounds grandiose and idealistic, but the fact is that it is there. The cornerstone of the scheme was the concept of African citizenship, transcending race and tribe, let alone the arbitrary and opportunistic boundaries of the colonial territories; and that has to be a high ideal. Indeed, that could be said to have been the fundamental reason for its failure.'[2]

Looking back 50 years to the time when David founded the Capricorn Africa Society in Southern Rhodesia, it is not hard to understand the complacency that was general among the white population, and the level of acceptance of the status quo in much, but not all, of the African population. In 1949, from the Sahara to the South African border, only Abyssinia and Liberia were independent, though hardly model democracies. It was a time when the people of Africa were only half way along the steep and difficult road from subsistence to the Internet, from family group to the complexities of the nation state. The settlers tended to ignore injustice to men and women whose skin colour was not white, while Africans appeared to accept the situation because there were few opportunities to protest. Today many Africans are oppressed not because of their colour but because their mother tongue is not that of the ruling tribe, and protest is still difficult and often dangerous. Under colonial rule in Africa, there were poverty and lack of opportunity; now, pressures of global commerce, population growth and endemic corruption ensure that poverty continues.

By 1985, 20 years after Capricorn had closed down in Africa, the only countries other than South Africa not yet independent under an elected African government were Namibia, controlled by South Africa, and Eritrea, then considered part of Ethiopia. Could Capricorn's founder, and its members, have anticipated how powerful the flood tide of African nationalism would be as it swept away colonial rule? And would they have acted differently if they could have foreseen the future of multiple coups, inter-tribal wars and maladministration? Could Capricorn's proposals have provided the time and the space in the settler countries of east and central Africa for the necessary changes to take place peacefully? These questions are in the background of many of these pages — to believe success might have been possible would give some meaning to all those years of effort.

Underpinning many voluntary organizations is a complex network of relationships: friendships from school, university or the war, family and social connections, loyalties developed through enthusiasm for the campaign and, for some, devotion to a charismatic leader. It is these links that hold committees together through tedious meetings and disagreements over policy, that keep volunteers working on menial tasks and that persuade people to pay subscriptions year after year. The geographical spread from central Africa to Britain made the connections in the Capricorn movement tenuous and difficult to maintain, but they were extremely important to its life and to its vitality. I have attempted to identify and trace the initial contacts and the continuing links between the key individuals to explain the powerful loyalties that the enterprise created, and in memory, still does.

The story of those years in Africa is also a personal one, for I was a member, and then chairman, of the society in Kenya and knew many of the people from the other countries. And I am still involved with the survivors from the Capricorn London office in the Zebra Trust. When I was 11, in 1937, I landed at Mombasa with my mother and sister to join my father in Tanganyika. As we moved around East Africa, I went to schools in Arusha, Dar es Salaam and Nairobi and then to a public school in Natal, South Africa. This education, plus 15 months serving with other young white settlers in the Kenya Regiment as the war approached its end, notably failed to encourage any thinking about the problems inherent in a multiracial continent. After leaving the army I trained as an architect in London, spending the intermediate year in Kenya where I met and married Anne, who has been an essential part of everything I have done since.

At the Architectural Association School of Architecture I was stimulated to think about the problems of the country where I had been brought up, and to develop tentative solutions in a paper written in 1950 and in my final thesis in 1953. On reading those optimistic texts, I am persuaded that I was forearmed and waiting to be exposed to Capricorn when Anne and I went home to Kenya in late 1955. From the early days David had discussed his ideas with the editor of the influential *Kenya Weekly News,* my father-in-law Mervyn Hill, who never joined the society on principle. It was he who suggested I should visit the Capricorn office soon after arriving in Nairobi where I quickly found myself involved in a citizenship committee working on the document we were to sign at Salima.

Although there is a chronological thread running through the story, some chapters deal with the franchise, adult education or politics as specific issues, and others with east and central Africa separately although they overlap in time. The London office, which became the Zebra Trust and Zebra Housing Association housing overseas students, has a separate chapter.[3] In Africa Capricorn survived as a coherent organization for a little more than a dozen years, while the London operation has continued for more than 40 years. It could be argued that in concentrating on the African side of the story I am undervaluing decades of constant and effective work in England. However, the period in Africa was a time of dramatic change in colonial policy when there was always the possibility that some of our proposals might be adopted, and the ideas developed in Africa were the genesis of all that followed in England. The early years of the Capricorn and Zebra Trusts, when properties were bought and hostels opened year by year, were as exciting as the meetings and politicking in Africa. When the trusts became Registered Social Landlords as the Zebra Housing Association, under the control of the National Housing Corporation the story becomes one of adverse reports, rent reviews and costly maintenance schedules for ageing buildings. In spite of bureaucratic controls the student communities continue to flourish, as do the Christmas parties, but the story became commonplace. Higher university fees in Britain combined with less hard currency available in Africa for overseas education have meant that now there are very few African students in the hostels owned and managed by the Zebra Housing Association. The Zebra Trust no longer owns property but maintains contact with the continent from which the original inspiration came by giving bursaries to schools in Africa.

Chapter 1
David Stirling Goes to Africa

David Stirling is said to have founded the Capricorn Africa Society in 1949, three years after he arrived in Southern Rhodesia. By 1955, when I joined Capricorn, there were branches with multiracial membership in Southern Rhodesia, Northern Rhodesia, Nyasaland, Tanganyika and Kenya with an office in London and ambitious plans for a convention to be held in the near future. Although I did not know it then, Capricorn philosophy had altered significantly since its inception — it had become concerned with the people of Africa and had abandoned dreams of an economically powerful dominion unifying the British territories of east and central Africa.

Two factors were responsible for the growth of Capricorn and the dedication of its members: the leadership of an extraordinary man, David Stirling, and the situation in colonial Africa in the 1950s.

David was born in 1915 into a landed Scottish Roman Catholic family whose tradition of service and religious conviction remained an influence on him throughout his life. As a young man before the war he went to Cambridge University, but the Newmarket bookmakers were too close to resist and he enjoyed life too much, so in the end he was sent down for an accumulation of minor offences. He went to Paris to be an artist, and when that failed, tried to be an architect working for a firm in Scotland, until he realized he could not draw. His mother, who was always a strong influence on her wayward son, forcefully pointed out to him that his brothers were making something of themselves, and so should David. This encouraged his determination to be the first man to conquer Mount Everest, for which he trained by undertaking physically hard climbing in the Rocky Mountains in America. In August 1939 these enthusiasms were interrupted by the serious possibility of war, and David flew home to join the Scots Guards. His dazzling and successful career in the North African campaign, as the founder and inspiration of the SAS Regiment, has been described in *The Phantom Major*[1] and by Alan Hoe in his monumental biography,[2] both essential reading for understanding David's complex character. Eventually, his extraordinary exploits were cut short when he was captured in early 1943, spending the remainder of the war as a prisoner in Italy and then in Germany, his attempts to escape ensuring that he was kept in Colditz Castle.

In the foreword to Hoe's book, General Sir Peter de la Billière wrote: 'David Stirling was a legend in his time and eccentric in his day. Tough physically and mentally, he was essentially a visionary. Of course he was a man of action. He was a leader of the greatest distinction whose personality inspired others although he needed his lieutenant (for it was a rôle he never played and for which he was quite unsuited).'[3]

The two powerful and contradictory sides to David's make-up, the dreamer and the man of action, made him a unique and innovative soldier when the British were in danger of being driven out of Egypt by the German army in 1941. After the war these characteristics inspired him in his battle to change the course of history in Africa. David described himself as a political agitator, and as an agitator for the Africa he believed in he deployed the same tactics he used at headquarters in Cairo to persuade senior officers to accept his apparently wild ideas. When I first knew David, I thought his cavalier disregard for authority, and indeed for veracity when it suited him, was the result of being a prisoner of war when it was a positive duty to dissemble and bluff. Later, reading about his early years and his part in SAS operations, I realized David's restless ambition and his belief that the end justifies the means were innate characteristics, reinforced by his upbringing. The Western Desert and Colditz Castle had not made the man; he grew up with the qualities he needed and with the confidence to ensure that they were used to the full. His sense of destiny, though he would have laughed at the phrase, was so strong that in war he often drove himself beyond exhaustion, and for Capricorn he frequently ignored ill health while there was work to be done.

David was an impressive figure: well over six foot tall, though not broad, with a powerful determination to have his own way, a type known as an alpha male by animal behaviourists. Typically, alpha males cannot allow rivals and the men with whom David had bitter arguments in the SAS, and later in Capricorn, were in the same mould: large and powerful. Alan Hoe has said[4] that David's second in command in the SAS, Paddy Mayne, was of a similar age and build, but broader, having been an international rugby forward. Their arguments were especially ferocious because Mayne was an Ulsterman with an inbred dislike of Catholics, especially upper class Catholics. Hoe thought the SAS would have had to divide into two units if David had not been captured.

David's personality and the reputation of his fledgling regiment made an impression on many men at British army headquarters in Cairo, but three were to be especially important to him when he was campaigning for Capricorn: Winston Churchill, General Ismay and Alan Lennox-Boyd. They were, or became, prime minister, minister of state for the colonies and colonial secretary. His family background also put him on familiar terms with members of the establishment at the centre of influence in Britain. His father, Brigadier General Archibald Stirling, was an MP during the First World War and his maternal grandfather was the 13th Baron Lovat. His sister Margaret married the Earl of Dalhousie, whose aunt was Princess Patricia of Connaught, a granddaughter of Queen Victoria, which gave David access to the monarchy and to the Salisbury dynasty, among others. I never heard David dropping names except for a purpose, or seeking any personal advantage from being close to people of influence and wealth, although for Capricorn he used his contacts mercilessly. The files[5] have many letters with salutations like 'My dear Andrew', 'My dear Bobby', 'My dear Aga'; which at the bottom of the page are addressed to 'His Grace the Duke of —' or 'The Rt Hon the Earl of —' or in the last case: 'His Highness The Aga Khan, PC, GCSI, GCIE, GCVO.' This letter opens in characteristic style: 'When we last met just after you had won the big race at Ascot I told you that we were about to publish our Capricorn Declarations. ... I should very much like to fly out to France to discuss the Declarations with you.'

After his release from Colditz in April 1945, David was faced with the problem of what he should do and where. The SAS unit he had created was then under the command of Paddy Mayne; Hiroshima ended the war against Japan before he could take a unit to the Far East, and the SAS was being disbanded (some years later, Churchill reinstated the regiment). He left Britain for Africa within the year, without waiting to be demobilized — he was not formally 'released to unemployment' by the army until late in 1946.[6] In 1941 when he sailed to Egypt round the Cape of Good Hope his troopship stopped at Cape Town giving him an opportunity to climb Table Mountain and appreciate the space and freedom of Africa. In the preface to a book he drafted in 1951, David described his feelings that in 1946 England's authority in the world was withering and that the country was at the tail end of its industrial revolution, with resources nearly exhausted. As a high Tory, he regretted the fall in standards and the general desire for social security, which led him to believe that England could not long sustain her leadership of the Commonwealth. In the war he listened to Rhodesians in the Long Range Desert Group talking about opportunities in central Africa, and in Colditz he read about the continent, so it seemed to be a place where he could settle and earn a living.

Alan Hoe recorded David's description of going to Africa, keeping his inimitable style and language. 'I was offered the job of managing director to a London-based financial development company and asked to spearhead a somewhat superficial study of the vast natural resources both of mineral deposits and agricultural potential of the continent. ... My main intention was to carry out a thorough reconnaissance of conditions and business potential. ... Lots of blackamoors and brownamoors had moved into urban areas during the past few years as the need for labour grew in industries supplying the war effort. ... Britain was pouring absolute sporrans full of money into East Africa, to be used to improve the lot of the African. I spent some months both in Southern Rhodesia, based in Salisbury, and in Kenya where I had many old friends in Nairobi. The whole period was hugely enjoyable. I did a lot of travelling and quite a bit of boozing – it was possible then to find some good backgammon, which helped the sporran considerably. ... Africa certainly seemed to me the place to earn the brasso and stock up on the indispensable stuff. I got my first real insight into apartheid in the Rhodesias. Not the apartheid of the South African, but certainly enthusiastic colour prejudice. ... Beyond doubt until there was an understanding between the different races of Africa there was no hope of prosperity.'[7]

David started a number of commercial ventures on his own or in partnerships with his friend, Sir Francis (Freddie) de Guingand,[8] or with his elder brother Bill Stirling. The construction firm, Stirling-Astaldi, operating in East and central Africa, and the family estates in Scotland were run by Bill Stirling who, as the eldest son, became Stirling of Keir on his father's death. He had followed David into the SAS, commanding the second regiment, and ended the war, like his younger brother, as a colonel. Also like his brother he was a gambler, though more dangerously than David so that eventually he lost almost everything, David said, 'on the turn of a card'.[9] The

Stirling family had supported David financially throughout his long campaign in Africa and Bill Stirling's catastrophic loss meant that David had to earn his living, which led, in 1959, to his resignation as president of the Capricorn Africa Society.

David was a romantic and attractive figure, a celebrated war hero, tall and handsome in a saturnine way with his soft voice and penetrating, rather hooded, eyes. His easy charm and mischievous sense of fun meant we were always delighted to see him and follow his lead. His confidence in the rightness of his ideas was infectious so that wherever he went he left supporters, some forever, and some until his personal magic had worn off and reality intervened. The loyal and unquestioning acceptance of Capricorn philosophy by three women – one in central Africa, one in East Africa and one in England – was strengthened by their lifelong and unrequited devotion to David. He met the first of the three, Jennifer Bailey Southwell, while staying in Johannesburg in 1947 at the time of the royal tour of South Africa when he attended a dinner for the King and Queen in Pretoria.[10] Jennifer says they were 'walking out', which in those days probably meant just that and no more. In due course Jennifer went to England to 'come out' where she married the Honorable Robin Plunket. Some years later they settled in Southern Rhodesia, both becoming staunch supporters of Capricorn.

When David went to Africa in 1946 he hoped, as many immigrants did, that Southern Rhodesia, or perhaps Kenya, would offer him a secure and prosperous future. Africa from the Sahara to the South African border appeared to him to be under the firm, and sometimes benign, control of a few European powers together with Emperor Haile Selassie in Abyssinia and the Firestone Tyre Company in Liberia. Although David had thought hard about Africa in Colditz, he found people in Britain generally ignorant about the problems of the continent – those who were interested in imperial and commonwealth affairs concentrated on the imminent independence of India, Pakistan, Burma and Ceylon.

The early histories of white settlement in Southern Rhodesia and in Kenya emphasize their differences: when the British South Africa Company marched north from Bechuanaland in 1890 there were between 400 and 500 Europeans in the column[11] – Southern Rhodesia was intended to be a white man's country from the start. Further north at the same time Frederick (later Lord) Lugard led his porters through East Africa with only three white men in the safari. When the railway was built through British East Africa towards Uganda to control the source of the Nile and suppress the slave trade, it needed agriculture to make it pay, so Britain had to encourage British settlers to take up and develop land along the line.

Southern Rhodesia had been granted self-government in 1923, controlled from Whitehall on a loose rein by the Dominions Office, not the Colonial Office which was responsible for the surrounding British dependencies. Commenting on demands by the settlers in Kenya for similar status, J. H. Oldham,[12] later an important figure in the Capricorn story, pointed out that 'self-government' was a contradiction in terms[13] – a minority both surrounded by, and fiscally dependent upon, a majority native population could scarcely be called 'self-governing'. His comments were always to the point and were respected by the Colonial Office although at the time he had not yet been to Africa. The charter granted to Southern Rhodesia specified that the terms of the 1898 Order in Council, prescribing respect for native religion and customary law on the holding of land, were to be respected and that the assent of the UK government to any change would be required.[14] The legislature was elected on a common roll but with education and income qualifications set too high for nearly all Africans. The white farmers and people in commerce thought they were firmly in control for the foreseeable future; there had been some major native rebellions and strikes but conveniently in the past. In the 1930s the ruling white minority passed legislation similar to that in South Africa, which established separate white and African areas and employment laws that resulted in an industrial colour bar. The year before David's arrival in the country the overwhelmingly white electorate had given a right-wing party 11 seats out of 30 in the first election since 1939.[15] Sir Godfrey Huggins, the prime minister, called another election two years later, which strengthened his position and marked a division between South African apartheid and the more pragmatic native policies in Southern Rhodesia. Nevertheless, in 1957 the white controlled government doubled the income qualification in line with inflation, and the result was that even fewer Africans were able to vote.[16]

In Southern Rhodesia, and in Kenya, David recognized the roads and the railways, the buildings and services as being similar to those in Britain, and admired the British enterprise that had created so much in the heart of the continent in only 50 years. He found the vast majority of the African population living in rural areas, or in menial employment in the towns. For the most part their concerns about the poll tax or discriminatory legislation went unvoiced and unheard by the other communities or by government, although a few young white Rhodesians were beginning to question the basis of the government's native policy. The two main tribes in Southern Rhodesia are both Bantu speakers, the Shona in the north and the Ndebele in the southwest. The former, like the Xhosa in South Africa, tended to provide the intellectual leadership of the country and is in the majority, while the Ndebele, though few in number, maintain the warrior culture of the related Zulu people. The differences between the two tribal groups, as in most African countries, have underscored political life since the early days of the white explorers.

The populations of neighbouring Nyasaland and Northern Rhodesia, both British protectorates, were divided into a large number of tribes, all of Bantu origin. Nyasaland was, and remains, a rural country with few natural resources except excess labour, most of which went to work in the South African gold mines. When the economy of Northern Rhodesia was transformed in the 1920s by the development of the copper mines, there was an influx of white workers and managers, demanding a say in government in order to follow the native policies of Southern Rhodesia. All three countries were landlocked and dependent on their Portuguese neighbours, or South Africa, for access to the sea. To the north, the colonial power in the Belgian Congo concentrated on extracting vast wealth from the country's mineral deposits to the exclusion of any form of political expression for settlers or for Africans, creating a spurious impression that all was peaceful in the country.

To the east and west of Southern Rhodesia were the Portuguese colonies of Mozambique and Angola, where steps were taken to link the colonies with the metropolitan government. In 1951 the territories were designated as 'overseas provinces' with three deputies elected from each to serve in the National Assembly in Lisbon. The deputies did not have to be African or even live overseas, so the African people correctly saw the proposal as an empty gesture doing little to appease the freedom movements whose internecine wars later caused so much havoc and bloodshed in both countries. The *assimilado* system, in which selected Africans were regarded as honorary Portuguese, was so limited it was equally ineffective in meeting the aspirations of the Africans in either country. In the early days of colonization, Cecil Rhodes failed to persuade the British government to buy Mozambique for £4 million and there was always considerable British investment in the country, particularly in the Beira to Salisbury railway, the essential link to the sea for Southern Rhodesia. Nearly a century later this relationship has been consummated by the country's acceptance into the Commonwealth.

Christian missionaries led the way in opening up the unknown eastern half of Africa in the 1880s to counter the Arab slave trade and to convert the heathen. As the European powers established approximate boundaries between their zones of influence the missions continued to provide the only education available to the African, a situation that continued well into the twentieth century. Accordingly, government expenditure on education was minimal: in 1924 government spending in Tanganyika on education was 1 per cent of general revenue and only 4 per cent in Kenya.[17] In 1926 Christian missions in Africa held a large conference at which education was an important part. Oldham, who had just returned from his first visit to the continent, reported with an excitement that heralds his long engagement with Africa. 'The whole work of the conference was done under a sense that a human drama of absorbing interest and deep significance was being enacted with the African continent as its stage. Within the lifetime and memory of many of those present the opening up of its vast interior had taken place. ... Now for the first time these peoples are being swept into the mainstream of human history, and what their development is to be under the impact of the new forces has become one of the major questions of the twentieth century.'[18]

In Kenya European farmers appeared secure within the borders of the White Highlands (agricultural land reserved for European ownership) and many of the settled professionals and businessmen in Nairobi and Mombasa were also white. The Asian community provided the day-to-day commerce throughout the country, most of the craftsmen, clerks and the essential middle level jobs, and some entrepreneurs and professionals. It was Asian labour that had built the vital railway from the coast to Lake Victoria, although the Asian was a second-class citizen in the eyes of the Colonial Office and the white settlers. In the 1920s it was pressure from the subcontinent, through the India Office in Whitehall, for equality with Europeans and more immigration that first led Oldham and other reformers to take an interest in East Africa. The African people were largely rural, growing subsistence crops in the areas reserved for them, with a minority working for government or for white or Asian employers. Government was controlled by the Colonial Office through the governor and an official majority in the

Legislative Council, with elected Asian and European unofficial members who generally felt they had a duty to dispute official proposals. The Europeans believed these were designed to favour the African population, while the Asians thought they promoted the interests of the settlers. Whatever the subject of debate – taxes, land reform or education, the elected representatives of the immigrant communities had to bear in mind the 1923 Devonshire White Paper, which was unequivocal. 'Primarily Kenya is an African territory, and His Majesty's Government think it necessary definitely to record their considered opinion that the interests of the African Natives must be paramount, and that if and when those interests and the interests of the immigrant races should conflict, the former should prevail. ... In the administration of Kenya His Majesty's Government regard themselves as exercising a trust on behalf of the African population, and they are unable to delegate or share this trust, the object of which may be defined as the protection and advancement of the native races.'[19] The 1923 statement was the result of intensive lobbying by Lugard, the Archbishop of Canterbury and Oldham, who first used the word 'paramount' in a memorandum to the colonial secretary in May that year.[20]

To assuage the settlers' loudly expressed demand for closer union of the three East African territories, particularly as some of them had powerful family connections in Britain, and as a *quid pro quo* for giving Asians the vote on a communal roll, in 1930 the imperial government compromised. A White Paper confirmed that 'The goal of constitutional evolution, in Kenya as elsewhere, is admittedly responsible government by a ministry representing an electorate in which every section of the population finds an effective and adequate voice.'[21] This allowed the Europeans to ignore the realities of the Devonshire Declaration and as their contribution to the economy of the country became greater they demanded increasing political rights. The various statements issued by British governments over the years fully merit Lord Hailey's comment that their 'abstract declarations of policy, framed for the most part to meet the political exigencies of the moment, have frequently been such as to combine the minimum of definite guidance to the colonial executive, with the maximum difficulty of interpretation'.[22]

In Kenya there are three distinct linguistic groups, which makes intertribal rivalry especially volatile. Bantu tribes are in the majority and are spread from the coast to the highlands, the Nilotic people live round Lake Victoria, while the Hamitic, or

Cushitic, people lead a nomadic life in the dry northern desert. Colonial rule generally controlled fighting between rival tribes and was even-handed between them, so a postwar immigrant to East Africa would not have found the differences between African tribes particularly relevant. Many years later, immediately before and after independence, when politicians sought election by appealing to their own people, the destructive force of tribal antagonism became, and remains, extremely damaging to stable government.

The three East African territories of Kenya, Uganda and Tanganyika appeared superficially similar: each was administered by the Colonial Office through the governor and Legislative Council with an official majority, but the legislative framework was different in each case. In all three countries commerce was in the hands of immigrant communities with an apparently calm African rural population. Uganda was a protectorate, with ancient African kingdoms with which treaties had been signed, making it unsuitable for white settlement. Tanganyika was taken from German control in 1918, to be administered by Britain under a League of Nations mandate until 1945, when the formation of the United Nations Organization created a new mandate, supervised by the UN Trusteeship Council. In practice, Tanganyika was controlled as part of the British colonial empire 'until the ultimate object of the trusteeship system, self-government or independence, is attained'[23] as Ernest Bevin said in the House of Commons in 1946. The requirements of the UN mandate were that 'the Administering Authority had to provide educational, social, economic and political advancement ... to encourage human rights and fundamental freedoms for all without distinction as to race, sex, language or religion.'[24] There were no settled designated white areas and fewer Asians than in Kenya. The majority of the African tribes were Bantu with four Nilotic groups, but there was no dominant tribe as there was in Kenya.

At the end of 1947 Field Marshal Montgomery made a tour of British Africa, studying defence issues, and offered the government his robust thoughts on the future of the continent, which he thought was bleak. On Tanganyika he wrote, 'We should have no nonsense from UNO about Tanganyika; it should be absorbed into the British bosom.'[25] This was firmly rebuffed by the colonial secretary, Arthur Creech-Jones, whose memo is significant for his reference to the influence of the United States on Britain's colonial policy: 'There can be no question of going back on the trusteeship agreement for Tanganyika. ... Any attempt to go back on it, quite apart from its other effects, would be violently opposed by the United States and would have a disastrous effect on the American attitude towards our African policy and perhaps over a wider field as well.'[26]

After the war, which left the United States and the Soviet Union as dominant world powers, African moves to independence were part of the change in international attitudes to colonialism. Americans' historic antipathy to colonialism became increasingly important to Africa as their power in the world grew. In 1941 the United States insisted on Point Three of the Atlantic Charter, which guaranteed 'the right of all peoples to choose the form of government under which they will live'. In 1942 a writer in *Life Magazine* expressed the popular American view that 'Great Britain had better decide to part with her empire, for the United States is not prepared to fight in order to enable her to keep it.'[27]

For colonial countries, one far-reaching result of the war was the setting up of the United Nations Organization. Because the only experience of colonialism for the growing number of UN members was limited to having escaped from it, whether in 1776 or more recently, debates at the UN became increasingly anti-colonial. The Soviet Union and China, as permanent members of the United Nations Security Council also called for the emancipation of colonial peoples (except those under their control). Colonial officials and European settlers, in their determination to keep Africa free of communism, tended to discount the importance of these calls for oppressed peoples to claim their freedom.

A quarter of a million Africans served overseas beside French and British soldiers from 1939 to 1945, and discovered that white men were not so different, or intrinsically superior, to themselves. The many who had not had the opportunity of much education beyond the most rudimentary at a local mission school, were taught to write and to read, giving them access to newspapers and world opinion. On their demobilization they were not prepared to accept the colonial situation as sacrosanct, and many, finding the skills they were taught in the army counted for nothing, became unemployed and disaffected. In some cases their military knowledge was used in insurrections against the colonial powers.

A small number of Africans from British and French territories had been to universities in South Africa, Europe or America where they were exposed to international anti-colonial opinion. While away from home, their reading and their experiences encouraged them to reject the assumptions of white rule. They were insignificant in number, but their eventual influence on events was fundamental, some becoming household names, first as detainees and then as presidents of independent countries. At the sixth Pan-African Congress held in Manchester in 1945 the future leaders of Ghana, Kenya and Malawi – Kwame Nkrumah, Jomo Kenyatta and Kamuzu Banda – had called for independence for African countries by 1950, which should have alerted the colonial powers and white politicians in Africa to what the future might hold. From 1947 French rule over her West African colonies was challenged by terrorism and riots in spite of the nominal inclusion of the overseas territories as departments of metropolitan France.

Slowly some officials and a very small number of Asian and European politicians in Africa became aware of the storm coming from West Africa and the seriousness of international anti-colonial rhetoric. In 1950 the Gold Coast, later to become independent Ghana, was granted what Lord Hailey called 'semi-responsible government'.[28] Two years later Nkrumah came out of prison to be prime minister. In the same year in Southern Rhodesia Huggins used the word 'partnership' for the first time, although he was said to be thinking of the partnership between a rider and his horse. In Kenya, colonial service officers in the field were reporting serious trouble among the Kikuyu people: warnings largely ignored by the governor, Sir Philip Mitchell.

Boundaries in Africa were established at the end of the nineteenth century round a conference table in Europe as the colonial powers divided the continent between them, often forcing disparate peoples into one country or cutting across tribal boundaries. Since the early years of the twentieth century inadequate or unequal natural resources have indicated the need for regional groupings – Cecil Rhodes, the creator of the countries named in his honour, was certain of it: his statue points north with the inscription 'Your hinterland is here.' Lord Delamere, the great Kenya pioneer between the wars, believed, like General Smuts, the South African premier and war leader, that 'the white backbone running up through the eastern segment of this vast black continent must at all costs be strengthened'[29] and he remained a champion of Rhodes's ideal. They believed that Africa could and should be on a par with the other dominions of the British Empire like Canada and Australia.

There had been proposals in 1925 and 1939 to link the two Rhodesias and Nyasaland together, both of which were rejected by their African populations. Philip Mason's last volume of autobiography[30] has a chapter entitled *Have You No Word for No?*

quoting the exasperated comment of an African in Northern Rhodesia, referring to repeated attempts at amalgamation. In 1953 the British succeeded in imposing federation on central Africa although the majority of the whole population was still against it. In Montgomery's 1947 report he went further, proposing three large federations: West, East and Central Africa. Proposals for a federation of the three East African territories seemed obvious and desirable to the settlers in Kenya, although resisted by Africans in Tanganyika and Uganda. In 1928 the British government appointed the Royal Commission on Closer Union in East Africa, known as the Hilton–Young Commission, after the chairman. Oldham was one of the four members who recommended, in 1929, a moderate, flexible form of union, but resisted the settlers' demands for an unofficial majority. The subsequent argument, in which both Oldham and Lugard were closely involved, led to the appointment of a further commission in 1930, which established that African interests were to remain paramount but with some concessions to the immigrant races.

For many practical reasons the East Africa High Commission was set up in 1948 to deal with a limited number of common services, including currency, posts, railways and harbours, customs and scientific services, but without dealing with political issues. Later, when the possibility of a political union of the East African territories was raised, the idea created strong reactions in Uganda where the people and their tribal leaders were fearful of coming under a government controlled by white settlers in Kenya, especially after the colonial secretary, Oliver Lyttleton (Lord Chandos), supported Capricorn's proposal of one great federation from north to south. Late in 1953 the Colonial Office denied the very idea in a repetitive and formal telegram to the Kabaka of Buganda. 'Her Majesty's Government has no intention whatsoever of raising the issue of East African Federation either at the present time or while local public opinion on this issue remains as it is at the present time. Her Majesty's Government fully recognizes that public opinion in Buganda and the rest of the protectorate will be opposed to the inclusion of the Uganda protectorate in any such Federation. Her Majesty's Government has no intention whatsoever of disregarding this opinion, either now or at any time, and recognizes accordingly that the inclusion of the Uganda protectorate in any such Federation is outside the realm of practical politics at the present time or while local public opinion remains as it is at the present time.'[31]

In economic terms, unions of neighbouring countries were logical and obvious, but eventually the Central African Federation and the East Africa High Commission both failed, and for similar reasons. Each was frustrated by fear: fear by white communities that they would be swamped by African majorities in adjacent countries, and more often and with more reason, fear by Africans that their needs would be ignored by white controlled federal legislatures. Although political systems have changed in many independent countries in Africa, the original territorial borders have remained inviolate and rigorously defended in spite of dividing tribes and being a hangover from an imperial past.

David Stirling, leaving what he described as a sad and socialist Britain, was aching to be constructive after his years as a prisoner of war. When he arrived in Africa he saw a continent waiting to be developed if problems of manpower and infrastructure could be solved and, having overcome great difficulties in war, he was confident he could win the battle to develop Africa.

Chapter 2
Two Pyramids

When Viscount Montgomery, the chief of the Imperial General Staff, was in Salisbury at the end of 1947, it is very probable that David Stirling discussed the future of the continent with him. In the Western Desert Montgomery had come to admire David, after initial reservations about his unorthodox proposals, and his chief of staff was Sir Francis (Freddie) de Guingand, an old friend and later business partner of David's.

In early Capricorn documents there are echoes of Montgomery's forthright report: 'It is impossible to visit Africa without being impressed by the following points: (a) the immense possibilities that exist in British Africa for development; (b) the use to which such development could be put to enable Britain to maintain her standard of living and to survive; (c) the lack of any grand design for the development of British Africa and consequently the lack of a master plan in any colony. The two primary essentials would seem to be: (a) to develop the resources with the necessary capital, capital goods, brains and manpower, as rapidly as possible; (b) to effect such a grouping of British (or Commonwealth) Africa as will break down the many existing barriers. Economic necessity and sound common sense should be the yardstick; these factors should take priority over all political viewpoints. ... We must think big and have vision. Difficulties will be immense; so they were when we went into Normandy in 1944.'

'Many people will say that what I advocate above is not possible *yet*: I could have written a paper proving the theoretical impossibility of a landing in Normandy in 1944. There will be many people in UK who oppose such a plan on the grounds that the African will suffer in the process; there is no reason whatever why he should suffer; and in any case he is a complete savage and is quite incapable of developing the country himself. ... Immense "drive" will be required to formulate the "grand design" and in fact to get a move on. Many people will say it can't be done: they should be eliminated ruthlessly. Bellyaching will assume colossal proportions: it must be stamped on.'[1]

None of the comments from the Colonial Office or from the Commonwealth Relations Office suggested the gallant field marshal had exceeded his brief in his wide-ranging comment on the future of a complete continent. The CRO note, however, was critical: 'but from the African point of view, it is not so much economic development, as individual freedom which is important. ... The CIGS's plans are completely divorced from their political context. From the purely military point of view they would undoubtedly have great advantages, but ... it is politically impossible to contemplate so drastic a rearrangement of the map of Africa.'[2]

As David travelled and explored the possibilities of the region he came to the conclusion that economic development in east and central Africa was constrained by the lack of trained workers of any race, and he could see no constructive proposals for change. At the time he arrived in Salisbury two Rhodesian-born lawyers, Hardwicke Holderness and Pat Lewis, with other ex-servicemen, started regular lunchtime lectures in Salisbury. The Rhodesian National Affairs Association was an attempt to explore, in a non-racial atmosphere, rational and liberal ideas for the future. They were home after the war in Europe, and as Holderness has written: 'I was quite obsessed with the notion that Southern Rhodesia, with its already considerable experience of self-government and continuing common voters' roll, possessed an opportunity perhaps unique in Africa of achieving peaceful reform instead of the probable alternative racial conflict or civil war, and that its electorate was capable of rising to the occasion if properly presented with the facts.'[3] They were naïve about the predominantly white electorate's capabilities in reaction to the facts, but over the years they did much good in bridging the divide between men and women of different races who hoped that the country could develop peacefully. In 1950 RNAA started a discussion group in Harare, the African suburb of Salisbury, for Africans who had difficulties in getting to the meetings in the white areas of town.

In 1949 David began his long campaign with discussions with an older man, N. H. Wilson, 'the most outspoken and able political journalist in the Colony'[4] who arrived in Southern Rhodesia in 1906, at the age of 20, to join the British South Africa Police. After four years in the police Wilson joined the civil service, becoming secretary to the Ministry of Agriculture and Lands, and then going into farming himself. He edited a number of journals and helped found an equal number of political parties, including the White Rhodesia Association, and was elected MP for Salisbury Central in 1933. At one time he was general secretary of the right wing Dominion Party and chairman of the central Africa wing of the League of Empire Loyalists.[5] In spite of his background in the police, Wilson always said he was opposed to the racial policies of the South African government. It was Wilson who christened the African countries lying between the Tropic of Capricorn and the equator after the tropic,[6] and provided many of the ideas that became the original Capricorn programme, ensuring they had wide circulation through his journalism.

Like David, he was a powerful character, used to having his own way, another alpha male, and in due course they locked horns in a bitter argument, after which he was written out of the Capricorn story and was not mentioned in David's reminiscences recorded by Alan Hoe.[7] When David began to take an active interest in the future of the country Holderness and his colleagues were suspicious of Wilson's background in right-wing politics and regarded David as an 'exotic import'[8] whose upper class contacts in London were irrelevant to the problems of a self-governing country. Holderness and Lewis, who were both Rhodes scholars at Oxford and had served with the RAF and the British army, were accustomed to men who spoke without a Rhodesian accent, but there was still a lack of cooperation. David thought their activities parochial, concerned only with Southern Rhodesia, while his objectives were larger scale, 'more high-flown',[9] so there was little collaboration, although Lewis later joined Capricorn.

David and Wilson planned to write a book, *Africa: Key Continent*, to set out their ideas on the future of Capricorn Africa. David wrote some notes about the book. 'We must admit from the start and emphasize that the medium in which we must activate our object is commerce. Immigration, movement of capital, creation of communications in support of commercial demand and finally the gradual integration of the economic interests of the territories concerned will create the necessary pressures, which will in time force requisite political recognition. This ultimate goal must be nothing less than the United States of Capricorn Africa. ... Also to the fact that we must accept ultimately the principle of native states within the Capricorn Federation. We must be emphatic in this last factor; but of course we must qualify it by being equally emphatic concerning the tempo at which the native is capable of advancing. ... We must provide evidence of the favourable reception of our pamphlet by the native and white population of southern Africa and UK.'[10]

In April 1950 they published one chapter as a pamphlet with forewords by leading politicians and approving comments from two bishops.[11] When I read it in the library of the School of Oriental and African Studies at the end of the twentieth century, it was difficult to believe it was a prelude to Capricorn – the ideas were

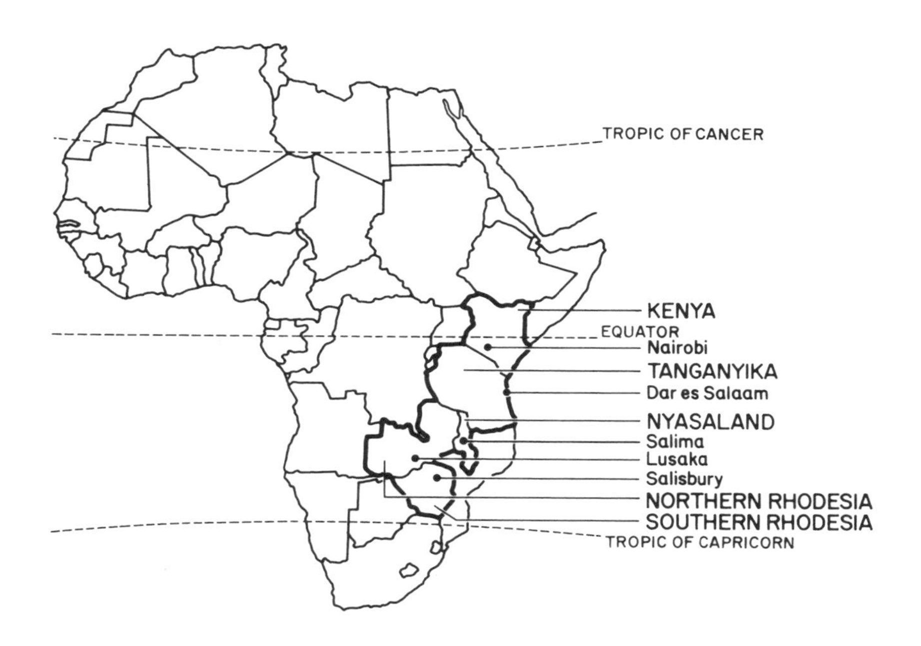

those of a paternalistic white Rhodesian settler. From Wilson's 40 years' experience and David's brief introduction to the realities of the continent, they evolved what they thought were sensible proposals to develop its economic potential. They believed that east and central Africa could become an area of great prosperity and, linked to Britain as a dominion, would be a bulwark against communist inroads into Africa. Their models were the white dominions of the Commonwealth and the United States of America but, aware of the fate of the native Americans or the Aborigines in Australia, they insisted that Africans must be protected from the pressures and stresses of a dominant white-run economy. Their pamphlet opens with: 'If there had never been any people at all in Africa south of the Sahara, or in the three million odd square miles with which this book is concerned (Capricorn Africa, i.e. Kenya, Uganda, the Belgian Congo, Ruanda-Urundi, Tanganyika, Angola, Northern and Southern Rhodesia, Nyasaland, Mozambique and Northern Bechuanaland – Uganda might possibly be omitted) the position would have been greatly simplified. The Europeans would have colonized the country as they did Australia, both temperate and tropical, but by now the white population would have greatly exceeded that of the younger country, Australia. ... The fact is, however, that Capricorn Africa is neither empty nor populated. It has about 40 million inhabitants in its three million square miles; or as many people as there are in England and Wales spread over a country half as big again as Europe.'

Developing this thesis, they concluded the only solution was massive immigration of white workers combined with setting aside adequate land to allow the Africans to develop at their own pace, explaining that this was not really like South African *apartheid*, which they said they abhorred. They thought history was on their side: 'African negroes were in touch with one of the earliest of all civilizations, the Egyptian. There has never been a time since, probably, that they have not been in touch with some civilization or other – Phoenician, Greek, Roman, Arab, European, Indian. Yet the black alone of all the great divisions of mankind has never produced a civilization of its own; nor, when it has adopted the civilization of a conqueror has it been able to sustain it when the support of the conqueror was withdrawn.'

When they were writing their pamphlet 50 years ago, the scant information on the indigenous culture that created the stone buildings of Great Zimbabwe was suppressed by a government unable to accept that Africans had built the ancient city.[12] In 1931 the archaeologist Gertrude Caton-Thompson concluded her report on the ruins thus. 'Examination of all the existing evidence, gathered from every quarter, still can produce not one single item that is not in accordance with the claim of Bantu origin and medieval date. The interest in [Great] Zimbabwe and the allied ruins should, on this account, to all educated people be enhanced a hundredfold; it enriches, not impoverishes, our wonderment at their remarkable achievement: it cannot detract from their inherent majesty: for the mystery of [Great] Zimbabwe is the mystery which lies in the still pulsating heart of native Africa.'[13] The white government of Southern Rhodesia regarded her ideas as heretical.

David and his older colleague were concerned that their proposals, though logical, should not be unjust, and asked themselves a number of questions: 'Does it involve taking the native's country from him? In what sense does Africa 'belong' to the present indigenous Africans?' Their answers were blunt. 'We cannot believe that to develop such an area, which belongs to humanity as a whole, is robbing the few million Bantu who happen to be occupying it at a certain conjuncture in the world's history. The world is aware that there has in the past been grave exploitation of primitive races by immigrant developers. ... The next possible injustice in the method of development advocated is that it may lead to the exploitation by the whites of cheap black labour. This is a real danger that must be guarded against, and it takes many forms. ... The best protection against the repetition here of anything approaching the appalling conditions of sweated wage-slavery of the English industrial revolution is the provision of ample native reserves, where the native can continue his tribal way of life, without payment to anybody for agricultural and pastoral land, for water and timber rights. Then, there must be ample opportunities for those Africans who are capable of becoming professional men and skilled workers, to develop along those lines. There must be nothing in the nature of an arbitrary division with skilled white workers above the line, unskilled black workers below it. Our native policy must not be such as will lead to the exploitation of cheap black labour, by European, Asiatic, or African employers, either industrialists or pseudo-aristocrats.'

They were convinced that the African worker must be better educated, that more skilled white people were needed and that Asian immigration should be strictly limited, believing in the superiority of the British Empire and the white race, and that the African would only be able to improve his position under European (preferably British) leadership. At the time this was a belief held by most Christian missionaries and colonial officers from which settlers and politicians differed only in believing that the African was incapable of improvement. Their pamphlet continued: 'It will be realized that the whole success of the two-pyramid policy depends upon the sincerity with which the development of the native areas ... is carried out. If that is not done with sincerity, then the whole policy is nothing but window-dressing, and could be used as a mask to impose repression upon the native. One must have a policy not only of today, but one that looks to tomorrow, but there is no need to meet at once a situation a hundred years ahead. ... It is too early probably by fifty or a hundred years, even to talk of setting up purely native states as part of the eventual Capricorn Africa political federation, union, or confederation. Anyone who really wants African development to benefit fully the Bantu, will want Europeans to occupy the country in as large numbers as is possible, compatible with provision of ample native reserves.'

They discussed the best type of white immigrant, some holding the view that bricklayers and craftsmen from Europe, especially Italians, were more efficient and hard working than British workmen and should be encouraged. Philip Mason, who was at the Salima Convention in 1956 and later director of the Institute of Race Relations in Britain, wrote in his magisterial study of the development of Southern Rhodesia, *The Birth of a Dilemma*, that it was the white workers in manual jobs in Northern and Southern Rhodesia who made sure the African did not advance.[14] During the war, when production was vital and trained Africans were scarce, white mine workers on the Northern Rhodesian Copper Belt won levels of pay and conditions well above the true worth of their jobs, a situation they were determined to maintain at all costs. The employment of Africans competent to do the same work, but accepting low rates of pay, would be a serious threat to the white mine workers' high standard of living who therefore fiercely resisted African training and advancement. 'Equal pay for equal work' was the hypocritical rallying cry of the white trade unions in South Africa and the Rhodesias. This was a paradox that David and his business friends who wanted more white immigration failed to confront.

The two-pyramid system was designed to allow whites and Africans to develop, each at their own pace, without integrating socially or politically. David and Wilson hoped that complete economies might grow in African areas, writing: 'It is intended that the native areas should be developed so that the skilled native artisan or professional man will be able to find occupation to the full limit of his capacity. The next step being considered is the founding of something resembling the old market towns of rural England, centres for native commerce, industry, schools, professional men, administrative officials, clinics, and so on. It is realized that the growth of a native middle class is essential to raising the mass of natives in the standard of civilization.' However, Professor Edgar Brookes had listed only 'three possibilities for native policy in Africa: (a) complete identification of the races; (b) domination and subordination, either way, and (c) differentiation.'[15] The two-pyramid system was type C plus kindness — 'apartheid with sugar icing'.[16]

Wilson was a man who thought about the issues and was aware of history, and there is something Victorian in his determination to solve the problems of the country, using logic rather than sentiment and starting from the position as he found it. The fundamental flaw in his thinking was the assumption that European control was a permanent part of the equation, and the other error to believe that people in the mass, black or white, were subject to logic. The white community and most politicians in Southern Rhodesia at that time were content to let the current situation continue with minor adjustments to keep the economy expanding. Some, like members of the RNAA, did what they could to maintain contact across the racial divide, discussing the issues and proposing improvements to the existing regulations on land, employment or the voters' roll. Wilson's two-pyramid system was unsympathetic and impractical in the world of the United Nations and growing calls for independence, but some people were aware of the larger picture. Kendall Ward, the executive officer of the European Elected Members (of Legislative Council) Organization in Kenya and later Capricorn executive officer there, wrote in 1950, 'But it would be foolish to disregard the increase in demand for autonomy or independent direction of affairs by the African territories within Africa.'[17] In the same paper he warned of the dangers of federation, which 'is suspect in every East African territory by official and unofficial alike. ... The UK pins its faith, naturally since it conceived such forms, in the development of High Commissions which are bound to fail as they have contrived to alienate the support of local public opinion.'

While David and Wilson were proposing the development of market towns in the African areas, in London I was working on something similar, but with a different emphasis. In the summer of 1947 I went to England by troopship to join the Architectural Association School of Architecture, generally known as the AA. I was as innocent, in every way, as when I had left the country ten years earlier and was unprepared for the ferment of ideas I found in the AA, or for the impact of the art galleries in London, a consuming passion that is still an essential part of my life, but which forms no part of this story. The AA believed in excellence, that form follows function, and that the practice of architecture could change social conditions for the better, particularly for the deprived and the poor. After the damage and difficulties of the war, for Britain was still rationed and exhausted, there was much evidence of the overwhelming need for fresh ideas in planning and building. The challenging attitudes of the staff and students at the Architectural Association School changed me into an idealist, with the confidence to propose radical solutions to the problems of Kenya, which I regarded as home. When Anne and I were married in Nairobi Anglican Cathedral, we did not question where we would spend our lives: it would be in the country where she had been born and where I had been raised, and where our parents lived and later died.

The mix of liberal social ideas at the AA and my African background meant that my third-year thesis, submitted in July 1950, was an examination of the problems involved in housing the growing African urban population of Kenya. The introduction included the following: 'If there is an answer to African building it lies in simplicity and the use of natural materials. ... Such an approach to the problems of building in East Africa would tend to minimize the gap that exists between methods for the African and methods for the European. To some extent I have acknowledged this gap, though merely from the economic aspect; for low cost housing must be built cheaply, not because Africans are to live in it, but because whoever is to live in subsidized housing cannot afford more than a limited rent.'[18]

Although the paper was on African housing, I also wrote about the larger issues of neighbourhoods and town planning, putting forward ideas I developed three years later. 'Grouped in the centre of the neighbourhood, serving all the races, will be the shops, police, dispensaries and market [while] restaurants, cinemas, hotels and the commercial area will stay in the heart of the town itself. In this way, the services each economic and racial group has to offer the others will be available. ... Such juxtaposition of the racial areas will facilitate the setting up of combined nursery schools. ... For children of any race up to the age of six years it would be admirable if they could mix freely with each other in a nursery school, mostly in the open air and taught by means of games and stories, told them by the nurses of whatever race. In this way from their earliest days children will learn a great deal about the culture and history of the people of East Africa. ... Throughout the child's schooling and later life, the early contacts and the discovery that children are the same whatever their colour, should enlarge their understanding of the country in which they live and the people with whom they share it.' The AA was sufficiently liberal to accept it as a valid thesis, though it was markedly different from the cinemas and town halls submitted by my peers.

Wilson wrote persuasive articles and letters to the press supporting the proposed Central African Federation, in which he was backed up by David, who believed the region would then develop economically to the benefit of all. They were joined by a small number of white businessmen in Salisbury who also thought federation and the development of the African population were essential to the country's future prosperity. Most were postwar immigrants, like David bringing a fresh approach to the country's problems and opportunities, who dismissed the conservative attitudes of the older white settlers. They were convinced the economic base of the country must include the African, which they realized meant facing up to the white trade unions. Key figures from this group were John Baines and Brian O'Connell, men with whom David felt comfortable, with public school backgrounds and good war records. Baines was three years older than David, educated at Sherborne School and New College Oxford, had been a colonel in the war and moved to Africa in 1950 to start an investment company. He believed in federation 'because it seemed good business to build a central Africa'.[19] O'Connell, a year younger than Baines, went to Shrewsbury School, trained as an accountant and moved to Southern Rhodesia in 1947 after leaving the army as a major in the Royal Artillery. He also reacted against the lack of constructive ideas for the future in local politics, and much later accepted the inevitability of black rule. After Zimbabwe's independence O'Connell continued to be involved in political and business circles where he was well respected.

Although Wilson had a lifetime's knowledge of local politics and the other two more business experience, they accepted David as the leader of their campaign. During the war David had the confidence in his own judgement and ability to take charge, naturally, in any circumstances in which he found himself, and in Africa his colleagues appeared happy for him to do so. But in August 1952 O'Connell resigned from Capricorn because he was 'fundamentally opposed to the present conduct of the Society'[20] and two years later Wilson very publicly abandoned Capricorn.[21]

One reason for David being accepted as their leader was his claim of access to the British establishment and press; in early January 1951 he wrote to O'Connell: 'You must not underestimate our strength. You have no doubt noticed N. H. Wilson and I have complete access whenever required to the *Manchester*

Guardian (we have had three leaders in this paper in the last four months); the *Daily Telegraph* (I know Camrose and Seymour Berry very well and they have given us ready access when required); the *Observer* (David Astor has recently taken this paper over and sent out Patrick O'Donovan with an introduction to me, and he has entirely accepted our African conception, and indeed has written articles supporting it); *The Times* (Gavin Astor, son of Bill Astor the owner, is a very good friend and supporter of his dominion and colonial editor, Oliver Woods – N. H. Wilson and I are in frequent correspondence); the Tablet (I have known Douglas Woodruff, the editor, for years and it is the leading Catholic weekly); the *World Review* (the recent article by Norman Angel on immigration from England was based on a memorandum prepared by N. H. Wilson for this purpose. I do not like Hulton, but he seems prepared to help us). I also know quite well the editor of the *News of the World*, and Beaverbrook's eldest son, who will certainly become available to us any time we like to approach them.'[22]

David followed this up with an enthusiastic and unrealistic letter to Oliver Woods of *The Times*: 'This Society has a wide membership in east and central Africa.'[23] Later in the year he wrote to Wilson: 'My brother Bill has been staying four or five days with Governor Twining [of Tanganyika] and I will know more of the Colonial Office attitude after dining on Sunday night with Cohen [Governor of Uganda] and Oliver Woods of *The Times*. I am soon to lunch with Oliver Lyttleton, the new colonial secretary and Alan Lennox-Boyd [minister of state in the Colonial Office] at the latter's house, at which I will concentrate mainly on the Tanganyika question, and pressing on with the federation proposals in central Africa.'[24]

The record of the inaugural meeting of the Capricorn Africa Society is dated 9 April 1951 although legend has it that the Society started in 1949.[25] Before the meeting David clearly had Capricorn already set up and was doing a good deal of organizing, if not bullying. In a letter written on the first day of 1951, he wrote: 'I am glad to be able to say that all the members of the Society have come completely to heel and I do not anticipate any further trouble from them in the future, in fact, they are all really pulling together at last as a real team. I must admit, on the other hand, that I had to bulldoze them during the first meeting or two but, thank goodness, the whole thing has worked out all right. Welensky [chairman of the elected members of Northern Rhodesian Legislative Council] and all the other leaders of the other territories are backing it [his proposed convention] most forthrightly and I think the whole project is now set for a really stunningly important contribution in Africa's progress.'[26]

The objects of the Society were: (1) the development of Capricorn Africa — that is roughly Africa between the Equator and the Limpopo — mainly by large-scale European investment and immigration; (2) the political and economic union or coordination of all Capricorn Africa, including Belgian and Portuguese Africa; (3) the promotion of a just native policy, based on the two-pyramid system, and adaptable to the changing needs of the times; and (4) the cultural and political and economic establishment of Capricorn Africa as an integral part and a pillar of Western civilization.[27] The constitution of the Society envisaged a small select band of 100 in Salisbury and in proportion elsewhere, paying a £5 membership fee (more than a month's wages for an African).[28]

There were grand proposals for Capricorn Africa institutes to be set up in various countries in Africa, Europe and the United States. The minutes of the inaugural meeting noted in clause 6: 'The Society does not at present do anything publicly as a corporate body; rather it will debate the issues, decide on the line to follow and then every member of the Society will use whatever influence he can in every direction to promote that line of policy.'[29] 'The president, David Stirling, stated his belief that if the West succeeded in harnessing the resources of the continent, then the West will have an immense strategic preponderance over the East [communism and Asia]. He added that Capricorn would be publishing a book to be called *Africa: Key Continent*, which it was hoped would be the bible of the movement.'

The minutes of a later meeting, with David in the chair, record: 'There followed a discussion on the whole question of Indian immigration. It was agreed that the only way, in the long run, that the problem of immigration in East Africa could be controlled was by the settlers themselves being responsible for the government of that area. The chairman reassured [a member] that the British Government and many socialists were with us in this matter of stopping further Indian immigration.'[30] This attitude was to cause David a great deal of trouble with Asians in Kenya who wanted to be sympathetic to Capricorn, but could not stomach the racialism of this policy. Eventually, there were a number of Asian members but they were always suspicious, with good reason, that Capricorn believed the future was between Europeans and Africans. As Satish Gautama, an elderly Nairobi lawyer who supported radical politics all his life, said sadly in 1998: 'Under the British we were second class citizens, now we are third class citizens.'[31]

That year, 1951, Penguin Books published a book of essays: *Attitude to Africa*,[32] which the Fabian Colonial Bureau reviewed in the December issue of *Venture*. The editor asked for comments from 'three young men from Africa: Mr Abrahams, a coloured novelist from South Africa, Richard Hughes from Kenya and Julius Nyerere, an African student from Tanganyika'. Nine years later the student from Tanganyika was elected chief minister of his country on the verge of independence and came to a meeting of the Kenya Party,[33] when Capricorn members were busy writing constitutional proposals, but by then we had both forgotten the page we shared in *Venture*.

In Salisbury, throughout 1951, David and Wilson continued to work on their book, *Africa: Key Continent*. In a draft preface they wrote, 'Attainment of our ideals is dependent entirely on whether the ideals are set within the inexorable trends of the century.'[34] Isolated in Southern Rhodesia as they were, the inexorable trend of African nationalism growing in West Africa was too far away to be relevant. They wrote of their moral reaction to the nineteenth-century grabs at African territory, which they believed could only be expiated by its gradual return to the Africans, a view that unfortunately was not expressed in their pamphlet on native policy.

In June Wilson went to Kenya to meet the European Elected Members of Legislative Council, writing on his return: 'After visiting Kenya, I am firmly convinced that (a) without help from Rhodesia, there is great danger of East Africa falling completely into Indian hands; (b) in her own interest Southern Rhodesia must press on with the Capricorn Africa idea to keep the Indian menace away from East Africa; (c) with help from Southern Rhodesia, Kenya at least, possibly also Uganda, can be included in that part of Africa which will be joined to the Western European civilization and culture.'[35] In Nairobi he enrolled some influential Kenya figures as members of the new Society, and gave them hope for the future. In Kenya, Kendall Ward enthused: 'I can only say that his visit here has justified itself more than I dared to hope. NH's mere presence here has done more than I can tell you.'[36]

In November 1951 David also went to Nairobi where he attended a meeting of the European Elected Members at which he impressed Wilfred Havelock, and to a lesser extent, Michael Blundell, the leading liberal European politicians in Kenya. The record of the meeting shows how David's ideas were changing: 'DS explained there were certain areas in the six territories which could be regarded as "native states", for example Uganda and Nyasaland [while] Tanganyika was so undeveloped that at the moment it was impossible to anticipate whether it would eventually be European, Asian or African. ... Turning to the "European states" DS discussed the impact of the lower grade white workers on the more intelligent native worker and that the industrial colour bar was one of the most powerful influences on race relations in Southern Rhodesia. The intelligent native, being unable to pass the colour bar, in too many cases used his excess energy and intelligence, which can not find an outlet in earning higher wages for a higher grade of industrial skill, increasingly in political agitation against the European. [He said] "this impasse could only be solved by creating opportunities for the increasing capacity for the native in industrial skills outside the area of European trades union practice, in fact in native Reserve Areas, and in SR in the native purchase areas." The general consensus was strong concern [against] increasing Indian involvement in politics.'[37]

Ward, as an officer of the elected members' organization, was in an ideal position to provide reliable and knowledgeable opinions on the political scene in Kenya and Tanganyika. He was a charming and entertaining Rhodesian with a clear grasp of politics in East Africa and the ability to explain his ideas clearly. He sent David eight pages of detailed analysis in which he listed four attitudes among Europeans in Kenya: the die-hards, the statics, the gradualists and the partitionists – which he called the fortress school of thought.[38] There was no recognizable group that supported liberal or non-racial politics. Ward continued, 'today the average European would oppose to the last ditch any federation of the three East African territories,' and could have added that the average African in Tanganyika or Uganda felt exactly the same. He listed the numerous political organizations and personalities with a frankness that justified the 'strictly personal and confidential' he put on the letter. He ended by asking himself what was wrong with East Africa, and concluded that liberal policies had for too long been choked by fear – 'if fear for the future could be removed then it would be found that the native loomed not as something alien but as a member of one's own community whom it would be a duty to cherish and protect.' He confirmed that the European Elected Members warmly welcomed David's proposed Settlers' Convention to be held in Salisbury.

David may have immigrated to Southern Rhodesia but Salisbury was more a base of operations than a permanent home. He was travelling almost constantly around central and East Africa, to Britain and to America. Some meetings were chasing commercial opportunities while many were to spread his ideas and develop contacts with leaders in each country. Visits to Britain also provided opportunities for fishing and shooting in Scotland, gambling at the Clermont Club, dining with friends in White's and asking advice from experts on Africa from all sides of the argument.

Chapter 3
The Declarations

When soliciting support, David Stirling believed in an ecumenical approach in spite of his Catholic upbringing; an encouraging letter is in the files from the Anglican Archbishop of Canterbury: 'I was very glad to hear from the Archbishop of Central Africa that you were coming to England and I welcome the suggestion that if possible I should see you while you are in England. ... It is a magnificent thing to see people intelligently sitting down to seek reasonable and peaceful ways of development of this multiracial society. I am perfectly sure that it can be solved. What you are doing is a magnificent assistance and encouragement. I wish you all prosperity in it. Sincerely, Geoffrey Cantaur.'[1]

David Stirling and his colleague, N. H. Wilson, after publishing the chapter on their native policies, put the idea of writing a book on one side, probably with some relief. Their next idea was to hold a settlers' convention at which a statement of convictions and proposals, at first called *The Salisbury Declarations*, would be published.

In a paper written early in 1952, which was unsigned but reads like David's prose, he summarized their basic principles: 'It is emphasized that the process will be a gradual one in view of the large gaps between the standards of life of the various races. ... The races will move forward in partnership, each possessing and earning social and political rights consistent with their capabilities and their constitution [contribution?] to the progress and welfare of the community. The paramountcy of any race, either in the majority or minority, is utterly rejected. The responsibility of leadership must remain with the European–Africans until such time as the other races are capable of playing their full part. This leadership (which is claimed solely on grounds of administrative ability and not of colour) should consider itself a trustee of all the peoples of east and central Africa and under solemn duty to assist their opportunity of economic, social and political advancement.'[2]

The rejection of superiority based on race, which had developed since the pamphlet on native policy was published in 1950, shows the first sign of a more liberal approach, which was to result, four years later, in the idealism of the Salima contract.

In spite of the warning by Kendall Ward on closer union in East Africa, David decided a successful amalgamation of the three central African territories would be a good start to his scheme of linking the five British territories in a dominion, of which Tanganyika would be the geographical centre. In March 1952 he wrote, optimistically (and inaccurately), that 'there is wide recognition that Tanganyika is the key territory of British east and central Africa. The reasons for this are that Tanganyika appears to be the richest in resources – more particularly all the requirements of a basic industrial economy, such as iron, coal and the ingredients for the manufacture of steel, her long seaboard and natural harbours. The highlands are suitable for European settlement.'[3] He immediately flung himself and his small society into the battle for central African federation, which was then raging.

He held meetings with the prime minister of Southern Rhodesia, Sir Godfrey Huggins, in London and again in Salisbury, and agreed to delay holding his convention, or publishing his declarations, until the debate on federation was won. David assured Huggins that Capricorn would do its utmost to support him in the campaign for federation. He added that funds were being spent on creating branches in the African areas of the three countries to provide 'concrete evidence of African support for the objects of the Capricorn Africa Society, thus combating the existing impression that the African is unanimously against closer political unity in central Africa.'[4] John Baines concluded that African opposition to federation was 'inspired by a small number of unscrupulous and politically inspired intellectuals,'[5] rehearsing a familiar and long-standing attitude to African aspirations held by Europeans in Africa, including many members of Capricorn. The Society published a 46-page paper by N. H. Wilson, A. Nyirenda and T. J. Hlazo, supporting federation of the three central African territories – *Federation and the African: The Case for Federation of the Two Rhodesias and Nyasaland from the African Viewpoint.* The pamphlet gave Capricorn a multiracial image but did little to change the opinion of the mass of the African population, which was unconvinced of the advantages of coming under a white-dominated federal legislature. Abel Nyirenda and Titus Hlazo, both school teachers, were paid £40 a month by Capricorn to campaign in Northern Rhodesia for federation. Hlazo remained a keen advocate for Capricorn ideas and later proposed starting a branch of Capricorn in Mashonaland.[6]

The mines on the Copper Belt in Northern Rhodesia, controlled by Anglo-American and Rhodesian (later Roan) Selection Trust (RST), were the mainstay of the economy of the country, and of the whole area after federation. In February 1952 Ronald Prain, chairman of the RST group of copper mining companies, provided £1000 anonymously from the chairman's fund to be spent in the African areas to encourage support for federation.[7] Sir Ronald, as he was from 1956, also supported the Capricorn convention at Salima in 1956, though he insisted that his name and that of RST should not be recorded as contributors. He was a consistent opponent of the industrial colour bar that the white trade unions were determined to maintain, although rivalry between African trade unions often made it difficult for Prain to give them the support they needed. In his autobiography[8] he wrote of his early enthusiasm for federation and his eventual recognition that the policies of the white dominated government made its dissolution inevitable.

While supporting the federal government Prain began to make personal contact with African nationalists including Kenneth Kaunda, later the first president of independent Zambia. Prain wanted to understand their intentions, while continuing the group's backing for Capricorn and the ruling United Federal Party until 1959, when he realized both were lost causes and withdrew financial support. Exceptionally, Capricorn was given £500 in November 1960 from his chairman's fund.[9] Prain's approach to African politicians may have been prudently ensuring that the group he controlled was on the right side in the long run, and was therefore good business sense, but RST actually was more liberal than most companies in southern Africa at the time. The other large mining group, Anglo-American, sounded less progressive than RST, while often being the first to introduce liberal measures for their African employees. Although Prain must have known David well, and they had many friends in common including the colonial secretary, Lennox-Boyd, his book makes no mention of Capricorn or of David, so he clearly intended his support for Capricorn to remain confidential. David, on the other hand, refers to contributions from Prain and RST in correspondence more than once without any indication that they were not to be published.[10] Perhaps they met in London over dinner at White's Club, of which they were both members, occasions that for Prain would have been social, and not to be mentioned in the story of his corporate life, while for David they were opportunities to canvas support for Capricorn.

The year 1952 was one of action and more travelling for David: in early February he attended a Capricorn meeting in Salisbury and then went to London to work on the draft of *The Salisbury Declarations*, which were to be a major statement of the Society's beliefs. David used his friendship with Lennox-Boyd and Lord Ismay, the minister of state in the Colonial Office, to arrange a meeting with civil servants at the Commonwealth Relations Office (responsible for Southern Rhodesia) and the CO to seek their advice and comments.[11] The notes of the meeting recorded by the officials read: 'It had been emphasized by Lord Ismay and was now again emphasized by Mr Baxter (CO) that this advice was wholly unofficial and without prejudice to any possible future attitude by the ministers of the departments concerned.'

The meeting went through the draft line by line, attempting to tone down some of the stronger statements in support of the settlers, generally making suggestions and comments, and in some cases noting that 'obviously no comment could be made on this item.' At the close, the officials reiterated that the discussion must be regarded as unofficial and confidential and should not be taken to mean that either the CRO or the CO agreed to the desirability of holding the Salisbury Convention or to the policy advocated by the Capricorn Africa Society. David clearly considered this to be civil servants doing what they did best, covering their backs, and that it could be ignored.

He wrote to the minister of state at the Colonial Office, 'The Society have adopted all the main suggestions put forward by the Commonwealth Relations Office and the Colonial Office. ... I hope you do not mind my giving this letter fairly wide circulation.'[12] This produced a sharp response from Lennox-Boyd who wrote to David saying how surprised he was to read widely circulated remarks that carried the implication that government departments and ministers approved of all Capricorn was saying.[13] He added that this would help neither Capricorn nor government, and if steps were not taken quickly to correct the inference, government would be forced to make a denial. There is no record of the inference being corrected or of the UK government issuing a denial. However, in spite of the official reproof, David could safely circulate an earlier letter from Lennox-Boyd: 'It is very largely on people like yourselves that the whole future of central Africa depends; and I and others are glad to know that men of responsibility are thinking out the great problems which face our fellow citizens in Africa.'[14]

David wrote from London to Baines in Salisbury: 'We must always remember that we are acting as custodians for those who believe in Africa's great destiny and the vital role the continent could play in saving the West. ... Our Declarations will establish once and for all time that the British settler is a worthy vehicle for the responsibility of administration in the six territories. Once this fact is established here and elsewhere, the protests of the African nationalist extremists will carry little weight and there will be little ground left under the feet of the Fabians.'[15] David's use of the word 'custodian' to refer to the settlers was a perversion of British statements, for since the time of Lugard colonial governments had been the custodians of the native people until they were in a position to control their own lives. His letter continued, confusingly, to suggest that the settlers do have a role as trustees over the African: 'Our proposals ... would save the European settlers from embarking upon a policy of fortressing themselves in the White Highlands [in Kenya] and denying their trusteeship and responsibility of leadership over the African. Such a denial must inevitably lead to the economic isolation and the eventual freezing out of the Kenya settler.'

He ends the letter with a paragraph that is pure Stirling, reminding Baines that his contact with the Colonial Office includes dining with the secretary of state and the minister of state, with a frank note in parenthesis on doctoring the evidence: 'Tomorrow afternoon I am seeing Lennox-Boyd and I shall be dining with him and Anthony Head in the evening. I shall give them those extracts of your letter which deal with the matter of African support (I hope you will not mind my altering your first paragraph).'

Some time in 1952 David wrote 'Further Notes for the Salisbury Convention' for consideration by his colleague, Wilson.[16] These powerfully expressed and, from our perspective, deluded expressions of David's ideas in the early days of the movement indicate how far he moved to the position he held a few years later. Note 3 was: 'The African continent no more belongs to the African than it belongs to the European. The only valid claims to a country are those based on conquest or on full and beneficial occupation. British east and central Africa is at present only occupied to a token of its capacity and is only yielding a token of its wealth. It is amoral and unrealistic in the face of the overcrowded conditions in Europe and India to reserve Africa's empty spaces for gradual occupation at a pace determined by the Africans' birth rate.'

In March 1952 the Tanganyika correspondent of the *Manchester Guardian* reported that a proposal for an unofficial Capricorn conference on federation of the six countries of east and central Africa had been published in the local press: 'Editorial comment [in the Tanganyika press], which represents general public feeling, was along the lines that the principle was good, but present discussion [of a federation] was premature.' He added, 'Tanganyika has a special interest in such a plan. It would be, for geographical, mineralogical and political reasons, the key state of a six-territory federation. ... The strongest support has come from ... the Tanganyika European Council.'[17]

Tanganyika was fundamentally different from the other countries involved, as the United Nations Mandate ensuring that African interests were paramount was subject to inspection by regular, and not always sympathetic, UN missions. The governor, Sir Edward Twining, hoped that Capricorn might be used to hold back the tide of African nationalism, and welcomed David to Government House. His ADC being ex-SAS helped, although David never hesitated to call on any governor or prime minister to give them the benefit of his advice. Twining had been appointed with instructions to prepare the country for independence, but he warmed to David's ideas, writing to him: 'The more I think of your Society's proposals, the more I like them. ... I imagine that any political party in England today faced with the more complicated affairs in east and central Africa ... must look for any straw to grasp to get them out of the difficulty. It seems to me that you have supplied them with a sapling. ... It will only be possible to get past our international obligations to Tanganyika if we can get the Africans backing the proposal.'[18]

The governor suggested David should meet Robin Johnston, an exceptionally able man who had ended the war as a much-decorated RAF wing commander and retired to farm at Ol Molog. Johnston said in 1974: 'Twining sent me a letter when [I was] a farmer and said "I've got a most interesting and dangerous man I'd like you to meet." I think that Twining felt that [Stirling] was a little too hot to handle. ... He rather pushed him on to me, where he could observe from a flank what Stirling was up to without being personally associated.'[19] High on the slopes of Mount Kilimanjaro, with long views north to Amboseli Game Reserve in Kenya, Ol Molog was a magical place, immune to the manifold problems on the plains below. When there, with the snow-covered crown of the mountain above the forest, it was easy to imagine that the small community of men and women who had created their productive farms from the bush would go on forever. The unofficial leader of the settlers at Ol Molog was Johnston, who hoped he would be able to play a role in the future of the country. When they met, he was impressed by David and became an enthusiastic member of Capricorn and an important link for the Society in East Africa.

In August and September 1952 David was in Northern Rhodesia on business, then went on to Tanganyika to meet Lady Chesham, the liberal member of Legislative Council, and persuade some bishops of the importance of his declarations, as well as visiting a wattle scheme and a coalmine. After calling at Ol Molog, he was off to Uganda to see a copper mine and then to Nairobi where he dined with Michael Blundell and my father-in-law, Mervyn Hill,[20] editor of the *Kenya Weekly News*. David left a draft of his document with Blundell's colleague, Wilfred Havelock, for comments, met Ward to persuade him to work for Capricorn on a retainer, and did some more business before flying to London.

The hectic pace produced results: Havelock wrote David a long letter with detailed comments and rewrites of paragraphs of the declarations.[21] He was rewarded with a letter about his new friend's connections. 'I had over an hour's talk with the Queen Mother last night, a lot of it about Africa, and told her our plans. She ... is immensely interested in Africa and is intensely looking forward to returning to Rhodesia.'[22] From London David meticulously wrote to those he had met in Nairobi, confirming their enthusiasm for his project and thus drawing them into the net of supporters. But he also created some typical misunderstandings: Blundell found it necessary to write dissociating himself from the proposed declarations after receiving a report saying he was involved.[23] David wrote inviting Rudolph Anderson,[24] an accountant and prominent member of Nairobi's business community, to join the executive committee of Capricorn.[25] Most businessmen in Kenya, as in central Africa, accepted the two-pyramid idea of the 1950 pamphlet, but firmly resisted any more liberal ideas.

After shooting in Scotland, David approached his friends for help with the polishing of his document. During November he sent out 'draft declarations' and 'final draft declarations' to a number of influential people in England and Africa for comment and advice. Some individuals received both editions within a week, so had little time to submit comments. It was a softening up process, to give as many people as possible the feeling that they were part of the drafting team so they would support the document when it was published.

Some did respond: in the files is an affectionate letter from Robin Darwin in which he returns David's draft with comments and amendments on the language rather than the sentiments expressed. Knowing David, he added that he hoped special effort would be made to give facts and figures about the size of Capricorn, 'for all anyone might know to the contrary, you might be the only member and the only branch'.[26] Darwin was then the principal of the Royal College of Art, which later produced a number of important artists, so I was intrigued to find him in the Capricorn files commenting on the future of Africa. Darwin was a little older than David, and although their paths did not cross at school (Darwin was at Eton while David was at Ampleforth), or in the war when Darwin was in the camouflage directorate, they met in London where both moved in 'society'. David's young ambition to be an artist attracted him to a man who was a successful painter and the head of the best art school in the country.

There were delays in publication to accommodate the wishes of the Southern Rhodesia government, which, according to David, was concerned there might be confusion between the official line on federation and that proposed by Capricorn. Eventually, under a new title, *The Capricorn Declarations*, it appeared on 8 December 1952. David had hoped the document would be signed by a large number of supporters of all races but in the end only David and Arthur Stokes, secretary of the Society in Southern Rhodesia, signed it, although Wilson was involved in the drafting.

The document was printed in London on heavyweight cream paper in 16-point Roman type with a note inside the cover:[27] 'This is number __ of a special limited edition of 250 copies' to suggest that it would become a collector's item. The grandiloquent opening phrases of the document, appropriate to its ambitious aims, presaged the contract signed at Salima four years later: 'We, the sponsors of the Capricorn Declarations, affirm the beliefs which have guided us in their preparation and which will inspire us in their fulfilment. We hold that all men, despite their varying talents, are born equal in dignity before God, and have a common duty to one another. We hold that the differences between men, whether of creed or colour, are honourable differences. We emphasize this simple precept of Christian teaching because it is fundamental to our beliefs, and also because we wish to dissociate ourselves from the barren philosophy which determines racial legislation in lands beyond our boundaries. ... We believe in the destiny of the British east and central Africa territories and their peoples.'

The text continues with support for 'a single self-governing federation under the British Crown' for the countries of east and central Africa, in the belief 'that to strive towards such a goal will provide a sense of shared purpose and dedication transcending racial differences [bringing] untold benefits to Africa ... and to mankind'. The basis for their proposals was set out in clause II: 'The peoples of Europe have two responsibilities in Africa, and these are complementary to one another. They have an obligation to mankind to develop that continent jointly with the Africans, so that it shall contribute from its great resources to the wealth of the world. They have an equal obligation to give to the African both incentive and opportunity to achieve higher standards of life, and so make possible a true partnership between the races.' And in the following clause they tried to establish their squatters' rights to the continent: 'The African peoples as yet lack the technical skill, the industrial maturity and indeed the numbers to secure by themselves the timely development of the continent. The twofold responsibility of the European cannot be discharged by reserving all Africa's sparsely populated areas for gradual development at a pace determined by the African's birth rate. It can be discharged, and Africa's development quickened, by an increasing combination of Western immigration and technology with the latent capacity of the African and other races.'

In clause VI they stated firmly that economic progress demands 'sound administration and political stability, which at the outset will call for European leadership ... claimed only by right of administrative ability and experience, not of colour. It will not endure, nor deserve to endure, unless it encourages the participation of other races.' Recognizing the importance of world opinion, the declarations noted that: 'success ... will depend essentially upon a policy of race relations which is flexible enough to meet the special requirements of each territory; and broad and liberal enough to face with confidence the scrutiny of enlightened opinion throughout the world. The Federal Government must hold in trust the interest of all Africa's peoples, and its constant duty must be to ensure that the federal structure corresponds to the growing capacities of all sections in the community. It must promote the spiritual, economic, cultural and political progress of the African. All Africans who have attained the necessary social and educational standard must be accorded the responsibility of franchise and be given no less opportunity than their European fellow citizens to play their part in an expanding, civilized community.'

Attached to the formal declarations were notes on the forthcoming convention, the colour bar, the role of the 'Asiatics' in the future, the common roll and comments on the Society's relationship with the Colonial Office.

The proposal that the ideal was Western civilization based on Christian precepts did not appeal to the Asian religious groups whose adherents helped to make the development of East Africa possible. Caught between the upper millstone of assumed European superiority and the nether of overwhelming numbers of Africans, the Asians had an understandable desire for better race relations. They were naturals for membership of Capricorn, had it not been for references to Christian precepts and the statement that 'unrestricted Asian immigration would damage the aim of encouraging Africans to achieve European standards and of moulding east and central Africa into a democratic state.' David recognized the difficulty and dealt with it like a politician, writing to Stokes: 'The question of Christianity is a difficult one. Talking about Western civilization standards is almost as meaningless as talking about true civilization standards. The measuring yard is obviously determined by Christianity. My stock answer when tackled on the subject by an Asian is to say the use of the word "Christian" has, in fact, already been superseded by the reference to the crown being protector of "spiritual values" rather than defender of the faith (namely Christianity).'[28]

In the notes is the first reference to the franchise that was to become a key element in Capricorn ideology: 'Western civilization can prevail in Africa, only if its noblest tenets are maintained by men and women holding the franchise not by right of birth, colour or creed, but by right of their capacity to sustain the responsibilities of citizenship. The Society recommends that no member of any race shall be admitted to the privilege of the franchise in the open areas until he has satisfied the federal authority of his worthiness. The Society believes that the franchise should be granted only on a test more exacting, although on wider terms than that at present prevailing in Southern Rhodesia. ... The Society ... believes that a strict qualifying test will produce citizens more truly free from racial discrimination and more capable of guarding the best in Western and African tradition.'

David may have been an amateur at public relations, but he was extraordinarily successful. The many files of press cuttings over the years show that David himself – the phantom major – was a star, whose name ensured press interest in both serious and popular papers. The distribution list for the declarations covered 234 publications in the UK and Africa, from *The Times* to the *Railway Review* and the *General and Municipal Workers' Journal*, with additional copies to American papers with London offices.[29] Copies were sent to 45 Roman Catholic bishops and 88 Protestant bishops and Jewish bodies, plus the many people David had met in Africa who had given the impression they were sympathetic. It was saturation bombing and, as David proudly announced, quickly produced a total of 360 column inches of press cuttings, virtually all being favourable. The exceptions were the *Observer*, whose editor David Astor did not support the settlers in Africa, and F. S. Joelson, editor of *East Africa and Rhodesia*, who described the declarations as 'careless and inexact and assuredly not practical politics ... badly timed ... and irresponsible'. Joelson added that Capricorn had disregarded the advice of 'the most influential and experienced political quarters', which indicated that he had not been consulted and was unaware that David had been through the draft with CO and CRO mandarins.

The Capricorn Declarations show David and his friends arguing the concept of a future partnership between the races provided Europeans remained in control. For the first time it seemed that new ideas on the future were coming out of Africa, which most of the overseas press welcomed with relief. A booklet to match the original production was produced, titled: *The Capricorn Convention: The World Press on the Capricorn Africa Society's Declarations*, listing journals that had commented with copies of supportive articles and headlines.[30] In the *Daily Express* Max Aitken, a contemporary of David's, called the document the most impressive event to emerge from Africa in the century[31] while the left-wing *Daily Herald* headline was 'They plan the birth of a nation.'[32]

Editorial comment on the right was encouraging: 'If only heed is paid to [those declarations dealing with race relations] in the right quarters these could the basis of a far-reaching advance. ... The Capricorn Declarations point the right way ahead ... this is a courageous attempt to get away from communalism in African politics – perhaps more courageous in its context than it seems at a glance from distant Britain.'[33] The liberal *News Chronicle* wrote: 'The unrest and disorders in east and southern Africa are bewildering and disquieting to everyone. There is a tendency in this country to see the situation in terms of one race oppressing another and to forget that men in Africa are in the throes of creating a new form of society. One of the most cheering of recent events in Africa is the publication yesterday of the Capricorn Declarations. In this document some of the farsighted Europeans who have made their homes in Africa have ... published to the world their conviction that civilized men of all races should live and work together as equals. ... The dream of a great federation extending from Ethiopia to the Limpopo may be visionary but is none the worse for that.'[34]

The *Economist* was judicious and responsible, as expected: 'A more reasonable criticism is that undue emphasis seems to be placed on the protection of European standards, and whereas in the native areas there are loopholes for Europeans, in the open areas there are nothing but obstacle races for the Africans who want to advance. But it has to be remembered that this criticism comes easily from British armchairs – many Europeans in the territories concerned will criticize the document for placing too much emphasis on African progress. At the very least, the 'declarations' can be said to be a sincere and constructive attempt to solve the racial problem from the point of view of the liberal settler. Unfortunately, the attempt is probably being made a generation too late.'[35]

Comment from Catholic papers would have pleased David:[36] 'It would be true to say that "The Capricorn Declarations" is one of the most Christian documents that has come out of Africa written by a non-religious organization. There may be scope for much discussion on its points, and also on its practicability, but it is of a far higher moral standard than sterile [South African] Malanism,' and *Truth* wrote:[37] 'It is encouraging to find men of Colonel Stirling's calibre concerning themselves with the grave problems of the African continent where they have gone to live. Their activities, given one provision, can lead only to good. That provision is that they never forget the truth of the saying that the ideal is the enemy of the real.'

Editors in Africa were equally supportive: the *Tanganyika Standard* said: 'we would urge that [sceptics] give the declaration most careful thought, for there is very much to be said in favour of federation on right lines – and those indicated in the draft proposals bear the hallmark of statesmanship. They have, moreover, the support of many right-thinking men in Britain and central and East Africa, both in the Labour Party and in the recent government. ... What is wanted now is interracial talks at which all, especially Africans, can express their views and listen to those of others.'[38]

In Salisbury the *Rhodesia Herald* commented: 'the Capricorn Declarations have two great virtues. Firstly, they are sufficiently liberal in their outlook to commend themselves to the native peoples and to overseas critics who suspect the British settlers' attitude to racial problems. Secondly, they suggest safeguards for the maintenance of the European ways and standards of living in the areas where white settlement already exists.'[39] In Bulawayo the editor wrote: 'As should be the case when a large idea is ventilated, there is a breadth and a liberalism about the Capricorn Africa Society's manifesto. It has been, and will be, termed visionary, but so have all ambitious plans when painted on a wide canvas.'[40]

In America comment varied from comparisons with the plot of a Western film to the knowledgeable. The *New York Times* said: 'Audacious plans to invigorate Britain's waning empire are now being hatched in this central African boom town [Salisbury], which, with its gaudy big new buildings, daily bustle and bold talk of new developments, is in many ways reminiscent of American Western cities that mushroomed during the last century.'[41] More thoughtfully the *Christian Science Monitor* wrote: 'A remarkable fact about these "declarations" however, is that they are not the product of studies remote from Africa, but are the work of men and women living in Africa – businessmen, professional men, industrialists, farmers, journalists – living in close daily contact with the problems of Africa, and with the Africans. It is fairly safe to say that no more liberal doctrines ever have been enunciated by such a group of Europeans in Africa south of the Sahara.'[42]

David made sure that his own interpretation was heard in Britain by writing an article for the *Birmingham Post and Mail* called 'A New Dominion in Embryo' in which he reiterated the points of the declarations with some changes of emphasis: 'Look at Africa on the map. Note specially the territories of Northern Rhodesia, Southern Rhodesia and Nyasaland. Nearby are Kenya – so much in the news today – Tanganyika and Uganda. Upon the destiny of these six territories may depend Britain's standard of living and her continued greatness in world affairs. The importance, however, of *The Capricorn Declarations* does not lie only in the economic aspects of the proposals, but also in the solemn recognition implicit in them that the future of east and central Africa can only be built on the partnership of all races, creeds and colours – and not on the principles of racial domination as expressed in Malan's [South

Africa's prime minister from 1948 to 1958] policy of apartheid. ... The apparently overwhelming problems of race relations in Africa would soon fall away if all the races of these territories accepted one goal for Africa and were prepared to work towards its attainment.'[43]

For the first time David suggests in this article that solutions to Africa's problems were being proposed by people of all races in Africa, although evidence for such involvement is difficult to find in the files. He continued: 'The Declarations represent a solution to African problems in terms of Africa. They embody principles agreed upon as the result of exhaustive investigation and discussion by white, black and Asiatic leaders throughout the territories and men and women of varying political beliefs in Britain.' In his use of the press, David echoed Frederick Lugard's campaign[44] almost 60 years earlier in support of the fight against the slave trade and bringing peace to Uganda. Both were known to the public as brave and resourceful soldiers and both had an almost manic energy in their advocacy for the cause they believed in. Lugard, like David, reported with some pride the many column inches devoted to his cause and the establishment figures with whom he dined and brought round to his point of view. Lugard published a two-volume book in which he presciently anticipated trouble with the Kikuyu, largely because of their mishandling by incompetent and callous European travellers.[45]

In December 1952, Jomo Kenyatta, the alleged leader of the Kikuyu uprising known as Mau Mau, who was to become the first president of independent Kenya, was on trial in the remote Kenya town of Kapenguria. His counsel, D. N. Pritt, QC, ensured that people in Britain knew all about what he described as the inequities of colonial justice. The British public, the Colonial Office and the settlers in Kenya had not yet realized the full extent, or the intentions, of the Mau Mau insurrection, though they were learning it involved some horrible oaths and was ruthless in attacking loyal Kikuyu and white farmers alike. Although it was not a good time to publish radical ideas, the *Kenya Weekly News* printed the text of the declarations in full and carried two editorial pieces that were supportive.

The *East African Standard* had a column in the news section without comment. David continued to believe that the future of Kenya lay with the settlers, and in December wrote from London to Havelock in Nairobi. 'The settlers [in Kenya] have behaved in such an exemplary fashion since the Mau Mau trouble started, and the blame for the existence of Mau Mau lies so obviously at the door of the Colonial Office, that there is little doubt that responsible public opinion in this country will increasingly favour the transfer of authority to the settler.'[46]

As *The Capricorn Declarations* were published only two months after the emergency in Kenya was declared, David repeatedly made clear that his campaign had begun much earlier, and that Capricorn's philosophy was not born of fear or in reaction to Mau Mau. It was about this time that David had the masterly inspiration that the zebra should be the Capricorn symbol. The zebra's stripes had symbolic resonance in being brown, black and white with one heart. The animal itself, plump and slightly ridiculous as it gambols on the African plains, avoids being pretentious, as would be the case had David chosen for his icon a majestic lion or a powerful buffalo. His first idea of adding the SAS motto 'Who Dares Wins' may have been appropriate for the size of his ambitions, but nostalgia for his days of glory in the Western Desert was not suitable for the situation in Africa, although the motto appeared from time to time. The zebra continues to be an enduring image in the name of the trust and student housing association in Britain, where its black and white stripes are now fashionable.

When David was back in Africa after the excitement and success of the Declarations he was brought down to earth, but only briefly, by a realistic letter from his friend, Tony McNaulty, in London. 'As you know, there is no concrete Capricorn organization in London. ... Please do not think, therefore, that you have left behind a crisp organization, but only a few limp and uncoordinated amateurs.'[47] During his frequent forays to London, David used the Upper Grosvenor Street office of the family firm, Keir & Cawdor, named after the Stirling properties in Dunblane and Lanarkshire. He realized that Capricorn needed a London organization and base of its own if it were to make any progress in raising funds and influencing politicians and others who would be making the decisions about Africa.

In his February letter to John Baines he discussed the possibility of taking on General Hollis, about to retire as commandant general of the Royal Marines, as 'a sort of secretary general, honorary in the first stage'.[48] It seems Hollis preferred to remain a general to becoming a secretary. In July David again tried to recruit a man for his London office, this time successfully. He wrote to Brigadier Dudley Clarke (who, in 1941, had proposed the name Special Air Service Brigade for David's unit) offering him the job of setting up an African intelligence room in Keir & Cawdor's offices. Although David referred to commercial intelligence, his main interest was to establish a Capricorn office in London. This, however, he did not make clear to Clarke, who wrote a careful letter to David, full of suppressed irritation that he had been let in for more than he bargained for, and did not like it.

He wrote: 'Before my very anomalous position in regard to the Capricorn Society leads us both into difficulties, I want to put down in writing beyond any possibility of later misunderstandings exactly where I stand. ... You referred to me as being the secretary of the London committee. This is not so: nobody ever asked me to be secretary nor – to my knowledge – ever made the appointment. ... I shall not in all honesty be able to take any office, paid or voluntary, in the Capricorn Society. You know that I have never made any secret of the fact that I was not 100 per cent in sympathy; and since the shift of emphasis, which has occurred since you returned, I feel that the difference between my views and yours has widened. ... I assure you that I will go on helping you *personally* as much as I possibly can – should you still want it. But it must be on condition you do not commit me publicly to a course which I have not so far been able to accept in full. If not, I'm afraid we should have to part officially – on, I sincerely hope, the friendliness of terms.'[49]

The Colonial Office had the power to impose federation on Northern Rhodesia and Nyasaland, but in the self-governing colony of Southern Rhodesia a referendum was required to endorse constitutional change. At the time the voters' roll was made up of 47,500 Europeans, 1000 Asians and coloureds and 430 Africans[50] although more Africans could have been on the roll under the income and educational qualifications if they had thought it worthwhile. Africans in the other two territories were British protected persons, not British citizens, so did not qualify for a vote even if referenda had been held. Although some white die-hards worried that it might lead to partnership between the races, in 1953 a two-thirds majority of the voters in Southern Rhodesia supported the proposed federation, which the white population thought would be good for the economy, as indeed it was for them. The Federation of Rhodesia and Nyasaland was inaugurated on 3 September 1953, and many Southern Rhodesian white politicians, including Huggins, promoted themselves to the federal parliament. There was anticipation in the white population, particularly in the urban areas, that partnership was a possibility, but preferably in the future.

Sir Robert Tredgold, the chief justice whose house later became Ranche House College,[51] wrote in his autobiography 'a great many ordinary people took the committal to partnership a good deal more seriously than did the politicians.'[52] Ian Hancock has written that: 'Existing social clubs dropped their colour bar and new ones proudly proclaimed their non-racialism, individuals organized tea parties and sundowners, societies called conferences and published journals.'[53] But Africans saw clearly that power would lie with the white dominated federal government, whatever safeguards might be written into the constitution, and they were proved right. David and his associates in the early days of Capricorn were more concerned with economic development than with the conditions of the African people and were able to convince themselves that federation would be good for all who lived in the region, whether they liked it or not.

Looking back, David's enthusiasm for federation makes no sense when African opinion throughout the region was against it; clearly his vision of a great dominion overcame his poor sense of what was politically possible. Supporting federation was an error that was to haunt Capricorn throughout its life, and was responsible for African antagonism to the Society, particularly in Nyasaland and Northern Rhodesia, where, for many, the word 'Capricornist' became synonymous with 'traitor'.

It was an error that might have been avoided had there been any real exchange of views between Capricorn and the Rhodesian National Affairs Association because Hardwicke Holderness was well aware of African opinion, having helped draft the Southern Rhodesia African Association memorandum on federation to the Secretary of State for Commonwealth Relations. The reasonably phrased final paragraph read: 'We think the time will not be ripe for closer association until there is some real evidence of partnership in Southern Rhodesia's native policy, for example in regard to the economic colour bar, the qualification for the franchise, [land] tenure in the towns and local government. Some evidence of the possibility of such a change would be provided if the government showed signs of making use of African opinion to help in solving the problems underlying these matters.'[54]

In September 1950 the RNAA had issued a résumé of its activities since 1946, which listed 200 lectures (one by Father Trevor Huddleston, some by African speakers and two by N. H. Wilson), 26 debates, a number of radio broadcasts and the production of a regular bulletin. As lawyers known to be sympathetic to the Africans' problems, Holderness and Pat Lewis were often involved professionally on questions of land tenure and discriminatory regulations, which gave them a greater understanding of the issues than most white liberals, and also close contact with educated Africans. Although some individuals were members of both, there was very little cooperation between Capricorn and the Rhodesian National Affairs Association. Holderness has said that there was little point in a merger with Capricorn because their ambitions and methods were so different.[55] RNAA concentrated on Southern Rhodesia, working for change through the existing parliamentary system, including Holderness becoming an MP, while David hoped that five countries would adopt his proposals without specifying how this was to be achieved within their different constitutions. Both were unrealistic: the white majority in the Southern Rhodesia electorate would frustrate effective change, however logical, while altering the laws on franchise, citizenship, land tenure and external relations in five different countries would be beyond the will or capacity of the British government. A combination of RNAA's understanding of the political realities with David's flair, drive and contacts in Whitehall might have achieved more in Southern Rhodesia than the two organizations working separately. The tragedies of unilateral and illegal independence and civil war, which followed, meant that both failed.

David kept travelling and lobbying: in January 1953 he was in Southern Rhodesia, then to the United States in March, to Tanganyika, Kenya, London and back to America at the end of the year. In the United States he was given a dinner by the establishment figure Bernard Baruch, at which he met a number of influential businessmen. He sought a donation from Harold and Walter Hochshild, of the American Metal Company, major shareholder in the Rhodesian Selection Trust, to whom he was introduced by

Prain, his anonymous supporter in Northern Rhodesia. David had hopes of the American connection, as it was proving difficult to raise funds for Capricorn in England.

African support for federation did not materialize, but David continued to believe British Africa could develop into a great dominion for the benefit of all its people, though he had not yet found the means to achieve it. In June he wrote to Julian Amery, MP, with copies to a list of notables in England: 'The ultimate purpose of the Capricorn African Society is to establish the United States of Capricorn Africa founded on a political philosophy ... [with] a common citizenship open to all those of any race who have attained the qualifications necessary to protect western civilization standards. The Capricorn Africa Society is convinced that political and economic concessions and other appeals to the head rather than the heart of the African will not arrest the progress of nationalism.'[56] The last sentence appears to contradict the first in that federation of the countries of east and central Africa appealed only to the head while Africans firmly rejected the idea in their hearts.

Chapter 4
Transformation and Growth

When I joined Capricorn in late 1955 David Stirling had abandoned the idea that economic development was the priority, and had become more sensitive to the aspirations of the African people. The inequalities of the two-pyramid system had been replaced by an approach that recognized that Africans could contribute more than merely labour to the future of Capricorn Africa. I was completely unaware of the earlier proposals until I went through the old files while writing this book. David's enthusiasm was always for the moment and the future and Capricorn's origins were never mentioned.

After federation in central African was achieved David concentrated on the relationship between the races in the countries of Capricorn Africa, and found that he needed to change many of his ideas. One of the influences for change was Laurens van der Post, the visionary writer and explorer who always made much of having been born in Africa and being of Africa, writing with some hyperbole: 'Africa is the oldest and the first country in the world. It was the first country to rise out of the waters in the beginning.'[1] When they met in 1952 van der Post was 46, nine years older than David, and the author of an acclaimed travel book, *Venture to the Interior*, published early that year.[2] Like David, he had been a prisoner from 1943 to the end of the war, but in a Japanese camp. The image of himself as visionary and man of action was made clear in the frontispiece of his book — a photograph of the author gazing soulfully into the distance, still in military beret and battledress, medal ribbons and colonel's insignia in view.

The soldier in van der Post recognized a man in his own mould, and the romantic side of David's nature responded to the passages in *Venture to the Interior*, a story of an ill-fated expedition to Nyasaland, in which the author romances about his feelings for Africa. 'People like myself, whose first memory is of a large, black, smiling, crooning, warm, full-bosomed figure bending over his cot and whose friends for years were naked black urchins, know that contact between Europeans and Africans is ... a significant, almost measureless two-way flow of traffic. The traffic can, with proper understanding and tolerance, enrich as well the life of the European. Or he can, with his own blind intolerance, divert and disorganize it to his own impoverishment and embitterment. ... Half the love we give ourselves would do for him [the African]; half for our bright morning selves, and half for him. ... He would go anywhere we ask for half our love. It is an irony so characteristic of our basic unreality to blame the problem on him, to shoulder him with our fears and our sin, to call it a black, a native, an African problem.'

Van der Post's romantic view of the African led him to make some extraordinary statements. In 1952, the year the Mau Mau in Kenya began their revolt, he told a meeting of the Royal African Society that it was: 'a legend that my black countrymen are hungry ... for a social and political system such as ours. ... They need medicines and doctors more than political slogans and trade unions. ... The black man needs a long sustained period of growth, of mental stability and security, of training and preparation. ... Given this, a hundred years or more can peacefully and fruitfully go by before he will need many of the things which are now being wilfully thrust upon him.'[3] At that stage in his odyssey David might have applauded, though there is no evidence that he heard or read his new friend's speech.

Alan Hoe recorded David's memories of their meeting: 'Laurens van der Post, who knew the country and the people better than all of us put together, was an inspiration, but he came later. ... By this time [1953, he] was firmly with us. It was reading his book *Venture to the Interior* which first drew my attention to him. ... I vowed that I would meet him. ... We were both just back from different parts of Africa and I told him of Capricorn and my years working for the Society and that I thought his help would be crucial to us. ... Laurens said he was ready to campaign for us. From then on his enthusiasm and knowledge of the African people propped up our morale. ... He constantly prompted our thinking and supported our sense of purpose.'[4]

David was intrigued and encouraged to meet a real Afrikaner with a liberal attitude to the African. Van der Post first appears in the record at a Capricorn meeting in Salisbury in mid-1952, when David and his friends were working on the text of the Declarations.[5] Memories long after events are sometimes self-serving: in

1997 van der Post issued a paper entitled 'The Laurens van der Post Foundation for Africa and the Worldwide Advancement of the Humanities'[6] in which he wrote: 'The first major step was van der Post's creation of the Capricorn Society of Africa with his great friend David Stirling.' He attended only a few Capricorn committee meetings but there is no doubt that van der Post's emotive and sentimental attitude to the problems of the continent contributed to David's philosophy at a moment when he was searching for a fresh approach. The tone of the documents produced after the meeting between the two men showed greater understanding of the feelings of the African people than those written with his businessmen friends in Salisbury.

In 1953 David began talent spotting among the African elite of Salisbury, and discovered young men who were educated and amusing with a self-deprecating sense of humour like his own. They had been to university, were better educated than the general run of the local whites who were determined to keep them in their place and although a tiny minority, they understood only too well the frustrations and indignities of their fellow Africans. David persuaded some to join Capricorn and a few stayed with the Society until after the Salima Convention in 1956: they were excited by the scale of his vision and, although some realized that it was only a version of the 'partnership' that was being offered as the basis of the federal concept, they really hoped that government sponsored partnership with the white population would work. In the atmosphere of the time they had to be particularly brave to join a white-dominated society, so their disappointment was bitter when they realized that it was a sham because little changed in the laws that controlled the life of the average African. It was then, to quote Hardwicke Holderness, that they became 'reluctant revolutionaries'. Although I met some of these interesting men at Salima, or briefly in January 1960, my memory is now unreliable so I asked Elspeth Holderness, who knew them well over many years, to remind me of their physical appearance.[7]

An early recruit was Herbert Chitepo, educated at Fort Hare University in South Africa and the Inns of Court in London, who was the first African from Southern Rhodesia to qualify as a barrister. Tall and athletic with a lively face and ready smile, he was relaxed, confident and a determined reformer, supported by his attractive and clever wife, Victoria. Although the Southern Rhodesian Bar was proud of admitting him as an advocate of the High Court in 1954, in his daily life he had to suffer the same problems as his countrymen. He was over thirty, a qualified barrister, but he was still called 'boy' and told to wait outside European shops. Philip Mason wrote of meeting him in Salisbury in about 1955, two years after the start of the federation and alleged partnership in central Africa,[8] and how Chitepo said, when they next met: 'Did you realize that I was breaking the law in three respects that evening? I was in a white area after dark. I drank whisky – and no native may drink whisky. I was driving a car in a white area.' After some years of living with these insults, 'with dignity and restraint' Mason wrote, in 1960 Chitepo turned to African politics to become a member first of the National Democratic Party (NDP) and then of the Zimbabwe African People's Union (ZAPU) when NDP was banned. In 1962 he left Southern Rhodesia to become director of public prosecutions in Tanganyika when Julius Nyerere was prime minister. In 1975 he was assassinated outside his house in Lusaka, allegedly by agents from Salisbury during the war in Southern Rhodesia, although it has also been suggested that his death was part of a leadership struggle within the independence movement. His remains were later buried in Heroes Acre in Harare and his widow, Victoria, was made a cabinet minister in Robert Mugabe's first government.

Lawrence Vambe I know as a friend in London and Harare and can appreciate Elspeth Holderness's comment that as a young man, tall and well educated, he had the same charm and slow, amused way of speaking as he has today. She has written that he was serious about reform and was one of the keenest and most determined leaders in all the projects that were started in the 1950s. He became a dedicated member of Capricorn in 1953 after he met David, whom he described as 'a breath of fresh air'.[9] He had been brought up as a Catholic, and had tried to be a priest before training to be a teacher and going to St Francis College, Marianhill, in Natal. In spite of the savage racial attitude of the government, South Africa did offer Africans an opportunity for a university education. Vambe joined the African Press in Salisbury in 1946, when he was 29, and by the time he met David he was acting chief editor of nine newspapers in various languages, wielding great influence with Africans in central Africa.

Vambe has said that, being a realist, he recognized the white Rhodesians were not easily going to give up power, so the solution was for the country to be governed by an elite of black and white together until the whites were prepared to accept government by the majority. Vambe supported the concept of a selective franchise in the interim and thought that David, being himself part of an elite, was not enthusiastic about one-man-one-vote. Vambe was never a political animal, and in 1959 went to London as information officer for the federal government, a job for which he was later appointed an MBE. After three years he realized that the policies of Roy Welensky, the federal prime minister, were so biased in favour of the white minority that he resigned. In 1963 he joined the mining group Anglo-American, for whom he worked in the information office in London for some years, staying on in Britain as a businessman and author[10] until 1979 when he went home to a country on the threshold of independence. Vambe has continued in business in Zimbabwe and observes contemporary events with wry detachment and great sadness.

Lawrence Vambe, 2000

A keen, but not active, Capricorn recruit was Jasper Z. Savanhu, a contemporary of Vambe and also a journalist. Savanhu had argued against federation when he went to London in 1952 with Nkomo and Sir Godfrey Huggins, the Southern Rhodesia prime minister, but after the event he accepted it and served as an MP throughout the life of the federation as one of the few African members of the federal parliament. In 1958 Welensky appointed him parliamentary secretary to the minister of home affairs, a post from which he resigned in 1962 in protest at the lack of real partnership. Savanhu became irrelevant in African politics after the dissolution of the federation, but he was not inactive: when he died in 1984 he left 13 children and 19 grandchildren.

A political survivor from the group is Nathan Shamuyarira, who has served as a minister in the government of Zimbabwe. During the war of independence he famously said, 'I am prepared to die for my country, but not to kill.'[11] Three Africans joined and worked for Capricorn as executive officers: Chad Chipunza and T. J. Hlazo, who worked with Peter Mackay setting up the convention at Salima in 1956 and, later, Leopold Takawira. Chipunza was a cheerful, short and round man who tried to help his people, serving loyally on committees. Takawira was more lively: short and energetic, spontaneous and brave: David called him 'Napoleon' and for the nationalists he was 'the Lion of Zimbabwe' when, in frustration, he turned to African politics.[12] He wrote to David of the true and lasting brotherhood between members of the old Capricorn group, adding that the relationship between himself and David had almost become a blood one: 'we are brothers.' Many Africans who joined Capricorn enjoyed the 'warm feeling about belonging to a wider movement which had branches and influential contacts in East Africa, Britain and the United States'.[13]

In mid-1953 the Interracial Association of Southern Rhodesia was formed to bring together people of all races prepared to do some constructive thinking about the future of the country. There was already the Inter-Racial Club in Salisbury, at one time in the same building as Capricorn, as well as the original Rhodesian National Affairs Association, which continued to hold lunch-time lectures for many years. The founders of the new group wanted to study the day-to-day issues that bedevilled race relations and politics in the country. They worked on detailed proposals for improvements in the law in a number of specific areas: restrictions on African ownership of land in the townships; the development of local government in African areas; pass and liquor laws, and the liberalization of franchise qualifications. They produced a quarterly journal, *Concorde*, edited by Mackay, later to be a Capricorn executive officer.

They believed that to concentrate on removing the day-to-day legal restrictions and humiliations suffered by the African in Southern Rhodesia was more effective than what they saw as the grand gestures on a continental scale proposed by David. The historian Ian Hancock (who lived in Southern Rhodesia for some years) has written that cooperation faltered because the Interracial Association members disliked the 'imperial' element in Capricorn and Holderness felt he could not work with David.[14] A letter from David to Jeannine Scott shows that an attempt was made in 1954 to coordinate activities, but only on his terms so it is not surprising that nothing came of it. 'We had a meeting last night of representatives of the United Races Club, the Interracial Association, the Federated Welfare Societies, and the Capricorn Africa Society. The meeting took place in my house and the Bishop of Mashonaland was in the chair. The Bishop made no bones about his conviction that the other three organizations should do their utmost to help the Capricorn Africa Society, as he felt that the true solution lay with them rather than the other groups. We agreed to set up a small coordinating committee to make quite certain that we did not overlap and that our separate organizations did not cause confusion with the public. Six weeks ago our membership was not much greater than that of the Interracial Association; it is now nearly twice as big.'[15]

In Kenya, 1953 was a bad year: the Mau Mau rebellion was at its worst with British troops flown in as thousands of 'loyal' Kikuyu were killed and more white families on isolated farms murdered. European farmers dined with a revolver on the table and slept with one under the pillow. For many settlers the worst was the thought that Kikuyu servants and farm workers, whom they had known and relied upon for years, might have been forced to take an oath to attack their employers. For many, the only solution was to dismiss their Kikuyu staff, regretting that they would join the unemployed in Nairobi, be rounded up and detained by the police or join a gang in the forest taking with them knowledge of the household's weak spots.

The Kikuyu, the largest tribe in Kenya, had the advantage of missionary schooling and the proximity of Nairobi as a centre for employment so, up until 1952, there were more Kikuyu employed in the city than Africans from other tribes. When the emergency was declared large numbers were rounded up by the police and detained or sent home to newly built villages in the reserve. The Kikuyu are a religious people, so the Mau Mau leaders adapted hymns and prayers learnt from the missionaries to create an alternative to Christianity and made sure of support by bestial oaths and the threat of an unpleasant end if the oath were denied. The subversion of Christianity crystallized opposition to the movement among African Christians, which explains the large number of Kikuyu who were murdered by the gangs. By nature and history they were clannish and excluded other tribes from their secret organization, which allowed the Colonial Office and the settlers to believe that Mau Mau was not a national uprising for independence but a localized and atavistic aberration – mass hysteria – to be suppressed at all costs. It was both, as Louis Leakey, the distinguished palaeontologist who had been brought up among the Kikuyu and understood them well, made clear when he listed the seven aims of Mau Mau: (1) recover the land stolen from us by the white man; (2) obtain self-government; (3) destroy Christianity;

(4) restore ancient customs whenever possible; (5) drive out, or subjugate, all foreigners; (6) abolish soil conservation; and (7) increase secular education.[16]

There were individuals of other tribes who subscribed to many of these aims and a few fought in the forest beside the Kikuyu. Although Mau Mau was crushed by 1956, at great cost in lives, historians have suggested that the end of white rule in Kenya began in October 1952, when Jomo Kenyatta and the other leaders of the Kenya African Union were arrested. During the emergency liberal-thinking Europeans and Asians began to doubt the possibility of a multiracial future for Kenya, while on the other hand, idealists redoubled their efforts to build bridges between the races in the belief that most Africans were not involved and did not support the aims of Mau Mau.

Living on a small farm at Limuru, 20 miles outside Nairobi on the edge of the Kikuyu reserve, was a couple whose distress over the horrors of Mau Mau did not diminish their sense of mission in Africa. Michael Wood was a surgeon who had come to Nairobi after medical training in London, because the high altitude helped his chronic asthma. The dry air and cool nights in Nairobi, at 5800 feet (2750 metres) above sea level were ideal, and Limuru at nearly 7000 feet (3300 metres) even better, and much colder at night. After two years at Winchester College, he finished his education in Switzerland because of his asthma, becoming a skilled skier and mountaineer. By nature Wood was a humanitarian, strengthened by his Church of England upbringing and a powerful determination. When he realized how much of the country was without any medical services, he learnt to fly to reach patients around the country, often in areas that had never seen a nurse, doctor or surgeon. His wife, Susan, born in Africa into an evangelical missionary background,[17] was soon involved in voluntary work with the Red Cross and the East African Women's League. The Woods were a striking couple: Michael tall and generally smiling, with hair brushed straight back from a broad forehead; Susan with red hair, bright blue eyes and a pale complexion. They were to become an essential part of Capricorn.

The surgeon whose practice Wood joined in Nairobi, Gerald Anderson, was a leading figure in the Moral Rearmament movement, whose members were known in England between the wars as Buchmanites after the American founder, Dr Frank Buchman. Capricorn was occasionally linked with MRA because both organizations gave the impression of being 'holier than thou' and both had a strong element of idealism. In the public mind it was a connection that was strengthened in many ways during the time Capricorn was active.

For two years in the emergency, a leading MRA man, Alan Knight, was in control of the large Mau Mau detention camp at Athi River, with a team from the USA, Switzerland and Denmark attempting to cleanse the detainees of their oaths. Anderson and Wood visited the camp regularly, Wood going only as a doctor. Canon Martin Capon, who had been brought to Kenya as a missionary by Susan Wood's father, was closely involved in both MRA and Capricorn.[18]

Michael Wood, c.1975 (photo: AMREF)

In 1953 David wrote in support of the movement to the colonial secretary: I am 'supporting an MRA team who want to visit Africa. ... [W]hile not operating members of MRA, [we are] convinced that they have helped to a most remarkable extent in taking the heat out of racial pressures in Africa.'[19] This letter in the files may have been why a later Colonial Office memo disparagingly bracketed Capricorn with MRA. The movement was also active in Southern Rhodesia, claiming Savanhu and Nkomo as adherents after they had been tempted to visit the MRA centre at Caux in Switzerland. Vambe was wooed with offers of a trip to Switzerland but resisted their offers.

In 1955 the Kenya Police Special Branch wrote an analysis of the security implications of the movement: Moral Rearmament (MRA) 'is clearly an attempt to practise Christian doctrines in a specific manner, and the only thing extraordinary about it is that MRA enthusiasts themselves should consider that the results are so remarkable. ... [In the Athi River camp] they failed dismally in their efforts to rehabilitate these hard-core detainees. They were, however, most unwilling to admit failure and in fact claimed that they had achieved striking successes. This unjustifiable claim was given wide publicity in Kenya and throughout MRA centres all over the world. ... The chief danger of the movement lies in the fact that it plays on emotionalism and exhibitionism, and so provides opportunities for the unscrupulous to make use of the movement for their own purposes. ... The movement in Kenya does not present a security risk at present and the activities of genuine converts would be most unlikely to result in subversion ... but some of its supporters are of unstable character.'[20]

This frank, and I believe accurate, analysis explains why members of Capricorn were not keen to be bracketed with MRA, however much the movements may have had in common. In spite of Special Branch comments, most MRA supporters in Kenya were people who did more good than harm, and only a few were also members of Capricorn.

On his visits to East Africa David enjoyed going to Ol Molog where his brother Bill Stirling had a share in a farm and where he felt at ease with the dashing ex-RAF types who flew him round Mount Kilimanjaro in a small plane. On one of David's visits to Robin Johnston, involving late nights and much whisky, he met the man who was part owner of the farm, Archibald McIndoe, who spent two months every winter recuperating from the hectic life of a busy and celebrated plastic surgeon in England. He had made his name at East Grinstead Hospital performing miracles of reconstruction on his 'guinea pigs' — badly burnt fighter pilots — during, and for many years after, the Battle of Britain. McIndoe retained traces of his New Zealand accent, and with his stocky build, white hair brushed straight back and horn-rimmed glasses, in a pair of shorts he looked far from the eminent surgeon. Even without his immaculate suit and Rolls Royce, McIndoe was an impressive and powerful character who recognized the same qualities in others. Johnston had been at East Grinstead briefly for McIndoe to operate on a damaged hand and they had become firm friends. Later, McIndoe went on safari with Johnston in Tanganyika and fell in love with Africa.[21] They bought 600 acres of bush at Ol Molog, which Johnston began to develop when he left the colonial service in 1951. On McIndoe's annual visits he worked on the farm and joined in the life of the small community on the mountain.

David persuaded McIndoe and his American born second wife, Connie, to become Capricorn supporters in London, and in 1954 McIndoe was chairman of the London committee, helping to raise money from his wealthy friends. During a professional visit to Nairobi McIndoe met Wood who became a lifelong friend and colleague in surgery and in Capricorn. Recognizing the need in East Africa for reconstructive surgery, and Wood's skill as a surgeon, McIndoe suggested that he should go to England for further training at East Grinstead.

As with many links in Capricorn, Sir Archibald McIndoe and Michael Wood forged another connection, more permanent than Capricorn, when Wood started the flying doctor service in East Africa.[22] As he flew to areas far from medical services, he realized that many patients needed urgent hospital treatment, particularly cases of serious burns requiring reconstructive surgery and specialized postoperative care. This suggested that a unit should be built in Nairobi to which such patients could be flown for treatment. I was closely involved for some years as the architect for the proposed reconstructive surgery unit, which in the end was never built, as is often the case with an architect's first big project. The idea of flying medical care to remote areas, or flying the patient to hospital, developed into the African Medical and Research Foundation, which continues to provide an essential service to the whole of eastern Africa, and remains Wood's monument. Although I knew David Stirling, Robin Johnston, Archie McIndoe and Michael Wood, and was flown to Ol Molog more than once, I was never present when all four powerful and extraordinary men were there together, arguing and plotting about the future.

It was through the Ol Molog connection and McIndoe that David met the Woods, who gave more to Capricorn in Africa than any of his followers. Susan Wood's passionate nature and commitment to Africa ensured her unquestioning loyalty to David for the rest of his life. She has said that her relationship with David was more intense than her husband's and that she was probably the driving force in their enthusiasm for Capricorn.[23] Not long after they met, David wrote to Wood: 'You and van der Post are the only two I have met so far who have really got to the heart of the matter and really understand the full purposes of [Capricorn].'[24] He went on to say he was pleased that Wood was prepared to take on the job of executive officer for Capricorn, at a salary to be paid retrospectively when they had collected the necessary funds. Wood was a busy surgeon with a growing family, lived 20 miles from Nairobi, and in the Kenya Police Reserve was liable to be called out to deal with Mau Mau incidents at Limuru. It is a measure of David's messianic powers of persuasion that Wood should consider the possibility of such a commitment, even assuming that he hoped his wife would help in the Capricorn office. The flow of letters continued with David writing to make sure that Wood's committee would be truly multiracial, adding, it is 'of enormous importance to the future to be able to say the Society was drawn from all the races.'[25]

When David found Michael and Susan Wood and realized that this was the couple to whom he could safely entrust the Capricorn flame in Kenya, he already had the beginnings of a network in the country. He had met Michael Blundell and Wilfred Havelock, both members of Legislative Council, and Kendall Ward, the executive officer of the European Elected Members Union. He could tell himself that they were all members of Capricorn, although they were involved in politics and David was suspicious of politicians — he thought they said what the electorate expected and were without his finality and lack of compromise. He had hopes that he could also include Sir Eboo Pirbhai, the leader of the Aga Khan community in Kenya and Mervyn Hill, editor of the *Kenya Weekly News*, with whom David corresponded and whom he also listed as a Capricorn member, although Hill, as a journalist, always took care to preserve his independence of any organization concerned with the government of the country.

Because of the emergency, it took time for a branch of Capricorn to be established in Kenya, particularly for a society that hoped to enrol African members. There were controls on African organizations, and the formation of any new society was approved by government only if its aims were considered safe politically and unlikely to be subversive. Working with Ward in the European Elected Members Union was Betty Couldrey, a young Englishwoman married to Jack Couldrey, a Kenya-born lawyer whose father owned the *Kenya Weekly News*, for which she wrote parliamentary reports. She was interested in politics, so it was not long before David asked her to work for Capricorn. Betty Couldrey in turn enrolled her friend Joyce Raw, one of the contingent who moved to Kenya following Indian independence after a lifetime in the subcontinent. They set about seeking members with advertisements in the local papers that brought in some replies, mostly from Asians and Europeans. Betty Couldrey and Joyce Raw remained members of Capricorn until early 1961, and did stalwart work at the Salima convention in June 1956.[26] They hoped that Capricorn's proposals would make it possible for Europeans to continue living and contributing to Kenya's development.

A supporter of the liberal European politicians in Legislative Council, and an early Capricorn member, was Eric Wilkinson, dapper and precise. As African affairs officer in Nairobi City Council he spoke Kiswahili fluently, was friendly with Africans in all walks of life in the city and it was through him that key African members were recruited.

One he did not persuade to join the Society was Tom Mboya, the rising nationalist leader, whose considerable power in the country came from his position as general secretary of the Kenya Federation of Labour (KFL) in the crucial decade from 1953 to 1963. For most of that period emergency regulations banned African political parties and nationwide organizations so the head of the trade union movement was in a unique position, a position of which he took full advantage. I met Mboya through Wilkinson in 1959 and was appointed architect for the KFL Nairobi headquarters,[27] which meant that I worked closely with him for over two years. Mboya was often accused of arrogance, and he was understandably impatient with those around him, as his intelligence and capacity for hard work were very rare. Blundell[28] said Mboya was the only member in Legislative Council of any race who had read and understood the papers before speaking in debate. Although he came from western Kenya he was popular and respected by Africans from other parts of the country and was elected to parliament for a Nairobi constituency. His non-tribal appeal was very important for the future and his assassination in 1969, at the tragically young age of 39, deprived the country of a man who might have saved Kenya from destructive tribal animosity had he succeeded Kenyatta as president.

Joram Amadi, 1998

Joram Amadi and Boaz Omori, both journalists in Nairobi, were close friends of Mboya but joined Capricorn because emergency regulations prohibited African countrywide organizations – in effect, they had nowhere else to go if they were to be politically active. Another journalist member who was later in local government and national politics was Musa Amalemba, who was to play a part in the citizenship college.[29] Moody Awori, one of a large family whose father was a well-known canon in the Anglican Church, became a keen member and a devoted follower of the Woods. Mboya, Amadi, Amalemba, Awori and Omori all came from western Kenya, near Lake Victoria, and were typically chubby, cheerful characters with wide smiles masking a considerable intelligence and political understanding.

Compared with the African university graduates recruited by David in Southern Rhodesia, Capricorn in Kenya could boast only one: J. D. Otiende, also from western Kenya. Educated at the Alliance High School near Nairobi and at Makerere University in Kampala, Otiende was the first African to teach at Alliance, which he did for ten years under the legendary headmaster, Carey Francis.[30] When the call of politics became too strong he became the first secretary-general of the Kenya African Union, later taken over by Kikuyu members and implicated in the beginnings of Mau Mau, although by then Otiende was no longer involved. He was minister of education and then health in the government of Kenya after independence. When I met him again in 1998, he was 81 and still active, grumbling that a one-party state cannot make the telephones work.

Enthusiastic though they were, none of the African members were Kikuyu, which was important for the future of Capricorn in Kenya. While emergency regulations were in force (1952–59) almost all Kikuyu were either in detention, rusticated to the reserve or fighting in the forest, which made Capricorn's African membership seriously unbalanced, as the Kikuyu were the most advanced and educated of all the tribes in Kenya. When emergency restrictions were removed, Kikuyu people began to reassert themselves in the economic life of the country, replacing other tribes who had taken their jobs in the interim. The lack of Kikuyu involvement in Capricorn was missed most acutely at the time when we were attempting to persuade politicians of all races to adopt Capricorn principles for the elections in 1957. If there had been Kikuyu men and women — many of whom were powerful and able — in Capricorn, we might have had some small influence on events. All Africans acknowledged Kenyatta, a Kikuyu, as the undisputed leader of the country, which gave the Kikuyu an enormous advantage, so that when he was released from gaol to become prime minister and then president, the Kikuyu were soon back in control.

For many years Africans throughout the continent had regarded Kenyatta as a major figure in the independence struggle, which reinforced his position as the undisputed leader in Kenya.

In spite of David's earlier proposals restricting Indian immigration, there were a number of enthusiastic Asian members in Kenya. The most flamboyant was Abdul Ghafur Sheikh, a handsome young businessman, with an MBA from Harvard and a yellow American convertible that was much envied, as was his ability to fill it with blonde young women. Nevertheless, Sheikh was a keen and important Capricorn member, becoming vice-chairman of the branch.[31]

The Johnston's farmhouse at Ol Molog continued to be a centre for endless discussions about the future of the country, although any realistic analysis would have shown that Tanganyika could never be a Capricorn country because of the terms of the UN mandate and anti-colonial sentiment among UN members. The proportions between the races in Tanganyika were more disparate than in Kenya: in 1955 there were 25,000 Europeans, 88,500 Asians and Arabs and 8,200,000 Africans while Kenya had twice as many Europeans and Asians and about 4,000,000 Africans.[32] Nevertheless, David's boundless enthusiasm encouraged the formation of a branch of Capricorn in Tanganyika with Johnston as chairman. For some years Johnston was obsessive in trying to persuade people of all races that Capricorn was the answer. Somehow, he thought, logic would prevail over the limitations of the UN mandate. His wife, Erika, wrote in her book about their life at Ol Molog that she thought he was bashing his head against a brick wall, but he kept on trying.[33]

In the early 1950s Tanganyika was undeveloped with poor communications and large areas of land unusable because of tsetse fly, and few Africans with secondary education or a university degree. There were pockets of prosperity: the Chagga tribe grew coffee on the slopes of Mount Kilimanjaro and were rich and well organized; there were European farms at Ol Molog and Mbeya in the south and large sisal estates along the coast. It seemed reasonable to Johnston and his friends that the country would need European and Asian skills and capital for generations if the life, and life expectancy, of the average African were to be improved.

One man changed the picture for ever, and it was not David Stirling, it was a small, modest, graduate of Edinburgh University: Julius Nyerere, who went home to Tanganyika in 1952. David met him that year and Johnston saw him in Dar es Salaam after he had formed the Tanganyika African National Union. Nyerere listened courteously to their ideas of partnership between the races, but was adamant that the country had to be governed by Africans on the basis of universal franchise, which made Capricorn an enemy to be derided and made irrelevant. Nyerere himself accepted the need for expatriate advice and investment, which he combined with a utopian concept of African socialism. Many of his followers were less subtle, taking a harder line, which made life difficult for Asians and Europeans, whether they supported Capricorn or not. The combination of African socialism and Nyerere's brand of African nationalism has kept Tanzania, as it was called after the amalgamation with Zanzibar, comparatively stable and poor in World Bank terms, although the people have land enough to feed themselves and are content.

During 1953 David continued to travel and lobby his friends and contacts in Africa, America and London. Peter Allsebrook, a director of the family firm Keir & Cawdor, had joined David's company, Central African Commerce Ltd,[34] and was soon involved with Capricorn. In July David wrote him a long letter from Salisbury with plans for raising a large sum of money and how it would be spent, very quickly it seemed. David ended, with some exaggeration: 'In the meantime I hope you will realize that literally tens of thousands of people of all races in Africa are pinning their hopes on the Capricorn Africa Society. If you had been recently in Africa you would understand the grave threat of the Pan African Nationalist Congress at present being organized by Nkrumah, Nehru and others. The promoters are trying their utmost to catch Kidaha [a senior chief in Tanganyika], Tshekedi [Khama, chief in Bechuanaland] and others of our Africans to join them. It is literally our convention against theirs. More and more people realize here that our convention is the last bid in Africa to get Asian and African leaders to join with the European settlers.'[35]

The following month David, in London, wrote a letter to Hill, which shows how he used his contacts and also how thoroughly he ensured that they received and understood the message. 'There seems at last an inclination at this end for the politicians to leave the initiative to us. I think this is at least largely due to the fact that Gordon-Walker [Labour shadow colonial secretary] has let it be known in no uncertain terms that he backs without qualification the Society's programme. This week Oliver Lyttleton [Conservative colonial secretary] is staying with my brother Bill in Scotland for a week's grouse shooting and Hugh Fraser (his PPS) will be staying with Bill the following week. Bill is as thoroughly acquainted with our aims and objects as any member of the Society, and I wrote him a long letter emphasizing the points to get over to Lyttleton, and I am ringing Bill each evening to make sure that he is putting over our case really fully. I shall see Lyttleton myself on his return from Scotland.'[36]

Another letter recorded his latest coup: 'Last night I had the good luck to run into Eddie [Rothschild]. Not only did he say that he thought it was time his bank reconsidered the Capricorn case, but also I managed to whip nearly £200 off him at backgammon, which he agreed to convert to a covenant which will yield the Society a good deal more than this.'[37] David never missed an opportunity to plug the Capricorn case, or to raise funds.

That year, 1953, I was in my last year at the Architectural Association School, completing my final thesis, which superficially was a development plan for a region in Kenya, but in reality was a political programme for a multiracial country. Terence Powell, also from Kenya, and I combined our theses — his for Imperial College on hydropower and irrigation and mine for the AA — to provide the region with a basic economy. I used town planning techniques and neighbourhood layouts to encourage Africans, Asians and Europeans to understand one another and live together amicably. Reading the introduction to the Maragua Development Plan I realize that I was ready for Capricorn, although at the time the word meant no more to me than a line of latitude on the globe.

'Our intention is to plan an environment for multiracial living. ... It should be stressed at the outset that no plan can solve the racial problem in Kenya — it can only provide the opportunity for the individual to solve it, and this we have tried to do. ... The great scourge of the world today is the rise of militant and uncompromising nationalism, and Kenya is no exception to this. If Kenya is to avoid nationalism on a racial basis the present leaders, the Europeans, must capture the imagination of the other races in the common future they share in East Africa. And they must show that there is a common future by deeds and not specious words like "partnership", which mean something different to each group so that each is doomed to frustration. ... It is an example of this common future we have tried to indicate in microcosm in this thesis. Its basis is the present, which in many respects is not ideal, but it is with us, and is real. We have accepted the differences between the various groups which make up Kenya today, and tried to provide an environment which will encourage them to diminish, in which individuals of each race may come to know, understand and respect those of the others.'

'In some areas [in Africa], the situation is complicated, almost to the point of being insoluble, by the presence of one or more immigrant races who consider Africa their home, though they rarely wish to share it on a basis of equality with the Africans. Kenya is such a country: Europeans, Asians and Arabs all live in Kenya in considerable numbers, and they intend to remain there. In the integration of these groups, so different in everything except their common humanity and future, one should avoid losing the valuable and varied characteristics which each race brings to the whole; the technical skills, capital and civic responsibility of the European, the social discipline (already almost gone) and the laughter and music of the Africans, and the religious strength, thrift and capacity for work in their own interest of the Asians. ... The Maragua Development Plan is intended as an example of economic and social integration. The details of the site itself are irrelevant to the main theme that real integration can only take place equably in medium sized groups sharing the facilities of, and enthusiasm for, their own neighbourhood and town.'

'Diverse groups can only be brought together of their own free will by giving them a common loyalty to a place or an idea. But such strong loyalties can only be induced when both the place and the idea are clearly defined and limited, and it is on these beliefs that this plan, at every scale, is based. As the majority gain in technical skill and political understanding, so will the minorities become redundant and their position in the country precarious. Only by canalizing the divergent interests of the various races through shared enthusiasms for places and ideas, towards a common loyalty to East Africa and its future, can the minorities hope to be tolerated once they have ceased to be essential to the country. ... The neighbourhoods have been arranged so that areas of different densities (the different racial groups in the beginning) alternate over the whole plan, so that pairs of racial groups cannot coalesce into larger communities, sufficiently self-centred to ignore their neighbourhoods.'

'The plan ... has allocated primary schools to the groups nearest to them in accordance with the relative needs of the group, with playing fields shared between two or more schools [serving different economic areas] where this is possible. From these beginnings, it is hoped that under the encouragement of the multiracial school in the town centre, will grow an educational system for the region which will be able to offer to every child a school most suited to his individual needs rather than to the colour of his skin. Each neighbourhood would have near the centre a nursery school for children of all races. They would spend time mostly out of doors playing games and listening to stories, so that the African children could share the heritage of fairy stories and folk laws that surrounds an English childhood, and the other children could learn

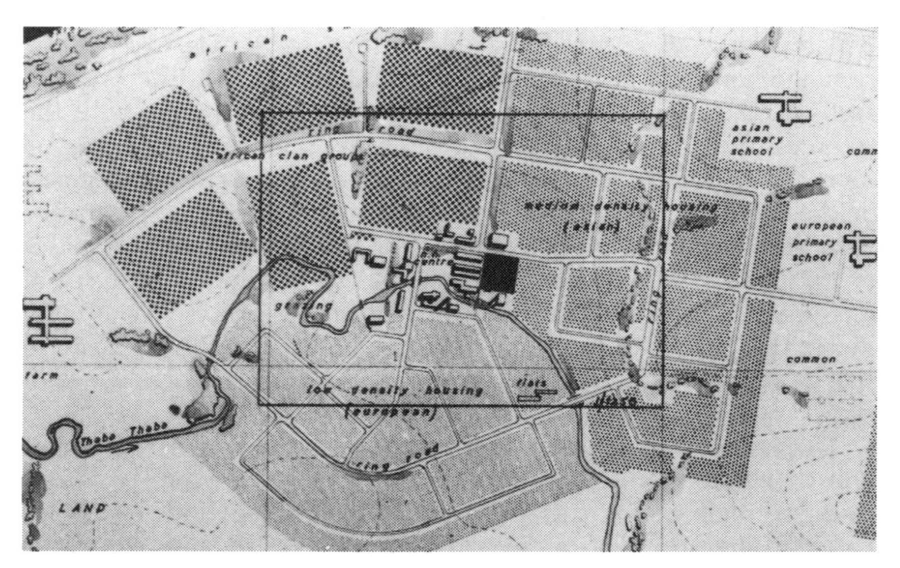

A Maragua neighbourhood with housing areas of different densities planned around the centre with local shops and community centre

more about the country they live in, its tribal laws, the characteristics of the people and the wealth of knowledge about the fauna and flora of the country which is handed down by word of mouth in African families. The lessons of tolerance and respect for individual capabilities regardless of race, if they are inculcated at an early age should be the ineradicable.'

The BBC World Service broadcast an interview and the scheme was exhibited at the Imperial Institute and the Overseas League in London, with attention from the daily press and specialist magazines.[38] Sir Hugh Dow, the chairman, and some members of the East Africa Royal Commission, including Margery Perham,[39] Philip Mason, later director of the Institute of Race Relations, and numerous others came to the exhibitions and read about the scheme in the newspapers and journals. But Kenya was at the worst of the Mau Mau emergency so there were more urgent matters to consider than innocent plans for a non-racial Utopia in Kikuyuland.

When I arrived in Nairobi in July 1955 after two years in America, Kenya was beginning to recover from the trauma of Mau Mau, although emergency regulations were still in force. The non-racial United Kenya Club, grown in numbers, was in newly designed premises, but little else had changed in relations between the races since I left Kenya four years earlier. The idealism that lay behind my first thesis and *Maragua* was still alive, and in Capricorn I was happy to find people of all races whose ideas matched my own, and with whom I hoped to be constructive.

Chapter 5
New Hope in Africa

Once a branch of the Society had been established in Kenya, David Stirling appointed Michael Wood as chairman and persuaded Kendall Ward to be executive officer. In one of his many letters to Wood he showed his continuing enthusiasm for Laurens van der Post's contribution: he 'has confirmed that he is determined to write a book on Capricorn. He tells me ... he has never felt more strongly the urge to write ... [this] should give our Society a useful boost when published.'[1] In another letter in the same vein on the same day David added, 'van der Post's book will in effect be a description of the twenty years he has spent in quest of an ideology for Africa and the finding of it in CAS.'[2] The book that gave the Society a boost was not by van der Post, who sublimated his urge to write about Capricorn, but was by a retired missionary, Dr Joe Oldham, whose contribution established a theoretical basis for Capricorn's programme.

In September 1953 the Society published a pamphlet with extracts from the constitution and objects, a signed essay by David and a list of 'leaders of all races' in Africa who were supporters, with the note: 'Nearly all those mentioned are members of the Society's central executive.'[3] This was more than an exaggeration as many of those listed were not even members of the Society, although they may have expressed interest in David's ideas. Like the declarations the previous year it was printed on heavyweight cream paper in a handsome red cover and was circulated among his contacts in Whitehall[4] and supporters.

David's essay showed that his views on race relations had changed since the publication of *The Capricorn Declarations* and that he realized federation was not the answer. With small modifications it appeared, four months later, as advertisements in newspapers in east and central Africa, sparking comment and resignations. In his essay David described the forthcoming convention to be held in Mbeya, in Tanganyika, which was to be preceded by multiracial citizenship committees whose task it was to agree a loyalty code. There was no mention of the franchise in the paper. David wrote: '*The Capricorn Declarations*, published on 8 December 1952, gave a preliminary expression to the aims and objects of the Society but the declarations constituted a statement of principles mainly from the European standpoint and over-emphasized the political aspect of federation. To broaden these principles and to plan for their implementation, the Society is now organizing a multiracial convention.'

He devoted most attention to the section on human relations in Africa. 'The aim of the black racialist extremists is to drive the European out of Africa; it is a movement which knows no territorial boundaries. On the other hand, the aim of the white racialists is to deny the black man forever the opportunity of advancement to full citizenship to which as a human being he is entitled. Black racialism was originally in the main a product of white racialism; in Africa today the one continues to stimulate the other. ... The Society is convinced that political and economic concessions and other appeals to the head rather than to the heart of the African will not arrest the progress of African racialism. An emotional force can only be countered by a stronger and more practical spiritual and emotional force.' In these words the influence of van der Post is clear, as it is in David's recognition that the fundamental issue was emotional, not economic.

He continued: 'The Capricorn African Society, however, operates on a scale at least as wide geographically as that of pan-African racialism, and judging from our experience, our Society has a strong emotional appeal to the African. ... Central African federation has not improved the climate of race relations in central Africa, in spite of the material benefits likely to flow from it for all races. The reason for this must be its subordination of human relations to economic and administrative values. ... But the only enduring foundation capable of taking the political structure of six-territory federation is an ideology embracing the loyalties of all races within those territories. ... To press for this federation now as the exclusive goal of European politicians will make its achievement almost impossible; or if railroaded through on grounds of administrative and economic expediency, the political structure would be founded on sand. What we need today in Africa is not discussions in political terms of the wider federation but closer understanding in human terms of Africa's three main races. We await the rising up from the smoke and turbulence of Africa's racial cauldron of an ideology to which European, African and

Indian politicians will willingly subscribe — an ideology truly set in God's values, combining the legitimate aspirations of each race, and one for which all contributing races will feel equally responsible. We submit that the Capricorn Convention is the first act in the emergence of this ideology.'

These powerful words and David's change of tack stimulated comment in Whitehall where officials were alternately impressed and irritated by his enthusiasm and advocacy. A Commonwealth Relations Office memo reads: 'Have the [Colonial Office] had a copy of this latest edition of the Capricorn thesis? Col Stirling has succeeded in the rare feat of transferring to paper some of that magnetism which he exerts in personal contact. I have seldom seen a more remarkable amalgam of high-mindedness and sweet reasonableness: if the document had been accompanied by a membership form, I should probably have signed up and produced my guinea before I knew what I was doing!'[5]

But a few weeks later a CO note records: 'Col Stirling had no more in mind than to promote amelioration of the attitude between white and black. I read his misty pronouncement, calling for some practical thing to be done, presumably in all the countries concerned ... if he did line up moderate Africans behind such demand, there would be set up all sorts of resistances and distortions. His head is too much in the clouds to see that the important thing is to make a success of such ventures as the multiracial university and the running in of the (multiracial) federal legislature. Col Stirling's vision never descends to realities. He wants to carry a torch, but the only torches likely to light up Africa will unfortunately be African and they could result in a conflagration of alarming dimensions.'[6]

David's tireless lobbying produced a positive reaction in the British high commission in Southern Rhodesia: an intelligence digest sent to the CRO in October 1953 must have been written after a visit from David. 'CAPRICORN AFRICA SOCIETY: Its leaders hope to find a workable compromise between the sometimes maladroit handling of racial problems in the Union of South Africa, and the irresponsible disregard of realities which usually characterizes what are called "liberal" circles. In a very different quarter, however, plans are being made for another African conference in 1954. ... It is being sponsored by the India Africa Council in New Delhi and pretty well every subversive influence in Africa will, no doubt, be represented at it if it materializes. An ideological battle has begun and it is a matter of the greatest moment as to who will win it. It may be those – such as the Capricorn Africa Society – who seek to weld a great area of Africa into an entity with a common loyalty to the progress and well being of all its citizens and a common loyalty to the precepts of Christian civilization. If, however, these projects are allowed to go by default, the struggle for Africa may be won by those who seek to use for their own purposes the evil and subversive influences in the Continent.'[7] The last paragraph has the sound of David's voice, especially as the writer added the addresses of the Society's offices for the benefit of putative members.

The head of the Africa section in the Colonial Office commented in a letter to the governors in east and central Africa: 'He [David Stirling] now seems genuinely decided that the whole conception of [the larger] federation must be relegated into the indefinite future and that the present role of his Society should be the improvement of race relations in east and central Africa; he now seems reconciled to the idea that his convention cannot be held until 1955 and I have the impression that he will be prepared to consult us about the timing of it in due course. He also seems reconciled – albeit a little reluctantly – to the view that the work of his Society can best be carried out behind the scenes for the time being, although he said that, if his interterritorial conception was too long postponed he feared his African supporters might grow restive.'[8]

There is no indication whether the Whitehall civil servant believed David's talk of his African supporters growing restive if the great federation were delayed, or the implication that there were so many that their restiveness would be significant. The letter continues: 'To sum up, I obtained the impression that he has moved a long way from the rather grandiose world of make-believe which surrounded his earlier conception; he now appears to be genuinely trying to make a more realistic approach to a limited objective, with which I do not think we have any reason to quarrel.'

The officials in the Commonwealth Relations Office were concerned that David's activities might disturb the steady and slow progress they intended for Southern Rhodesia and that the Colonial Office proposed for the territories under its control. A letter to the British high commissioner in Salisbury from the CRO enclosing CO comments shows their alarm and, by extension, that they were taking David's activities as a serious threat to what they regarded as a stable situation. Had David seen this letter, he would have been flattered as well as irritated: 'we do not suggest that you pass ... the [following] tentative Colonial Office reactions to either the Federal or the Southern Rhodesian governments. I think that we shall be right if we continue to try to put a brake on Stirling. His aim – to ameliorate the relations between white and black – is admirable. But he is an unpractical fanatic and does not reckon the probable consequences of his activities, which I believe may give rise to all sorts of resistances and distortions to imperial stability and ordered progress. He seems to aim at some grandiose movement, which will transcend frontiers, whereas the position and potentialities in each country are different. If he succeeds in lining up moderate Africans in a demand for some sort of "code" he may well start something with some sort of resemblance to a forest fire which neither he nor anyone else will be able to extinguish, [and] which will not be to the immediate or ultimate good of the territories in general or the African inhabitants in particular.'[9]

The response from Mr MacLennan, in the high commission in Salisbury, shows that he knew his Bible, and gives an idea of the effect of David's eloquence, even on a resistant official: 'I doubt whether we shall have any great success in trying to put a brake on Stirling. He is, as you say, a fanatic and he takes little account of the views of the "practical man". I am always left after one of my talks with him feeling either that I am Gallio, or when David has been more than usually eloquent, King Agrippa after St Paul's speech. I suppose that there is a danger that he and his friends might start a forest fire but my own guess is that their movement will excite hostility and suspicion among the general mass of the Africans, especially in view of the quite undeservedly bad name which the Capricorn African Society obtained in its previous manifestations [in recommending federation]. In which case I shall be sorry for Stirling because however unpractical he may be, he is a likeable character and his motives are of the highest.'[10]

Not having the advantage of MacLellan's theological education, I looked up his biblical references. Gallio was the first-century Roman proconsul in Palestine who dismissed the charge against St Paul brought by the Jews because religious conflicts were not within his legal remit (Acts XVIII, 17: 'And Gallio cared for none of these things'). King Agrippa II (also known as Herod) heard St Paul's defence when he was on trial in Rome that he was called by God and asked: 'Are you trying to persuade me to be a Christian?' (Acts XXV, 23–6).

After issuing his new paper David went to America to raise

funds for Capricorn. The flavour of his time in the United States is caught in a letter in the Whitehall files: 'I saw David Stirling and heard a certain amount from him about "Capricorn Africa" which I think may be of interest to you. After hearing David Stirling talk about his views on two or three occasions when we were lunching or dining together I find myself sharing the opinions expressed by Bill Gorell-Barnes [of the Colonial Office] to the effect that the group's ideas are "good in parts but not in the last analysis very practical". I must admit, however, that I suffer the disadvantage of knowing practically nothing of these problems myself. Furthermore, our main conversation wound up at four o'clock in the morning in the Yukon Bar on 3rd Avenue [New York] so my recollections of what David Stirling said are perhaps not quite as crystal clear as they ought to be!'[11]

David was convinced that proposals for the future of Africa would be unacceptable were they not formulated by people of all the races who lived there. In London, on his return from the United States, he saw a paper from the Capricorn office in Salisbury, which stimulated a strong letter to Arthur Stokes: 'The thing that really shakes me ... is the fact that neither the Indian [n]or the African has yet been consulted. It was most clearly laid down time and time again that there will be no virtue in a definition of citizenship and the loyalty code unless the African feels as much concerned with its definition as the European.'[12]

In February 1954 David published his manifesto in one-and-a-half-page advertisements in central African newspapers, laid out like news pages with headlines, 'editorials', photographs and approving articles by distinguished people about the Capricorn Africa Society.[13] In an attempt to mollify those who thought he was a dangerous radical criticizing everything the white man did in Africa, David wrote an article for *East Africa and Rhodesia* in which he said, 'I am not suggesting that our attitude in Southern Rhodesia has been wrong in the past but that it is becoming wrong in the present and will be disastrously wrong in the future. Those attitudes were understandable while there were only a few educated Africans, but are now quite untenable.'[14]

The editor commented that this was a great improvement on the earlier declarations, but that the statement was still ambiguous and marred by extreme exaggeration when it suggested that the Society is the only agency that has any hope of preventing a dangerous increase in African racialism. He added: 'If that were true, the outlook would indeed be bad, for there is no convincing evidence that the Society has made any marked contribution in that direction since it was established.' Newspaper comment in Africa was warmer – many papers reporting an approving statement from Garfield Todd, the Southern Rhodesia prime minister, that 'human values should be safely guarded in a new and clearly defined concept of citizenship – a citizenship common to each of the states concerned – is a worthy idea.'[15]

In Tanganyika the local paper quoted an African as saying that the document was the first really to capture the imagination of the African in southern Africa, adding that it was 'of real statesmanship behind which lies a deep recognition of the fundamental causes of Africa's unrest'.[16] The paper continued with a long interview with David's associate in Dar es Salaam, Tom Tyrell. A letter to the *Observer* suggested that the concept was 'based on outside standards, imported by small majorities' and that a civilized standard should be a 'democratic standard, *with all that this implies*'.[17] The Roman Catholic paper *Truth* preferred David's earlier proposals, writing: 'In view of Stirling's about-face on the federation issue it is difficult to see what useful purpose his ambitious venture can possibly serve now.'[18] In Kenya, the *East African Standard* refrained from comment, merely reporting an enthusiastic speech by Wood.[19] Jasper Zavanhu was quoted in *African Weekly*: 'With the delusion of [equal rights to all civilized men] in their heart, is it not natural that my people everywhere are now suspicious of this new term "partnership"? Into this atmosphere of mistrust comes the clear vivid light cast by the Capricorn Africa Society's announcement.'[20]

In spite of so much editorial approval of the manifesto, N. H. Wilson resigned from the Society, although David may not have expected that he would signal his resignation in a series of acrimonious letters to the press, in which David's running of the Society would be criticized. Wilson wrote to the newspapers: 'I am reluctantly compelled to disassociate myself from the advertisement in your issue of February 26 in the name of the Capricorn Africa Society, with many features of which I disagree most strongly. Without any desire to wash dirty linen in public, I must point out the following: (1) the text of the advertisement was not communicated to, or approved by, any meeting of the Society ...; (2) there has been no resolution passed at any meeting, council or committee of the Society ... abandoning the Society's objective of pressing, on political and economic grounds, for the closer association of the states of central Africa ...; (3) There has been likewise no resolution authorizing the Society's spokesmen to abandon its firm opposition to further Asiatic immigration into Africa ... an opposition which, to the best of my knowledge, the Society has maintained since its foundation. As I feel most strongly that the Society's original objectives in these two latter matters are of vital importance to Africa; and as I have been publicly identified, to a certain extent, with the Society ... I have no option but to ... resign from the Society in protest and oppose its new policy.'[21]

Arthur Stokes, writing as secretary of the Society, wrote a strong reply: 'The Capricorn Africa Society gratefully accepts Mr Wilson's resignation but regrets his wilful attempt to misinform the public. I will take Mr Wilson's accusations ... in the order he made them. It will be rather like picking a saboteur's limpets off the side of a ship.'[22] He went on to underline the Society's commitment to Africans at all levels of society in central Africa, and also to Asians already living in the country. There were more letters to the press from Capricorn supporters and from Wilson himself, who was an old hand at letters to the editor and was convinced of the rightness of his position. Wilson went on to expand on his criticisms in a long article in *East Africa and Rhodesia* in which he said that there were 'such grave defects in the proposals that if they were accepted it would be completely disastrous for West European Civilization and for the White Man as its chief custodian' (his capitalization).[23]

Relations between Wilson and David had been deteriorating as the elderly journalist stuck to his original two-pyramid idea. David suggested to Stokes that he 'allow NH to slide out of CAS. Don't hurt the old boy's feelings: put down his whipping round like a weathercock to the erosion of old age on his brain. Tragic in view of his immense contributions to CAS.'[24] During the previous year a number of high profile African members had been recruited, none of whom knew that Wilson was involved in Capricorn. Lawrence Vambe told me that Wilson did not come to any meeting he attended and, had he done so, the Africans would have left immediately because Wilson's policies were notorious and obnoxious.[25] (It was a total surprise to Vambe when, in 1999, he saw *A Native Policy for Africa*, which David and Wilson wrote together in 1950.)

Ignoring this public disagreement, David wrote with enthusiasm to Wood in April 1954 that 'the manifesto has been really extraordinarily successful in breaking down the remaining opposition to the Society. It has undoubtedly hugely increased our prestige. Some very hard-headed editors say it is the most statesmanlike document in their view that has ever come out of Africa. As you can imagine this is rather good for the morale.'[26] This letter illustrates his style of leadership: to exaggerate success and influence while ignoring adverse criticism or reality. In most cases it achieved its objective in keeping members of the Society focused, and it also worked on David himself, as he clearly believed his own hyperbole. An example is his letter in 1954 to Sir Philip Mitchell: 'It was splendid news to hear from Michael Wood that you have decided to join the Capricorn Africa Society.'[27] Mitchell, who had served as chief secretary in Tanganyika and governor of Uganda and Kenya, had by then retired in Kenya, determined to 'keep right out of affairs' as he told his successor, Sir Evelyn Baring[28] and would not have joined any society more political than a farmers' cooperative.

David continued to issue orders by correspondence to the Salisbury office when he was away, and no doubt verbally when he was in Salisbury. In May 1954 he sent a testy note to the committee in Salisbury: 'I cannot understand why the Salisbury Committee is so slow to accept the point that I have been trying to hammer for so long. It is not the function of the Society to pontificate various African problems, such as land tenure, immigration etc. It is our object to create a citizenship and an electoral system from which problems can be considered without racial prejudice.'[29] The previous year the Interracial Association of Southern Rhodesia had published its *Draft Declaration on African Affairs* with which Vambe and other Capricorn members had been closely involved. David's letter suggests that he thought some were continuing to work on solutions to 'various African problems'. However, had they been solved or ameliorated, they might have made his common citizenship more palatable to the African majority in the country.

In August 1954 David held the first interterritorial Capricorn meeting in Salisbury,[30] with Wood and Johnston attending from Kenya and Tanganyika, which confirmed that there should be no weakening of the standards set by Western Christian civilization. Also on the agenda was a proposed visit to East Africa by two Rhodesians to appreciate the links between the two arms of David's future dominion. Wood flew David, Vambe and Savanhu to Kenya where they addressed groups of Europeans, Asians and Africans, and met Mervyn Hill, whom Vambe thought was 'charismatic, influential and much respected by David'. They noticed the lack of Kikuyu people among the African members they met who, they thought, were good men but not the type to set the world on fire.

At the height of the emergency they found Kenya a sad country with the only major figure, Jomo Kenyatta, in prison and vilified by government and the white population.

Johnston flew them to Tanganyika where they met Chief Marealle, whom they thought was hostile to Capricorn, although David claimed him as a supporter. Then they went on to Dar es Salaam where they had lunch with the governor, Sir Edward Twining, and met Julius Nyerere and Tom Tyrell. To complete the tour they stayed at Ol Molog, where Johnston showed them off to his friends, and the Rhodesians met white farmers who they found were different from those in Southern Rhodesia, though only in degree. Vambe has said[31] that the Ol Molog settlers were clearly aware of the UN mandate and the threat Nyerere posed to their hopes of a Capricorn future. He thought that Johnston was firm in his antagonism to African nationalism, and detested black lawyers, which was a familiar attitude among settlers.

At this point in his odyssey David was clear about objectives but uncertain about method. This changed when he met Oldham, who was to be of fundamental importance to Capricorn. On 15 March 1954 a young woman recently back from Tanganyika, recovering from a disastrous marriage there but having fallen in love with Africa, wrote a fan letter to the colonel. Jeannine Scott praised his article in *East Africa and Rhodesia* and told him about Oldham and the YMCA college and conference centre at Dunford, near Midhurst in Sussex, where she worked with the administrator, Edwin Townsend-Coles.

David responded enthusiastically,[32] enclosing copies of manifestos and articles about the Society and saying how interested he was in coming to Dunford. It is difficult to know whether David realized at the time how crucial Oldham and Jeannine Scott were to be to Capricorn. He was to write an influential book about the Society and she continues to this day maintaining total belief in its basic philosophy and providing devoted encouragement to everyone involved with Capricorn and its successor organizations in London. Warm and smiling with curly brown hair she was, and remains, attractive and energetic with the added advantage that she has connections on her mother's side with the Kleinwort banking family. Another strand in the social network so important to Capricorn was her godmother, Princess Patricia of Connaught, a connection of David's through his brother-in-law, the Earl of Dalhousie.

With Susan Wood in East Africa and Jennifer Plunket in central

Africa, Jeannine Scott in England completed the geographically well-placed trio of women who gave David their absolute loyalty and devotion, however unrequited it may have been. Of the three, Jeannine Scott was the only one who was unattached, having divorced for good reason her first husband, Alan Scott. But marriage was not on David's agenda; although he was attractive to women and enjoyed their company, he thought he would not be able to live up to the solemn vows of the wedding service, and a wife would have cramped his style. In answer to my impertinent questioning, Jeannine Scott said he was windy if romance looked likely, as it did on the many occasions when she acted as hostess for David's London dinner parties.

Jeannine Bartosik, 1998

Dr J. H. Oldham, CBE, DD, then 80 years old, was widely respected for his unrivalled knowledge of colonial affairs and especially education. He had written an influential book in which he said that 'the responsibility of trusteeship means more than the protection of the native from injustice. It calls for active exertion to help the African to make the best of himself.'[33] For nearly 20 years he was secretary of the International Missionary Council and for almost as long a member of the Advisory Committee on Education in the Colonies. His biographer has written that during the First World War, Oldham 'recognized race to be one of the key issues of the day, and attempts at racial domination to be one of the symptoms ... of the malaise underlying the "Christian" West'.[34]

Between the wars Oldham worked closely with Lord Lugard to bring a sense of humanity to Colonial Office decisions of the day. Margery Perham describes their relationship from her personal knowledge of both men: 'Lugard's ... intimates were few but very close. ... And his partnership with Dr Oldham was perhaps the most complete and effective of these later years. Dr Oldham is a man whose great gifts have had diverse expressions – ecclesiastical statesman, writer, administrator, teacher, ... diplomat and politician. He was destined to leave a deep if, in part, a secret mark upon Africa. It was through his interest in missions that he was drawn into educational problems. ... Sincere, selfless, thoughtful, a small man and very gentle, but with steel behind the gentleness, he and Lugard fitted perfectly in character and aims. ... Oldham was above all the diplomat[;] ... he illustrated the meaning of that rather startling injunction of Christ, "Be ye wise as serpents and harmless as doves". A Christian of an ecumenical cast of mind, his political principles were based upon religious belief. ... [Lugard and Oldham] chose to work quietly in the background; both recoiled from extremists.'[35]

Michael Wood, Joe Oldham and David Stirling, 1954 (photo: Jeannine Bartosik)

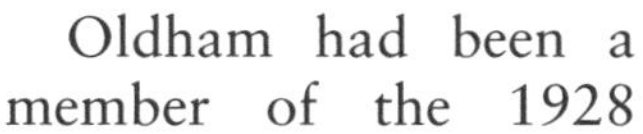

Oldham had been a member of the 1928 Hilton–Young Commission on the Closer Union of the Dependencies in Eastern and Central Africa[36] set up to counter the clamour from the settlers in Kenya for an unofficial majority in Legislative Council and union of Kenya and Tanganyika.

The parallel a generation later in central Africa is close except that Oldham and Lugard were not available to defend the rights of the Africans, so the settlers won their federation in central Africa but in the end were overwhelmed by the rising power of the African majority in the two northern territories. Lugard in the 1890s and Oldham in the 1920s and 1930s used the medium of the press to influence government. Lugard believed that while Africa was the place for action, Britain was the place for decision, often driven by public opinion, very much as David did in the 1950s.

The YMCA had set up five adult education colleges in Britain for people of different ages – Dunford for the oldest was where Oldham was the first resident fellow. Townsend-Coles, fresh from Durham University, had been appointed to initiate and run the centre and to help organize meetings, often about Africa, which Oldham chaired. In 1959, after listening to talk of Africa and meeting people of all races from the continent, Townsend-Coles asked the YMCA for a posting to Southern Rhodesia, where he soon became a member of Capricorn and a key figure in the development of the College of Citizenship.[37]

After the exchange of letters with Jeannine Scott, David moved quickly, staying at Dunford over the Easter weekend where he met Oldham and his wife, Mary. David and the elderly churchman hit it off immediately: within a few weeks they were addressing their letters 'My dear Joe' and 'My dear David'. Oldham believed that commitment and adventure were the very life of the human soul[38] and in David he found a classic example of both.

He was moved to write to David in poetic terms: 'Beacon of hope ye appear! / Languor is not in your heart / Weakness is not in your word / Weariness is not on your brow.'[39] Although he had never lived in Africa, Oldham could speak with warmth and emotive power about the continent. At a missionary conference in 1926 he said: 'Our attention has been directed ... to the powerful new forces that are reshaping the life of African peoples. ... Not to rest content with being in Africa and preaching on African soil, but to get as near as we can to the throbbing heart and centre of the movement of African life is the further call that comes to us.'[40] Oldham was fired with a renewed enthusiasm for Africa and offered to set up a powerful consultative committee for working weekends at Dunford. In describing his mental return to Africa, Oldham's biographer described David as 'a Roman Catholic and an idealist' and added, with less ecumenism than his subject, 'There are many of [Oldham's] admirers who could wish that he had not tried to do so, at any rate not quite in the form which his attempt took.'[41]

Jeannine Scott willingly found herself acting as honorary executive officer to what became a Capricorn office, soon to be inundated with files and papers from Salisbury and London. David wrote to John Baines with copies to Wood in Kenya, Tyrell and Johnston in Tanganyika, to tell them the news: 'I have always been worried that there was no intellectual rallying point or political philosophy in this country [UK] to combat the African nationalism and negative sentimentalism of the [Fabian Society] Africa Bureau. It is therefore of tremendous importance to us that there is being established at Dunford a centre which can become a rallying point in the intellectual sense of all those who believe that a basis can be found for racial cooperation in Africa.'[42]

From the time that David met Oldham, the Society began to concentrate on the practicalities of government in a multiracial country. Until then the vision was that if people of different races in east and central Africa could come together in a common loyalty and citizenship, everything else would follow. Officials in Whitehall, who were sympathetic to the general idea, but were running an empire, with budgets to be met and legislation to be passed, had described David as an impractical idealist, and some who suffered his intensive lobbying added that he was a fanatic. Now the Society was to put forward proposals that demanded analysis and serious consideration, and the Colonial Office was prepared to give advice, provided their support was not publicized.

David was excited by the idea of an expert team[43] working out the details of citizenship and the franchise in Capricorn Africa, writing to Betty Couldrey in the Nairobi office, full of enthusiasm after the first weekend meeting: 'Joe Oldham's first Capricorn group meeting was an exhausting but interesting affair. Walter Elliott and Creech-Jones came in order to give the Socialists' and Conservatives' standpoint, but the rest of them were professors of one sort or another and I had to get quite tight the first evening in order to overcome my natural shyness in this atmosphere, having been sent down so early in my own academic career at Cambridge!'[44] In spite of David's alleged awe of his advisors, he was adamant that 'we will put nobody on our consultancy committee on citizenship in this country until they have accepted entirely without qualification the entire aims and objects of the Society.'[45]

Oldham wrote a long memorandum in mid-1954 outlining the results of the discussions at Dunford. David's comments,[46] covering nine pages of advice and admonitions, show that he had lost what he called his natural shyness if it ever existed. He hoped that Oldham would emphasize that there was no vehicle other than Capricorn to bring about the enduring rapprochement between the races in Africa, adding that the extensiveness of the evidence and the number of witnesses available to the Society could not possibly be matched by a royal commission or a parliamentary select committee. David suggested that an African leader who joins the Society would maintain and even increase his African following. Vambe has said[47] that this bold statement would not have been borne out by evidence on the ground.

David described African nationalism as an evil equal to white racialism: 'Concessions granted as a result of African nationalist pressure tend merely to wet [*sic*] the appetite of the agitators and thereby demonstrate the rewards attaching to agitation.' Oldham took a more understanding view, writing: 'African nationalism is the primary, volcanic force to be reckoned with in Africa. It must be directed to constructive, not destructive ends. ... [It is] a force to be cordially welcomed because of its creative possibilities.'

An important division of opinion arose between them over the eventual transfer of power. Oldham wrote realistically and hopefully that the passing of power from the European to the African by virtue of their superior numbers should take place naturally and peacefully so that the European could continue to play a part as the creative minority. David countered this, even more hopefully, by insisting that power would pass from predominately European control to 'organically non-racial' control because the Capricorn revolution will succeed in establishing a new patriotism without regard to race. In a powerful and moving expression of faith, David continued. 'In Africa the elimination of the colour bar restrictions can either be regarded as a slow process ... a rearguard action by the European seeking to retain power as long as possible (as in Rhodesia) or, and this is the Capricorn way, as the remaining and therefore priceless material which the European must be prepared to expend in one great act of faith in order to establish his sincerity of purpose in creating a new integrated multiracial community.'

Oldham's next draft, 'The Fundamentals of the Capricorn Movement'[48] dealt obliquely with the issue that bedevilled Capricorn for most of its life – politics. 'The primary aim of the Capricorn Society is to serve as the vehicle of a creative idea, as an agency for bringing about a psychological change in the minds of all races, and as a driving force to promote legislative action. ... But while the best advice available must be sought, it is desirable to recognize from the start that in politics things seldom turn out the way that is expected. The most carefully prepared proposals may undergo large modifications in their translation into legislation, and legislative decisions may be found in practice to work very differently from what was expected.' This realism, based on his long involvement with the problems of India and Africa, contrasted with David's absolutism.

Oldham's memorandum developed into a slim book, *New Hope in Africa*, which he introduced with the words: 'This is a book about the Capricorn Africa Society. It is not in the ordinary sense propaganda for that Society. ... To the ends which the Society seeks to serve I am completely committed. ... None of us can measure how much may be lost if the cause should fail, nor how bright a future may open in Africa if it should succeed.'[49] Although his stand in the decades before the war had been against closer union until the Africans themselves demanded it, the only comment Oldham made on the subject was to note that the Society had acknowledged that it had been a mistake to press for administrative and economic unity before achieving integration between the races. He concentrated on the twin aims of the Society – the creation of a common loyalty for all regardless of race and the maintenance of civilized standards.

The publication of *New Hope in Africa* in 1955 was of great importance for the Society. It was an inspiring and elegantly written analysis of the human and political situation in east and central Africa, and of Capricorn's proposals, by a man widely regarded as uniquely independent and knowledgeable. For Capricorn members in Africa, it became a talisman, to be read and reread, as we struggled to develop proposals for the future. My copy, with many annotations of approval, bears the scars of much use, having been carried to many meetings and to Salima and back. To have our ideas described and praised by a man of Oldham's stature, a man no one could call an idealistic fanatic, was enormously encouraging.

Echoing David, the book was a call to arms: 'The battle will not be won by drawing up paper schemes or by high sounding pronouncements, but only by a living political faith and resolute action. ... The greatness of men and nations is measured not only by their wealth and power, but by their ability to bear burdens and to overcome difficulties, to pursue excellence, and to maintain a just and stable social order.' Less securely based on fact was an echo of David's enthusiasm: 'Africans and Asians have played a full part in the movement from the beginning and are among its most ardent supporters.'

Oldham's only knowledge of the Society's strength in Africa came from optimistic assessments by David, van der Post and the Woods, who hoped that such statements were true. With gentle logic Oldham analysed racial differences, the adjustments Africans have to make as they become part of a technological and alien civilization, the nature of that civilization itself, and the problems inherent in systems of universal franchise. Although he resisted discussing proposals for electoral systems because he did not wish to pre-empt ideas from the citizenship committees in Africa, his comment introduces the possibility of a qualified, multiple vote. Presciently, he wrote: 'Perhaps the most difficult and urgent social problem in Africa is to enable Africans to make the transition from the (relative) collectivism of tribalism to the free society of responsible individuals, without succumbing to the collectivism of the totalitarian state.' What would that good and thoughtful man have written if he could have foreseen the future, in which large numbers of Africans would suffer grievously from tribalism and totalitarian rule?

The book was well received by the press, *Time and Tide* calling it 'this lucid, graceful and profound little book'. *East Africa and Rhodesia*, whose editor F. S. Joelson did not always approve of Capricorn, described it as 'an important and absorbingly interesting book'. It went down well in Whitehall, as a Colonial Office memo records: 'The Colonial Secretary is obviously impressed by the work of the Capricorn Africa Society and recently he had informal talks with Col David Stirling. Mr Lennox-Boyd spoke with enthusiasm of the book *New Hope in Africa* in which the 81-year-old author, Dr J. Oldham, sets out with a degree of critical detachment to interpret the purposes and aims of the Society. The book – a fascinating one according to Mr Lennox-Boyd – is focused on the Central African Federation and East Africa.'[50]

From memos written in the Colonial Office in the mid-1950s, it is clear that Whitehall genuinely believed that a multiracial political future was possible for the countries under their control in east and central Africa. Lennox-Boyd's approval of *New Hope in Africa*, even making allowance for his friendship with David, confirms this. But after the political advances in West Africa the UK government realized that power could be transferred peacefully only if it were done without undue delay, and made plans to hand over government to African majorities. The settlers had feared, and the Africans hoped, that a Labour government in Britain would instigate rapid moves to independence, but they were both wrong. Conservatives were in power from October 1951 to October 1964, the period covering the time when the countries with which we are concerned, except Southern Rhodesia, became independent under democratically elected African governments.

In central Africa, Sir Roy Welensky (prime minister of the federation) and other European politicians continued to hope for a real amalgamation of the two Rhodesias. The African people in Northern Rhodesia believed that wealth from copper was financing new roads and other services in Southern Rhodesia while Northern Rhodesia was poorly served by the federal government. The country was different from the other candidates for David's great federation in that most of the white population were on contract to the mines or in government service, unlike the farmers and businessmen in Kenya or Southern Rhodesia, and it was rich. Members of the fledgling Capricorn branch in Northern Rhodesia were sincere in their desire to break down racial barriers, but Capricorn was intent on creating a situation in which votes would be cast regardless of race. This was never feasible for many reasons, including the vehement antagonism of Africans to the federation, which Capricorn had supported. Nyasaland was even less promising for the Society, having little natural wealth, few settlers and an equal aversion to federation.

In Kenya constitutional changes under the 1954 proposals proposed by the Conservative secretary of state, Oliver Lyttleton, resulted in what the Colonial Office described as 'the first mixed government in an African country with a settled European population'.[51] There were African, Asian and European members of Legislative Council, although ultimate power remained with the official members and the governor. Elections were on communal voters' rolls, criticized by Capricorn as encouraging candidates to appeal to the racial attitudes of their constituents instead of proposing ideas for the good of the whole country. During the election campaigns, this was the case in most election speeches. Once elected, some members of Legislative Council made efforts to form a united front across the races, but they were unable to overcome established positions and difficult personalities. Commenting on the new situation the governor, Sir Evelyn Baring, wrote with some truth to the Colonial Office that 'the Europeans in general dislike the idea of party politics, and would be happier as permanent critics of an irremovable government.'[52]

The governor's ADC was Colin Campbell who later became a close friend and business partner of David's. As with so many of the connections in Capricorn, this relationship came through family and the army: Campbell's cousin, Guy Campbell, commanded the Kenya Regiment during the Mau Mau emergency, with his headquarters on a coffee farm in the highlands near Mount Kenya owned by a Capricorn supporter, Peter Marrian.[53] Campbell spent many weekends on the farm, sometimes taking the governor's daughters with him, and it was through Marrian that Campbell met David, whom he described to me as tall, bronzed and impressive, although not conventionally handsome. The governor listened to Capricorn ideas from both Marrian and David without indicating whether he agreed with them or not. He was, after all, a career colonial officer from a line of distinguished diplomats.

In May 1955 the report of the East Africa Royal Commission was published, after two years and thousands of submissions.[54] It was a fair and balanced analysis of the many factors influencing the future of the region. The chapter on race relations described the level of distrust and resentment to be found among the African people over the question of land, while the commissioners recognized that the wealth of the country, and therefore improvement in conditions generally, depended on the farms in the White Highlands. The commissioners wrote: 'non-African settlement aggravates the situation. Where fertile land is scarce ... such settlement appears not as the harbinger of greater wealth and better jobs but as an intruder. Particularly is this the case when there is an immense disparity between the size of the settler estates and the overcrowded holdings of indigenous cultivators about them, especially if the estates are undeveloped.'[55]

They continued: 'The value of efficient European ranches and farms as a guide to right usage by Africans has been submerged in a resentment that, unalienated, such lands might have eased their own grazing and cultivating problems. The European settler himself, busy with the pioneering task of discovering how to farm efficiently in an untested environment, has had little time as an individual for considering his African neighbour and, when challenged as a class by African claims that his presence is restricting their means of survival, feels that these claims are unjustified when the Africans do not practice proper farming in the land which they have.'

Further quotations illustrate the sympathetic and realistic approach of the commissioners to the intractable problems involved in land and productivity. 'Those who follow the whole history of land disposal in East Africa can understand how strong a sense of rightness is derived from achievement on the immigrant side and from checked customary expansion on the indigenous side. ... The approach on a tribal basis to questions of land tenure and land use is incompatible with the development of a modern economy, and this applies equally to a purely racial approach to the highlands question.' Even the most extreme settlers should have recognized the importance of the report's conclusions that the highlands could not be a white enclave forever.

The commissioners wrote: 'We have said that East Africa needs the skill and capital of the non-African more than the non-African needs East Africa and this is true in economic terms.' They added: 'A policy without the cooperation of the indigenous people is no policy at all.' Capricorn citizenship committees[56] in Kenya considered the Royal Commission proposals together with Oldham's words when drafting the sections of the Capricorn Contract on land reform, labour relations, education and immigration. The commission's terms of reference did not include politics, so for ideas on the electoral system we turned to the report by Walter Coutts,[57] published in the same year.

Chapter 6
Outposts and Officers

After five years of great effort and some significant changes of direction, David Stirling believed he had an organization capable of the task he set himself. By 1955 there were offices with staff in London, Salisbury, Bulawayo, Nairobi, Ol Molog and on the Copper Belt, plus supporters in America. And David could genuinely claim an African membership, although in very limited numbers.

In London, David had landed a catch: Marshal of the Royal Air Force Sir John Slessor. He had served in the Royal Flying Corps during the First World War; in 1939 he was an air commodore, then air chief marshal, becoming marshal of the RAF in 1950. He was an impressive and influential figure to have as chairman of the Capricorn London committee and his career gave him a useful range of contacts: he had served in Europe and the United States and was twice ADC to the King (1938 and 1948–50). Jeannine Bartosik describes him as a lovely man, warm-hearted and upright, a perfectionist who insisted everything should be done correctly, which brought him into conflict with David's attitude that the end justifies the means.

Early in 1955 there was a serious row in which Slessor accused David of being 'hopelessly irresponsible' and of playing fast and loose with finance. David played the ultimate card by threatening to resign, writing that he could not possibly remain as president 'if the fantastic charges made by Slessor remain standing'.[1] This tactic seems to have worked because I could find nothing in the files about it thereafter. Conflict between the two men, both tall and powerful, had been building up for some months. David had expressed his irritation with Slessor in a letter from Salisbury to Jeannine Scott (as she then was): 'You have got no idea of how thoroughly impatient such lack of robustness makes us out here when we are busting ourselves in every way to put Capricorn on the map. I feel sure that it must be equally distasteful to Joe [Oldham] and yourself.'[2]

Jeannine Scott worked with Joe Oldham and his powerful consultative committee with the important addition in August 1955 of Jonathan Lewis as executive officer. Lewis, a few years younger than David and a friend from before the war, had served as a colonial service district officer in Nigeria until retiring through ill health. With his Irish background, Lewis's charm and cheerful eccentricity made him a very attractive character who soon became a vital part of the small group of London supporters. David was keen to have him, with one reservation, writing that: 'there is one element of doubt I have about him, and that is his studiously scruffy appearance. Do you think if he was doing the rounds of the city, raising money for Capricorn, he would consent to constrict his neck in a hard collar, and to have a comb leaving its mark in his hair?'[3] The appointment was a masterstroke: in spite of his dishevelled appearance Lewis was a good organizer with a powerful intellect who was passionately concerned about Africa. Although Oldham's committee met at Dunford in Sussex, the Capricorn office was in 43 Cheval Place, Jeannine Scott's house in Knightsbridge. It soon became a centre for people involved with the future of Africa – Capricorn members from abroad called in for a gossip with Lewis, and would perhaps be offered what he called a 'jar' of Jameson's Irish whiskey. The lucky ones might be taken for a spin in one of his vintage Rolls Royces, or watch his nonchalant handling of a penny-farthing bicycle.

Jonathan Lewis, 1956
(photo: Jeannine Bartosik)

It was Lewis's sympathy and understanding of the problems faced by African students in Britain that created the hostels in central London,[4] which continued the spirit of Capricorn after its ambitions failed in Africa. Jeannine Scott and Jennifer Plunket, who was then living in England, built up a network of wealthy and well-connected people to organize a piano recital, film previews and society balls to raise funds for the cause. Jeannine Scott persuaded Princess Margaret, a friend of her sister's, to become patron of the non-political Zebra Trust and later the Zebra Housing Association, a duty which she undertook with enthusiasm until her death in 2002.

The Capricorn office in London provided intellectual muscle to David's ideas and was vital as a source of funds for the whole movement. This led to friction between London, demanding evidence that the organization they were asking their friends to subsidize was effective, and those in Africa, who appeared to be holding back on the drive for new members. The main protagonists were Slessor in London and David in Africa. Slessor wanted membership numbers and information on local fund-raising activities with audited accounts, which the Salisbury office was reluctant, or unable, to supply. In September 1955 Slessor wrote to David reiterating the points about finance that he had made two years earlier, to which David replied that the membership drive had to wait until he was back in Africa to ensure that the European members being enrolled were not the kind that might prejudice existing African support.[5]

While London was unwilling to provide more money without evidence of real members, Salisbury reiterated that funds were needed to mount the membership drive, so the debate continued without conclusion. Although David was making bold statements about a future mass membership, he was curiously hesitant to start building it up. He insisted that the drive to enrol African members depended on having suitable European members, while the reverse applied to the growth of European membership. Meanwhile, the London committee waited for news of members of any colour. David had spent five years trying to build Capricorn into an effecttive movement and, although there is no indication in the files, it is possible that his prevarication over the membership drive was because he was just enough of a realist to know that it might be futile.

In July 1955 Jeannine Scott, Lewis, Michael and Susan Wood prepared a paper in London that set out the main issues. They concluded that financiers in the City would not support Capricorn because: (a) the movement was political; (b) its aims conflicted with those of South Africa (where there was much UK investment); (c) there was insufficient evidence of backing in Africa; and (d) the City had been bitten before. Success in Africa was the one and only factor that would ensure support in London. Between February and June 1955 the London office tried to raise £20,000 from A and B lists of possible donors, but in the end the majority on both lists declined the invitation to subscribe, and a total of only £3260 was raised.[6] Minutes of a Dulverton Trust[7] meeting from 1956 record that an appeal for funds had been rejected because the Society was 'the subject of political controversy in Africa, that there some doubts concerning its charitable status, and that its funds were not well administered'. In 1957 in response to 'a renewed and urgent appeal' the trust[8] made a grant to the Society of £2000 'towards its work among African peoples' but insisted that it be anonymous. In the Salisbury office the minutes record examples of the problems of fund-raising faced by a multiracial organization in a divided and bigoted society — a dance was proposed, which would, by law, have to be for one race only. The committee naturally responded that any Capricorn affair must be open to all races.[9] Meanwhile, the president's office with a secretary, and the branch office in Salisbury with two executive officers and a secretary and committees around the country, cost £500 a month,[10] more than any other political organization had to spend, but it was also more than was available. In 1955, the two executive officers in Salisbury were Chad Chipunza and Peter Mackay.

Peter Mackay, 2000

Following local custom, if not Capricorn philosophy, Mackay was paid £90, Chipunza £40 and the female European secretary £50 per month. Chipunza, like many members of the African elite who joined Capricorn, was educated at Fort Hare University in South Africa and became a school headmaster. He was not respected by other Africans, perhaps because of his family background — an ancestor, Chief Chipunza, had sided with the white invaders in a battle in 1896. He became national chairman of the United Federal Party under Sir Roy Welensky and leader of the official opposition in the Rhodesian parliament during the period of white dominated unilaterally declared independence. Unlike many of his contemporaries, Chipunza was never detained by the Smith government, which also damned him as a stooge in the eyes of Africans.[11] His contemporaries say that he worked for Capricorn only for the money, but he appeared genuine in his belief in the possibilities of a multiracial future.

In his detailed report of a tour on behalf of the Society round Northern Rhodesia his comments were frank: 'I visited the Mine Workers' Union Offices in Kitwe, where I met the general secretary, the vice-president and others. After about an hour's deliberation I came to the conclusion that they are incapable of comprehending national issues and placing them in their proper perspective. They confused politics with trade union matters throughout the session and they appeared to be too drunk both with power and liquor to appreciate anything. They told me categorically that their first and foremost duty was to fight for the miners and if there is no trouble there is no work for them.'[12]

His comments on those who were running the African National Congress was equally honest: 'it became very clear to me that the members of the congress executive (who all receive salaries) have realized that in order to maintain their comfortable positions they should brand all their critics (who are their peers) as informers, traitors, or Capricorn, in order to get rid of rivals.'

Mackay arrived in Southern Rhodesia in 1948 to take up farming and freelance writing for local papers. He was a handsome young man with a military bearing and moustache who had done his national service in David's old regiment, the Scots Guards — he was very much David's sort of man: middle class and single who had done well in the army. He was not religious but had the inner strength and single-mindedness of a priest or a monk. After editing *Concorde* for the Interracial Association, Mackay wanted to work full time in the campaign and agreed to act as executive officer for Capricorn from January 1955, reporting to the branch chairman, John Baines. Later, he came to believe that democracy meant majority rule and joined his friend Leo Takawira in the National Democratic Party where he gave help to the families of gaoled black activists.

It was not his nature to dissemble, so whatever his principles were at the time, they would have been inviolable, causing him a great deal of trouble when, in 1963, the government required all Europeans to register for military service. Mackay refused to fight the people of the country he had made his home, and served four months in gaol, where Takawira was also detained in the African enclosure. On his release Mackay again refused to register and, before he could be deported, went into exile in Zambia where, during the war in Rhodesia, he 'became a foot-soldier in the African National Congress, obeying orders',[13] smuggling men and arms in and out of Zambia along what was known as the 'freedom road'. The Rhodesian government and most of the white population said that Mackay was a communist, or a KGB agent – the standard epithet for any white man who actively supported African nationalism – and he was a prohibited immigrant in Rhodesia and other colonial territories. After Zimbabwe's independence he devoted himself to working with local people on development schemes, until his quiet and solitary retirement with his books and collection of African maps and carvings.

Mackay's experience as a journalist helped David in writing and producing the *Handbook for Speakers*, which had questions and answers on 'political philosophy', 'citizenship and franchise', 'social relations and colour bar', 'labour relations', 'land tenure', 'immigration' and 'economic development'. It reminded some critics, thinking of David's upbringing, of the Roman Catholic catechism. The technique of question and answer (even if the answers actually came first) produced statements on all aspects of the Society's philosophy and organization. Drafts went back and forth between Salisbury and London as points were added or clarified. In June 1955 Slessor wrote detailed comments on the introductory section after working with Dudley Clarke[14] and the editor of *East Africa and Rhodesia* on the draft, and Oldham and his consultative committee added their thoughts.

An appendix to the handbook proposed an elaborate administrative structure developed by David.[15] He proposed 12 different organizations including the board of patrons, the president's standing committee, a number of regional executive committees and citizenship committees, plus urban and rural area controllers and roving agents. The structure was grandiose and cumbersome, and only a few of the units were actually set up. The handbook defined the structure and duties of the citizenship committees, with a timetable leading to the convention in June 1956,[16] then expected to be in Mbeya, Tanganyika, the central point of the future dominion. The principle of the multiple vote was introduced into Capricorn thinking and unequivocally supported,[17] with the explanation that it would balance experience against numbers in a multiracial common roll. The handbook is an important document because it was produced at a time when the concept of areas reserved for African ownership was replaced by the clear statement that the Society 'believes that ultimately all land in a Capricorn territory should become an area of equal purchase opportunity for all citizens of that territory'.[18]

In February 1956 there were meetings, often more than one, held in Salisbury, Zomba, Blantyre, Cholo, Que Que, Bulawayo, Umtali, Rusape, Mashaba, the Copper Belt, Kitwe and Marandellas, in which Africans, Europeans, some Asians and Coloureds debated the clauses of the proposed document and tried to raise funds. Local financial support came from a few wealthy and upper-class settlers who accepted David's passionately argued concept of a future in which race and colour would be irrelevant. By upbringing they were paternalistic in their attitude to those less fortunate than themselves, and generally suspicious of politicians.

Foremost among the donors were (later Sir) Stephen Courtauld and his Italian-Romanian wife, Ginny, who had built themselves a beautiful house, La Rochelle, at Umtali when they moved from England during the war. Enormously wealthy from textiles, in the 1930s the Courtaulds had restored and enlarged a medieval palace at Eltham, outside London, equipped with the latest under-floor heating, built-in vacuum cleaning and a music system throughout. The palace and the Art Deco interiors have recently been restored and opened to the public by English Heritage, although the many works of art were taken to Umtali by the Courtaulds and eventually given to the National Art Gallery in Salisbury (now Harare). In late 1956 the Capricorn treasurer, Charles March, went with David to stay with the Courtaulds. On the Sunday morning David vanished, leaving March to make conversation. When David reappeared, having been to mass, both Courtauld and his wife produced their chequebooks and wrote out cheques for £3000, a large sum at that time.[19] After the expenses of the Salima convention,[20] which they had attended as observers, the money was badly needed.

My memory of staying at La Rochelle in 1960, when the Courtaulds were both over seventy, is of the large plate glass window on which distinguished visitors signed their names with a diamond. I cannot remember whether Wood and I signed. Ian Hancock, who interviewed Capricorn members in 1974, has written: 'The Courtaulds and the Plunkets ... were exceptional. Most [white] Capricornists were not rich and titled, even if their accents were unmistakably of the public schools, the Guards, the Colonial Service or the City. It was true, however that the CAS was no place for the white artisan or the Afrikaner farmer.'[21]

The formation of a branch in Northern Rhodesia was inspired when Jeannine Scott had lunch in London with Charles Fisher and his wife Monica, two doctors on leave from the Copper Belt. She told them about Capricorn and David with her usual enthusiasm[22] and a visit from David to Luanshya in March 1955[23] encouraged them to open a Capricorn office. In contrast to the racial attitudes of the white mine workers, there were a few individuals in Northern Rhodesia who realized that the barriers between the races were indefensible and, in the long run, unsustainable. They included Sir Ronald Prain, chairman of Roan Selection Trust; Fisher himself, who became chief medical officer of the Roan Antelope Mine and later of RST, and Monica Fisher's uncle, (later Sir) Stewart Gore-Browne, an eccentric aristocrat who lived in style on a great estate in the northeastern corner of the country.[24] Gore-Browne, although he often treated his servants as if they were medieval serfs, staunchly believed in equality between the races and supported African moves to independence, becoming a close friend of Kenneth Kaunda, Zambia's first president. As another alpha male, he never succumbed to David's charm and thought the qualified franchise was a delaying tactic.

Fisher and his wife Monica were convinced Christians and it was their faith and innate sense of justice that directed them to work for greater understanding between the races. In 1940 Fisher had been appointed by the governor to represent African interests in Legislative Council and, although the demands of his medical work meant that he later resigned, his opinion continued to be sought and respected in the country. Fisher was a large, kindly man, fluent in African dialects, and devoted to Northern Rhodesia, the country of his birth where his widow still lives.

The chief personnel officer of RST was Robert Menzies, whose career in Africa began as a colonial service district officer in Uganda. He had been an athlete at university and found himself taking a team of Ugandans to the 1954 All Africa Games in Lusaka, where it was clear that his sympathetic approach to coaching produced better results than the authoritarian style usual in southern Africa. After a Ugandan was successful in the high jump, a South African coach, thinking perhaps of how effective a rhino-hide whip could be, complimented Menzies, saying: 'You certainly know how to make a kaffir jump.'[25]

Menzies joined RST as personnel officer, and quickly became involved with interracial affairs, working with the Fishers in the Capricorn branch. Of Fisher he has written: 'Charles was always there, utterly dependable; his example gave us courage to expose unpopular points of view. We lesser ones took shelter from heads of departments and management under his solid spreading branches. No one dared say we were irresponsible or even ridiculous to hold such views because Charles held them and his wisdom was not questioned. ... He lives most vividly in my mind for his example; solid and genuine; and he was right.'[26] Menzies has described that period in his life as 'halcyon days — times when life seemed to be in technicolour — when there was constant stimulation and when David made everything, if improbable, still possible, and of course great fun. ... Events were there to be engaged in — things were there to be done in the excitement of great ideas about a future to be created.'[27] I remember the same excitement in Kenya.

Menzies helped set up three citizenship committees on the Copper Belt and opened a Capricorn office. After being asked by his employers if he wanted to work for RST or for Capricorn, Menzies decided it would be unwise to attend the convention at Salima.[28] Mackay wrote in his annual report for 1955: 'We should like here to mention the work of the Copper Belt executive committee where, under the guidance of Dr Charles Fisher and the brilliant management of Mr I. R. Menzies, the Capricorn organization has opened its own office, is in process of building a Capricorn hall, and has established a firm and ever-growing foothold.'[29] Menzies was typical of many Capricorn members, more concerned with social issues than politics, who joined Capricorn because it claimed to be non-political. After Salima he reluctantly realized that events would be resolved only through political action, which was unlikely to produce a Capricorn solution. Enthusiasms begun in the Northern Rhodesia branch were to result in much generosity when the London office turned its attention to the plight of African students in Britain.[30] Oliver Carruthers worked as a temporary Capricorn executive officer from the Fishers' house in Luanshya in 1958 and from 1965 Theo Bull lived in the country as a journalist and publisher of the *Central African Examiner* with support from the Courtaulds, Gore-Browne and Prain of RST.[31]

Mackay made a three-week tour of Nyasaland in December 1955 to set up the nucleus of a Capricorn organization. He reported 130 interviews with 94 people while he was there and was able to leave an executive committee in Blantyre and five citizenship committees or discussion groups in the country. However, he reported that the small European community held the conviction that the country's government would inevitably pass into

African hands and the only point of disagreement was the time factor. He found reactions to this conviction varied from indifference to a determination to postpone the time for as long as possible. In spite of Mackay's enthusiasm, the small number of Europeans, many of whom were government servants, and the large African population made the possibility of a Capricorn outcome unlikely.

In Tanganyika it was becoming increasingly obvious that Africans were not joining Capricorn for two reasons – its early enthusiasm for federation and because it appeared to be, and indeed was, dominated by Europeans. In the files there is an encouraging letter from David to Tom Tyrell, the Capricorn man in Dar es Salaam: 'My sister stayed with John Elphinstone ... and the only other guests were the Queen and Prince Philip. Both my sister and Simon Dalhousie [her husband] are ... supporters of Capricorn ... and were able to work on our behalf. P[rince] Philip more than interested.'[32]

However, in spite of Capricorn's useful contacts, it was decided to form a new organization to be based in Tanganyika in order to combat the charge that the Society was controlled and funded from outside. In November David wrote to Robin Johnston in Ol Molog: 'stayed at GH [Government House] with Twining. Saw Ivor Bayldon [MP, who thought that] Capricorn name caused suspicion ... and would not ... provide a vehicle for interracial political action. Also emphasized by Twining. [I] proposed to change name to Tanganyika National Society.'[33]

Following instructions, Johnston and his committee published the Tanganyika National Society manifesto in December 1955, after much agonized discussion with Susan Wood, who was emotionally attached to Capricorn. The timing of the launch was designed to pre-empt the formation of the similar, but less liberal, United Tanganyika Party, supported by the governor[34] to keep Julius Nyerere's Tanganyika African National Union in check, realizing that Capricorn was unlikely to succeed. Nyerere responded to the formation of both multiracial parties with two powerful pamphlets that demolished the gradualism implied in the phrase 'maintenance of civilized standards' and the idea of the qualified vote, writing that Capricorn was an attempt by imperialists to hang on to some shreds of privilege.[35] Nyerere himself was not a racist, but he saw clearly that any compromise over the principle of universal franchise was dangerous to the belief that Tanganyika was to be an African country in which other races would be welcome, but only as guests. Nyerere's tactics and the overwhelming number of his supporters ensured that the plans of the governor and the rival multiracial parties came to nothing. The Tanganyika branch sent six delegates to the Salima convention and Ol Molog continued to be a centre for long talks about the Society, especially when Wood was there at the weekend, but as a practical proposition in Tanganyika it was effectively dead.

In the Nairobi office the Woods were supported by Betty Couldrey and Kendall Ward, whose political awareness was important in steering debates in the citizenship committees. David's optimism and encouragement on his visits, and the enthusiasm of the African and Asian members of the committees created a feeling that Kenya really could be a country in which Africans, Asians and Europeans could live together and prosper. This was the atmosphere when I joined Capricorn in late 1955. I found a group of impressive people of all races, educated and confident, who contributed time and effort to attending meetings and preparing drafts in committees around the country. Those I knew best, who have remained firm friends, were in Nairobi but there were also European farmers drafting clauses on land tenure that would remove the protection they enjoyed in the White Highlands. There were three committees in the Nairobi area and nine around the country, meeting every week or ten days.

I joined a local citizenship committee and see from my old files that in March 1956 I was chairing and writing the minutes. The other members were two Africans, two Asian businessmen, the wife of an American oil executive and a young Kenya-born European who had distinguished himself in the forests fighting Mau Mau, earning the George Cross. We argued and debated the issues as individuals with a common aim, but in retrospect the approach to many of the social questions must have been different – the Africans and Asians sought improvements in access to education, health facilities, land and jobs, whereas the European members were working to reduce their privileges and isolation. With the emergency regulations still in force, the lack of any Kikuyu members in the Society seemed to us at the time only right and proper, not having the foresight to recognize how serious this omission would be in the years to come. It appears that we did have at least one Kikuyu member: a letter dated October 1955 from Ward to Mackay in Salisbury records that he was 'still very concerned about the security aspect of Capricorn. For instance, a Mau Mau general had signed on. This was discovered after he had been shot in the Aberdare [forest] and on his person were found [CAS] membership papers.

This has meant that I have had to send the whole of our membership [list] over to the [police] special branch for scrutiny.'[36]

Suggestions and amendments to the draft contract proposed by the citizenship committees were sent to the Nairobi office and then on to David. The minutes show the depth of our debates as we analysed the clauses sent from Salisbury. Our committee prepared a questionnaire on requirements for citizenship and the franchise and tried to balance David's demand for one document, relevant to all the countries of east and central Africa, and our ideas of what would be right for Kenya. In our attempts to develop a programme for the future we were unaware of David's attitude, expressed the previous year in a letter to Johnston: 'The organization was not to be for the discussion of the Society's policy [which] was a given, but instead to provide support facilities. We must not broaden our membership for the purpose of discussing our future plans; rather we must invite membership on the widest possible scale to back our plan when it is cut and dried. ... Our Society must be prepared to be authoritarian up to this point, otherwise people joining will imagine they are doing so to help formulate an idea rather than serve one.'[37] David set a deadline of the end of May 1956 to have the document ready for the convention in June. We tried hard to meet it, little realizing that there would be changes at Salima, many made by Philip Mason and myself working overnight.[38]

In early 1956 the possibility of any of the countries in east and central Africa being granted self-government within a few years seemed remote, and all the members of our group thought that a generation would be required. As we worked on the details of the document in our committees, we believed that we were creating the structure that would allow the country to develop at a sensible pace to eventual independence, with all the races that had contributed to its development being involved in government. We were, of course, naive. India, Ceylon and Burma had been independent for eight years, but we knew they were ancient civilizations and did not have entrenched white settlers who had created the economy and intended to continue managing it.

Colonial Office files in the Public Record Office give an idea of how Capricorn was perceived by the authorities in Kenya. Comments on the Society by police special branch in their monthly reports to the governor are especially illuminating.[39] In October 1955 their informer reported that Kendall Ward had quoted membership as 526 Europeans, 573 Africans and 127 Asians. In November that year, the informer wrote that 'the Society does not appear to be increasing its influence or membership, and Africans see it as a way of opening the [white] highlands and limiting European immigration. Asians remain disinterested, seeing little benefit to themselves.' In January 1956, special branch reported several meetings having been held but 'no indication of headway. Finances precarious, Europeans perhaps disposed to ... good intentions and integrity, but the majority regard it as an ideal rather than a practicality. Asians remain on the fence and Africans reluctant to grasp Capricorn concept.' In April and May the report was of a number of meetings at which van der Post was the principal speaker, 'but it cannot be said, however, that the Society's prospects have been noticeably advanced thereby. The Africans are suspicious, viewing with disfavour any policy which appears to postpone African self-government.' In spite of the special branch informer's jaundiced though probably accurate opinion, van der Post's inspiring lectures drew large crowds in Kampala, Nairobi, Mombasa, Dar es Salaam and in the Rhodesias and Nyasaland. In Mombasa he enthused a young Englishman, Robert Dick-Read, to seek out Lewis in London and come back to Kenya the following year to work for Capricorn in Nairobi.

David drove himself hard and was often unwell – in the 18 months leading up to the convention he made 14 trips out of Salisbury – though he seemed to be strong and in control of Capricorn and himself whenever I saw him in the early months of 1956. Nothing could dim his enthusiasm or his ability to exaggerate the situation, even to his friends. In November 1955 he wrote to Lewis in London expressing dismay about an article in the *Observer* by Arthur Creech-Jones, the Labour colonial spokesman, which had said Capricorn was more European than African.[40] David responded by asking Chipunza to write to the editor saying that there were a hundred active African members for every European and that the *Handbook* was as much an African as a European effort. This was neither true nor good tactics: of course Capricorn was more European than African and needed to be because it was European attitudes that needed to change first. In 1953 David had written, accurately, that white racialism encouraged black nationalism. The humiliations and restrictions of the colour bar were imposed and maintained by individual Europeans and the government machine they dominated in the countries of Capricorn Africa. The editor of *East Africa and Rhodesia* thought that many Africans in central Africa regarded joining Capricorn as a real test of the sincerity of Europeans who professed liberal intentions.[41]

Chapter 7
An Essential Difference

Many members of Capricorn, myself included, believed that our proposals for the franchise were fundamental to our project. It was the qualified multiple vote that gave our ideals some bite, an edge over other organizations whose members believed, as we did, in the oneness of humanity and that racial discrimination was a bad thing. We sought a practical programme to underpin sentiments of goodwill, and believed that the qualified vote was a logical solution to the problem of three disparate groups of people sharing the governance of one country. The opening precepts of the Capricorn Contract, which we signed at Salima,[1] set out beliefs that were generally acceptable, even if some are observed in the breach, but the essential difference was in Provision One on the electoral system: 'The right to elect members of the legislature is open to all citizens who have attained the statutory qualifications and they will be registered on one common roll. The vote is not a natural right but a responsibility to be exercised for the common good.' David Stirling described his philosophy on the franchise as 'the supreme gamble' lying at the heart of the Capricorn approach.[2] He believed 'that the inevitable statistical predominance of the African, in the long run, would have no significance if the common loyalty proves emotionally valid for each race.'

Joe Oldham's group in England and David in Africa refined the concept of the qualified franchise by adding the possibility that individuals could have more than one vote. *The Handbook for Speakers* said: 'The Society views with approval the principle of the multiple vote. It believes that members of all races who deserve well of their country and who have positions of more than average responsibility should be candidates for additional votes. The decision to incorporate the multiple vote into the Capricorn electoral system would make possible the broadening of the base of the vote quantitatively without diluting its overall standard in the qualitative sense.'[3] We were convinced that a system in which voters had to qualify to be on the electoral roll, and in which some individuals would have more than one vote, could help to balance experience against numbers. In any case, as Oldham wrote in *New Hope in Africa*, universal suffrage was comparatively new in Europe, and could not necessarily be regarded as an unqualified success.

It was not clear to those of us on the citizenship committees whether our proposal was set in stone, applicable for all time as an absolute good, or was an interim measure that would evolve into universal franchise. Clause IV of the Contract said: 'We declare and agree that the foregoing precepts fundamental to our mutual contract define the basic and permanent principles which shall be written into the new constitutions of any of these territories on their attainment of full self-government. At the same time we acknowledge that a constitution must be subject to amendment if, in the constantly changing circumstances of the world, confidence in these principles is to be preserved and renewed.' It seemed that some changes of detail would be acceptable provided canon law expressed in the precepts (that the vote is not a natural right) was not breached. This absolutism came from David, who believed that Capricorn's principles would last forever.

Philip Mason thought that David did not appreciate the necessity for flexibility and quoted Disraeli: 'Finality is not the language of politics.'[4] Mason had attended some citizenship committee meetings in Salisbury, had been an advisor to the London office (where he was known for being a stickler for correct punctuation) and had broadcast on the BBC about Capricorn. He differed from David in that he never regarded Capricorn's electoral proposal as a permanent solution to the problems of multiracial Africa but as a transition to eventual full democracy. He wrote in *A Thread of Silk*: 'I went to several meetings of one of these committees [in Rhodesia], and there the basic difficulty emerged. The black African would say: 'Why not one man one vote? That's what you have in England. If it is good for you, why not for us? You are thinking up a device for prolonging white supremacy. To my mind, the answer to that was that perhaps the plural vote was only a step on the way – one stage in a developing situation; once the new state was achieved it would grow on its own lines. But David would have none of that. The plural vote was to him something absolutely good, better than the single vote and, what is more, the new state must have absolute principles built into its constitution guaranteeing what each party had promised to the other. It was to be a national covenant – eternal, indissoluble, a sacramental marriage.'[5] Some 18 months after Salima Jonathan Lewis quoted Mason: 'It sounds as though everything [on the franchise] we put into an appendix at Salima has been discarded. As you know, I am not sorry about that.'[6]

While citizenship committees were working on proposals intended for all the countries of Capricorn Africa, the Interracial Association was preparing a memorandum for the franchise commission of Southern Rhodesia. Their draft conclusions, published in *Concord*, included (their emphasis): 'We hold that the country's ultimate goal must be *universal adult franchise*. We recognize that this is *not immediately politically possible* but urge that unflagging progress towards that goal be maintained. The plan must be politically possible, i.e. acceptable in the main to the present electorate and to enlightened African opinion. We feel that a common voters' roll is acceptable because it already exists, is simple and workable, gives hope to the Africans, and lessens the possibility of future racial politics. In the eyes of the Africans it has to such an extent become the foundation of hope and the touchstone of sincerity that its abolition or dilution would destroy any hope of interracial cooperation. ... We criticize proposals for a *multiple vote* as complicated, cumbersome and not easily workable.'[7]

In its ideals the Interracial Association was more radical than Capricorn but their caveat that the plan must be acceptable to the existing electorate meant their goal would be unattainable. The overwhelmingly white voters were resistant to reducing the qualifications for the common roll and were totally against the idea of universal franchise.

During 1955 and early 1956 David and the Salisbury office issued pages of notes and questionnaires for the many committees (there were 30 in central Africa) working on the draft contract. The central Africa office also undertook research on behalf of the citizenship committees and collected copies of constitutions from countries around the world to provide models and ideas. Peter Mackay prepared graphs to illustrate the relationship between education and income or between meritorious service and age in assessing the number of votes to be allocated. The assumptions on which the work was based included the statement: 'That special exemptions will be necessary for those citizens who have not got access to the conditions (such as education, income etc.) which would enable them to qualify for the vote.' There were questions to be considered on the administrative measures to operate a multiple vote system, including verification of qualifications. Mason and members of the Society submitted papers with their ideas, most were variations on the same theme with trenchant comments on universal adult suffrage.

A typical paper was that submitted by Sir Thomas Chegwidden, from Salisbury. 'Thoughtful observers of the political scene in Western democracies are inclining more and more to the view that adult suffrage is showing itself to be fundamentally unsound ... the result in an election is the counting of heads, most of which are empty of thought or intelligence, but full of desires and emotions. We have a chance — and only one chance — of getting away from this form of idiocy, and giving the vote to those and only to those who are equipped by age, education, experience or achievement to form reasonable judgements on current affairs. ... It so happens that we shall for the next 25 years at least ensure that political power remains predominantly in the hands of the white man. But this is a temporary by-product.'[8]

An early draft of an appendix to the Contract put the question into a historical context: 'In Britain universal adult suffrage was the culmination of a long process in which it gradually replaced a system of high franchise and plural voting. It was not introduced until primary education had been universal and compulsory for some time. ... In Germany, Italy, and Spain it has led to dictatorship. In France it can hardly be called a success. It is certainly too soon to say that it is working well in India, the Sudan and other countries where primary education is not general.'[9] Although many of the papers submitted by white members, particularly in Southern Rhodesia, expressed views that might be expected at the time, David and Mackay did a great deal of work collating comments on the whole question of democratic representation and the parliamentary framework within which the franchise would operate.[10]

To go out with the first draft of the Contract David wrote two long papers of notes and tactics, which included: 'We are establishing a committee of top-rating literary experts to advise us on the choice of language in the document. ... The Capricorn document when completed will have been thought out to a conclusion and so presented as to make self-evident its practical application to each territory. Towards this end the Society has continuous access to the best consultant brains in Africa, Britain and America to help solve problems of political philosophy, constitutional law and anthropology. At the same time the document will be emotionally valid and exciting to all races in Capricorn Africa. To the European it will provide a political order and way of life which will at last enable him to "square his conscience" with the Christian ethic and with British tradition, which will provide the real basis for the effective protection of civilized standards, and which will enable him to exercise his powers of leadership constructively towards an unparalleled scale of development of the African continent. To the African it will be valid and exciting because it will remove the frustration of racial discrimination, open a way to self-fulfilment and participation in the creation of a great nation. To the Asian, the Euro-African and Coloureds it will mean at last full membership in the citizenship of their country. The Society looks on its document as a contract of agreement between Africa's races. We cannot conceive such a contract being long regarded as binding by each race unless each had participated not only in the drawing up of its terms, but also in the early initiation of the whole proposition.'[11]

These stirring statements gave the members of the citizenship committees the feeling that they were indeed embarked upon a unique and important enterprise. David appeared to be completely confident that our Contract, when dedicated and issued, would change the future of the countries in which we lived, and we believed him.

In Kenya citizenship committees were encouraged by government proposals on the multiple vote and qualified franchise developed by Walter Coutts in 1955.[12] He was the administrator of the West Indian island of St Vincent when the Colonial Office posted him back to Kenya to work on franchise proposals for African elections. We made abortive attempts to coordinate submissions to Coutts from the Kenya European elected members of Legislative Council, the Capricorn Africa Society, the Christian Council of Kenya and the Akamba (a tribe related to the Kikuyu, but not involved in Mau Mau) Association. Coutts was a Presbyterian with an intrinsic belief in the goodness of man, but the franchise he developed for Zanzibar was not a success. It allowed the Arab population to continue control of the island's affairs for their own benefit, which led to the African majority becoming increasingly radical and eventually to revolution and infiltration from China and East Germany. This was clearly not the intention, and proved how delicate a balance was required in drawing up voting qualifications, even assuming that those responsible intend a particular outcome.

In his report,[13] which was copied and circulated to citizenship committees by the Salisbury office, Coutts wrote: 'I should mention at this point that it has been interesting to me to find that quite independently the Capricorn Africa Society has been thinking along the same lines in trying to assess qualifications for a common citizenship with a common roll in Capricorn Africa. To quote from one of their pamphlets: "The Society views with approval the principle of the multiple vote. It believes that members of all races who deserve well of their country and who have positions of more than average responsibility should be candidates for additional votes. The decision to incorporate the multiple vote into the Capricorn electoral system would make possible the broadening of the base of the vote qualitatively without diluting its overall standard in the qualitative sense." And again: "The gravest defect of the high franchise system which does not incorporate the multiple vote is the extreme severity of the penalty to the individual who does not quite qualify for a vote and the exaggerated award to the individual who qualifies by a narrow margin." Remembering that all of the above refers to conditions in Africa of the present day and age I wholly concur.'

This comment cut no ice with a Colonial Office mandarin in Whitehall, who was dismissive of Coutts's reference to Capricorn, writing in an internal memo: 'Mr Coutts has sought to draw strength from the fact that the ideas which the Capricorn Africa Society are beginning to develop are similar to his own. As you know, it is my view that, since they abandoned their ideas of a federation of east and central African territories, the Capricorn Africa Society has been doing valuable work and, with your approval, we have, behind the scenes, been giving them what help we can. ... In these circumstances I doubt whether the inclusion of this reference to the Society will be a bull point for the report when it is published. ... I gather that [Coutts] had already told Mr David Stirling that he was intending to include a passage of this kind. If, therefore, we ask for it to be taken out, this will become known to Mr Stirling and will no doubt give him and others the impression that our declarations of "benevolent neutrality" have not been sincere.'[14]

The Coutts Report said: 'The Government is in agreement ... that universal adult franchise [for Africans] should not be introduced into Kenya at the present time, but that, instead, there should be a limited qualitative franchise based on education, experience, public service and character.' It added that those exceptionally qualified would be accorded additional votes. Coutts proposed ten qualifications, any three of which would qualify for one vote, with another vote for each additional point. In theory it was possible for an elderly, ex-service, intellectual, female paragon to earn the maximum additional seven votes, but such were considered to be sufficiently rare that the possibility could be discounted. The qualifications proposed were: age over 21; intermediate standard schooling; university degree; five years' service in the armed forces; income of £120 or property worth £500; age over 45 or elected as an elder of the tribe; award of a civil or military decoration; five years' service on an African district council or court; ten years' responsible service or 20 years' good service; or the holding of a women's club badge.

The Kenya government ran a pilot scheme and found that only half the population would be eligible for even one vote so the requirements were simplified and the maximum number of votes set at three. The government said that the system was too complicated for voters and returning officers alike. Coutts, like Capricorn, hoped that the system would eventually be applied to all races in the country voting on a common roll but the Europeans, who had universal franchise in their elections, refused to consider a diminution of their rights and Sir Evelyn Baring, the governor, thought it would be political suicide for any white politician to suggest such a proposal. Comment in *The Times* was unequivocally headlined 'A Bad Project',[15] although the paper failed to offer any alternative solution to the dilemma of developing democracy in a largely illiterate society. The leader writer analysed the history of selecting representatives for the House of Commons and established that for most of British history, members of parliament were elected to represent groups or interests and not a majority of the population. He added that the recent idea that power lay with the individual stemmed from the current of thought flowing from the French revolution. The paper was convinced, rightly as it turned out, that Africans would naturally choose the system that the white man had for himself — universal franchise — and that they would feel cheated if offered anything less.

In spite of cerebral thoughts in *The Times* and back-tracking by the Kenya government on the Coutts report, our citizenship committees continued to develop a system of qualifications with a maximum of six votes. Precept Six of the Capricorn Contract stated that the vote was not a natural right but a responsibility. Provision One affirmed the principles of the electoral system, while an appendix provided details of voting qualifications as an example for further study. Whereas Coutts's report was concerned with Africans voting communally, Capricorn's proposals were for everyone voting on a common roll. Capricorn committees working on details of the franchise assumed that every European would earn one vote, on age and minimum education qualifications, with a number having additional votes for higher education or income. An important clause in Provision One affirmed 'the introduction of a qualified franchise must be accompanied by a vigorous interpretation of Precept Three, which states that it is an obligation of the state to afford to the limit of its economic capacity such facilities for education in all its forms as will give every individual the opportunity ... of gaining the vote.'

We considered it important to provide a wide range of qualifications for African and Asian voters and particularly for women. Debates in the citizenship committees on the inclusion of qualifications for an apprentice, or the right for the senior wife to gain from her husband's income, were long and good-natured. They were also largely based on ignorance, as neither Coutts nor we had access to any statistics that might have quantified our ideas. Perhaps this was just as well, for it meant that our qualifications were proposed as being right in themselves, without consideration of how the numbers might turn out.

Capricorn's qualifications were similar to Coutts's although ours were intended to produce a responsible electorate without consideration of race. Our voters needed two points to be on the electoral roll, with a maximum of six votes. We gave temporary qualifications for Africans: the mother of two or more children who have passed form 11; a master farmer or an African warrant officer in HM armed forces and police. To encourage women voters a wife gained an extra point by virtue of her husband's income or property qualification. Committee minutes also reported that: 'a great deal of arithmetical guesswork was done which seemed to show that on the suggested qualifications in almost any constituency in Kenya there would be an overwhelming preponderance of African votes. Some on the committee felt this was no more the Capricorn ideal than domination by any of the other races, although we realized that in time the African vote would be in the majority.'[16] In this we were acknowledging reality, while hoping for the ideal.

Like David's early enthusiasm for federating the countries of Capricorn Africa, our franchise proposals were eminently logical and generally unpopular. The mass of African opinion, however many votes individuals would earn, regarded anything less than universal franchise as a delaying tactic by Europeans designed to hold off the day when they would lose power. When it was suggested to David that our proposals would result in an African majority among voters and in parliament his optimistic answer was vague. He was convinced, and convincing, that an 'organically non-racial' electorate would develop, so to him the question was irrelevant.

Question E12 of the *Capricorn Handbook* dealt with the issue of Asian voters in East Africa and explained that the layout of constituencies should prevent an overall Asian majority in parliament. No question was posed in the *Handbook* on the possibility of an African majority. At a meeting of Northern Rhodesian white miners Laurens van der Post addressed the question head on. 'We do not believe that the white man can secure his destiny in Rhodesia and in Africa, nor that this country ... can achieve its economic potential until the black man has a majority of the votes and the same access to land purchase as the white man. Our proposals for the right to vote, based on the multivote system, would establish perhaps the most intelligent electorate in the world; but it would certainly yield more votes to the Africans than to the Europeans.'[17]

Press comment on the convention at Salima underlined the importance of the franchise proposals. Rex Reynolds wrote in the *Kenya Weekly News*: 'The franchise is, of course, the most complex and controversial subject that has to be dealt with. The Society – refreshingly, in these days of *demos* – regards the vote not as a natural right but as a responsibility to be exercised for the common good.'[18] The leader writer in the Salisbury *Sunday Mail* was enthusiastic: 'The Capricorn Society is to be commended on its multiple vote plan. We believe it is far superior to any plan so far put forward. The Society does not itself claim that its suggestions cannot be improved on. But there is no doubt that here is a scheme which could succeed and, in succeeding, set an example to those parts of the world where there are wide differences in culture and standards of civilization.'[19]

In the *Illustrated London News* Sir Arthur Bryant put our franchise proposals into historical perspective. 'It has taken us centuries to evolve our present system of representative government ... and anyone with any knowledge of our history knows that our fifteenth- and sixteenth-century ancestors would have failed to make our present system work because they were not then sufficiently mature in political experience to be able to do so. This does not mean that they were inferior as human beings to us; the men who could build King's College chapel and the lovely stone towers of our perpendicular churches, or write and sing the kind of music that has come down to us from their civilization of faith and instinct, were certainly not our inferiors.'[20]

European resistance to the qualified vote on a common roll was based on the belief that it was less valuable than the universal adult suffrage they already enjoyed, but their abhorrence of the common roll recognized that it would be the thick end of the wedge — the huge disparity in numbers would lead inevitably and quickly to an African government in which the European would have no influence. African politicians disliked our proposals because they assumed, correctly, that it was a device to increase the power of the educated and prosperous voter, whom they thought would be white or Asian. Capricorn members believed that the common roll was essential if politicians seeking votes were to offer proposals that would appeal to the entire electorate, for the good of the whole country, and that the qualified multiple vote would ensure that candidates' manifestos were judged with some experience. Communal rolls encourage candidates to play to the fears and hopes of their racial group. Recent history in Africa has shown that tribal consciousness has increased under universal franchise as candidates appeal to narrow chauvinism, which in turn increases the differences between language groups.

When early independence in Kenya looked likely, there were suggestions in the Society that the provisions of the Capricorn Contract should be brought up to date. This was a move I resisted, writing: 'My personal reaction is that the Contract remains a valid ideal though it may be less attainable now ... than it was. ... The Contract itself should remain as a firm statement of our beliefs, for they are certainly my beliefs, even the qualified franchise provision. ... If we changed our beliefs to suit the new circumstances, there would be little to distinguish Capricorn from the "common roll, universal franchise with possibly a few reserved seats" school of thought. If our ideas were good in 1956 then they are still good.'[21] In this letter there are seeds of the disagreements that erupted in the following year between those who felt the Society depended for its validity on the terms of the Contract, specifically the franchise proposals, and those who believed the essential character of the Society was in the concept that all men are equal before God.[22] I was firmly in the former group, believing that once events showed our proposals were no longer attainable then there was no further role for Capricorn in Kenya, at least. Others members felt passionately that the Society must continue the good fight.

Chapter 8
Salima

For members of Capricorn the word 'Salima' represented the high point in the life of the Society – a moment when we believed a new Africa was born. For those fortunate enough to have been there, it was a unique and moving experience, for others it became a legend. Two generations after the event it is difficult, almost impossible, to realize how extraordinary Salima was in 1956: 250 men and women, black, white and brown, living and eating together and debating their common future with understanding and good humour. In the 1950s relations between the races in America and Europe were grounded in misunderstandings and ignorance while in colonial Africa they were generally non-existent. It is a measure of David Stirling's vision and his powers of persuasion that Salima took place at all and was widely recognized as a resounding success. The reality, which subsequently clouded our confident memories, was rooted in the euphoria of the last morning when we signed our document without thinking what to do with it.

We were encouraged by press reports in Africa and throughout the world; a typical comment was by Rex Reynolds, a hard-bitten journalist in central Africa, writing from Salima. 'To my mind the most remarkable thing about the convention of the Capricorn Africa Society is that such a conference was not held long ago. ... The elimination of racial discrimination that is inherent in many of the clauses of the Capricorn Contract has long been recognized by thinking people as inevitable. ... It is high time some representative and responsible body not only acknowledged the inevitable, but frankly affirmed and welcomed it as a real and necessary contribution to progress.'[1]

The intention to hold a convention at which a formal statement of Capricorn principles would be published had been in David's mind for some years. It was to have been held in 1953 and then 1954 at Mbeya in the southern highlands of Tanganyika, at the geographical centre of David's proposed federal dominion, and even more awkward for access than Salima. The intended convention was taken sufficiently seriously in Whitehall to cause anxiety among civil servants at the Commonwealth Relations Office, who tried to pass the buck to the Colonial Office. A CRO official minuted: 'I think it is much more of the CO than us. At this stage [September 1953] Col Stirling's convention might not be much more than a nuisance to us.'[2]

When the 1954 Mbeya convention seemed imminent the CRO recorded its alarm at the proposal: 'The Governor of Tanganyika felt that politically it would be a most undesirable thing to take place. He considered that the vast majority of people in Tanganyika, of all races, fear any suggestion of an East African federation and the conference might therefore have a disturbing effect on them. ... The governors of Uganda, Northern Rhodesia and Nyasaland have all replied to the Colonial Office that the proposed conference would undoubtedly have a disturbing effect on their territories and they are anxious to persuade Col Stirling not to hold it.'[3] The CRO minute continued: 'Accordingly, the Colonial Office approached us asking whether we could intervene with Col Stirling in an attempt to persuade him to postpone his convention on the grounds that "it might very well stimulate opposition to central African federation." ... In the present state of Africa we feel at the official level that the less philosophical discussion of racial problems (in the blare of publicity) there is, the better. ... Stirling's proposed activities seem to me likely to raise apprehension and unsettlement in both Africans and Europeans – the former by presenting further vistas of the unknown and the latter by the very gestures of sentimentalism towards the African.'

The 1954 Mbeya proposal was abandoned: funding was precarious, David realized that the troops were too thin on the ground, and Kenya was in the grip of the Mau Mau emergency. During 1955 David's agenda changed from announcing a declaration of principles to developing a contract to which people of all races would subscribe at a convention. In towns and country areas of east and central Africa small groups of Africans, Asians and Europeans met in citizenship committees to debate the drafts of the document and study papers coming from Salisbury. The arguments were often tense as they tried to imagine how the proposals would affect their lives. Multiracial schools and hospitals, differential pay scales or the reservation of land were highly charged and sensitive issues, undermining long established demands and fears of one race or another, and sometimes of all three. Comments and suggestions from the committees in Africa and ideas from Joe Oldham and his group at Dunford were sent to Salisbury where David accepted those that agreed with his ideas.

While the citizenship committees saw the issues in terms of local conditions, David was determined to have a document applicable to all the countries of Capricorn Africa, so committees were sometimes overruled or cajoled into accepting clauses about which they were doubtful. At Salima we discovered how David's shuttle diplomacy had succeeded in getting the document he wanted. On flying visits to Nairobi, he would say: 'I know you're not happy with this section but in Rhodesia they absolutely insist on it.' Then, after reluctant acquiescence in Kenya, next week in Rhodesia would be the same, except that it was the Kenyans who were said to be immovable on the clause, so the Rhodesians accept the change without enthusiasm. With David's persuasive charm it was very effective; fortunately we were all working towards the same goal so there were no rows at Salima when we discovered that the views of our friends were not exactly what we had been led to believe.

Whatever the subsequent failure of Capricorn to affect the larger events in Africa, the influence of citizenship committees on all who took part was important and long lasting. They were far from the patronizing 'tea and cakes' liberalism of which we were sometimes accused. Vigorous argument about difficult choices established relationships of trust and understanding between individuals of different races that have lasted for the rest of our lives. In Kenya the move to independence and the years following were remarkably free from racial animosity, which was partly due to the influence of the friendships across racial barriers that we established. In later years meeting Boaz Omori, G. N. Shah, S. T. Thakore and many others was always an occasion of warmth and affection. In 1998 when I went to Kenya to talk to old Capricorn hands, J. D. Otiende and Joram Amadi greeted me as an old friend — Amadi and I walked around Kisumu hand in hand exchanging news of the years since we last met.

As late as March 1956 the executive committee in Salisbury discussed where the June convention might be held.[4] Peter Mackay had identified the site in a letter to David earlier in the month: 'When in Nyasaland last week ... it transpired that there is only one place which will satisfactorily meet our requirements. This is the Lake Nyasa Hotel ... empty of furnishings and unoccupied. ... It is well out of the general stream of the country's activity but is only four miles from an airstrip and twelve miles from the railhead.'[5]

Salima was a small village on the western shore of Lake Nyasa

370 miles (600 kilometres) by air from Salisbury and 900 miles (1400 kilometres) on a long and tortuous road across the Zambezi River, through Northern Rhodesia, and round the Tete salient in Mozambique. An advantage was that the site was far from any town that might encourage local delegates to go home overnight, but also meant it was far from suppliers of furniture and food. Mackay used his considerable administrative ability to organize the major exercise involved in repairing the buildings and equipping the camp with the necessities for 250 people over three days and nights. Jimmy Skinner, newly arrived in Nyasaland and working for Bookers, remembers Mackay appearing at the Lilongwe trading centre with purchase orders for a long list, including flags for the countries represented, 20 staff uniforms, 350 ashtrays, 200 anti-malarial tablets and a snakebite outfit.[6] Mackay made detailed lists of everyone's duties and produced a complex diagram, like a modern critical path network, to establish the route, timing and overnight stop of each plane to and from the various centres over the period of the meeting.

Once the empty hotel at Salima had been selected, there was much work needed to make it habitable and suitable for the convention. As an advance party to organize the arrangements for the delegates, observers and press, Jeannine Scott and Susan Wood flew from Nairobi to Salima in Michael Wood's small aeroplane, which he had learnt to fly the previous year. In Susan Wood's book *A Fly in Amber* she describes the hectic days before the convention opened: 'The staff were detailed to complete the new grass houses which had been built to extend the accommodation, while the others put up the tents which had begun to arrive. ... Because of the cost of hiring equipment, the date for its departure had been delayed as late as possible. As day after day passed without news of the two pantechnicons from Salisbury, local inhabitants began to warn us that they were very unlikely to arrive in time. They were to bring chairs, tables, linen, blankets and a vast quantity of essentials. ... Our anxiety became frantic as 48 hours before the delegates and press were due to arrive there was still no sign of either rail trucks or pantechnicons. At last we heard that a pantechnicon had been sighted passing through Zomba [capital of Nyasaland, 200 miles to the south]. Next day it arrived. On the day on which the main delegations were due to arrive, the railway trucks pulled calmly into Salima and all available transport was rushed to the station.'[7]

The Kenya delegation was photographed with their zebra symbol in front of the chartered aircraft at Wilson airport, outside Nairobi, before leaving for Salima. Flying south we passed the snow-capped grandeur of Kilimanjaro, across the vast and largely empty spaces of Tanganyika and down the length of Lake Nyasa to the airstrip near Salima. Many of our delegation had never been in an aeroplane before, so there was much excitement at seeing the landscape from the air and the strange experience of flying into a

The Kenya branch off to Salima, 1956: Eric Wilkinson on left, RH on right

cloud and out the other side, unharmed. The surroundings at Salima reminded the settlers among us of hotels on the Kenya coast, where each room was a separate hut, set in a profusion of flowering shrubs, with sandy paths among palm trees to an open-sided, thatched dining room and bar overlooking the ocean. At Salima the open sided thatched building was the meeting hall — a *bwalo* to the locals — with rows of metal chairs facing the podium.

Having been a member of Capricorn for less than nine months, some of the Kenya delegates were strangers to me and it took some time to establish who was who, particularly as David gave me a job that kept me out of general circulation. Among the Kenya members were white farmers whose support for opening the White Highlands was unequivocal, an Asian cabinet minister, A. B. Patel, who later retired from Kenya politics to an ashram in India and Clem Argwings-Kodhek, president of the radical Kenya African Congress. The Kenya delegation made themselves felt in a number of ways, as Reynolds reported: 'they were the youngest delegation and the most provocative. ... A number of the Kenya ladies were helping dish out bacon and eggs from the kitchen [where] there was a shortage of eggs, and one of the Kenya ladies spotted an

African kitchen boy idling about and taking bites out of a bacon and egg sandwich. He seemed somewhat surprised when the good lady clouted him across the head with a frying pan.'[8]

Betty Couldrey, Molly Hodge, Gillian Solly, Susan Wood and Joyce Raw (of frying pan fame), all from Kenya, did much of the housekeeping and, with Jeannine Scott, were the moving spirits of the camp. They were always cheerful and willing to undertake any job that needed doing, however menial (and some were very menial indeed), as well as being closely and emotionally identified with the serious purpose of the convention.

As more delegates arrived by plane, car and coach, I began to discover that there were differences in attitude between the white Rhodesians and the Kenyans. The latter were more radical and realistic than most of the Rhodesians, for whom the ultimate in liberal thought was Cecil Rhodes's famous dictum 'equal rights for every civilized man' though few completed it: '—south of the Zambezi'. A white Rhodesian reaction to the experience of Salima was described a few years after the event by Peter Gibbs, a delegate from Matabeleland: at Salima 'we were shown the little thatched roofed huts in which we would sleep; we were in no way to be crowded together because there was plenty of room ... nevertheless, the sudden realization that I was actually going to sleep in the same room as an African, probably alongside him, gave me another shock — just another manifestation of my strangely conditioned mind.'[9]

Once Gibbs and his friends had found the bar there was another shock: 'To someone like myself who had spent 20 years in the carefully segregated world of Africa the spectacle before me was almost incredible. I was so conditioned to white exclusiveness that the situation seemed at first entirely incongruous, as if certain inviolable rules were being broken. ... Here were Europeans talking to Africans as if they were their equals, laughing with them, buying them drinks, and here also were Africans and Coloureds going to the bar and ordering drinks themselves as to the manner born. ... I had often heard it said that the relative cultural advancement of the races being what it is, it would take a hundred years to break down the social barriers between them. I found in practice that it took about a hundred minutes and by then they had gone altogether. ... What really broke down the barriers between the races was not the airing of common political problems but the impact of the common problems of where to hang your clothes at night and getting hot water to shave in the morning. ... Now we were meeting our intellectual equals, some of them our intellectual superiors, and it was as if a thick cloud, which had been hanging between us for years, had been suddenly blown away and we were seeing each other clearly for the first time and were able to make contact with each other without misunderstanding.'

The team from London – Jeannine Scott, Henry Crookenden and Jonathan Lewis – were just names to me, but it did not take long to realize how crucial they were to the whole project. Crookenden had been a friend and admirer of Jeannine Scott since they first met at the hospital where he had both legs amputated after being wounded in the Italian campaign in 1943. Handsome and distinguished, with a natural gift for words, Crookenden, as chairman of the London working party was a steadying influence on David and the ebullient Lewis. With his artificial legs Crookenden found the loose sand at Salima hard going, but he was a key figure behind the scenes, discussing the issues and persuading delegates that the Capricorn Contract was the only answer.

Almost 30 observers and the same number of press (a few of whom were also delegates or observers) were accommodated, fed and provided essentially with a bar in the evenings. Reynolds's second dispatch captured the Salima atmosphere precisely: 'Even for a hardened newspaperman, the convention was an inspiring as well as a stimulating occasion, rich in human experience, idealism, wisdom and plain common sense ... life was uncomplicated, although it was unique in any territory in British Africa. ... The most interesting thing was that there was little or no self-conscious effort to "get together, bridge the gulf" or arrange people in the chequer-board pattern so beloved of the [Fabian Society] Africa Bureau. Delegates could and did talk to friends and strangers of all races and joined the chat in any circle they liked, but as often as not they gravitated towards the groups with whom they had most in common, aside from the ideals of the Society. Dress was informal – from khaki drill to natty tropical suitings: on the whole, the Africans and Indians were rather better dressed than the European delegates and, of course, far better than the press. The general feeling seemed to be summed up by a snatch of conversation overheard in the bar. "How odd it will seem," said a white delegate, "when we are back in civilization and can't have a drink together." "Civilization?" said the black delegate, "Ah, well, in the meantime, it's my turn: let me get you another beer."'[10]

Alistair Ross, in his paper 'Capricorn in Tanganyika',[11] analysed the make-up of delegates by country and by race, noting that

Capricorners themselves would have discouraged any breakdown by race. I have recalculated the results, based on my list from Salima: out of 138 delegates, 39 per cent were African, 15 per cent Asian or Coloured and 46 per cent European. Including members of the central African executive committee, most of whom were from Southern Rhodesia, there were 42 delegates from Kenya, 61 from Southern Rhodesia, 17 from Northern Rhodesia, 9 from

'Delegates could and did talk to friends and strangers of all races,' Salima, 1956

Nyasaland and 6 from Tanganyika (all from around Mount Kilimanjaro) and 3 from Britain.

Before leaving Salisbury for Salima David issued a press statement setting out his ambitions for the convention. He wrote: 'Everywhere in British Africa north of the Limpopo, there is benevolent government conscientiously trying to meet the needs of the less advanced sections of the community, but everywhere it must be admitted that there is a steady worsening of the relationship between Africa's different peoples. Opportunities for social and economic advancement and increased participation in the political management of the territories are too often given [to] the African by governments — whose officials are predominantly European — in a spirit of concession, and are too often taken by the African as a reward for agitation and political pressure. ... The Capricorn Contract is an effective challenge both to militant black nationalism and to the Strijdom [South African premier 1954–58] creed of apartheid. The contract makes no pretence at compromise between the two, but sets up an idea that is valid in its own right.'[12]

The Salisbury office produced handsome files for everyone, with the Capricorn crest of a rampant zebra bestriding the map of Africa on the cover. It contained the tenth draft of the Contract and the very full agenda for the two and a half days of the convention; I still have my folder, with its rusting clip and pages heavily annotated with corrections and alterations. Meetings started at eight o'clock, except on the Sunday when time was allowed for church parade taken by the bishop of Nyasaland, who was an observer. The timetable was tight throughout, with only an hour and five minutes allocated on the last day for debating the crucial question of what we were to do with our contract in the real world.

The first morning in the *bwalo* was a brilliant set piece with short and powerful speeches to establish the tone of the convention and identify the breadth of support behind the Capricorn philosophy. After David was elected chairman he spoke quietly, but with great intensity and absolute conviction, of his hopes for Africa, and then introduced the selected keynote speakers. A white woman from Kenya who had been born in Africa, a respected black lawyer from Southern Rhodesia, a senior Asian politician from Kenya, a well known Afrikaner liberal born in South Africa, the white chairman of the Society in Southern Rhodesian, and lastly a Methodist missionary, also from Southern Rhodesia.

Susan Wood made the first speech, saying she spoke as a European: 'I can without hesitation say that no other moment in my life has carried a greater privilege. For it is my task to try and describe for a whole race the frustrations and perplexities which it is experiencing at this point in time and to express its great hope. I am the third generation of my family to live and work in Africa. My grandfather lived, worked and died in the heart of the Ituri forest in the Belgian Congo. My father lived for 25 years travelling all over East Africa, the Congo and Ethiopia. I was born in the Congo and now live in Kenya. Living in Africa today one has the feeling that all one thinks and believes is facing perhaps the greatest challenge in history.'[13]

She said the European living in Africa found that a system of colonial administration, which was largely sound and just, was not enough — there was something lacking — because man lives by inspiration and not by economic factors alone. European domination in the past had arisen from circumstances, but as they changed, the moral force of that domination fell away and then relied on force. The dilemma she identified was that domination by force was not in the British democratic tradition, which was the cause of her perplexities and frustration. She proposed that a future free from racial antagonisms would let the European live within his own ethic, at peace with himself.

Herbert Chitepo, vice-chairman of the central African executive committee, was unable to be at Salima so his speech was read for him: 'Because of the continued refusal of the Europeans to accord Africans the dignity, freedom and security, which [are] the right of every human being, new African organizations are arising which seek the removal of the Europeans. Time is short and this is not only a unique opportunity for Africa, it is also the last, for if we cannot succeed together, Africans will be driven to adopt open racialist nationalism. ... For the first time in the history of the conflict among the three races in Africa, members of each race have come together to declare to the world the terms of their coexistence and to pledge themselves to preserve those terms to eternity. Now, for we Africans, Salima heralds the realization of our desire to live in peace and harmony with Asians and Europeans. Our common patriotism ... is more compelling and emotionally more satisfying than anything that mankind has seen.'[14] Chitepo continued by calling for refusal to compromise and for resolute determination to put the Contract into practice. He ended by stressing that Christianity plus Capricorn results in equality before God and that there would be no democracy without it.

The third keynote speech was by the leader of the Asian elected members in the Kenya Legislative Council and vice president of Capricorn, A. B. Patel. He said he had been involved in Kenya politics for many years and was well aware of the strength of vigorous African black nationalism. His theme was simple: 'Asians have not played a fully constructive role in East African development because the policies and practices of racial discrimination have not allowed this to happen. The Asians have fears that South African conditions may be repeated in East Africa since a whispering campaign was conducted against them and hostility was openly expressed. I am sure that the Asian community of East Africa will lend full support to the praiseworthy aims and ideals of the Capricorn Society.'

Laurens van der Post stayed in London to answer queries as he explained many years later.[15] The more likely reason was that he knew he would be unwelcome in Nyasaland after his book about the country, *Venture to the Interior*, had raised local hackles.[16] We had to imagine his South African accent and slightly guttural voice as Kendall Ward read his speech, characteristically rich in language and mysticism. 'This is a fanatically extrovert age, which grossly overvalues the external and material factors of life and undervalues criminally the inner and invisible realities. ... To all of us in Capricorn, the idea is the beginning of doing: unless we have the idea right, we can never do right. We make sense only as the vehicle of an idea; flesh and blood have meaning only as an idea made alive. One of the reasons why racialism is for the moment in command in my native country [South Africa] and why the indigenous people of Africa are increasingly turning their imaginations and minds to a racial line of advance is because no truly honourable indigenous alternative has been put before them. Here, for the first time, we have a movement dedicated to a concept which is concerned no longer with these crippling and paralytic preoccupations with race, but is concerned only with the maintenance and advance of fundamental human values. ... We are both seed and natural seedbed for the new non-racial African world to come. ... With 300 years of Africa in my blood, I know what an immense inflowing of strength comes to the individual who has burst through the racial barrier and stands free to accept Africa and all that is born of it as an inviolate part of his own nature and innermost belonging. ... Out of this will come a new and greater way of life in Africa!'[17]

John Baines, chairman of the Society in Southern Rhodesia, affirmed that Cecil Rhodes stood for real understanding between the races, not only because it was right but also because it alone could create the climate in which economic progress could flourish. He continued: 'with the death of Rhodes much of the driving force behind the development of Capricorn Africa was cut off. ... We have never regarded material advantages as a substitute for political and social justice, but political advancement is an empty thing unless it is supported by efficient social services, notably of health and education. ... If this Contract is incorporated into the life of Capricorn Africa, the ensuing economic development will astonish the world. In no other way can overseas capital be persuaded to venture here in sufficient quantity. ... We believe, in humility, that Rhodes would approve and applaud.'

The Reverend Fred Rea, who later became a key figure in keeping Capricorn alive in Southern Rhodesia, speaking as a missionary invoked both David Livingstone and Rhodes, saying that they had:

'discovered that there is a vital nexus between the kingdom of heaven and the kingdoms of commerce and trade. Livingstone foresaw that in the salvation of Africa trade and government had a significant part to play. This convention has stamped itself indelibly upon the missionary policy of central Africa. In few parts of the world have the temporal and the spiritual needs of the people shared so equal a place in the heart and labours of the missionary church. ... The Capricorn Africa Society says to the sons of Rhodes: "Here is the faith of Rhodes translated in terms of the needs of our generation. If you seek, like him, to build a world of commerce in the heart of Africa, here are your blueprints." To our generation has been committed the responsibility and privilege of laying the foundations of Christian democracy in a multiracial society. For the next generation it will have been too late.' In the debate on education on the second day, Rea also said: 'make a blunt statement on interracial education in Southern Rhodesia, and you will destroy Capricorn.'

The style of the Contract was modelled on the American Declaration of Independence, opening with the ringing phrase: 'We, the signatories of this Document, drawn from all the races living in the self-governing colony of Southern Rhodesia, the Colony and protectorate of Kenya, the protectorates of Nyasaland and Northern Rhodesia and the Territory of Tanganyika wish to affirm our faith in the greatness of our common destiny and our resolve to reject the barren doctrine of racial nationalism.'

Of the eight clauses in the contract, the third contained six precepts to establish the philosophy of the document, opening with Precept One: 'All men, despite their varying individual talents and differences of race and colour, are born equal in dignity before God and have a common duty to Him and to one another.' After Clause VIII and space for delegates' signatures there were provisions on the electoral system, land reform, labour relations, education and immigration. The document balanced idealism with recognition of current realities. Clause VI said 'the final elimination of some aspects of racial segregation will take time and reforms towards this end too hastily carried out might cause injustice to individuals and communities and might jeopardize the preservation of civilized standards.'

Provision One dealing with the electoral system and the accompanying appendix on qualifications for the vote have been described in the previous chapter. Provision Two on land reform confirmed that: 'The state, while respecting in the spirit of Clause

VI the desire of certain tribes to maintain their communal system of land tenure and way of life, shall allow and encourage the conversion of all land, by successive stages, into areas open to purchase by all persons irrespective of race. ... Land shall not be reserved in perpetuity for members of one race or tribe.' We recognized the importance of land as security for old age in Clause (f): 'Even those Africans who have spent most of their lives and earned their living in European areas are finally dependent, when they are not employed or can no longer earn their living through old age or sickness, on the means of subsistence available under the communal system of land tenure. The gradual opening of reserved and tribal lands to individual tenure will create two new classes, one of specialized farmers and the other of employed persons without land. ... The state shall be under obligation to provide by legislation new forms of security better fitted than the old to the individual way of life towards which the African is graduating.' Back in London Crookenden later wrote: 'No inhabitant of Africa, whatever his race, is entirely sane about land, and on no topic has the Capricorn movement been more misunderstood and misrepresented.'[18]

In the provisions on labour relations and on immigration there were echoes of the 1952 Declarations, but with different meanings in the context of the document as a whole. 'Individuals holding positions of equal responsibility and producing work equal in quantity and quality shall be entitled to equal rates of pay.' The Contract continued: 'In order to attract capital it will be necessary to encourage the immigration of technically skilled and qualified persons from outside the territories until the number of skilled and fully trained persons within the territories is sufficient to meet all requirements. We believe that when it becomes evident to all sections of the community that racial discrimination no longer exists and that their own training to fill technical posts is being pushed forward as rapidly as possible, fears of immigration will diminish, since it will be seen to contribute to the welfare and progress of all.'

On the sensitive question of interracial education the Contract was ambivalent: 'We hold that all children, regardless of their race, should receive the best education the country can afford and should grow up in understanding of each other and free from racial prejudice. We agree that these objects can ultimately be achieved and our concept of common citizenship best be served by interracial education. We hold that the implementation of a policy of interracial education should be encouraged but can be achieved only when a more advanced cultural and social status has been reached by the majority of the community, when the English language is more fully in use and when the teachers of each race have attained the same qualifications in their profession.' There were proposals on interracial teaching centres and out-of-school activities and a call for the establishment of courses on citizenship.[19]

To quote Reynolds again: 'there was a good deal of debate. Some of it quite lively, and only the darkness stopped the proceedings each day — leaving subcommittees to complete their homework by lantern light. ... Some amendments were so hastily conceived and loosely framed that, unless they have received a little postoperative treatment, they are liable to give the Society trouble in the future. The president, elected to the chair, handled the meeting with characteristic individualism, and frankly steamrollered through provisions that discussion outside the bwalo had shown to be contentious, but on the whole there was a high degree of unanimity on principles.'[20]

When I arrived at Salima David asked me to sit behind him on the podium as a drafting subcommittee with Philip Mason. We were to incorporate any amendments that came from the floor and generally polish the document — 'postoperative treatment' in Reynolds's phrase. This meant working through the siesta hour and late into the night with paraffin lanterns while others were making friends over a drink, or asleep, which limited my memory of Salima as an occasion. Mason was then director of Studies in Race Relations at Chatham House in London doing research for *The Birth of a Dilemma*.[21] When we were at Salima he was 50 with a list of successful books, written as Philip Woodruff, and a distinguished career in the Indian civil service behind him. He was white haired and carefully dressed, even in the informal surroundings of Salima, and I was in awe of his background and experience. His approach to race was unsentimental, based on common sense and a belief in man's common humanity. Looking over the document we amended, I think that we worked well together and although he had reservations about it, he made no attempt to influence my enthusiasm.

Mason later wrote in *A Thread of Silk*: 'I also had an uneasy feeling at the time, which has since grown stronger, that a bargain is not the way to start a new state. Either there must be a real basis of agreement on fundamentals — as between the 13 American states — or it must be recognized that the majority will have its way, and any minority is there on sufferance. "Guarantees" cannot last; the good sense of the minority and the magnanimity of the majority are the only lasting source of amity. In Southern Rhodesia, there was one inescapable fact ... blacks wanted to change almost everything, whites almost nothing. Besides, the idea of a bargain, or covenant, pictures two parties clearly separate and is fundamentally divisive.'[22] Going over the Contract in my old Salima folder, I am surprised at how much treatment we gave the text. Comparing the draft, covered in my untidy pencil corrections, with the printed document issued later, it is clear that almost all our changes were incorporated.

The precepts, which open the document, suffered only a few commas added or subtracted and capital letters rationalized, but the provisions on the electoral system, land reform, labour relations and education are covered in amendments, and in a few cases replaced paragraphs, one in Mason's upright fountain-pen script. Some alterations liberalized the tone of the document and some unfortunate phrases were deleted (shown below in square brackets): 'In the special circumstances of east and central Africa, [where there is no background of long established civic responsibility,] universal suffrage would give rise to the danger of irresponsible politicians [appealing to that section of the population that has yet to emerge from the communal tribal state and] being elected to the legislature on grounds irrelevant to the common good.'

In the same provision deletions and additions were made to make the document less absolute: 'We affirm our belief in a common voters' roll as the [only means of preserving harmony between different races] best means of promoting political stability.' We made some small, though significant, changes to the provision on education: '(d) The extension of educational facilities of all kinds for African women and girls' became 'for women and girls of all races'. And in (e) we added to the clause on courses for citizenship: 'in all forms of adult education'. This became significant some years later when Capricorn initiated the colleges of citizenship in Southern Rhodesia and Kenya.[23] There were numerous changes to the complex details of voting qualifications, and we added an important proviso: 'we submit the following scheme as a basis for further study and as an example which may be modified where necessary.'

Betty Couldrey has since said, firmly and characteristically, that David was not a democrat, and had run the convention sessions briskly to avoid changes being proposed from the floor, and in any case there was no time to debate alterations to the wording. Mason, just before he died, told me that he could no longer remember the details, but he would not have hesitated to amend the text as he thought best. Although it is doubtful whether David had time to read the revised document, he seemed happy with the outcome, writing to me from Salima as the camp was dismantled to say how grateful he was for the help I had given in drafting. He added a postscript that he disagreed with one paragraph and was redrafting it, so we did not have everything our own way. Critics of Capricorn have quoted David's dictatorial manner as one reason for its failure, yet Mason and I made a number of substantial alterations to the text of the Contract, which David accepted, or did not notice.

The Capricorn Contract was a document to be proud of, and we were proud of it. We thought its proposals were so obviously right, and reasonable, that any sensible political party would adopt them and that when Capricorn countries adopted constitutions based on our contract, David's great federation would evolve naturally. But we were not politicians and had little sense of the realities of political life. Newspaper headlines, designed to alarm Europeans, on the lines of 'CAPRICORN PROPOSES END TO RESERVATION OF LAND' or 'CAPRICORN PROPOSES COMMON VOTERS' ROLL' told only part of the story. We needed to explain the subtleties of our proposals, but in the period after Salima no political organization was prepared to examine our ideas, while Capricorn continued to maintain that the Society was non-political.

On the last morning of the convention, the amended contract was signed by David, followed by the delegates and many of the observers, moving forward to the podium in a long queue. Then there was approval of an illuminated loyal address to the Queen, which David formally signed on our behalf. Signing the contract took up the crucial time, short though it was, allocated to discussing the next steps for the movement, a lapse for which we paid dearly over the coming years.

Colonel Hickman, who was at Salima, and became a short-lived chairman of the Southern Rhodesia branch,[24] wrote in a memo after the event: 'There was great disappointment expressed during the last morning that time was wasted on ... irrelevant matters when we felt that the future policy of the Society should have been outlined by the president. Worldwide interest had been created in the convention – there was a sympathetic press and a strong feeling by all present that they wished to go into action to further the aims of the Society. Now was obviously the moment to take the next step and yet that opportunity was missed.'[25]

Before we dispersed, there were presentations to David and 'For He's a Jolly Good Fellow', which we sang with genuine enthusiasm, recognizing the unique and total contribution that he had made over the previous seven years, and for the way in which he had chaired the convention with firmness and good humour for

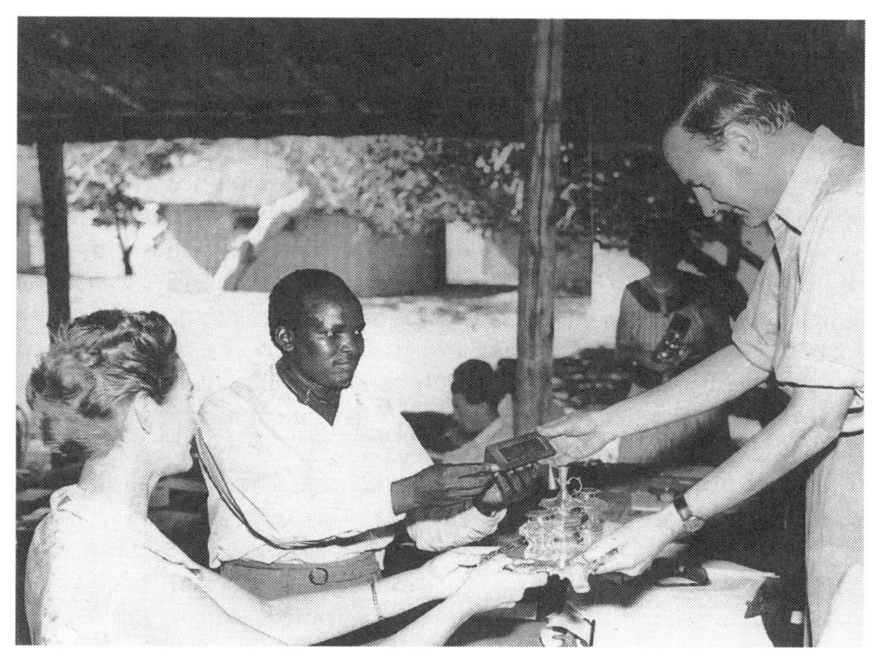

Susan Wood and Joel Ojal making presentations to David Stirling at the close of the Salima Convention, 1956 (photo: Rhodesian Herald)

three hard days. After what seemed too short a time, we boarded our planes back to the realities of everyday life.

Mackay wrote later that it was gratifying that leading British, Commonwealth, American and European continental newspapers, news agencies and journals had taken so much trouble over news and feature coverage of the occasion. This was because he had arranged for telephones, teleprinter services and a Morse code circuit to be installed for the press and for a delegate from Ol Molog to fly tape recordings and press photographs to Salisbury during the convention. Daily news items in east, central and South African papers and the extraordinary amount of coverage in the British press, as well as in India and Egypt, which were not so flattering, made the public aware of Capricorn's proposals and ideals. Later, David had excerpts from press comment with the text of the Contract printed in a booklet to match his 1952 Declarations for circulation in London. Reading the press cuttings, generally kind and accurate, many pure reportage, some approving commentary, gave us great hope at the time. Now it creates a feeling of an opportunity lost forever.

The day after the convention closed the *Sunday Mail*,[26] published in Salisbury, carried news items from Salima on three pages and wrote a leader that must have surprised its white readers, describing the contract as a 'blueprint for harmony'. The paper approved the crucial section of the Capricorn proposals on the multiple vote, although it retained its general position that the Society was unrealistic. 'The Capricorn Society is to be commended on its multiple vote plan. We believe it is far superior to any plan so far put forward. The Society does not itself claim that its suggestions cannot be improved on. But there is no doubt that here is a scheme which could succeed and, in succeeding, set an example to those parts of the world where there are wide differences in culture and standards of civilization. ... We do not by any means accept the "Capricorn Contract" in its entirety. We think that the Society still has its head in the clouds in many ways.'

This stimulated a great deal of correspondence, for and against, in the Rhodesian press. Alan Paton,[27] who was at Salima, wrote that if the Capricorn Contract had no chance in Africa, then nothing had. Joshua Nkomo, the Southern Rhodesian nationalist leader, expressed 'his total disapproval with the aims of the Society and demanded immediate majority rule'.[28] On the other hand, the editorial in the *Manchester Guardian* approved of the effort at least: 'Whatever one's reservations, it is impossible to withhold respect and admiration of the tone and spirit of the convention, and for the high spirit of endeavour voiced by the delegates of all races.'[29]

A reporter for *The Rhodesian* wrote: 'The air of haunting unreality which clung to the opening of the Capricorn African Society's interracial convention ... lifted as the initial unanimity gave way yesterday to candid argument ... though the convention meets in the Federation, the planning of earlier drafts of the contract by interracial committees occurred mainly in Kenya and it possibly fits the Kenya situation more neatly than the Federation. ... The African section of the Southern Rhodesian delegation is particularly representative. One feature ... is the obvious alarm among some Asian delegates at the growth of a vigorous African black nationalism in East Africa, fermented by Swahili broadcasts against colonialism from Cairo. Another [aspect] is the high percentage of practising Christians among the European supporters who obviously wish to live up to Christian principles of brotherhood with other races.'[30]

The Christian principles were implicit in the article written by Joyce Raw, a practising Catholic, in the London Roman Catholic *Tablet*. 'A noticeable feature of the convention on which many of the observers commented was the atmosphere of goodwill, understanding, and gaiety which emanated from Salima. This was so genuine, so spontaneous and unforced that it surprised even some of the earliest members of the Society. The convention will long remain in my memory as one of the most moving and stimulating experiences of my life. On the first day the atmosphere was solemn, but laughter came later and there was a great deal of laughter of the right sort, of affection, understanding and tolerance. I must say that the contribution made by the Kenya delegation was outstanding. This was especially true of some of our African speakers who showed a keen insight and true understanding of what is implied by the Capricorn philosophy.'[31]

An encouraging commentary was by the historian Sir Arthur Bryant in the *Illustrated London News*: 'The British people seem in their history to have been forever alternating between two points of view. One is the ideal and the other is the practicable. ... Take the vexed and frightening subject of race prejudice and the colour bar. ... If one takes the purely realistic and cynical view, that because a Hottentot tribesman happens in some respects to be much nearer the primitive savage of 4000 years ago than his European contemporary, the latter is entitled to treat him for the next 4000 years, or even forever, as an inferior creature, one will get a shock.'[32] In contrast to the eulogies, the *Times of India* from Bombay commented: 'Minutely examined, the Capricorn African Society constitution cannot wash. It is nothing better than a hotchpotch of paradoxes. Inherent in the principles of the Society is unity, under God, in a single loyalty to the British crown. This has been, and is, the ambition of every British settler in Africa; but the principle cuts at the roots of the aspiration of the African for the right of self-determination.' The editor in Bombay suspected that 'unity' would be between the settlers of east and central Africa, and that the God would be a white man.

Back in Kenya, the branch kept up the momentum with letters to the local newspapers. The leading paper in Kenya, serving mainly the European population, was the *East African Standard*, which failed to comment on Salima, although it duly reported the main items of news. In frustration I wrote a pompous letter to the editor. 'Responsible newspapers and periodicals in Great Britain and other parts of Africa have commented editorially on the Capricorn proposals. However, you Sir, as editor of the leading daily paper in a country which badly needs liberal and realistic political thought, remain silent. An objective appraisal of the Capricorn document might annoy the reactionary ostriches among us, but I suggest that it is a duty that your paper can not avoid if it is to maintain its reputation for responsible and objective comment on matters of importance to the future of these territories.'[33]

On the same day, Omori, who was a Nairobi journalist and had been a keen member of a Nairobi citizenship committee, also wrote a strong letter to the editor. 'According to Mr Herbert Chitepo, this was not only a unique occasion but also the last chance to save Africa from racial conflicts and ultimate social, economic and political destruction. I cannot agree more with this Southern Rhodesian African barrister who has the vision and courage to state that the African's advancement and greatness depend on how well he gets along with other races who have made their homes in this continent. Some Africans suspect that there is some ulterior motive behind the Society. ... It can be a great tragedy if the African is held responsible, and his name recorded in history, for any failure, or part of it, in harmonious and prosperous living in this part of the world. ... Let us throw in our lot and give the Capricorn Society the support it so richly deserves.'[34]

Later in the month, the *East African Standard* carried a contrary view from two Africans writing from Nakuru, in the White Highlands: 'The Capricorn ideas are some of the most disastrous and misleading notions which prevail in the country. The Society worships the quotation of Cecil Rhodes 'Equal rights for all civilized men'. As you can deduce, this is already a barrier between the civilized and the non-civilized, who need special help from the former.'[35]

Elspeth Huxley, born and raised in Kenya and well known for her two-volume biography of Lord Delamere,[36] and who was later to be a member of the Monkton commission on the future of the central Africa federation, wrote in a London journal.

'The Capricorn Contract is a new declaration of the rights of man designed for Africa. There is nothing revolutionary about the rights and duties which its six precepts define; they are those generally accepted as lying at the heart of our western democratic philosophy, but there is something revolutionary about trying to apply them in a practical form to the multiracial countries of Africa. The Capricorn Society is disliked and distrusted by extremists on both sides. Quite clearly and unequivocally it renounces all forms of apartheid, it advocates the common voters' roll, and, by proclaiming that all should be free to own land in any area, it would sweep away the whole system of European and African reserves in Kenya and the Rhodesias. This is revolutionary indeed ... in countries where the whole economic and social pattern rests upon tribal and racial rights to specific areas of land. The Society also draws the fire of those African nationalists and their supporters in Britain who wish to see Africa as a giant reserve for the dark-skinned, and believe that whites have no future there save as temporary technicians. The black nationalists who find support among such bodies as the Africa Bureau and among some Labour members of the House of Commons are as bigoted as Mr Strijdom and his followers. The idea of a qualified franchise is too revolutionary for those nurtured on the notion that democracy is somehow equated with one man, one vote. Unless the idea can be got across ... that the status of a citizen can involve hard, slogging work, intelligence, and restraint, and does not consist merely in being served sugared tea in an ever-open welfare canteen, there will be a dim future for these African countries.'[37]

For a movement that was perennially hard up, the costs of the Salima convention were daunting. As a new member of the Kenya branch, it did not occur to me to question who was paying for the chartered flight, accommodation, food and furniture, arrangements for the press and the excellent secretariat. Individual members were neither asked nor expected to contribute – for one thing, many, including myself at that time, would have found difficulty in doing so. The costs were covered by donations from London and from individuals in Kenya and Southern Rhodesia, although there was some doubt that the total amount was available before we went to Salima. It would have been surprising if David had waited until all the money was raised before the convention – he never allowed shortage of ready cash to prevent him campaigning for what he believed so passionately.

Among the survivors, Lawrence Vambe now remembers Salima as 'an interesting occasion with nice people' who were critical of existing society and were looking for an answer. He wonders whether they knew what they were doing, and asks: 'Were we naive, was it too good to be true?' I, too, remember optimism and hope at Salima, but the question now is whether we had the slightest chance of making our proposals a reality. Over the next four years we were to discover the answer. Tragically, when Capricorn was enjoying praise and publicity for the success of Salima, within months the Suez debacle[38] signalled the end of European power and influence in Africa.

Chapter 9
Against the Odds in a Self-Governing Colony

After the excitement and undoubted success of Salima, David Stirling, Philip Mason and Jeannine Scott flew to Salisbury where Mason addressed the Rhodesian National Affairs Association[1] about the convention, at which the RNAA president, Hardwicke Holderness, by then an MP in the Southern Rhodesia parliament, had been an ironic observer. Nearly 20 years later Holderness described his memories of what he called an 'improbable international gathering' in terms that hint of an element of rivalry in the lack of cooperation between the RNAA and Capricorn. 'The Salima Convention was boycotted by the African nationalists ... and had no special political impact afterwards, but it was a romantic occasion. ... White Rhodesians hobnobbing with black ex-Mau Mau Kenyans under the stars.'[2] African nationalists were unlikely to be Capricorn members or delegates to the convention, and the suggestion that every black Kenyan was a member of Mau Mau is a measure of how isolated from the rest of Africa even liberal white Rhodesians were. One reason for the distance between Capricorn and both the RNAA and the Interracial Association was that David did not engage with (kept aloof from, some said) Southern Rhodesian politics while Holderness and his friend, Pat Lewis, as lawyers, believed that change must come through parliament.

Although David, publicly and privately, stressed that the philosophy and membership of Capricorn came from all races, in retrospect it is clear that it was essential to concentrate first on changing the attitudes of the white settlers — governments were controlled by Europeans, whether in Nairobi, Salisbury or Whitehall. There is no evidence that this was David's strategy when he sought out Colonel Selwyn Hickman, recently retired as commissioner of the British South Africa Police — the nostalgic title of the Rhodesian police force – and enrolled him as a member of the central Africa executive committee of Capricorn.

In seeking supporters David had always looked for leaders and in Hickman he had a key figure in the white community of Southern Rhodesia. He was a local historian, a keen member of the Anglican Church, the Samaritans, St John Ambulance Brigade, Film Censorship Board, National Monuments Commission and the Rhodesiana Society. His position as the chief of police, upholding the many regulations that controlled and restricted African life, recommended him to the Europeans as much as his appointment was an insult to the African members of the Society. In spite of Hickman's background he was a man who tried to build bridges – the historian Peter Garlake, whose father knew Hickman well, said he had 'an enormously kind heart and an enormously narrow mind'.[3] Hickman was a powerful figure, accustomed to speaking his mind and having people agree with him. It was not long before he clashed with David, opening hostilities by suggesting that Moral Rearmament were claiming credit for Salima because David had been to Caux, MRA headquarters in Switzerland.[4] David had to acknowledge that he had been there to see for himself what was going on but robustly denied being influenced by MRA ideology.

At the end of July 1956 David left for Britain, stopping in Nairobi on the way. He had devoted seven years to Capricorn – years of travelling up and down Africa, visiting Britain and the United States, cajoling and encouraging citizenship committees, lobbying politicians and charming possible donors. Although he revelled in it, he was physically and emotionally drained, suffering from migraines and needing time to recuperate. After shooting in Scotland, in November he was in Addenbrooke Hospital, near Cambridge, for tests on his circulation. He badly needed time away from the action but, while Capricorn was in the news, it was time the movement could not afford to lose. Although there were loyal, hard-working members who supported the cause, without David's leadership and drive Capricorn floundered and lost direction. Clearly, it was dangerous for an enterprise with such ambitions to be dependent on the health and stability of one man.

At a meeting of the central Africa executive at the end of August 1956,[5] Hickman's election as chairman of the branch was seconded by Lawrence Vambe, although he shared African feelings about the police background. S. J. T. Samkange was elected deputy chairman and Fred Rea joined the committee. Hickman was now in a position to take control, examine how the Society had been managed and decide what changes he would like to make. He was not impressed. As executive officers, the branch had Chad Chipunza, Titus Hlazo and Peter Mackay, who was about to resign at the end of the 18 months he signed on for. In his handing over notes[6] Mackay recorded that the Society's membership in central Africa amounted to: 'European 468, African 935, other races 80, total 1483. NR Membership: E[uropean] 88, A[frican] 10, o[ther races] 7, Nyasaland Membership: E[uropean] 34, A[frican] 11, o[ther races] 1.' He meticulously prepared the accounts for the convention and was warmly congratulated for having born the brunt of the organization for the event. Funds were set aside for a presentation, which Mackay (who was just 30 years old) declined to accept on the grounds that he never accepted presentations.

In October David was still away, writing to Hickman: 'My dear Colonel, I have decided to postpone my return',[7] and to Mackay: 'I do hope that now you are free from the Society you are having a complete rest before engaging in other pursuits. You certainly are a mystery man. I had a splendid time in Scotland killing quite a few stags and lots of grouse and walked up to the top of very many hills, including Ben Nevis.'[8] At the end of November 1956 David arrived back in Salisbury with Charles March and a young Etonian, David Hamilton. A few days later Hickman met David who displayed no interest in how the Society had fared in his absence and said he had personal plans so would not be available for Capricorn affairs until early 1957.[9] David handed over a letter he and March (CAS treasurer) had written in Nairobi containing orders that Hickman's branch office was to be closed, though the president's office would continue, plus instructions on how to pay in cheques and other management details.[10]

This lack of tact to an experienced and senior man was not a good omen for the relationship between the president of the Society and the chairman of the local branch and within a month it had broken down irretrievably. Hickman called a special meeting of the Southern Rhodesia executive on 7 January 1957, at which David and 20 members were present together with Chipunza and Mackay's successor, K. M. Stevens.[11] The minutes record that Hickman opened the meeting by outlining 'the Society's progress since the [Salima] convention and said it was felt that a statement on policy should have been announced then. Without such a statement the tremendous enthusiasm which had been aroused could not be kept up.' Hickman continued by reporting that 'the independent treasurer [March] had made recommendations for a budget which the president proposed should be approved and accepted, but the chairman felt that in view of his differences of opinion with the president over various matters, he would have to tender his resignation as chairman.' He added that notice of termination of employment had been given to Mr Stevens and the secretary, Mrs Coombe, as there were no funds available for their salaries.

The minutes reported: 'The president regretted that he had not given a directive after Salima due to a breakdown in his health necessitating a holiday and due to his undertaking to carry out a mission in Europe' (which sounded better than the grouse moors and hospital). David continued by stating that a political party independent of the Society was vital, following which 'Mr Rosin, Mrs Tarican and Mrs Brickhill tendered their resignations. Mr Hickman resigned and Mr Samkange was asked to take his place.' After the meeting the short-lived executive officer, Stevens, wrote to Dr Dewe of the Midlands branch that 'It seems impossible to obtain any final ruling on which way the Society is going. It is a great pity, but with all this muddle I shall be pleased to get out of this office!'[12]

Hickman, the amateur historian, meticulously recorded each step of the dispute in two long memoranda, now in the Zimbabwe National Archives. Like Wilson before him he was written out of the Capricorn story and he omitted any mention of being a member, or chairman, of the Society in his biographical details. His second memorandum, running to 25 pages, gives the story from his point of view, and is corroborated in correspondence from others involved. Of the meeting on 7 January he wrote: 'I then outlined the ... points of disagreement ... since the return of the president to Southern Rhodesia. I spoke very forcibly and I was told afterwards that several members present felt quite sorry for Stirling. During various stages he offered to resign but it was pointed out that this was out of order in a SR executive meeting ... for the most part he sat, as described by one member, weak and flaccid, receiving punches but having no stomach in him to fight back.'[13]

David must have been more ill than he realized, because even when he was exhausted he never gave in. Hickman continued: 'I informed the president that as I personally had no confidence in him, I must resign ... and would remain as a private member as I believed in the ideals of the Society, apart from its administration. Stirling's defence of himself, and his attitude, was pathetically feeble. ... After Stirling's statement, which lasted half an hour, a number of members resigned and left the meeting.'

Hickman attached a memo from Dewe who commented: '(1) There is no departure from the principles of the Capricorn Contract by any proponent in the dispute. There is however, a basic disagreement as regards administration, formulation of policy and financial arrangements. (2) It is common ground that the inspiration, leadership and drive which culminated in the Capricorn Contract will be associated for all time with Col Stirling personally. His exceptional resource and courage in the crusade, which has resulted in the firm establishment of the Society as an increasing force in the salvation of Africa and for the world, is unmatched and was given at a crucial period of time. ... It is fundamental to the Capricorn Contract that it was produced as a result of the combined effort of all races in central Africa. ... It is ineluctable that subsequent policies should be similarly derived. ... There is a danger at present of giving an impression that the policy of the Society is dictated from without. Acceptance of Col Hickman's resignation would be disastrous to the Society in Southern Rhodesia. It is obvious to those people who are in close contact with the ordinary Rhodesians that Hickman's accession to office has profoundly impressed a great number of [white] Rhodesians and immigrant South Africans who have grown up in the old tradition, on account of his background and experience, and his obvious total sincerity. This effect Col Stirling could never have hoped to emulate with the best will in the world.'

European members of Capricorn believed that having Hickman as chairman made the Society's ideas more acceptable to the settlers, not only because of his background as a senior policeman but also because he was a genuine Rhodesian who had lived in the country for over 30 years.

In February David went to Que Que in Midlands with Hamilton and Stevens to explain himself. From a letter written by Dewe, the branch secretary and treasurer, to his friend Guy Savory, David failed to persuade them. Dewe wrote: 'Col Stirling ... was strongly attacked on all sides on his treatment of Col Hickman and the executive in Salisbury. It was pointed out to him that his actions since his return to the country had done immense damage to the Society's cause and we requested him to try to make amends by coming to terms with Col Hickman. I recommend that the office of honorary life president be offered to him, with no entrenched executive rights. If Col Stirling refuses to accept this, or some similar role, I fear we are, as a Society, heading for a complete breakdown, which will be exploited by our enemies and misunderstood by our friends. ... Apparently Mr Hamilton returned to Salisbury with a very rosy view of the effect of his visit.'[14]

Hamilton was also an optimist in his assessment of the situation in the country, writing to Jonathan Lewis: 'Outside Salisbury, Bulawayo and, perhaps, Umtali [the African National] Congress has virtually no support whatsoever.'[15] In reality there was much discontent in the countryside over land. Hamilton, who had joined the office in Salisbury to work for a year, was murdered in Brixton 30 years later by his male lover who disposed of his body in a particularly grisly fashion.[16] In the 1950s Southern Rhodesia was a male oriented and tough society so it is questionable whether it was a wise move to import a rather effete upper-class young man as Capricorn executive officer.

From the correspondence in the files he did not impress some of the older members. Savory in the Midlands branch wrote to Michael Wood in Nairobi: 'We are deeply distressed about the catastrophic results of David Stirling's headlong dash through the country in a seemingly quite irresponsible and unbalanced mood. We regard David's new young man, Hamilton, as ... a negation of the principle that we must be inspired and grow from within Africa. I understand that his only experience of the continent is as adjutant to the Ethiopian Navy (*sic*) for a year. Good show, but we won't accept him.'[17] From Bulawayo, Aleco Pilavachi expressed the feelings of his branch in a letter to Hamilton which could have been expressed more tactfully: 'One can sum up the general attitude in a nutshell by saying that everyone is dead keen, but they won't be buggered about.'[18]

Aside from the primitive clash of personalities between Hickman and David, there were two issues of substance in David's battles with his erstwhile European supporters. It appears that the African members of Capricorn played no part in the affair, and their views do not seem to have been considered by the participants. One issue was the use of American money and the other David's determination that Capricorn's ideals must be carried on by political parties. David was, of course, right, but his antagonists were against both ideas, though for different reasons. Suspicion of American money was based on the white settlers' dislike of anti-colonial rhetoric from the USA, and as 'gentlemen' they distrusted politicians. John Olivey, a Melsetter member without a dictionary, wrote later: 'I think the mirkey business of politics are far better left to those mirkey people who understand mirk, to which level I find it all too easy to drop when once one has a vote. I could not at present support [a] party whose chief aim is to bring the African into politics.'[19]

The London office files give no indication that Jeannine Scott, Jonathan Lewis, Henry Crookenden or March appreciated the strong feelings that the Hickman affair aroused in Southern Rhodesia, while rank and file members in Kenya, like myself, heard nothing at all. Once the pressure of producing the Contract was over, the branches in east and central Africa concentrated on local problems with less correspondence between north and south. From talking to those close to him at the time, it seems that David was going through a breakdown, with characteristic highs and lows, which made his friends deeply concerned about his health and the effect that his actions and statements were having on the Society.

In the branch executive committee meeting in March 1957 Samkange was formally elected chairman[20] with the unenviable task of trying to mend broken fences. He had the help of three executive officers – Chipunza, Hamilton and Hlazo, none of whom was especially qualified to mollify the angry white Capricorn members around the country after the Hickman resignation. Later in the year, when Chipunza left, David appointed Leopold Takawira as executive officer. Takawira had chaired a Salisbury citizenship committee in 1955, been to Salima and remained devoted to David, Mackay and the Plunkets until the end of his life.

In March 1957 David gave a powerful lecture to the Royal African Society[21] in London. Back in Africa in August he was again ill, sending Jeannine Scott a reassuring, but not exactly truthful, cable from Nairobi: 'SITUATION ENTIRELY SOUND AND ALWAYS WAS STOP IMPLICATIONS AND DIFFICULTIES ENTIRELY IMAGINARY STOP WOODS IN TOP FORM = DAVID.'[22] In October he produced a powerful and persuasive paper, 'Proposals for the Future', which announced that adult education was the way forward for Africa and for Capricorn.[23] Writing 28 foolscap pages and, one assumes and hopes, debating and defending the contents with his colleagues, added to the toll on his physical and mental health. It was the start of a project that gave the Society a real and positive role in Kenya and in Southern Rhodesia, where it continues to make a contribution to the life of Zimbabwe.

At the end of the year David decided to take over the chairmanship of the SR branch himself as it was, he wrote, 'in bad disarray'.[24] At the same time he also wrote a letter from Salisbury on his personal notepaper announcing that after much deliberation he had decided to resign as president of the Capricorn Africa

Society. The copy in the files[25] has no addressee and no signature, although it appears it was sent to key people in the Society in Nairobi and London. The reasons he gave for resignation were his failure to persuade the London committee to recommend the conversion of covenants to cash and the state of his own finances, allied to the withdrawal of promised financial support from the family business. The latter was probably a consequence of his brother Bill's considerable gambling losses.

David recommended that Michael Wood take over the presidency, adding that no statement should be made until his successor was installed, to avoid the resignation being interpreted as due to differences of opinion on policy or programme – he was determined to deny Hickman and his supporters an opportunity to claim victory. David's close confidante, Jeannine Scott, reacted immediately: she wrote to his sister, Lady Dalhousie, then in Salisbury as the wife of the governor general of the federation. 'We are all dreadfully worried about [David]. ... I have had letters from him saying he is resigning from being the president of the Capricorn Society. ... If he is going to resign now it can only be, I feel, on health grounds and it should be clearly indicated also that it was only a temporary measure. ... I was devastated by David's letter to me – obviously we are at a moment of crisis both for him and the Society. ... I am sure David is heading for a serious mental and physical breakdown. ... He is talking wildly of abandoning Africa altogether, going to Canada ..., but to suddenly disappear into the blue would obviously be a most frightful let down. ... From all I saw during my recent tour in Africa, and my knowledge of the "this end" Capricorn, I cannot stress too strongly that if David should do what he threatens doing, he will sabotage his work of nine years which will involve the letting down of many hundreds of people who have put their faith in him and the cause and in his leadership particularly.'[26]

On 23 December 1957 David complicated the resignation issue in a letter to Crookenden in London in which he quoted a cable he had sent to Wood in Nairobi and to Charles Fisher in Northern Rhodesia. 'RESIGNATION WARNING ORDER NOT INTENDED TO BECOME EFFECTIVE IMMEDIATELY STOP HAVE AGREED TO DEFER IT UNTIL PARTIES FULLY ESTABLISHED IN ALL FIVE TERRITORIES AND EDUCATION SCHEME ADOPTED BY EACH BRANCH OF SOCIETY STOP THIS PROGRAMME SHOULD BE COMPLETED BY END MARCH AS ORIGINALLY PLANNED STOP.'[27] With scanty files and selective memories, it is difficult to have a clear picture of the situation, but

David's erratic behaviour had little regard for the sensibilities of his supporters, or for the situation on the ground. Imagining that there would be political parties based on Capricorn ideals in all five territories within a few months was to fly in the face of reality.

David and Takawira kept the office going during 1958, devoting much of their efforts to the development of the adult education proposal. In March they held a successful AGM[28] with over 300 people, including representatives of the consular and diplomatic corps in the front row. In his chairman's address David appealed for support to be given to other organizations that aimed at better relations between the races. The executive officer reported enthusiastically on progress since his appointment seven months earlier.

In June, after the liberal Garfield Todd had been replaced as prime minister, the success of right-wing parties in the Southern Rhodesian elections showed Africans and liberal Europeans where the future lay. Realists in Capricorn and in the Interracial Association began to lose heart as they recognized that the fight for a sensible future was almost lost. Africans who read of their contemporaries in East Africa being elected to parliament reflected bitterly that there had never been an African in the Southern Rhodesia parliament, or in the civil service at a professional level, in spite of having the highest literacy rate south of the Sahara. While continuing to work in the Capricorn office, Takawira became increasingly involved with the African National Congress (ANC). The conflict of interest and the use of the Society's facilities as an office for an African political party worried some of the white members, but was not an issue for David as his sympathy grew for Takawira's belief that Africans themselves must organize and press for change.

Philip Mason described David as a prophet but not a politician.[29] I believe he had the foresight to grasp the realities of the changes in West Africa and realized that they would be inevitable in the east, although publicly he continued to encourage his troops to keep the Capricorn banner flying. Susan Wood has said 'David hated losing and did not want to be associated with failure — perhaps that was one reason why he resigned when he did.'[30] The sense that the battle was lost, added to ill health and financial worries, drove him to take the step his many supporters dreaded: irrevocably resigning as president of Capricorn. This he did in September 1958. Michael Wood, the chairman of the Kenya branch, was elected unopposed to the post of president, and I was elected Kenya chairman in his place.

Jennifer Plunket has said Capricorn ended when David resigned: branches continued for some time, but his resignation undoubtedly hastened the Society's decline. David's irrational optimism was no longer available to keep us believing we could change our world against the odds, and against history. In December 1958 the new president made plans to visit Southern Rhodesia, writing a complacent letter to Lewis in London: 'The agonizing reappraisal of our position continues and I shall know more of the total position when I have visited Rhodesia. I am acutely aware of the temporary slump in affairs there, but this has happened before and I am not unduly perturbed.'[31]

Wood was in New Zealand in January 1959 at a Commonwealth conference when Lewis wrote to him in his usual robust style: 'Morale in central Africa seems to be at the lowest ebb ever. ... Why the hell can't the chaps get cracking instead of moaning/groaning and talking about setting up a new network of local groups. ... With such contemptible feebleness on the part of the Europeans, one simply daren't think of what is happening to our African/Asian following and your visit is clearly all important.'[32] This crossed with a long, handwritten letter to Lewis from Wood in Sydney, detailing his successes in persuading Commonwealth delegates of the importance of the Capricorn idea.[33] He also reported constructive discussions with Todd about setting up a combined liberal front in central Africa.

In spite of the worsening situation and reservations by many of the European members about political action, there were a few thoughtful individuals who were thinking hard about the role of the Society. In early 1959 Humphrey Amherst wrote to Rea: 'The Capricorn Contract is a thesis in political philosophy and the implementation of its philosophy can ultimately be brought about only by political action. Consequently the Society must be a political or quasi-political body whether it likes it or not. ... I have some fear of the Society degenerating into a mere welfare organization and if, as it almost certainly would be, the welfare were from one race to another it would not be a non-racial activity but a racial one, and as such not a proper function of the Society — it would be just another handout.'[34] This analysis went unheeded.

In his extensive tour of Southern Rhodesia, Wood addressed a meeting of the Rhodesian National Affairs Association in Salisbury and chaired the annual general meeting of the central Africa branch.[35] Takawira continued the tradition established by David in 'striking a note of considerable optimism' and reporting that 1958 'had been an exciting year of achievement'. He reported that he had visited 16 local associations around the country, some as many as four times and that the chairman had addressed meetings at a number of local associations and encouraged as many as 200 members to join the society.[36] He noted that 'the lady members, Lady Courtauld of Umtali; Mrs Snell of Marandellas; Mrs Plunket of Melsetter; Mrs King of Salisbury; Mrs Ranger of the University College in Salisbury, Mrs Ireland of Umtali and Miss Elisabeth Murphy had all been particularly keen and active.'

Jennifer Plunket, responding to comments by Africans that Capricorn meetings were only for men, had started the Capricorn mobile unit. She raised £1000, Jeannine Scott found £1000 in London and Laurens van der Post gave the old Land Rover from his Kalahari expedition. Two women, an African and a European, 'manned' the mobile unit, known as Kalahari Kate, to talk about hygiene and nutrition to African women's clubs around the country. The Capricorn mobile unit has continued to keep the Society's name alive in central Africa. Reading Takawira's report on this useful activity makes it difficult to refute the comment by Amherst that Capricorn was becoming an organization providing welfare from one race to another. A resolution that the Society 'urged the removal of all those conditions which are likely to excite any section of the community to violence was passed by 27 to 14'. It was then proposed that the vote had not been strong enough to publish the statement. Lewis's apposite and prophetic phrase 'contemptible feebleness' had been written a month earlier.

Disappointment after the general election results had led the ANC to propose a 'declaration of social war' by defying the colour bar.[37] In February 1959 the new prime minister, Sir Edgar Whitehead, declared a state of emergency under which the ANC was banned and hundreds of its supporters, including Takawira, detained without trial. This led to further breakdown in the fragile trust between the races that the Society and others had been fostering. Capricorn members campaigned for Takawira's release, and took him back into the office when he was freed. The incident did stimulate the Society to set up a civil liberties committee, which led to the holding of a study conference on 'Democracy: Its Rights and Responsibilities' at the University College of Rhodesia and Nyasaland.[38] During the year Herbert Chitepo, Takawira and others founded the National Democratic Party (NDP), which, as could be expected, was more militant than the banned ANC.

In January 1960 Wood and I went to Southern Rhodesia to discuss the Society's submission to the Monckton Commission on the future of the federation and to address Capricorn meetings. Our fortnight in Southern Rhodesia and our comments on the situation are recorded in the letters we wrote to the London office. Wood wrote: 'The situation has deteriorated a good deal since I was here last, and there is great depression in many quarters. Capricorn still valiantly tries to put forward a moderate view, but the Africans are tending to think that only extremism pays. One can hardly blame them. We have had a series of interesting meetings with Garfield Todd, the new National Democratic Party and the Courtaulds.'[39]

I had gone to Salisbury some days before Wood to take part in a weekend conference on the Society's submission to the Monckton Commission. I reported to Lewis: 'At a meeting with 30 to 40 people, slightly more Europeans than Africans, with half a dozen Asian and Coloured members, we discussed evidence for the commission. Terence Ranger, an academic from the university, Chitepo and a constitutional expert from Harvard proposed matters that should be raised. I wound up the day, speaking on East African developments and the impact on Rhodesia that political changes in the rest of Africa would make. The general affect of Ranger's talk and mine was to make the conference think along more liberal and urgent lines than they had been prepared to do.'[40]

Many of the white Capricorn members I met seemed isolated from the world outside central Africa and regarded me as wildly left wing when I reported what was happening in the west and north. When Wood arrived we held a general council meeting and worked on the Monckton submission, which included the following statement. 'Unless there can be some quite massive demonstration of the fact that within the next few years this territory is determined so to amend its discriminatory legislation as to ensure all its peoples an equal status as citizens, there can be no hope, either of maintaining present goodwill, or of reclaiming the goodwill of those who at present desire the dissolution of the Federation.'[41]

My report to London continued: 'One evening Leo Takawira and I went to address a meeting in the bush, where we found our local contact standing alone in the hall, although we were very late, having been lost. In an hour or two the word got round and people began to trickle in, and were still trickling in when we left after a long meeting with excellent cakes and strong tea. Peak attendance about 30 who asked good questions and were completely spellbound by Takawira's oratory. He is magnificent on an occasion like this, and I was extremely impressed with him in everything he did. When discussing the situation in East Africa with groups of Africans, the question they all want to ask is, are the advances a direct result of Mau Mau violence? It is a difficult question to answer because ... Mau Mau did jolt the European population and government into recognition that all was not well. One continues to say, however, that in Rhodesia violence is not the answer, though privately one cannot help but feel that against repression, and the total ignoring of the African's point of view, there is very little else left to them.' Before Wood and I left Salisbury on the Comet, we held a press conference at which we issued a statement. 'There has been some economic advance and relaxation of the colour bar in recent years but in the present tempo of events in Africa these developments have been totally inadequate. The political awakening of Africa has precipitated a condition where only rapid and drastic changes can prevent the destruction of society. It is useless to expect that the African will continue to accept economic or even educational advancement as a substitute for progress towards political and social equality in the country.'[42]

At the 1960 AGM in February, with Rea in the chair, David was reported as saying: 'One couldn't be but immensely encouraged with recent trends: (a) many political organizations, including HMG, were seeking to achieve the ends the Society set themselves 11 years go; (b) there was no sign of Capricorn diminishing in vigour or strength, and (c) he was especially happy about Tanganyika where Nyerere had said all nationalities should be made to feel at home'.[43] Takawira accepted his hero's wild optimism in these remarks, made at a time when large numbers of moderate Africans were detained without trial in Southern Rhodesia. Takawira continued to be in thrall to David's enthusiasm, writing to Lewis: 'The founder had just left after doing a tremendous piece of work. David and Fred Rea together have cleared the ground for future policy by deciding that the Society had to act very fast in a rapidly changing country. Their statement on African nationalism was devastating, and left Capricorn's opponents petrified. A European headmaster resigned from the Society but in exchange about six new people joined.'[44]

In March and April 1960 Takawira and John Michael Gibbs, who was to be the first principal of the College of Rhodesian Citizenship,[45] made a long tour of Northern Rhodesia for the Society. Takawira's day-by-day report[46] is factual and occasionally disingenuous. After attending a conference in Mindola on the future of the federation, which unanimously found that it must be abandoned, they went on to Luanshya where Yvette Menzies took

Takawira to the African township. He reported that the 'name "Capricorn" had been painted extremely black'. At Ndola he attended a mammoth rally where he found, to his 'surprise there were cries of "Freedom" "Kwacha" and all sorts of African slogans' when he appeared. He was conducted amidst applause and cheers to the dais to be introduced as a fellow freedom fighter. Takawira reported: 'here was an executive officer of the hated Capricorn Africa Society received so tumultuously. It did not sound quite correct or true to me; of course, the majority of the people there did not know I had any connection with the Society.' He could have added that they obviously knew a great deal about his connection with the NDP. In his report he commented that across the country's northern borders, in the Belgian Congo and in Tanganyika, people of the same tribe and levels of development were about to achieve their independence while Africans in Northern Rhodesia 'are not considered capable of being entrusted with similar responsibility'.

The next day Takawira met a small group of Capricorn enthusiasts and learnt that the Society had definitely proved unacceptable to the Africans and that it was useless to spend too much time on either organizing Capricorn or discussing it. He added that history had shown that imprisonment, detentions and other physical sufferings are the heralds of majority rule in any country, and that this struggle is not a racial one, having happened in Russia, France, the United States of America and indeed in Great Britain herself. Takawira pointed out that although there were many genuinely liberal white people, only one white man had been detained compared with many hundreds of Africans. At another meeting he heard the phrase 'so and so is a Capricorner', that is an African who attends national meetings with other Africans during the day and at night slips off to report to the police. Takawira concluded his report with the observation that the existence of the Capricorn Africa Society in Northern Rhodesia was impossible 'because in Northern Rhodesia the mere mention of the name Capricorn defeats straight away the reason for which the Society was created'. He proposed that people who shared Capricorn ideas should cause them to be implemented through other organizations rather than insisting on perpetuating the name itself.

In June 1960 Takawira described the current situation with sadness and honesty in a letter to Lewis, quoted in a Capricorn newsletter. I am 'fully committed to non-racialism and while partnership must be made to work if we are going to survive, I have discovered that unless Africans organize and unite, Europeans will not enter a real partnership with us. Multiracial organizations ... cannot speak for the blacks without that natural and native emotion which can only be arrived at from personal and physical suffering and humiliation which Africans encounter day in and day out. European friends will always be sympathizers but can never be physical co-sufferers.'[47] A few weeks later David wrote to Vambe: 'most moderate Africans are now NDP. If I were an African so would I [be]. As the position now exists in central Africa there is no alternative to Africans closing ranks behind NDP to force the government's hand and I believe, provided transfer of power doesn't take too long, Africans will exercise their power in a way generous to Europeans.'[48]

After the riots in Salisbury and Bulawayo in July 1960 Takawira was again arrested but soon released. In August he reported casually to the members: 'Since we met on 4th July nothing of great significance and worth reporting has happened,'[49] explaining that his arrest had some repercussions on the Society when the offices were searched, and that it caused many members anxious thinking and some embarrassment. He continued: 'Africans ... now cannot see how their presence in the Society can bring about the famous Capricorn national patriotism. The move, they say, must come from Europeans who have the power to bring the races together. ... Our future plans should be in the light of this argument.' Although Mackay was no longer in the Capricorn office, it was to him that his friend Takawira turned in confusion and disgust when, in November 1960, he was offered £50 by Hickman for inside information on NDP activities, the ex-policeman still in touch with his special branch friends.[50] Takawira continued to work out of the Capricorn office until he went to London as the NDP director for foreign affairs.

Capricorn was active in a national convention, an indaba, in late October 1960 at which the Society's chairman, Rea, spoke of the desire of the people to strive towards Rhodesian nationhood and stability. Edwin Townsend-Coles has written: 'In the short space of a week, 174 people (89 white, 72 African, 5 Coloured, 8 Asian) met and lived in a Salisbury hotel, debated the most pressing political and social issues of the day, and came up with proposals for the government. ... A final report of 112 pages was produced and finally adopted.'[51] Sadly, within days it was rejected out of hand by the Southern Rhodesian government. The convention also agreed that the college of citizenship[52] should be supported.

This was the year when Lewis made a tour through east and central Africa and submitted his devastating report on the health of the Society, which led to the general council meeting in January 1961.[53] Possibly stimulated by the Lewis report, the Southern Rhodesia branch held conferences on education for a multiracial society and on local government in 1961. More disappointingly, at the AGM the branch recorded the results of a questionnaire to members, which resulted in 51 replies saying that they would not continue, against 87 prepared to fight on.[54] These numbers gave a false impression as the executive committee had recorded a total of only 82 members and an income of £45.5.8. Some of the staunchest supporters said that the time had come for the Society to wind up its activities, although the decision finally reached was that the movement must continue and extend its work.

Rea told the AGM: 'Your executive is acutely conscious of how inadequate we are in the face of the tremendous task of strengthening the dykes of democracy in central Africa. We would be only too willing to make way for any other organization if such should emerge to tackle the task with larger resources, and we would gladly have merged our resources with theirs. But none has appeared and now we see clearly that for us to abandon the field at such a time as this and leave a vacuum would be a betrayal. We are resolved go forward with renewed confidence and determination.' On recruitment of new members he said, significantly, 'membership ... is not dependent upon meticulous adherence to every aspect of the [Capricorn Contract], parts which may now be out of date.'

In December 1961 the NDP was banned in its turn and the Zimbabwe Africa People's Union (ZAPU) was formed under Joshua Nkomo, which also sent Takawira to London as secretary for external affairs. Back in Salisbury he was once again arrested and released and then went to Tanganyika and Northern Rhodesia, where he joined Robert Mugabe in forming the Zimbabwe Africa National Union (ZANU), of which he became vice-president. Only four years earlier some members of the nationalist groups had been members of Capricorn, hoping to find a middle way that would allow their country to develop intelligently and with justice. The selfishness of the overwhelming majority of the white population and their ignorance of the world beyond their borders had dashed any hopes of a peaceful resolution.

Amherst's 1959 letter saying that welfare was not a proper function of the Society stated the obvious for an organization created to bring about constitutional change, a view that was to be echoed in the 1961 general council meeting in Nairobi.[55] The branch in Southern Rhodesia, aside from supporting the important citizenship college, degenerated into welfare, in spite of the efforts of Rea and the branch secretary, Herbert Carter. The executive committee in October 1963 recorded[56] a report on Ranche House College from Robin Plunket, and then noted help given for school fees, assistance to a local Scout group, and a grant to a young woman to study nursing, while the item on constitutional talks and racial discrimination was 'deferred owing to pressure of other business'. Later in the year a decision was made to try again and a conference held shortly before Christmas 1963 resulted in *Southern Rhodesia: The Price of Freedom*, published in April 1964 with a subsidy from the Capricorn Trust in London. The booklet, edited by Rea, had contributions from nine Rhodesians – Africans and Europeans, and sold in sufficient numbers to make a small profit. The authors included Sir Robert Tredgold, retired chief justice and Todd, both well-known liberals, who took a moderate position on the need for change in attitudes and policies if the country was to advance peacefully. It was a brave try, but too late to have any influence in a country governed by Ian Smith and the Rhodesian Front.

That year, during an unwise visit to Southern Rhodesia, Takawira was arrested and locked up for six years until his early death from untreated diabetes. After Zimbabwe's independence Takawira was reinterred in Hero's Acre, Harare, and a major street in the city is named after him, as there is for another old Capricorn member, Chitepo. Two months before Takawira died in prison, during Rhodesia's illegal independence, he wrote to Jennifer Plunket a poignant letter full of his warm personality: 'My dear Jennifer, Things are rather gloomy, Jennifer, in Rhodesia. ... This is cruel to the cause of sanity and broad humanity. ... Racial politics poison the mind and poison good taste. Those of us who believe that the whites are here to stay cannot fail to be concerned with what is going on. ... Well, this morning my good [wife] Sunny was here to see me as usual. ... I have a hunch that I may leave this or early next year when the prevention bill is passed into an act. I don't see what they are really keeping me here for so long. But on the other hand I'm quite prepared and strong to last here as long as it will please them, with still smiles on my face and happiness in my heart. ... Of course this is not pretending that I don't feel the physical tortures I daily go through day in and day out. ... Greetings and love to you and Robin, as ever, Leo.'[57]

The year 1963 was one of major changes in Capricorn Africa. Kenya became an independent country under majority rule and Tanganyika was already a one-party state. In central Africa the federation, which had been a key part of David's original programme, was dissolved, leading to independence for Zambia (Northern Rhodesia) and Malawi (Nyasaland) in 1964. When Smith's right-wing Rhodesian Front began to agitate for independence from Whitehall, the Southern Rhodesia branch of the Society issued an uncompromising press statement in March 1964. 'It is our conviction that it is not in the best interests of our country that the government should seek independence until a large number of Africans join in the request. ... The present demand for unfettered independence by the Europeans while they are still in power can, in the opinion of Africans, have only one possible implication, namely the attempt by the Europeans to entrench their present political power. We believe that the Europeans have rights which need to be safeguarded both before and after the coming of majority rule. But the honourable way of achieving this is not by unilateral action: no man (and no group) has the right to be judge in his own cause.'[58] In spite of momentous changes taking place in Africa, Capricorn in Southern Rhodesia bravely struggled to keep the Society relevant, but by this time the branch was the only survivor of the original Capricorn Africa Society. Individual members continued to make their views heard in the increasingly hostile climate.

In 1972 Rea, Brian O'Connell, Muriel Rosin, Kenneth Mew[59] and others were members of PARD (People Against Racial Discrimination),[60] which campaigned, unsuccessfully, for a sensible end to the deadlock over UDI when the Pearce Commission held hearings on a political solution to UDI. Mew in particular was articulate in publicly defending a balanced position on race and politics in the country, believing that the extreme position adopted by the white government and the equally intransigent demands of the African nationalists would only be resolved by force. Tragically his forecast was right, though he may not have anticipated that violence would reappear in Zimbabwe 30 years later.

Chapter 10
Action in East Africa

In the five years between the Salima convention and the effective end of Capricorn in Kenya we tried welfare, politics and education as the means to make the Contract a reality. After Salima, which we knew had been unique, and hoped would be significant, each branch of Capricorn concentrated on local issues as a reaction to the powerful coordination David Stirling had imposed during the drafting of the Contract. In any case, in the months after the convention when post-Salima euphoria was at its highest, there had been no central directive on future policy from David. In Kenya, we did not miss the lack of control: we had our script in the Contract, and we set about trying to put it into practice. Before June 1956 was over, strong campaign committees were set up with plans for issuing a précis of the Contract in English and Swahili and enlisting new members.

The indomitable Joyce Raw was appointed Nairobi campaign agent for Europeans and a public meeting was arranged to explain our proposals for the future. Separate committees were organized to encourage African and Asian membership, particularly in the Nairobi area, where it was thought the most politically aware were to be found. In July 1956 the local paper reported: 'Membership of the Kenya branch of the Capricorn Africa Society is increasing at an encouraging pace, the chairman, Mr Michael Wood, told the annual meeting of the branch in Nairobi on Friday. The present membership figure was 1418 – 624 Africans, 184 Asians and 610 Europeans. A year ago, there were 1105. Concluding his review of the year's work, Mr Wood said: "I would like to remind you all that we are on the threshold of great things".'[1] The numbers the chairman reported were the peak of our membership, and although the proportion between the races was reasonably balanced, we could not claim a mass membership in the country.

After David had survived the personality clashes that welcomed him back to Southern Rhodesia, of which we in Nairobi knew nothing, he made a number of visits to Kenya. Until mid-1957 when he proposed adult education as the answer, the orders were to do something, anything, to keep the Society active. We tried welfare, we wrote letters to the papers, some helped form a political wing, others attempted to open up Nairobi's social clubs to members of other races, and some were involved in proposals for multiracial schools. In the meantime Africa, especially in the west, was changing fast and not on Capricorn lines.

Before we went to Salima the Kenya branch rented a shop in Racecourse Road, Nairobi, as a Capricorn club. Although we worked hard to turn the old shop into a club, including painting the walls in bright colours selected by Susan Wood with my enthusiastic support, the club did not survive. The most important decision to be made was whether our club should operate jointly with the United Kenya Club, which was a thriving multiracial social club with regular weekly discussion meetings and residential accommodation. This question of overlap was one that would undermine most of the ideas we proposed in the years after Salima.

In February 1957 Michael Wood circulated a memorandum[2] listing some ideas for the Society, including a citizenship centre with library, information bureau, economic section, and facilities for entertaining foreign visitors; a mobile citizenship caravan to travel throughout the country; a non-racial restaurant as a meeting place for educated and civilized people of all races, and a junior branch with lectures in schools and expeditions out into the country. He then realized that almost all these ideas were already covered by the activities or aspirations of some other organization, and in some cases by more than one.

However, he continued: 'first and foremost we have the most important idea in Africa today. We must not allow ourselves to be deflected from our one main task of getting that idea across. The time we have to do it is so short.' Wood continued that the mobile caravan was worth concentrating on and also setting up a radio station, 'which would include programmes to assist African advancement and give publicity and encouragement to all other efforts for racial harmony. ... We believe that there is no better way to diffuse our idea in the two to three years that we have at our disposal.' The proposed caravan and radio station, which might have helped to alter public opinion in the country, were not followed up because the considerable sums of money required were not available. The London office had been having difficulties over raising funds for some time and, in a period when each branch was concentrating on local affairs, they were becoming increasingly involved in hostels for overseas students in London.[3] Their charitable status made it impossible to fund a radio station in East Africa intended to propagate what was in effect a political message and the idea, good though it may have been, was not taken further.

A telling incident, known as 'the St Julian's affair', blew up after our return from Salima and lasted for nearly a year. The passions and problems it generated were an indication of the paranoia of many settlers in the White Highlands and of the significance of the Society, if its connection with the simple sale of a small parcel of land near Tigoni, north of Nairobi, could create such excitement. Richard Frost, in *Race Against Time*, summed it up: 'This story of four women and twenty acres at Limuru is like a microscope under which we can study the fears and emotions, the hopes and the prejudices which beset the progress of interracial harmony in Kenya. The word "multiracial" was certainly anathema to a certain section of the white population.'[4]

In the context of the importance or otherwise of the Capricorn Africa Society, the facts need to be recounted. The Woods wanted to sell their small farm and house at Limuru to an Anglican religious community from England as a place of rest for people of all races suffering from the pressures of modern life. The area was listed as agricultural land and was therefore within the White Highlands, so some local settlers known as 'Tigoni Tigers' (after the name of the district) reacted with fury to the idea that there could be people of other races staying there, and tried all possible means to prevent the sale. They misunderstood, perhaps wilfully, the legalities as Mervyn Hill pointed out in the *Kenya Weekly Guardian*: 'the wise policy of the settlers is to keep quiet about the White Highlands and to treat the reservation as an economic and agrarian measure which is amply justified ... by the contribution of European farming to Kenya's economy. ... For many years the reservation has been in respect of ownership and occupation of property. It has never been a question of who lives and works in the highlands.'[5]

The governor, Sir Evelyn Baring, wrote a despairing letter to the Secretary of State. 'At the moment the most contentious issue is that of the St Julian's Community, a Church of England organization which wishes to buy a house and some land belonging to Mr Wood, the chairman of the Capricorn Society in this country. Unfortunately, this is in Limuru, exactly where the most foolish and noisy Europeans live. The missionaries, somewhat unwisely, describe St Julian's as a "multiracial centre". Objection was taken by the local Limuru Farmers' Association which is now dominated by extremists. ... I have let those concerned know that should the [highlands] board recommend against the transfer, on the grounds that Africans would be lodging in the community house, I would regretfully have to reject.'[6]

As the governor foresaw, the affair died down eventually with much muttering from the settlers and the Woods suffered some abuse from friends and neighbours.[7] The sale was completed two years after the publication of the East Africa Royal Commission Report, which was unequivocal in its comment that reservation of land on tribal or racial grounds was untenable, although at the time government had taken no steps to implement the commission's proposals.[8]

Shortly after the St Julian's affair hit the headlines the Woods were again in the news over an exclusive party at their Limuru house given for Princess Margaret. Jeannine Scott was the connection with the Princess, who was never a patron of Capricorn because of its political aims. Peter Marrian, who had been a Capricorn candidate for Legislative Council mentioned the occasion in a letter to David: 'Our little party for Princess Margaret was the greatest fun. "This is Capricorn," shouted the Tigoni Tigers. Fortunately nobody paid much attention.'[9] But at least one member of the Society who had not been invited did pay attention and spoke to the press, which led to his comments being reported by Reuters in central Africa. 'Mr Wood, chairman of the Capricorn Society, which campaigns for racial equality, was today criticized by the Society's vice-chairman, Mr Abdul Ghafur Sheikh, an Asian, for not making his party for Princess Margaret tonight multiracial. ... Mr Sheikh said it was impossible for the Capricorn chairman to disassociate the principle of racial equality from his personal actions ... [adding that] it was now more than ever necessary for the Capricorn movement leaders to practise their policy in their lives especially on the social side.'[10] When we met more than 40 years later Sheikh raised the issue of that party, and he was not comforted to hear that I had not been invited either.

A year after Salima Eric Wilkinson, the Kenya branch treasurer, wrote to Jonathan Lewis in London saying: 'Once again we are broke and it has now been decided to cut our current expenditure to a minimum. ... This paragraph sounds awfully blunt but I think it best that way.'[11] He continued to be even blunter: 'We have wired David and asked him not to come to Kenya and hold any meetings. It is felt that the present time is not a good time to hold any large Capricorn meetings as we have no master plan. We feel that he would serve a much more useful purpose if David spent this time with you in London and thrashed out the question of this plan and the present financial position of the society. We've got the best blueprint for racial cooperation ever produced, but we want to know the plans for putting this into operation.' From a member of Capricorn with more understanding of the local political scene than most, this letter underlines the dangerous reliance we placed on David's leadership.

Wilkinson continued: 'It is no good thinking that a non-racial political party in Kenya can be started in the near future. There is no indication that the Europeans here would support it and without such support the Africans would not come into the fold.' Michael and Susan Wood were in London when this letter arrived and Susan reacted immediately, writing from the Capricorn office in Cheval Place: 'You cannot know what distress it caused me to read your letter. ... I was very distressed to hear David's meetings were cancelled. It seemed to me that it was the perfect thing with which to open CAS activities again and fill the gap till the [proposed September] convention. ... Nothing I have read about the political situation in Kenya has altered my view that the country desperately needs CAS and needs it now. ... I have never believed that Capricorn will win by playing politics and waiting for the politic moment. ... There is no foundation in the point that David is an outsider. He is not an outsider in any part of east and central Africa. He is infinitely better informed that many of us. He belongs to Africa and is well known. He could have given a great lead.'[12]

Abdul Gafur Sheikh (Gaby), 1992
(photo: Ali Sheikh)

This exchange, only a year after the solidarity of Salima, epitomized the dilemma Capricorn faced in Kenya. On the one hand were the Woods with a romantic vision of David's omniscience on African affairs, while on the other there were those, including Wilkinson and myself, who were also true to the ideas of the Contract but aware of the realities and the need to be effective in whatever programme we developed.

In June 1957 Kendall Ward resigned as executive officer leaving the Kenya branch without his keen understanding of the situation and his familiarity with local politicians, experience that had been invaluable. In September Robert Dick-Read came as a volunteer executive officer in Nairobi and soon reported to the London office his disillusionment. 'I note your comments to Southern Rhodesia regarding Capricorn not a "thing of the people". I personally whole-heartedly endorse your feeling. Whilst the very back-bone of Capricorn is that it "thinks big" and puts forward an "all-embracing" philosophy I can see now that in Kenya we have been very definitely missing the boat with regard to more down to earth day-to-day action.'[13]

Dick-Read's interest in African art, which I shared, led in December 1957 to the Kenya branch organizing an exhibition in Nairobi of paintings from the Académie des Beaux Arts in Elizabethville in the Belgian Congo. Dick-Read wrote to Lewis: 'The paintings have arrived from the Congo; and among them are some staggering jobs. Colouring is terrific. Design enormous. Perspective totally lacking. Observation considerable. Humour definitely present. The law of the jungle rife. Death and horror widespread. The subjects are almost entirely birds, animals, fishes, snakes, crocodiles, butterflies, flowers, trees, and general jungle. I believe they will hit Nairobi with a bang.'[14] Dick-Read later wrote a light-hearted account of his travels in search of African art with one of the Elizabethville paintings on the cover.[15]

In July 1957 spokesmen for the League of Empire Loyalists arrived in Nairobi to propagate their brand of white extremism. They came from central Africa where N. H. Wilson, once an influential member of Capricorn, had been chairman of the local branch some years earlier. The league had held some bad tempered meetings in Salisbury, at one of which David was unwise enough to debate with their leader the proposition: 'The ideas of the Capricorn Africa Society, if adopted, would mean the ruination of the British Empire.' The editor commented in the *Kenya Weekly News*: 'The league gained the day by 278 votes to 191 but I doubt if that proved anything except that the League was more efficient in getting supporters to the meeting than the Society. ... I am not a member of the Capricorn Africa Society, but I am convinced that the Society is more likely to make a constructive contribution to a solution of east and central Africa's problems than the League. At least the Society is thinking ahead while the League is gallantly advancing towards that period of history when arguments were settled by the arrival of a British gunboat. ... In these days racial problems will never be solved by racialists.'[16]

I went to the League's Nairobi meeting in Torr's Hotel and was shocked at the behaviour of the 'civilized' Europeans in the audience who shouted and booed when I stood up to speak so that I had to wait on my feet for long minutes until the chairman called for calm. I accused the League of spreading a trail of calumny and hate in their tour through Africa. Standing in the double height ballroom with the white businessmen of Nairobi – doctors, dentists, accountants and probably architects – looking down from the gallery and around me on the main floor, it was disconcerting to see the fury with which they greeted the idea that a young man could suggest that the days of white supremacy were numbered and that the future for the European in Africa depended on accepting change. Hill commented in the *Kenya Weekly News*: 'I dislike the intolerance and the bitterness displayed at Torr's Hotel last Friday when the meeting set a poor example to Africans whose meetings are so often criticized. There was, for instance, the gallant loyalist who shouted at an Indian gentleman "Go back to Bombay". The retort was inevitable: "You go back to UK, I was born here".'[17]

Although Capricorn made little progress in changing public opinion, it is clear from correspondence between the governor and the Colonial Office that the British government at the time intended Kenya to be a multiracial state. A letter from the secretary of state to the governor says in part: 'I do in fact agree that African representation [in Legislative Council] must increase, but not in a way which would lead us on the clear road to destruction of the multiracial idea. ... We must keep faith with the Europeans – even if I was not determined to do so anyway, I would have no answer to Welensky [Prime Minister of the Central African Federation] if we didn't.'[18]

In late 1957 the secretary of state, Alan Lennox-Boyd, said in the House of Commons. 'I do not foresee a date at this moment when it will be possible for the Colonial Office to relinquish control. The ultimate purpose would be to enable all who have made their homes in Kenya of whatever race to feel that they have an enduring role to play and that the standards they have set shall be maintained.'[19] Two years later his successor, Iain Macleod, was planning the conference that agreed terms for self-government with universal franchise in 1962. Tanganyika was to be given independence even sooner, in 1961, and dreams of a multiracial future were only to be found at Ol Molog. Long talks with Robin Johnston when Wood was home for the weekend kept the flame alive as they worked out the possibilities of political action with Derek Bryceson, a local Capricorn member, who was later encouraged by David to stand for Legislative Council.[20] The change of name to Tanganyika National Society had done little to change the fortunes of Capricorn in that predominantly African country.

After David's resignation as president in 1958, there was a change of pace. Wood, as the new president, was strengthened in his belief in Capricorn ideals by religious conviction and by Susan's devotion to David, but he was a busy surgeon with responsibilities to patients, colleagues and family. From early 1957 Wood was setting up a reconstructive surgery unit in Nairobi and the flying doctor service that later became the African Medical and Research Foundation, still a vital service in East Africa today, and for which he was knighted in 1985. To add to the pressures in their lives, it was the time when the Woods moved the household to their farm at Ol Molog, to which Wood flew every weekend. On his frequent and demanding visits to central Africa, Europe and America Wood combined fund-raising, surgery and Capricorn, but his contribution to the Society could never be the same as David's total dedication. When new ideas and firm direction were imperative, the demands on his time and energy made it impossible for him to initiate ideas and direct Capricorn as David had.

As the new chairman of the Kenya branch I was in a similar position, at a lower intensity than Wood. In 1957 I had started work as an architect from a room in our house and worried whether the practice could survive. Nevertheless, over the two and a half years I was chairman in Kenya, my diary lists more than 400 meetings, meals or interviews on Capricorn affairs, including writing to the London office, the formation of the Kenya Party and the beginnings of the citizenship college, but not including working as an architect on the college buildings or Wood's reconstructive surgery unit.

Capricorn members in Kenya kept busy with a new political party, setting up the citizenship college and in good works. As the college was even less political than Capricorn was supposed to be, it did little to further our basic aims. But these activities could not hide diminishing African support – we told ourselves we were a pressure group in which numbers were irrelevant compared with the importance of our message. There were attempts at facing reality: in early 1958 Denis Acheson, a Salima veteran from central

Africa, was in London and tried to explain to Jeannine Scott and Lewis that there were almost no African members in Northern Rhodesia and that the word Capricorn was a term of abuse.[21] They did not believe him and took some offence at the idea.

In 1930, at a time when African education was limited and provided mainly by missions, Joe Oldham had written: 'The fundamental business of government in Africa is education.'[22] Two generations later we were also convinced that education was fundamental for the improvement of race relations. Oldham in *New Hope in Africa*[23] and the Capricorn Contract were equivocal on the immediate introduction of interracial education, Provision Four of the Contract stating: 'We hold that the implementation of a policy of interracial education should be encouraged but can be achieved only when a more advanced cultural and social status has been reached by the majority of the community, when the English language is more fully in use and when the teachers of each race have attained the same qualifications in their profession.'

In spite of these caveats, which would effectively delay implementation for a very long time, some Capricorn members in Kenya became involved in interracial education. Like many of our activities, it was difficult to know whether we were acting as concerned individuals or on behalf of the Society. Aims for education were easier to enunciate than to carry out in a country with three racial groups, each with their own hopes and needs. The Colonial Office, some churchmen and a few individuals believed that multiracial schooling was essential if Kenya was to develop peacefully, but none of the racial groups and few families wanted racially mixed education for its own sake. Europeans already had adequate government and private schools and were fearful of intermarriage following friendships at mixed schools; Africans simply wanted more and better publicly funded education; the Asian and Arab communities already had better schools than the Africans, but ambitious parents wanted improvements, and were also fearful of their daughters developing relationships across racial, religious and caste barriers.

The inequality in funding was stark: in 1957 the Kenya government spent £2 on each African child in school, £23 per Asian pupil and £61 for each European, although the total expenditure on each race reflected the huge difference in numbers.[24] With European politicians having a majority among the unofficial members of Legislative Council and many white civil servants having children at local schools, there was little chance of government starting a non-racial school, or of voting the substantial funds needed to improve and expand education for Africans and Asians. In any case the country could not afford the large sums required from local taxation.

John Karmali, a Kenya born Ismaili pharmacist and his British wife Joan, also a pharmacist, found the situation intolerable. At any level their children should have been educated with their peers at a government European school in Nairobi, but an Asian father, however well educated, made this impossible. In January 1950 the Karmalis and some Asian friends started a small school in a private house, and later in an ex-army wooden hut on an adjacent plot. At first there were no European children and only a few Africans, but as the school's reputation grew the racial proportion became more even. The governor, Sir Philip Mitchell, ensured a small government subvention to help with staff salaries[25] and promised a site in the grounds of Government House, Nairobi. His successor, Sir Evelyn Baring, agreed and in 1953 the school moved to its new site facing on to Hospital Hill, giving the school its name. From the beginning it was decided to control the numbers of each race to avoid the school rapidly becoming purely Asian because, of the three main communities, they alone wanted better standards and could pay the fees. African parents wanted higher standards too, but most could not afford to pay, while the majority of Europeans distrusted the idea even though expense was not a problem. By 1956 there were 12 Africans, 20 Asians and 9 European children.

The school recognized the importance of religion but followed no specific faith. Teachers were exceptionally devoted and enthusiastic, finding it rewarding to work with children from a variety of backgrounds and languages, and the school soon developed a reputation for interesting and good education. This in turn meant that parents tended to be liberal and well educated, some from embassies or foreign aid agencies accustomed to living and mixing with people of other races and experience. Both our daughters went to the school while it was in Government House grounds, making close friendships with children from other parts of Kenya, Japan and America.

With independence under an African government imminent, the number of European children declined and the Education Department foresaw empty government schools in Nairobi. In 1963 after long negotiations, Hospital Hill School was offered the premises and playing fields of a European primary school in Parklands, a largely Asian area of Nairobi, not far from where it had started. At the time I was chairman of the Parents Teachers Association and in 1963 the Karmalis asked me to join the board of governors where I served until the school was taken over by Nairobi City Council education department in 1975. Karmali was an outstandingly talented photographer but in spite of his contribution to education (or perhaps because of it) the Kenya Arts and Crafts Society continued to vote against admitting artists of other races at each successive annual general meeting. With Richard Frost,[26] the British Council representative in Nairobi who did so much to develop interracial understanding, and a very few others I proposed changes to the constitution of the society year after year without success. Strangely, while Europeans fiercely resisted opening their clubs and schools to other races, they accepted that organizations like Outward Bound, Boy Scouts, Girl Guides and the annual music festival were multiracial in theory and in practice.

Hospital Hill governors were keen to develop a non-racial secondary school where their pupils could continue their education, but this was a far more difficult enterprise than starting a small primary school. Over the years up to independence in 1963 five different groups of people struggled with the problem of creating a non-racial secondary school, some in competition, but all requiring large amounts of unavailable capital. I was involved in four, either as a school governor, sympathetic (that is to say honorary) architect or chairman of Capricorn, and the fifth group, the Christian Council of Kenya, were clients of mine. From late 1958, the Kenya branch of Capricorn was in serious discussions with government and members of Legislative Council on the possibility of the Society developing and running a non-racial secondary school, which would have merged with the Hospital Hill proposals. The ebb and flow of the ultimately hopeless project is recorded in the memoranda and correspondence in files at the Public Record Office.

The minister of education, Walter Coutts,[27] and officers in the ministry supported the idea, writing: 'So far as the management of the school is concerned, we are inviting the Capricorn Africa Society to be the managers of the school in terms of Section 16 of the Education Ordnance'.[28] The Ford Foundation had offered $50,000 provided the US International Cooperation Administration (ICA) supported the project, which in the end they failed to do. ICA worried about adverse publicity for 'dollar imperialism' and also had doubts about the management of the school being 'entrusted to the Society, whom they assessed as a band of rather woolly-thinking eggheads who carried with them no significant body of public opinion in the country'.[29]

The Colonial Office wrote a powerful letter to the American embassy in London supporting the school: 'The Ministers of Finance and Education and the Chief Secretary [in Kenya] have all strongly urged the setting up of such a school but because of European susceptibilities and the shortage of capital, capital assistance cannot be given by the Kenya government. ... It [is] of considerable importance to the general trend of the government's policy that the Hospital Hill experiment should be extended into secondary education and there is no other educational institution for which ICA help would be more welcome. It is quite true that some sections of Europeans will probably raise an outcry. On the other hand there has been quite a lot of favourable press comment on Hospital Hill in the more liberal papers. As regards the Capricorn Society, they have a reputation in some quarters for woolly minded liberalism ... but for some time now they have concentrated on the central aspect of multiracial life; they have instituted recently plans for adult education – colleges of citizenship. ... Christian missions are ruled out as managers of the school because of its multiracial character; the CAS have close links with the churches and are the only suitable body already in existence who could run the school. There is every reason to believe they would do so competently.'[30]

A confidential memo from the minister of education, labour and lands to the Colonial Office recorded: 'At his request, I saw Mr R. Hughes of the Capricorn Africa Society on the subject of the multiracial secondary school. In the light of an earlier conversation I had with him he was anxious to know whether we had any further news on the prospect of ICA assistance. ... I told him that I was, if anything, more discouraged over the prospect of ICA assistance since [they] were tending to feel that this particular project would, if supported, lead them into political difficulties. ... He went on to say that Capricorn was concerned at competitive efforts being discussed. He understood that the Christian Churches Educational Association (CCEA) was also studying the problem on the basis of financing a £200,000 Christian multiracial school. [Hughes] felt that a school that adhered exclusively to one of the monotheistic religions could not cater for the mixed communities in Kenya and might only withdraw support from the multiracial project. ... In the light of this conversation I had an interview with Mr Dain of the CCK [Christian Council of Kenya] on 18

November. I told him that the government had decided that it would assist the Capricorn Africa Society in Kenya as an instrument to manage such a school should the necessary funds to launch it become available from external sources. Mr Dain said that the Christian churches would much prefer to see such an enterprise launched on a declared Christian basis with every safeguard of conscience of parental choice available in the spiritual structure of the school. This [he said] had been the attitude adopted when Hospital Hill primary school was launched but he was afraid that the departure of the first principal had led to a weakening in the Christian force inspiring the school and that it was liable to drift into largely Asian hands. For this reason he was unhappy about the designation of Capricorn as the chosen instrument. ... He continued that the best African Christians had a profound distrust of Capricorn and the latter's association with such a venture would deter and discourage a large number of important European and African groups.'[31]

At the time I was suspicious of Ronald Dain's hearty professions of Christian friendship but had not realized, until examining the Colonial Office files for this book, that he was so devious in pushing his own proposals, or so inaccurate over the launch of Hospital Hill School. I would have felt more confident had I seen the minute in the Colonial Office files which read: 'If the ICA make a grant then I think we really must see that the CAS get home and dry'.[32]

In December 1958 the Specially Elected Members of Legislative Council announced their intention to start a 'leaders college' based on the best public schools in Britain at which boys of all races would be educated. The new minister of education wrote, in some despair, to the Colonial Office: 'I am afraid that there is a degree of confusion prevailing here at the moment. As you know, the Capricorn Africa Society in Kenya were appointed by my predecessor as the "chosen instrument" for this development, and Mr Richard Hughes is persistent in reminding me of the fact. I have never been wholly convinced myself that they were the best agency to promote sound and acceptable development here in this field and the failure of the ICA application, only now confirmed, gives us an opportunity to review this arrangement. The CCK, which has no very positive plan for separate action, is convinced that a Capricorn association would be the kiss of death to such a project and they in turn regard it as essential that multiracial education should proceed on an avowedly Christian basis, accepting the infidel as a fellow traveller. The latest in the field is the Specially Elected Members [of legislative council] although the implication of their collective action is less substantial than might appear at first sight. Whether this will produce more than a nasty mess I do not know, but clearly such a confrontation cannot take place before the Secretary of State is obliged to answer the question in the House of Commons.'[33]

The minister followed this up with a letter to me, with a copy to the Colonial Office in London: 'you asked for confirmation that the Society had a definite invitation from government "to run this project" and in his reply of the 15th October the Chief Secretary expressed satisfaction that the Kenya branch "were prepared to carry out the proposal". When we met at Legislative Council in November I explained that the Kenya government had made an application to the International Cooperation Administration of the United States seeking assistance for the purpose of establishing a multiracial secondary school for boys [?] under an independent management to be brought into being through the initiative of the Kenya branch of the Capricorn Africa Society. In a subsequent conversation in the ministry on the 17th November [1958] on the same subject, when you expressed some anxiety over competitive efforts which might be sponsored by other organizations, I said that I was afraid that the prospects of a favourable response from ICA had been diminished. ...'

'Meanwhile, there has been the development of a project sponsored by the Specially Elected Members on broadly similar lines to yours but with considerable differences in emphasis and details. My view is that competition by varying groups with varying political identities in this field can only be harmful. I do not believe that any single organization or association could in these circumstances have any monopoly conferred on it by government action. But particularly in view of the long-standing interest and amount of work devoted by the Capricorn Africa Society to investigating the requirements of a multiracial school, I should very much hope that this interest and experience could make a contribution towards launching such a project under the general sponsorship of all groups, associations and individuals who have at heart the cause of promoting harmony in [the country].'[34]

The minister reported to the Colonial Office in February: 'I succeeded in inducing the Specially Elected Members education committee to hold a meeting attended by representatives of other groups interested in furthering this project, namely the Capricorn Africa Society, the Christian Council of Kenya and governors of

Hospital Hill School. Before this meeting came off [Humphrey] Slade [who initiated the proposal] had struck another blow for the European mystique by issuing a "Signed Print" in the *Kenya Weekly News* of the 23rd January where the word "European" occurred 21 times and the idea of "European predominance" was stressed. ... An independent committee has now been set up to work further on the project. The existence of this committee is not "public knowledge" as opposed to being generally known.'[35] The Slade concept was a transposed Eton (Slade himself was an old Etonian) to which boys of other races might graciously go, provided they remained in the minority, which was far from the intentions of the Hospital Hill governors or of Capricorn. In October 1959 the minister of education wrote to the Colonial Office: 'We shall, as a government, have to try to formulate a policy on non-racial education. At present we have none, except to be frightened of it'.[36]

Later in 1960 I was involved as honorary architect (again) for a proposal by Lady Eleanor Cole for a non-racial secondary boarding school for girls at Gilgil. Many on the committee, including Susan Wood, were members of Capricorn although the Society was not mentioned in the brochure, which had my sketch design on the cover. This, too, came to nothing: by 1961 when the scheme was published, European government schools were making tentative steps to integrate girls' education. After some careful lobbying of parents by the heads of the secondary schools in Nairobi, one well-qualified daughter of an Asian doctor was admitted followed by four African girls. The new girls did well and the sky did not fall in, so steps were taken to open up the boys' schools. In the end it was the Roman Catholic Church through Opus Die that created the first multiracial senior school in Kenya – Strathmore Sixth Form College. This was built on church land in Nairobi and open to students of any colour or religion, with a high standard of accommodation and staff.

An exchange of letters in early 1959 between Wood and Charles March is a pointer to the reality of approach in the London office. Wood wrote: 'I myself had two to three weeks with Garfield Todd in New Zealand persuading him to do just what has been done in the Federation. Susan has been doing some stalwart work with a number of other people in Kenya with Tom Mboya [the leading African politician while Kenyatta remained in detention], and I believe that any change of heart that occurs there will be largely due to Capricorn effort. ... I do want to assure you that [this sort of action] is being done, and I think it sometimes is not appreciated in England as to how effective it is.'[37]

March responded to Wood's letter with tactful congratulations but firmly put his claims of influence into context. 'I do not underestimate what the Society has done in general terms in affecting the overall situation in east and central Africa and I agree that the matter of measuring its effort is one of our real difficulties. On the other hand, I don't think we must confuse what certain individual members do and achieve with what the Society is doing and achieving. All of us here admire tremendously the terrific efforts you and Sue have made but ... influencing Garfield Todd and Tom Mboya cannot be claimed as efforts or achievements by the Society. In the first place, these particular efforts were concerned with the political field in which the Society cannot effectively operate, but more important than that they were the efforts of two individual members of the Society acting on their own initiative. I expect that you and Sue feel that in these situations it is really the Society that is operating but unfortunately it does not appear like that to outsiders and certainly we cannot claim that you are acting on the Society's behalf. [I suggest] an individual member is acting on behalf of the Society when the action he is taking has been discussed and authorized at a meeting of one of the Society's committees and when the individual makes it clear to all concerned from the start that he is acting on behalf of the Society. ... We are not likely to gain more support or to raise money for future action unless we can show and claim that action by the Society has played a substantial part in bringing about certain changes. Secondly, we are much more likely to be seen to be at work in a particular situation if such action as we take is carried out by a group of members of all races rather than by individuals, particularly by an individual European.'[38]

Reading this correspondence now, as it was not copied to me as chairman in Kenya, makes me realize that there were two Capricorns – an inner circle of close friends who corresponded privately, and the bulk of the members and office bearers. The inner circle took for granted that, being close to David, they represented the Society and acted accordingly, although this sometimes created confusion. Throughout 1959 I met Mboya regularly about the new headquarters for his Kenya Federation of Labour for which I was the architect, and Wilkinson was also in contact[39] with him, but neither of us knew what Susan Wood was doing or saying.

When I reviewed *East African Citizen*[40] by Ronald Wraithe for the *Kenya Weekly News* it seemed to be a textbook for the future: authoritative, clear and rational. He said it was written for nationalists in East Africa who want self-government, and included analysis of the issues – methods of voting, education, taxation, and ownership of land. I asked the London office to buy a bulk order for us to circulate widely in Kenya, which they did. Europeans thought it was over-optimistic while Africans considered it unduly cautious (events proved that the African view was correct).

In mid-1959 the Nairobi office was enlivened by having a young, attractive and efficient secretary/executive officer, Bridget Jenkin. Through her enthusiasm a group of young members of Capricorn, known as the Nomads, was formed. They opened their activities with a dance at our house and went on to arrange discussions, tennis parties, and visits to the theatre and game parks. They were an example of how easy it was for people of different races to act normally together. Although the intention was not propaganda, this was achieved when banner headlines in the press reported that Capricorn members Daleep Mangat and Archdeacon Ken Stovold had been ejected from a hotel at the coast.

The Kenya branch set up a study group on human rights – a subject of particular interest to those who could foresee an African government in the near future when the immigrant races might welcome the protection of a declaration of the rights of the individual. In February 1959 Philip Mason sent Susan Wood a textual analysis of the UN Declaration of Human Rights, which he considered confused and unenforceable.[41] While he was writing his analysis he told my father-in-law, Hill: 'the country is already lost'.[42] We worried about the issue but made little headway in changing public opinion or government policy on protection of African rights or those of the immigrant races in the future.

In 1960 we were given an opportunity to challenge the sanctity of the White Highlands when the Society was offered 100 acres of farming land at Kaimosi in western Kenya. The land was owned by a retired Colonial Office doctor, Fairfax Bell, who had built an interesting house and a large aviary for his collection of birds on the edge of the forest, much of which he left undeveloped so that he could study the butterflies, birds and mammals. Bell suggested that the land should be developed as a settlement for African and Asian farmers, a proposal we accepted with enthusiasm, except for the perennial problem that capital of about £8500 would be required. We hoped that the project would demonstrate that families of different tribes and races could live and work amicably together and that land in the White Highlands could be successfully farmed by Africans and Asians. The project had the support of the Kenya National Farmers' Union but, as always, foundered on the difficulty of raising finance.

While we tried to develop a secondary school, or breach the White Highlands, or persuade the public of the validity and importance of the Capricorn Contract, many members were also involved in the development of a political party[43] and, with greater success, in setting up the college of citizenship.[44] The realists recognized that we were a dwindling band, fighting a rear-guard action, but it was not until Lewis came out to Africa in 1960[45] and looked dispassionately at what was left of the Society that the true situation was brought home to us.

Chapter 11
Playing at Politics

In many ways the relationship between the races in colonial Africa was similar to the class structure in prewar Britain with ignorance and arrogance on the one side stimulating envy and enmity on the other. Whatever efforts welfare and religious organizations made to ameliorate conditions among the disadvantaged, the only solution, short of revolution, to the problems raised by such divisions in society had to be political. Capricorn's dilemma, and failure, was in attempting to deal with these issues without being involved in political action: indeed a number of key figures in the Society disdained the very idea of 'playing politics'. In the end that was exactly what we were doing – playing at politics without wanting to get our feet muddy.

The Capricorn Africa Society was a non-political organization with charitable status in Britain, but the programme and philosophy set out in the Contract could only be made effective through politics. David Stirling increasingly came to recognize this truth, particularly in Tanganyika, where African nationalists were growing in strength under the powerful leadership of Julius Nyerere. The governor, Sir Edward Twining, tried to balance the increasing popularity of Nyerere's Tanganyika African National Union (TANU) by encouraging the formation of a multiracial party. The governor's chosen instrument, the United Tanganyika Party (UTP), was formed in early 1956 and not one candidate of any race came within sight of success in the elections.

A Colonial Office brief noted: 'The United Tanganyika Party, a non-racial political party, was formed ... by 23 unofficial members of the Tanganyika Legislative Council representing Europeans, Asians and Africans. They pledged to work for the political and social integration of all races with the aim of self-government within the commonwealth. Sir Edward Twining, writing in November 1956, said "it had only limited support and is not very well run or led but getting it going had served the useful purpose of giving the Europeans a chance of demonstrating whether they do possess that much vaunted political know-how and leadership or whether they are bankrupt in these commodities. I am sorry to say that the bankruptcy is becoming transparent to almost everyone." In its pamphlet it says the aims are: "To ... evolve the more suitable form of franchise for the circumstances in Tanganyika and to resist all proposals that would lead to the domination of one racial group over the others ...".'[1] Later, the governor, still hoping for a multiracial solution, wrote to the Colonial Office: 'We must work for the day when everybody who is domiciled here will regard themselves as Tanganyikans.'[2]

By November 1957 the governor had recognized how difficult it was to mastermind a political outcome, particularly if it differed from the will of the majority of the population. Disappointed with his promotion of the United Tanganyika Party, he wrote to the Secretary of State: 'David Stirling is here and intends to produce a new party to fight the election. I do not expect he will have a great deal of success but he will probably destroy UTP and produce something better.'[3] In the same month an extract from the Tanganyika intelligence summary recorded: 'Col David Stirling intends to encourage his party to develop as a counter to UTP. Stirling is of the opinion that leaders to form the nucleus of the party will be moderate African nationalists. It is his intention that the policies of the new party should appear to originate from the Africans themselves. Stirling is determined that the new party will not in any way be associated with UTP, the Tanganyika National Society [the name adopted by Robin Johnston for Capricorn] or the Capricorn Society.'[4]

The preamble to the new party's brochure was, however, almost identical to the Capricorn Contract. The Governor's comment on the bankruptcy of European leadership applied to David's new party as much as to the UTP, and the moderate African nationalists on whom David placed his hopes were not interested: unsurprisingly, they were attracted to Nyerere and TANU. David was discovering that one man's enthusiasm deployed on occasional visits was not enough to change the politics of a large and diverse country, but he continued to be optimistic about the chances of success for his rebadged Capricorn in Tanganyika. The man he selected to lead the charge was, typically, an ex-RAF farmer from Ol Molog, Derek Bryceson, a local Capricorn member. In 1956 he had written to David after talks with TANU leaders: 'they will consider nothing less than universal adult franchise and aim at one million members. ... We must beat them to it.'[5]

In February 1957 David had suggested that his brother Bill Stirling should buy the Bryceson farm, adding the tempting suggestion that Bryceson could then join the board of Stirling-Astaldi, the family construction firm. He added, with uncharacteristic frankness: 'my motive in this is wholly to get you launched in the political field in Tanganyika. If we could hang Capricorn on you in that territory, I believe we will undoubtedly win our cause. If we cannot we have little hope.'[6] Bryceson turned down the offer to sell his farm but accepted the post of assistant minister for social services when appointed by the governor, possibly as a result of David's lobbying in Dar es Salaam. The governor told Johnston that he was not appointed a minister because he was too closely identified with Capricorn.[7] Nyerere personally was tolerant of individual Europeans and Asians and recognized their value to the country, but he was determined to create a government run by Africans and hence regarded any multiracial party as an enemy, to be crushed. The overwhelming success of TANU, and recognition by white politicians like Bryceson that the future lay with the Africans, meant that both multiracial parties made virtually no impact and quickly closed down.

In the 1958/9 Tanganyika elections, in which each constituency elected a candidate from each of the three races, Bryceson stood successfully as a TANU candidate, abandoning his Capricorn connection in order to do so. His apostasy caused a rift among Capricorn members in Ol Molog as Johnston was chairman of the Society in Tanganyika and thought to be the obvious choice as the parliamentary candidate, and one who would stick to his principles. A Colonial Office note quotes Bryceson's naive political comments. 'I travelled with Mr Nyerere, the President of TANU, and the official TANU (African) candidate extensively throughout the constituency. Through their organization I had the pleasure not only of addressing some thousands of Africans myself but of hearing Mr Nyerere expound to them the advantages of a harmonious multiracial state with all the different races working together for the common good. ... I place great significance on this change of policy, this liberalizing, and am personally much encouraged by it.'[8]

However, in September 1959 Nyerere, with Tom Mboya and others from Kenya, attended a meeting of the Pan African Freedom Movement of East and Central Africa (PAFMECA) in Mwanza, on the shores of Lake Victoria. They adopted a charter stating: 'Freedom is our birthright; self-government our heritage as sons and daughters of the free men and women who inherited Africa for the

Africans. Every hour that passes under imperialism takes in its train a measure of our freedom and a portion of our noble heritage as Africans, the true, just and rightful masters of Africa's destiny. Every hour that passes means one more hour of subjugation, degradation, exploitation and humiliation by imperialists, white supremacists and foreign self-seekers. We therefore pledge: (1) That democracy must prevail throughout Africa from Senegal to Zanzibar and from Cape to Cairo; (2) That colonialism, the so-called trusteeship, the so-called partnership, apartheid, multi-racialism and white settlerism are enemies of freedom and can be eradicated only by African nationalism — virile and unrelenting; (3) That the right of self determination is God-given and no man or nation is chosen by God to determine the destiny of others.'[9]

A letter from Michael Wood to Charles March paints a picture of the situation some months after Bryceson's election. 'Sue and I have had a prowl round the northern province [in Tanganyika] and bearded a few of the red eyed settlers. Derek [Bryceson] and Julius Nyerere are doing a great job on the unofficial side of [Legislative Council], but this new found unity has not percolated to many levels in this large and largely primitive country. ... The echelon below Nyerere is very difficult to handle as they are not as educated as [he is] and are liable to be racial and stupid. Nyerere is well aware of this, and says it is his biggest problem. So you can picture the business of imposing democracy from the top when the infrastructure is pretty feeble and unreliable.'[10] For some years after independence Bryceson's career continued with a series of ministerial posts: his pragmatism in joining TANU meant that he could influence government decisions as it struggled with the many problems of a newly independent and poor country, which would not have been the case had he uncompromisingly stood firm on the Capricorn programme and failed to be elected. In 1959 the Johnstons left Ol Molog to live and work in Dar es Salaam, by which time Capricorn, both as a name and an ideal, was only a memory for a small group of friends in Tanganyika.

In Kenya the opportunity to put Capricorn policies to the public arose shortly after our return from Salima. Communal elections for Europeans and Asians were held in September 1956 under proposals known as the Lyttleton Plan, one of the increasingly complex constitutions imposed by the Colonial Office. There was no time for Capricorn to set up a political party, and we did not approve of communal rolls, but nevertheless we thought it important for the philosophy in the Capricorn Contract to be tested against public opinion. The police special branch reported: 'Mrs M. Wood, wife of CAS Chairman, will contest Nairobi North on Capricorn policy. Mr P. Marrian will oppose Group Capt Briggs in Mt Kenya constituency as an independent on Capricorn Contract.'[11] Peter Marrian was a coffee farmer at Mweiga, near Mount Kenya, who had been to Salima and supported the opening of the White Highlands, so did not expect much support from his fellow European farmers, who were only too aware, particularly after Mau Mau, that their white salient was surrounded by land hungry Kikuyu. Marrian was a handsome, aquiline man with the easy self-confidence that comes from having been to a good school, like some of his neighbours who had left India after partition. The rich soil, good rainfall and high altitude on the slopes of Mount Kenya were ideal conditions for growing coffee and creating beautiful gardens with green lawns and indigenous and exotic flowers under forest trees. Five years after his first attempt Marrian was elected to Legislative Council as a national member and became a junior minister.

Capricorn thought it important not to split the fragile 'liberal' vote, so avoided constituencies where candidates who supported Michael Blundell stood a good chance of success. Marrian's opponent, Briggs, was a notorious right-wing politician who believed in the absolute sanctity of the White Highlands and the superiority of European civilization. Those of us helping Susan Wood in her campaign in Nairobi learnt many lessons about politics and the public's perception of our ideas, most of which was depressing. We made posters with what we thought was a catchy reference to her striking red hair: 'PUT GINGER INTO NAIROBI' and brought out the motto developed before going to Salima: 'FOR KENYA, ONE LOYALTY, ONE CITIZENSHIP, ABOLITION OF RACIAL DISCRIMINATION, PROTECTION OF CIVILIZED STANDARDS WITH RESPONSIBLE GOVERNMENT ELECTED BY A RESPONSIBLE ELECTORATE'.[12]

In her powerful and honest manifesto Susan Wood made no attempt to evade the central issue. 'We are a people of democratic tradition. It is part of our history. There is no device within the framework of democracy which can prevent 6,000,000 Africans one day being numerically preponderant over 50,000 Europeans and 150,000 Asians in the voting power of the country. If, therefore, we are to remain for all time in the councils ... of the land we need to make ourselves wanted, not just as technicians and experts, but as a people. For the first time in the history of Kenya the African population is to take part in the political life of the country when, in March 1957, it faces its first election. African opinion is at a watershed. If we return racists and segregationists they will match them with the most bitter racialists we have known and the country will once more be torn with racial strife. If we set an example by returning people who put the good of the country before race they will have the confidence to do the same. It is for us to choose.'[13]

The election candidate, 1956

Bryceson came up from Ol Molog to canvass for Susan Wood and later wrote to Jonathan Lewis in London that he found Capricorn's connection with MRA was 'constantly raised' which he found difficult.[14] In spite of a visit from David during the campaign and much amateur enthusiasm, neither Susan Wood nor Marrian made much impact on the majorities of their opponents, which was disappointing but not unexpected. A Capricorn member, N. S. Mangat, QC, was successful in the Asian communal elections, usually decided by caste and religion, with all candidates demanding more say in running the country because of the number of Asians and their considerable contribution to the economy.

The overall results were serious for the future of the country for the right-wing Independent Group led by Marrian's opponent, Briggs, won eight seats compared with Blundell's more liberal United Country Party, which finished with six. One consolation was that the extreme right-wing (European) Federal Independence Party failed to win any seats, although they polled a worrying number of votes. As Susan Wood prophesied, this encouraged African politicians to be equally intransigent in their elections the following March.

After the European and Asian elections Marrian wrote to David: 'I never had the slightest illusion about standing on a Capricorn ticket in this constituency. ... I think it is most important that we don't pull wool over our eyes, but make a reassessment in the light of reality. The first thing to face squarely is that the Capricorn philosophy is not acceptable to five-sixths of this electorate at the present time. ... I do not believe that a non-racial approach to a racial electorate will ever be successful and that will apply equally to the African elections next year. On the one hand a racial electorate will reject a non-racial approach and on the other a non-racial electorate, which might accept it, cannot come into being by virtue of such rejection. Patently therefore our aim cannot be achieved through a democratic process and we must act either as a pressure group on those elected by the democratic process, or a governor or a secretary of state must impose a constitution for the good of all races, which will probably be opposed by all races – certainly by the Europeans and Africans. ... I would not care to assess whether our entry directly into politics has been an advantage or not. I think it was inevitable as a proof of good faith to the African. ... Political action while the electorates remain racial will be a waste of time.'[15]

Mervyn Hill, editor of the *Kenya Weekly News*, wrote after the 1956 elections: 'It is clear that the political ideas of the Capricorn Africa Society are commonly regarded as impracticable and immature. Time may well prove that outlook to be mistaken. On a recent journey of some 2000 miles, mainly through Tanganyika, almost everyone I met with an interest in the political affairs of East Africa told me that African nationalism was spreading like a prairie fire, and that the Capricorn idea was the only effective answer to it.'[16] Among the settler community the *Kenya Weekly News* and the opinions of its respected editor were considered sound, but this comment made no impact on the irrational fears that lay behind the views of most Europeans.

In the African elections in March 1957 Francis Khamisi was elected at the coast with our support and we could claim that a few candidates supported the general idea of a multiracial future for Kenya. Pressure from their colleagues made it impossible for them to maintain a non-racial stance once they were in Legislative Council. Although the African elections were held on a qualified multiple vote system, much simpler than our proposals, they nevertheless allowed the election of politicians who held extreme nationalist views. Even if the qualifications for the vote had been higher it is doubtful whether the results would have been different. A Colonial Office minute in June noted: 'Five Kenya Legislative Council members are Capricorners but (except for Mr Mangat) they have shown no signs of it since their election. Indeed the distinction between them and their fellows is so indistinct as to be invisible. As regards Mr Mangat, his exceedingly amusing speech does nothing to dispel the prevalent impression of a trimmer, and an "odd man out" (he does not even belong to the Asian members' group) whose support should lead the Capricorn Africa Society eventually to cry for salvation from its friends.'[17] Mangat became a member of the Kenya Party on its formation, but made few public promises of support for its programme.

Before the 1956 elections Wood announced in Mombasa that a separate political party would be formed, completely divorced from Capricorn, though he recognized that African membership would be made difficult by the continuing emergency restrictions on Africans joining countrywide political organizations.[18] Those involved included G. N. Shah, Joyce Raw, Boaz Omori, Abdul Ghafur Sheikh, Susan Wood and myself, all of whom had been at Salima. In September Sheikh invited influential Africans, Asians and Europeans to a public meeting in Nairobi to which over thirty discussed a long agenda. On 20 September Reuters reported: 'Many observers are looking to the non-racial thinking of the Capricorn Africa Society and a new multiracial party about to be formed to fill the vacuum in the centre and the left.'[19]

At the end of October 1956 the name 'Kenya Party' had been agreed and Sir Ernest Vasey, the most far-sighted European politician in Kenya, chaired a meeting to discuss policy, at which Sheikh was the only non-European.[20] After serving as mayor on Nairobi city council in 1941 Vasey was elected to Legislative Council in 1945 and again in 1948. In 1950 he resigned his seat to be minister for local government, and in 1952 became a successful minister for finance, a post he held until 1959 when he left Kenya for the same job in Tanganyika, then approaching independence.

Vasey, the illegitimate son of an actress, left school at the age of 12 with little formal education. He went to Kenya in 1935 on holiday and stayed as the manager of a Nairobi cinema, something that superior European opponents did not allow him to forget. Although his grandfather had been an Anglican vicar, both Vasey's wives were Jewish, as were many of his supporters and friends in Nairobi.[21] The typical British settler discriminated against Africans, distrusted Asians and was suspicious of a clever man who had not been to the right school, was probably Jewish and hence unacceptable as a member of Muthaiga or even Nairobi Club.

A 1959 note in the Colonial Office files set out his situation. 'Sir Ernest Vasey's relation to Kenya politics must be seen in the light of the following facts: (1) he holds a deep ... grudge against the Kenya Europeans as a community because he feels that they have never given him the enthusiasm or acceptance he deserves. He has never been elected to any of the main clubs in Nairobi; (2) he has envy of, and dislike for, Mr Blundell; (3) he has a great following among Asians ... and not inconsiderable influence among Africans, although his capacity for restraining Mr Mboya and Dr Kiano is less than he tries to make out; (4) he is anxious to be guide, philosopher and friend to the eventual rulers of Kenya, and regards Mr Mboya as virtually "unstoppable". He would probably like to play in Kenya the role of Mr Bryceson in Tanganyika – but Mr Mboya is not Mr Nyerere.'[22] Most of this must have come from the governor, Sir Evelyn Baring. Although he admired Vasey's acute mind and his skilful handling of the economy, Baring was a patrician to his fingertips and would have shared many of the prejudices of his class about a man of Vasey's background. Baring's biography[23] records that the governor relied on Vasey as a contact with the Asian and African politicians while Blundell was his link with the settlers; both being equally important to him.

Blundell described Vasey in his memoirs as a man who 'had an uncanny knack for presenting the essentials of a case and of dropping a judicious remark at the right moment with a view to influencing vital decisions. He was also far-sighted, and his judgement and imagination on the developing African scene would have been an advantage to his elected colleagues had he stayed with us.'[24] On the African elections in 1957, Blundell added: 'Vasey wrote a far-sighted note at this time to all the European Elected Members in which he pointed out the dangers of allowing the first African elections to be held on a purely racial as distinct from a common roll. He emphasized that by the time the second election came round, racialism would be so entrenched in the minds of the African majority that European and Asian interests would be swept away.'

My own memories of Vasey are of a smiling, kindly, short man with heavy glasses, who was supported in everything he did by his wife Hannah, probably the more radical of the two. Blundell was different in almost every way. He was a large, handsome man from a middle-class background who had gone to farm in Kenya after leaving Wellington College. Musical and sometimes emotional, his intelligence and sympathy made him an instinctive liberal, but representing a rural, white, electorate he had to tailor his views to the necessity of being re-elected. In talks on his farm at Subukia and in Nairobi I tried hard to persuade him to support Capricorn publicly, to which his answer was that he would be of no use to us, or to Kenya, if his constituents rejected him. Nevertheless, he put up with much vilification for having 'sold out' to the Africans after the 1960 Constitutional Conference, when the path to early independence was clear.

Although the political scene was in a ferment of change, in the Kenya Party we were in no hurry to establish ourselves. By October 1956 we had settled on the name and started a series of policy meetings, and in July 1957 the files show that I called a meeting to discuss the name of the party, again, and some fundamental issues arising from David's recent visit.[25] In London *The Times* reported on 8 July 1957: 'A new interracial political party, based on the Capricorn Contract, will be launched in Kenya, before the end of the year. Announcing the probable date here today, the president of the Capricorn Africa Society, Col David Stirling said that the 1960 elections [would be] on the principle of a common roll with a qualified franchise. ... The party would envisage the retention of the British government's control in the executive council "until it is clear that common economic and other interests secure the minorities from the risk of Africans exercising their immense numerical superiority to their racial advantage rather than to the interests of a common citizenship and of Kenya as a whole".'

In Nairobi David called on the governor to discuss the new party, telling him that both Vasey and Blundell were involved, which was not strictly true. Baring replied that in view of the incompatibility between them David should not seek to recruit either as leader. He recorded the meeting in a memo to the Colonial Office. 'Blundell, Mr Nathoo and Sir Eboo Pirbhai [two senior and respected Asian politicians] had previously all told me that they felt to publish in the middle of November [just after the colonial secretary's visit to Nairobi] the formation of a new political party, linked to the Capricorn Society, would be a mistake and would be premature. I was however unable to move Colonel Stirling. ... I said that I believed that very few elected members of Legislative Council would join the party in November. On the other hand, over a period of time the mood in the country among Europeans, Asians and Africans [might change] and the elected members and ministers might alter their views. In other words the appeal should be to the general public and only later to the politicians. ... I hope I made some impression on him by describing the extent of the opposition which he is likely to find from existing political interests and the various racially elected members organizations.'[26] The governor should have known that David would find the likelihood of serious opposition to be an irresistible challenge to advance rather than retreat.

In August and September 1957 there were more Kenya Party meetings, some chaired by Sheikh, others by myself, in which we worked on the details of a proposed constitution for Kenya, and discussed how and when we were to present our memorandum to the colonial secretary, Alan Lennox-Boyd, when he came to Nairobi in October. As chairman of the steering committee I signed and delivered the letter to the governor with which we enclosed our statement to the secretary of state, signed by four Africans, three Asians and four Europeans, listed alphabetically.[27] The statement referred to the new party in formation and quoted the precepts from the Capricorn Contract with the hope that they would be considered in the deliberations on the future of Kenya.

A note in the Colonial Office files dated November 1957 records that Wood also went to see the governor about the new party: 'It is necessary to recognize that, if the communal [universal adult] franchise for the other races in Kenya remains as it is, the introduction of universal adult suffrage for Africans is ultimately inevitable. If the Kenya Party is the first in the field with the demand for the other races to adopt the Coutts [qualified, multiple] franchise, it will to some extent capture Mboya's political clothes. If the demand has ultimately to be granted, as I believe it must, it is far better to have to reach this stage under pressure from the centre than from the left wing. It is recommended that the governor should give Mr Wood the all clear for his party.'[28] After the governor's advice to David the formal launch of the Kenya Party was put off until January 1958, 18 months after the success of Salima.

In November 1957 Blundell wrote to Joyce Raw, who was closely involved with the Kenya Party, saying: 'I find a curious inhibition in each racial group to the effect that anybody who thinks non-racially is automatically a stooge of the other groups. This applies equally to Asians, Africans and Europeans. I hope that the new party goes well.'[29] Blundell added, 'I have raised already with the European elected members my sympathy towards a multiracial party and to my surprise I received unanimous support save with usual dour Kenya warning "Now is not the moment – these things must grow".'

By December 1957 the steering committee had become the party council under the chairmanship of a retired major, Frank Sprott, said to be an adherent of MRA. We appointed an executive committee, a constitution committee and committee for membership and organization. At the time political parties, groups and movements in Kenya were forming, dissolving and coalescing with some politicians signing up to more than one. It is unlikely that their leaders had the time or the inclination to develop the bureaucratic structure that we spent so much effort creating. In the long run they were no more successful than we were in influencing or deflecting the inexorable march to universal franchise. Eventually, in January 1958, the Kenya Party was formally launched at a public meeting with speeches by Mangat, both Woods, Joel Ojal and Sheikh. Vasey was in London and sent a telegram summarizing the party's position on a number of issues including self-government, which he said was a distant objective that could only be achieved through economic self-sufficiency and an attempt at common citizenship.

The Kenya Party recognized that the ends desired would only be achieved by a gradual process of change. Comment in the Colonial Office was muted and resigned: 'I see nothing to object to in Mr Vasey's draft proposals of the Kenya Party. Like all Capricorn based documents it goes for the idea of a common roll and qualified franchise and a common citizenship. Like all ideas about common citizenship it raises complex technical problems. Any party hoping for support on the basis of these ideas would find little support in the country.'[30]

In March 1958 a party council was called to discuss candidates to be elected by members of Legislative Council sitting as an electoral college. The theory was that the Specially Elected Members, as they were to be called, would have a non-racial outlook being free from the pressures of a racial electorate. Vasey sounded out some of us on the possibility of being candidates, an invitation I declined without regret. Almost all the Africans we put forward could not resist pressure from Mboya and his colleagues to boycott the election, and did not stand, only Musa Amalemba being elected and nominated as minister for housing. In July he joined Mangat and Vasey as the third member of Legislative Council on the Kenya Party council. The election failed in its intention of creating non-racial members as nearly all the candidates, including Blundell, were already in Legislative Council elected on a communal basis, and continued to react to the views of their communities. Because of the African's boycott the election became a farce in which

Vasey, for whom the non-racial seats might have been designed, tied with Humphrey Slade at the bottom of the poll and lost on a draw from a silver bowl. An African member, B. A. Ohanga, wrote to the Colonial Office at the time: 'Mr Vasey ... is the man where interracial or party politics are concerned. ... His great personality, his good natured humour and foresightedness easily make him an asset for all communities.'[31]

In a letter to Lewis in London early in 1959, between items on the college of citizenship, I set out my thoughts: 'We are still much concerned with the idea of a statement on the future of true democratic states in Africa. ... I am feeling more than ever that it would not be wise for a basically European group to make a statement on "Democracy being unsuitable for Africans". It is too liable to be misunderstood. I feel that we must define what we mean by [a] true democratic state as one in which freedom of the individual ... is absolute and in which there is a free opposition offering valid and alternative policies on which every adult has the opportunity [to vote]. Capricorn can say that it was in recognition of the unsuitability of universal democracy for Africa that we defined the qualified franchise suited to the special conditions we have here — the great differences between tribes, peoples, economic levels and religions. ... Whether our precise ideas in the Contract of one common roll with a qualified franchise is still valid remains to be seen, but some form of qualified democracy is vital to the maintenance of Africa as anything but a dark continent in the future, and I regard this conception as absolutely basic to Capricorn's work in Africa.'[32]

My view of democracy offended the London office and some of their advisers so in February I wrote to explain that when I denigrated democracy I was referring to universal franchise and not the Athenian concept.[33] This paternalistic view of the future was, I believe, shared by most European Kenya Party members, with the possible exception of Vasey. Colonial Office files of that time indicate that the secretary of state and his officials still believed that a truly multiracial country could develop in Kenya. It was not long before this was shown to be disingenuous and optimistic.

Although Vasey was a key figure in the politics of the country and in the Kenya Party, where he regularly attended committee meetings, he had his own agenda and was in a position to put his ideas directly to Lennox-Boyd, the secretary of state. Early in 1959 he submitted a confidential memo to the Colonial Office in which he said: 'It is now more important than ever that Her Majesty's government should issue a statement of policy and intention with regard to Kenya, and unequivocally say that the objective of political advance in Kenya is a democratic state of the pattern that has characterized the advance of other colonial territories towards independence during the postwar period.'[34] Vasey clearly meant the countries in West Africa and elsewhere that had achieved independence with universal adult franchise – not at all what the Kenya Party was advocating. He proposed that all ministers should be nominated by the governor for a period of ten years and that there should be common roll seats in 12 to 15 years.

The Colonial Office files do not indicate any reaction, and it soon became clear that the new secretary of state (Iain Macleod) had in mind a far shorter time-scale than Vasey. Within a fortnight his confidential memo was being discussed, on the basis of hearsay, among the European elected members. I wrote to David: they have 'announced the discovery of a dastardly plot against the European community. ... I was relieved to hear that it was just Vasey and Mboya asking for a ten-year standstill followed by undiluted democracy.'[35] If the European politicians had been more prescient they would have jumped at the chance of ten years' standstill instead of panicking about plots. Mboya, a friend of Vasey's, may well have had a hand in the proposals as Susan Wood reported to David[36] that Mboya talked of 'a time for preparation' after common roll elections on a low qualified franchise. In my letter to David I referred to his plan for Africa (which Susan Wood called 'the master plan'), which he was drafting, and suggested that it should include provision for compensation for white farmers who had been invited and encouraged by the British government to develop land in Kenya.

March and April 1959 was a time of much activity. Blundell resigned as minister for agriculture to lead the New Kenya Group whose policy 'openly faced the fact that Africans would ultimately rule the country, and advocated the opening of the White Highlands to experienced farmers, qualified entry of all races into all schools and a common roll on a selective franchise.'[37] At the same time Musinde Muliro and S. V. Cooke formed the Kenya National Party, which was interracial to the extent that there was one European with a number of Asian and Africa politicians. In spite of close contact with the leaders of both these groups, the Kenya Party made no progress in creating a common non-racial front. Blundell's party had European politicians who were nervous about going too fast while Muliro's party had Africans and Asians who were suspicious of going too slowly, and we had inadequate numbers of any race to influence events. At one point Cooke wrote to me asking if one of us could join their delegation to London.[38] I replied that they would do more good by staying in Kenya to work out a common policy with the Blundell group.

I wrote to Lewis at the time: 'Manifestos from newly formed groups are falling on us like snowflakes at the moment. ... It is a full-time job for an agile mind to keep up with the situation, which can only be described as fluid but hopeful. ... Tom Mboya is becoming much more sensible in the last few months. Julius Nyerere of Tanganyika has seen Mboya on a number of occasions and is, I think, influencing him into a more moderate policy and making him realize that these countries cannot do without European and Asian enterprise, capital and skill and the "scram out of Africa" policy of the Accra [PAFMECA] conference is not the way to build a sound country here, whoever is in control of the government.'[39]

In April the Kenya Party executive committee decided to support Blundell's New Kenya Group in principle.[40] I wrote to Blundell saying that it would not be a good idea for his group to receive our public support, as 'some politicians were already saying, as if no condemnation could be worse, this [Kenya Party] looks extraordinarily like Capricorn.' He replied with a warm letter saying that he would like to suggest how we could best organize support to our mutual advantage.[41] The files show little progress on this except for a letter from the New Kenya Group's executive officer asking for a subscription, and Blundell in his memoirs *So Rough a Wind* makes no mention of David Stirling, the Kenya Party or Capricorn.

Realizing that Blundell's group would welcome subscriptions but little else, we continued to hold political evenings with Vasey and individual members of both the New Kenya Group and the Kenya National Party to debate the future. Susan Wood and I used the sessions to prepare the politicians to accept David's master plan when it was published. In August 1959 a group of African and Asian members of Legislative Council met informally meeting to see what common ground there was between the Kenya Party and the Kenya National Party.[42] Their only European member, Cooke, was an individualist described by Richard Turnbull, the acting governor, as 'a man of sterling hall-marked unreliability',[43] which made negotiation difficult. Over the following months there was much agonizing in London and Nairobi on whether, when or if, our party should merge with the Kenya National Party. By the end of the year its African members found that contact with Asian and

European politicians damaged them in the eyes of their followers, so an influx of mostly European Capricorners would not have been welcome. The party was disintegrating in any case as the Africans discovered that the Asians also wanted to farm in the White Highlands.

In October 1959 I was asked by Clem Argwings-Kodhek, president of the Nairobi District African Congress, to address a large meeting at Makadara Hall in the African area of Nairobi. The police licence recorded that the speakers were Argwings-Kodhek, S. G. Amin and myself and specified the items on the agenda as 'Can we be united – How? and Collection of funds as per permit.'[44] It also specified that no songs could be sung, no prayers uttered and no music played unless the exact words to be used were submitted in writing to the district commissioner and approved by him before the meeting. It was an exciting experience to speak to a large African audience, attentive and friendly, though it is doubtful whether my enthusiasm for a multiracial future changed their minds in any way.

That year Susan Wood was invited by Philip Mason, director of the Institute of Race Relations, to write a book on Kenya politics.[45] Published in 1960, it is a sympathetic and professional analysis of the politics of the different races and tribal groups, recognizing that African unity was unlikely to last beyond independence. She quoted Dr Kiano, a Kikuyu politician and academic, as saying: 'The desire to be rid of colonial government is the nearest thing we have to "one-ness", or to being a nation.' Continuous intertribal tension in independent Kenya since 1963 has proved him right. Susan Wood accurately described the changing mix of parties and groups that made Kenya politics so confusing, frustrating and ineffective, with a brief recognition of the Kenya Party, Capricorn and the United Kenya Club as outlets for 'non-racialists'. Susan Wood has said recently that the book 'had nothing to do with Capricorn at all ... and there was no discussion with Capricorn'.[46]

This reinforces my memory of the surprise that her friends in the local branch and the Kenya Party had not been canvassed for ideas. The files show, however, that drafts were sent to Jeannine Scott for comments by Lewis, Charles Janson and others in London.[47] It is unlikely that the book would have been any better if we had been involved, but a semblance of collaboration would have been good for the cohesion of our small group as we worked together for the future of the Kenya Party and the country.

In the period leading to independence the UK government

imposed constitutions on Kenya after consultation round the conference table at Lancaster House in London. They included communal and common rolls with primary elections for minorities, a council of state as a safeguard for minorities and a council of ministers with specified numbers from each race. Although each brought universal franchise nearer, the elaborate arrangements were designed to give time, expected to be some years, for Africans, Asians and Europeans to adjust to the idea that race was not relevant in a country where power would eventually be in the hands of the majority, the African people.

Pressure from African nationalists for early independence and the decision of the United Kingdom government to be rid of the difficult and expensive problems of running an empire, meant that the years for adjustment became months. In a minute in early 1959 a Colonial Office official had written: 'I cannot help feeling that we should try to take more positive steps to harness the energy of African nationalism instead of trying to fathom out ways of frustrating it and ultimately our own ends.'[48] Whether they harnessed that energy or simply gave in to it is debatable. The phrase 'African nationalism', used in the Colonial Office and by PAFMECA, implied that Africa, south of the Sahara, was inhabited by people homogeneous in culture and background though admittedly speaking in an enormous number of languages. This created the convenient myth that because West African countries were self-governing in the 1950s, people in east and central Africa were equally experienced and ready to manage their affairs. Aside from the inconvenience of settler populations in some of the latter, there were vast differences in political experience between the two sides of the continent.

Many people in West Africa, not only in areas with centuries of Muslim influence, had lived in and managed large towns and cities for many generations. In other parts of the continent, aside from Buganda, experience of organizing numbers of people was limited to the extended family group, often moving across the land without a settled base or permanent buildings. However, after nearly half a century of independence, there is now little to choose between the levels of maladministration and corruption in east and west.

During 1959 the Kenya Party continued to hold regular council meetings, at one of which Bryceson encouraged us with news of developments in Tanganyika, where the pace of change was well in advance of Kenya. Nyerere also came to a Kenya Party meeting at

Sprott's house at Karen and charmed us with his logical and reasonable attitude to the future. However, we made little impact on events in Kenya, and when David and Wood visited the secretary of state in London before his visit to Kenya in December 1959, his officials noted that the Kenya Party had been dormant throughout the year.[49]

The real action was in London where David, advised by Janson, James Lemkin, March, Lewis and others, was busy refining his master plan and lobbying members of the Cabinet and opposition so that when his proposals were published they would have all-party support. Janson was editor and part owner, with Lemkin and March, of *Africa Confidential*, an influential newsletter published in London, and Lemkin had close links with the radical Bow Group in the Conservative Party. During the year Joyce Raw, Susan Wood, Wilkinson and myself were all writing separately to Janson and to David with ideas and questions that must been confusing for those in London, and ineffective in developing a coherent Kenya Party policy.

While David's plan was being developed Janson wrote a long letter to me, which shows his knowledge of the situation in Kenya and the reality behind the title 'London working party', which he said really consisted of himself being contradicted by David Stirling. He wrote: with a timetable for self-government 'the Americans (and to a lesser extent the Germans) would have a starting point for programmes of economic aid. Without their aid (and much more British aid) it is idle to talk seriously about the political development in Africa [which] cannot take place unless there is also an economic revolution, especially in agriculture and education. ... The British role is to found electoral and parliamentary procedures which will work now: that means procedures that the African politicians will accept ... as a basis for action. That was why I rejected proposals for "new democratic techniques". They seem too likely to be lampooned as "devices"; too complicated for the understanding of the half educated Africans; and also too liable to give a false sense of security to the Europeans. ... You remark that the straight common roll would mean the defeat of all, or nearly all, non-African candidates in the first election. Would this matter decisively? What counts, surely, in the beginning of, say, a seven-year transition period, is precisely a good innings for the Africans. ... I am not hopeful of the multiracial future since it seems to me to demand a sort of saintly heroism from the Europeans, or at least those who are on the land. But equally I can see no other conceivable outcome than self-government in Kenya. Therefore better fairly soon than fairly late. If this argument is accepted, then the supreme need is to get Africans into the jobs while there is some goodwill left and, above all, while Mboya is accessible. To this end mechanics is surely secondary. ... Clearly the new programme in the Belgian Congo sounded the death knell of the present regime in Kenya ... and that scuppered us.'[50]

Although David was no longer president of Capricorn and said he was acting as an individual, Susan Wood and I were firm that it was not feasible for David, whose name was synonymous with Capricorn, to pretend that the Society was not involved in his plan.[51] At the end of April 1959 David sent me[52] the draft of his 'Plan for British East and Central Africa'.[53] The essential points were: the UK government must make an early statement on self government without a time-scale; constitutions must be developed in consultation with leaders in Africa in readiness for independence; there should be a common roll for all races with low qualifications; a citizenship bill must be prepared; land reform as proposed in the East Africa Royal Commission must be put in hand; and the Colonial Office be reformed and the word 'colony' abolished as a term. David concluded: 'HMG [should legislate] to secure the political and social status of the individual rather than that of each separate community. When independence comes, members of the minority groups, whether African, Asian or European, will be secure in their rights as ordinary citizens of the country or not at all.'

David, free of the shackles imposed by the Capricorn Contract or the limitations of carrying the members of the Society with him, was free to be as radical as he thought the situation demanded. In May he wrote to me: 'Herewith a more advanced copy of the memorandum for the Prime Minister. My three chief helpers in parliament are Iain Macleod of the Conservative Party (he is the chairman of their policy making committee), Patrick Gordon-Walker (now very much back in favour and a member of the Labour shadow cabinet) and Jo Grimond (head of the Liberal Party). All are individually doing all they can to win the acceptance of the paper by their respective parties. ... Next week I address the Bow Group and two weeks after that the Conservative Parliamentary Association.'[54]

In the archives there is an ecstatic letter from Jeannine Scott to Susan Wood in which she reports: 'Iain Macleod rang up during the afternoon to say that he had been with Mr Macmillan [the prime minister] that morning and that two-thirds of the time he was there they were discussing [David's] paper. We could hardly believe our ears. He asked Iain Macleod to let David know personally ... [that] he was immensely interested and David will be seeing him next week. I do so wonder what your and Richard's reactions are. ... David asks every day if anything has arrived from the Kenya front.'[55]

In June David wrote to Susan Wood and myself: 'Herewith paper in form that it is being sent to all MPs. I saw the Prime Minister yesterday (more than hour with the old boy). Everything went well.'[56] David's extraordinary level of access to the British establishment was being used to the full – after the October election his friend Macleod was appointed secretary of state for the colonies, to be the architect of the radical 1960 constitutional proposals for Kenya. I could find no reference in Colonial Office files of the period to David's plan, perhaps because he often discussed his ideas at private dinners or in the smoking room of White's Club, without a civil servant to minute conclusions for the file. His plan probably influenced Macmillan, a realist able to recognize the inevitable, whose 'wind of change' speech in the following January was to have profound implications for Africa.[57]

David's plan shows how his ideas were changing in advance of ours in Kenya, and history shows that his assessment of the inevitable was correct. Susan Wood wrote to me from London, after talking to David and Janson, that David 'feels that if we do anything it should be going out to meet African nationalism and identifying ourselves with their struggle. On the franchise David said that he himself had come to feel that it was comparatively unimportant compared to the citizenship bill and that he himself would be prepared to accept a universal franchise if it were necessary in order to win African cooperation.'[58] That attitude may have derived from David's reading of Mboya's character. In a letter to March he wrote that he had 'high regard for Mboya, who unlike others is not concerned with drive for power and Kikuyu domination'.[59] This was a misreading of Mboya's ambitions and incidentally of his tribal background, which was not Kikuyu.

In December 1959 Macleod went to Nairobi in preparation for the constitutional conference to be held in London the following January. The Kenya Party submitted a memorandum to the Colonial Office constitutional advisor with a map of Kenya, which I had drawn to show our proposed 'open constituencies' and 'reserved constituencies' and the anticipated numbers of members of each race.

While the future of Kenya was being settled at Lancaster House in London I wrote to Janson hoping that he could stress 'that ... European or Asian [communal] electoral rolls would be a disaster. ... The easiest way of being elected on a racial roll is to be racial, and as their numbers and power decrease such members are likely to get more racial, not less.'[60] I added that Vasey, fresh from London on his way to Dar es Salaam (where he was then minister of finance) had told me that Macleod said that our proposals were the very least that he would expect to get out of the conference.

Macleod's constitutional proposals at the end of the 1960 conference set up a common roll with certain seats reserved for minorities, an African majority in Legislative Council and a non-racial policy on land ownership. There was also a clear statement that Kenya would be a self-governing independent country with parliamentary institutions on the Westminster model. Macleod's 1960 constitution was more radical and urgent than politicians in Kenya, including the Africans, expected. While Lennox-Boyd had supported a policy based on partnership between the races, Macleod, a leading figure in the radical wing of the Conservative Party, took an unemotional view of the situation, without allowing feelings for 'kith and kin' to interfere with finding a rational solution.

The Kenya police special branch recorded European reactions in their monthly report at the end of the year. 'The results of the Lancaster House conference in February 1960 left the European community appalled at the apparent volte-face performed by the British government. ... Having only just accustomed itself to the official line of "multiracialism", the provisions of the latest constitution smack strongly of outright capitulation to the forces of African nationalism at the expense of civilized standards and values in the colony. That the community was so stunned ... must be contributed ... [to] the extent to which HM Government's colonial policy was being increasingly sublimated to the exigencies of its foreign policy. ... Before these new circumstances had time to become accepted as the current political norm, another event took place which plunged morale to hitherto unplumbed depths and inflated the ranks of those prophets of doom whose slogan was "I told you so". This was the granting of independence to the Congo and the calamitous events which it set in train ... although there has been no indication of panic among the immigrant communities. On the whole, Europeans regard [the situation] with feelings compounded of apathy, resignation and inevitability but, at the same time, many are said to be arranging for wives and children at least to be out of the country in the immediate post election period.'[61]

The election based on the Macleod proposals was held in 1961, comparatively peacefully, and with predictable results. Jomo Kenyatta was still restricted, although he had served his seven-year sentence for managing Mau Mau, and once he was completely free he was returned unopposed at a by-election in 1961, becoming Kenya's first prime minister. Many Europeans were anxious and frightened about the future but slowly the atmosphere changed as Kenyatta travelled the country, speaking to groups of farmers. At a meeting in Nakuru, in the Rift Valley, he helped to relax the tension by saying: 'I am a politician, but I am a farmer like you. ... I believe that the most disturbing point among us is suspicion, fear. This is created by not knowing what the other side is thinking. If we must live together, we must work together, we must talk together, exchange views. ... All of us, white, brown and black, can work together to make this country great. ... Let us join together and join hands and work together for the benefit of Kenya.'[62]

With Kenya making rapid strides to independence with universal franchise, the remnants of Capricorn needed another role if the Society was to continue. In April 1961 an MP made a visit to the Colonial Office, for which the CO brief reads: 'The Capricorn Africa Society having, so to speak, run out of business with the introduction of the Lancaster House constitution in Kenya, would like to find some other useful activity – possibly anti-Communist propaganda. ... Our view in the office has been, however, that since the Society has dabbled in a number of things fairly inefficiently it is hardly the medium for this sort of activity if we want to see results!'[63] In October that year Susan Wood and a Colonel W. H. Howell submitted proposals 'by some Kenyans of all races' on Capricorn Africa Society Kenya branch notepaper, for an elaborate constitution for the country, including a federation of the East African countries. The Colonial Office noted: 'this is another example of amateur constitution making which Sir Patrick Renison [the governor] told us about. Although some sound points are made, I doubt whether serious study is warranted.'[64]

Guy Hunter, whose advice and experience was invaluable to Capricorn in the creation of our colleges of citizenship, wrote of this period: 'The younger African leaders represented not merely an opposition to the Europeans but simultaneous political and social revolution within African society – the emancipation of a new class not only from the rural tribal society but from traditional leadership. They gathered in the discontented literates, the progressives in rural areas, the insulted and injured, the young professionals, the unemployed of the towns. ... Knowing their own, they were ruthless with waverers, and they played consistently on every grievance, real or imagined, both of the country and the town. Against settler governments, ammunition was ample – land, wages, colour bar, minority rule; the main difficulty was to break the attitude of dependence. Against the administration in non-settler territories, still experimenting with chiefs and native authorities, with tentative county councils and complex franchises, their impact was as simple and direct as a hammer blow – modern elected government by universal suffrage, neither more nor less. On such a simple programme, TANU in Tanganyika, typical of such a modern party, swept over that huge area in a flash of time, presenting an astonished government with its national force and ubiquity where before there had been scattered and contradictory grumbles. ... As soon as the government made the first major concession to the young leaders, the situation was in danger of becoming wholly out of hand. ... The first concession led to a second, for "the hatred of authorities is most marked just when they seem most full of goodwill", and soon government was mainly concerned to conduct at least a dignified retreat without having to swallow its own words and constitutions too often.'[65]

By acting as a bridge between the various political groups in Kenya, if not in Tanganyika, Capricorn and the Kenya Party may have helped to ease some European politicians into accepting the inevitable, and some African politicians into recognizing that the immigrant races were an important part of the economic future at least. As Lord (Denis) Healey, the veteran Labour politician, once said: 'liberals are always useful: they are a bridge to march over.'

Chapter 12
Education for Nationhood

The Capricorn colleges of citizenship in Southern Rhodesia and Kenya were the only real successes we could claim in Africa. Although the college in Kenya[1] had a comparatively short life, Ranche House College[2] in Zimbabwe continues to provide a wide education to many thousands of all races in the region. When David Stirling had recovered from the bruising experience of his return to Southern Rhodesia at the end of 1956, he was in Kenya in mid-1957. He had been invited to talk to the students at Jeanes School, the Kenya government training centre at Kabete, near Nairobi. After the lecture David spent the evening with the principal, John Porter, hearing about his tour of Scandinavia to study adult education for UNESCO. Porter had worked in education most of his life, in England and Kenya, and had the advantage of a clever and creative Danish wife, Kirsten. David was excited by the possibility that the folk high school concept in Denmark could foster a common patriotism among the peoples of Africa.

After that evening at Kabete, and discussions with Joe Oldham and others in London, David proposed a network of similar colleges in Africa. Oldham's advice was important; he was familiar with the 1948 Colonial Office paper on education,[3] which mentioned the importance of Danish folk high schools in adult education for citizenship and he had been concerned in the development of Jeanes School in 1926.[4] Edwin Townsend-Coles, who was later to be closely involved with Ranche House College, has written that at the time 'there was throughout the English speaking world a new impetus regarding adult education.'[5] Universities in Africa were setting up liberal extra-mural departments, 'which enriched but awarded no qualification to the student'. He added, in the context of Southern Rhodesia, 'It has to be remembered that adult education is a pretty dangerous commodity. It was considered such by colonial governments, since encouraging people to think was seen as a threat.' This thought would have encouraged David.

Early in September 1957 David was back in Salisbury where he expounded his new idea to an executive committee meeting.[6] He wanted to infuse Capricorn ideas into adult education to create the cultural, social and economic foundation for the common citizenship he believed was essential for the future. He proposed that pilot schemes should be established in Salisbury and in Nairobi, supported by funds from charitable foundations, missionary societies and, surprisingly, government. Characteristically, the idea was for citizenship committees involving all the races to draft a document that in turn would be endorsed at a convention. The committee congratulated him on his 'comprehensive and masterly proposal' and declared that the future of the Capricorn Society lay in the field of adult education. In the draft charter for the colleges David wrote that they would primarily 'serve the spirit of the individual and thus play a part in the creation of a great nation'.

Humphrey Amherst, an influential member of the Society in Southern Rhodesia, responded to David's paper with a memo in which he raised a number of cogent points, including: 'I do not feel that CAS, at least in Southern Rhodesia, as yet commands sufficient technical and administrative ability and experience to embark on a project such as this.'[7] He suggested working with the existing interracial adult educational organization – the new university, which already had buildings, finance, staff, educational standing and public goodwill. He recognized that the Society evidently needed to be reanimated by a new objective, but did not think the proposed schools a feasible way to do it. David was not deterred – he rarely was – and continued to work on his proposals, which he was convinced would give Capricorn a new lease of life and be of great value to the people of Africa.

The adult education proposal was discussed at a Capricorn meeting in Kenya in the garden at St Julian's, in September 1957. Robert Dick-Read, the executive officer in Kenya, described the event to the London office. 'Saturday saw the gathering of nearly 30 invited members from all over Kenya to discuss the Society's future in the field of adult education. The conference was held ... in the perfect atmosphere of the house and gardens that once were owned by Kenya's chairman. On Sunday morning from the lawns of St Julian's we were greeted with a superb view of the whole range of Kilimanjaro to the southeast, and the dazzling spectacle of Kirinaga [Mount Kenya] 240 miles to its north ... this rare sight seemed almost an omen that, after a period of inactivity, at last the clouds were rising on the Capricorn scene and that the way ahead lay clear. Members who were present at Salima agreed that the atmosphere of the conference was as stimulating as that at the convention and, as one who had not been present [at Salima], I can only say that over the weekend the enthusiasm and oneness of purpose of all races was a moving experience.'[8]

My memories of the occasion are also of enthusiasm, mixed with relief that the Society now had a tangible proposal to work for. Although David proposed that committees should develop the charter for the colleges, he wrote the document himself without waiting for committees. His memorandum recorded the proposal unanimously adopted by the meeting: 'That the Capricorn Africa Society adopts the creation of residential adult citizenship schools and adult extra-mural activities ... as its main task for the future, and the Society should forthwith undertake to establish schools of citizenship in east and central Africa.'[9]

After analysing why such colleges would not achieve the Society's aims if they were built and run by governments, David wrote with honesty and passion: 'The Capricorn idea could be described in the one word: integration, but to do so would be to risk a faulty interpretation of the Capricorn purpose. Integration used today in the context of human relations is accepted reluctantly by many people as an inevitable compromise. In most European minds, integration implies a gradual levelling down of standards and of the debasing of their way of life, and to the African nationalist (and nearly all full-blooded Africans are nationalists) it implies the gradual extinguishing of their exciting dreams of an Africa gloriously ruled by the Africans. For both it means a dreary descent from the peaks, forced on them by regrettable but inexorable economic and political considerations. It is understandable that, while this drab concept of integration persists in people's minds, the forces and passions of racial nationalism will be constantly on the increase, simply because people prepared to accept integration are not sufficiently inspired or roused by it as an idea to fight with any vigour on its behalf. But to us in Capricorn, integration means something positive and splendid. We believe the integration of all races into one common citizenship will enhance, rather than threaten, the standing and integrity of our respective races and religions. We believe that integration will release tremendous cultural and economic energies for Africa's development, and will lead us to higher rather than lower peaks of attainment, and an enriched rather than an impoverished way of life. We believe that our concept of the reintegration of the human race is the final and highest form of nationalism, and that the winning of it by mankind is perhaps the crucial challenge implicit in all history.'

The document proposed a punishing programme for David himself over the ensuing months, with trips to both Rhodesias, South Africa to talk to Alan Paton, to England for discussions with Oldham, to towns in Kenya with Michael Wood, to America and Canada, to Copenhagen and then back to east and central Africa. He was not well that year so some of these visits may have been abandoned. Oldham wrote an enthusiastic and expansive note on the subject in which he said, 'It is widely agreed, even by many outside the membership of the Capricorn Society, that there can be no great future for east and central Africa except on the foundation of the Capricorn idea.'[10] He warned of being known as a society concerned only with education when there was so much else to be done and raised, in his fifth point, a question that was to come out later, the use of the word 'citizenship'.

'So long as Africans are subject to colonial government, or are ruled by a dominant European minority, the danger can hardly be avoided of education for citizenship being interpreted by many of them as meaning education to become what the European regards as good boys. Is it necessary that the Capricorn Society should be saddled with this psychological handicap?' He went on to recommend that the new movement should have the best and most skilled leadership that can be found, adding that 'the history of education shows that notable educational achievements have been the work of exceptionally gifted individuals.' David confirmed at an executive committee in Salisbury that to attract influential sponsors the colleges would be entirely separate from the Society.[11] He recommended that experts should be co-opted to the college committees, suggesting Walter Coutts (who had proposed the qualified franchise and was later chief secretary in the Kenya government), the principals of the university colleges in east and central Africa, members of African and Asian teachers' associations and representatives of companies like ICI, Shell and Lever Brothers.

In early April 1958 Capricorn organized a conference, Education for Nationhood, under the chairmanship of Wood, in the hall of the Royal Technical College (later the University of Nairobi). Many of the stalwarts of the Kenya branch were not involved, including Betty Couldrey (who was busy with a new baby), Joyce Raw, Eric Wilkinson and myself. At the time we were busy with the Kenya Party, and David thought that his education proposals stood a better chance of success if they were not tainted with politics. In any case, the conference was not a Kenya affair even though the branch organized it. There were 30 patrons of the conference, of whom six were members of Capricorn, including Wood, who was then the chairman of the Kenya branch. Of the 11 speakers, each an acknowledged expert in his field, only four, including David, were members of the Society.

The pamphlet produced later noted in the introduction: 'The conference was attended by students and education experts, ministers and priests of many religions, farmers, agriculturists, medical men, economists, leaders of thought and of industry, government representatives and civilian well-wishers, Africans, Asians, Europeans and Arabs, men and women.' It could have added, less modestly, that among the speakers there were two distinguished ex-colonial governors, the minister of finance, the minister of agriculture and the chief secretary in the Kenya government and the principals of three universities.

David, in his address to the conference said: 'I believe that only a nation founded on the idea of a common patriotism, dedicated to truth and love, can resist the easy attraction of racial nationalism, communism and other propositions which betray truth and love. ... We have here in Kenya the most fully equipped laboratory in all history for the solution of the problem. Within its boundaries live three of the great race divisions of the world and, among them, believers in all the great religions. Other laboratories, such as in North America and Switzerland, have succeeded in meeting somewhat lesser challenges in national integration. And to establish a patriotism acceptable to all Kenya's races and religions will be to establish a patriotism which may gradually become valid for all mankind.'

David then referred to the success of the Danish folk high schools of 100 years earlier. 'At that time, the Germans were threatening the invasion of Schleswig-Holstein. The Danes had no heart to fight in self-defence because it seemed there was nothing worth defending. The country was bankrupt in spirit as well as in resources. Yet, within four years, Denmark was a flourishing country with a robust sense of patriotism. The secret of these schools — and the miracle they accomplished — lay partly in the way they were run and partly in the concept of patriotism which powered them.' For many of the large number of people of all races attending the conference it was an exhilarating experience to be part of a movement that was full of enthusiasm and hope for the future. One African delegate, as he was leaving the hall, turned and said quietly, 'I think the Kenyan nation began here.' Another said: 'During the conference new friendships grew up between people who had never met before.'

Six study groups were set up; one subject they discussed gives an indication of depth of debate, which was often heated: to what extent does the achievement of nationhood in Kenya imply westernization? Another group considered the question of multiracial education, which some felt was premature, although there was agreement on training in citizenship, and that the time had come for the formation of a secondary school open to all races. Almost half the membership of the study groups was African.[12]

Holding a conference for nearly 400 people over five days with speakers from other countries in Africa, and from England, required an enormous amount of organization by the Capricorn Nairobi office and considerable financial support, which had to come from Britain. In January 1958 the Dulverton Trust voted £1400 'towards salaries and travel expenses' for the conference.[13] As was so often the case in Capricorn affairs, the London office raised the funds that made the work in Africa possible. Jeannine Scott had encouraged Sir John Nelson, a Dulverton trustee, to take an interest in Africa, though his knowledge of Kenya politics was scanty. When he visited the College of Social Studies in 1963, shortly after Jomo Kenyatta became prime minister of a self-governing country, Nelson astounded the staff and African students by saying to the principal: 'I hope you're telling these chaps not to ask for independence too soon.'[14]

After the conference, which left everybody enthusiastic that practical steps towards building a nation were under way, David went to London to continue the fight. By July that year his publicity machine had instigated a leader in *The Times*, which read in part: 'The Capricorn Society's latest project is certainly one which deserves to succeed. It is the establishment in both Rhodesia and Kenya of colleges of citizenship. ... The subjects taught would include philosophy, politics, and problems of government at all levels, as well as purely practical subjects. ... The object of the courses would be to instil the spirit of partnership and of common nationhood as opposed to racial nationalism.'[15] *The Times* added: 'Governments naturally are chary of establishing such institutions because of their wide and sometimes controversial political implications. Controversy, however, is a diet on which Colonel Stirling and the Capricorn Society have always thrived. They deserve backing in their new venture.'

The English language press in Kenya reflected the atmosphere among the European settler community: in the *Kenya Weekly News*, between pieces by Mervyn Hill on golf, cricket and the breeding of racehorses, there were pessimistic views on the future of the country after the recent constitutional conference. An article in mid-September 1958 quoted farmers as saying 'the Africans have won' and 'look at Ghana'. In the same issue there was an article about the conference on education for nationhood and the proposed college of citizenship.

As the newly elected chairman of the Kenya branch of Capricorn I wrote to the editor saying: 'The theme of both leading article and "Signed Print" in your issue of September 19th is a dismal one: the pervasive belief that there is no stable future for Kenya. Although you rightly call for an end to this alarm and despondency, neither articles attempt to examine what has caused this sudden lowering of confidence, nor how to end it. I would suggest that the cause, not the symptom, of the trouble is that the majority of Europeans in Kenya have now realized that the past is gone for good; African nationalism is on the march, and they see no potent idea to stand against it. British people have always been at their best when the future looked bleak, but confidence drops when the future is indecisive and there is no leader to give the people an idea to follow. This is why the article on the proposed college of citizenship in the same issue is so important. Here is a great idea, which I hope will soon appear in concrete form to stand against the extremes of both sides. To rebuild morale, the country's immediate need is for a dynamic and positive conception of the future. The idea that a common national purpose is possible among the disparate peoples of Kenya may seem too vague, but the creation of adult education centres designed to build this sense of common purpose is a precise and practical idea to work for. Positive action is the antidote to despondency. The first steps have been taken: a conference was held in April to determine the need, at the end of which there was an overwhelming demand ... that the conception of adult education for citizenship should be made a reality.'[16]

College of citizenship associations were set up in Kenya and in Southern Rhodesia to carry the proposals into reality. In Kenya realization was protracted and complicated while Salisbury was quicker off the mark, perhaps because David was on the spot to maintain momentum – his enthusiasm and wild optimism sweeping away doubts or hesitations. Reading the brochure he wrote for the Rhodesian college is a reminder of what an extraordinary man

David was, and how we were inspired by his confidence and ambitions for the countries of his adoption.

David wrote: 'The college must make the idea of Rhodesian nationhood, and an understanding of how best to serve it, really live in the heads and intellect of its pupils. It must help to bring reality and definition to the word *partnership* before this word, on which our federation was founded, becomes wholly discredited. In Britain the idea of nationhood was built up by her people through two thousand years of history; America gained her concept much more rapidly, but its influence on her leaders in every walk of life is none the less great. Where would the United States stand today if each of the separate races and nationalities which inhabit that great country had different sets of leaders – as we tend to have in Africa – seeking to protect their different ways or life and their different aspirations?'[17]

He continued: 'The leaders of opinion in all communities in America accept and pay tribute to the basic tenets of her nationhood – tenets which are sacred to all the different races. ... It is the purpose of the college to help establish foundation tenets, which will become equally sacred to all Africa's peoples. But we must do better than merely attain the present degree of national solidarity in America and Britain. ... In both countries the idea behind their national purpose seems to be ever less clearly understood, and their peoples seem ever less prepared to accept the minimum disciplines needed to secure decent standards of morality and of individual behaviour. The idea which will power our college could prove more compelling on people to reach for higher standards of behaviour than any other idea in the contemporary world. This claim is understandable when it is realized that we are responding to the challenge of helping to teach a common national purpose for three of the great race divisions of the world, living within one environment. ... The reward for the successful meeting of the challenge would be an incalculable scale of prosperity and happiness for all who live in the Federation. We look on the College of Rhodesian Citizenship as only the beginning of a great movement in adult education.'

In parallel with events in the south, the College of Kenya Citizenship Association was set up with six vice-presidents, including Oldham, Laurens van der Post and the principals of the university colleges of east and central Africa, a board of trustees of well-known figures in Kenya and Southern Rhodesia, including David and Wood and many sponsors. The chairman of the management committee was a Capricorn supporter, Martin Capon, an Anglican priest and member of Moral Rearmament, who had chaired a study group at the conference. The association adopted the stirring and optimistic charter that David wrote for the Rhodesian college. The pamphlet produced by the Kenya association set out the need for an expert consultant to prepare a report on how a college of citizenship could be translated into a reality and to form the basis of an appeal for funds.

In September 1958 the *East African Standard* printed an article by Wood under the headline KENYA UNITY SPUR TO CITIZENSHIP COLLEGE PLAN, in which he described the proposals, writing: 'The Association believes that courses should start early in 1959 so it will concentrate on becoming operative with all possible speed. ... The day of pioneering in Kenya is not over, for those who have eyes to see and the courage to act, exciting and challenging prospects are offering themselves today. The Association for the College of Kenya Citizenship is one such opportunity, and should attract the support of all who call Kenya their home.'[18]

The association in Southern Rhodesia obtained funds from the Beit Trust for the appointment of a consultant whose terms of reference included: types of course, numbers and age groups of students, staff and running costs, relations with the university institute of adult education and the financial assistance required. Guy Hunter, assisted by his wife Lou, was appointed in October 1958. He had worked in adult education in Britain as the warden of Urchfont Manor from 1946 to 1955 and Grantley Hall, both short-term residential colleges for adults, and in 1956 was the director of studies for the first Duke of Edinburgh's conference. Hunter was a colleague of Philip Mason's and a friend of Charles March and Oldham – the London office had again used their formidable list of contacts to find the right man. Hunter's book *The New Societies of Tropical Africa*, an important and scholarly contribution to the study of changing societies in Africa, was published in 1962 under the auspices of the Institute of Race Relations.[19]

A quotation shows his sensitive approach to the problems inherent in settler societies. 'Too often [European] wives generalized on African character from their knowledge of inexperienced servants stumbling blindly through the routines of a European household. Certainly, these European attitudes were more marked in the settler countries, and above all in the Rhodesias, where a class of white artisans and clerks was potentially threatened by African advance. The attitude of many Rhodesians and of much of the

Rhodesian press towards Africans has been described by many writers; it is only necessary to record here the deep sense of indignity and bitterness and the appalling damage to race relations which the worst examples of it have caused. The employment of European women as secretaries and clerks, giving orders to Africans, was often especially unfortunate. But even elsewhere, as more Europeans appeared who were neither missionaries nor administrators (both in their way dedicated men), sourness and hostility began to grow.'

Hunter was 47 when he was appointed as consultant to the Rhodesian college, grey haired, tall and slightly stooped with a self deprecating air that hid a fine brain. Lou Hunter was a constant support and strength to her husband and they worked together as a team: she was a strong personality while he appeared shy, with an almost painful sense of decency, talking in a quiet educated voice with his head on one side. Hunter wrote in his preface to *The New Societies*: 'Finally, this book should really have my wife's name on it in addition to my own, since she not only took part in almost every interview and visit in Africa and the full rigours of travel, but brought back some 80,000 words of notes taken and written up *en route*. She has throughout contributed enormously to the ideas and balance of the book by suggestion and comment; typed the first manuscript; and sustained the author through two years of intensive work.'

This would have applied equally to the gruelling and extensive tour they took through Kenya and central Africa at the end of 1958 and early 1959 to report on the citizenship colleges. They completed the 80-page typescript, with long lists of the individuals interviewed and places visited, by April 1959. From the perspective of the end of the century, with laptop computers, laser printers, faxes and mobile telephones, it is difficult to remember how hard the Hunters worked to produce an immaculate and thoughtful report with only a spiral notebook and a portable Olivetti typewriter in their hotel room.

The minutes of the Dulverton Trust record: 'Lord Dulverton felt that it was vital for the Dulverton Trust to obtain reliable information about the proposed Capricorn college of citizenship for Kenya, [with] which the Beit Trust was not concerned. He had accordingly arranged for Mr and Mrs Hunter to spend up to four weeks in Kenya on their return journey from the federation in order to make a special report to the Dulverton Trust on the Kenya college. The Trust would be responsible for all expenses Mr and

Mrs Hunter incur in Kenya, over and above those paid for by the Beit Trust. These expenses might amount to a maximum of £400.'[20] Dulverton's initiative over the Kenya part of the Hunters' tour encouraged the trust to try to appropriate the project. Some 18 months later Hunter wrote to the principal of the Kenya college, Harold Wiltshire, saying: 'The Dulverton Trust, (and the Beit Trust for Rhodesia), pressed me very hard to accept direct instructions and direct payment from their bodies – they were already wanting to keep the college as separate from Capricorn as possible.'[21] However, Hunter insisted that he was responsible to Capricorn management committees who had appointed him. His report was presented jointly to the Beit and Dulverton trustees and to the management committees in Nairobi and Salisbury. Reading some of the aggressive correspondence later in the project from the secretary to the Dulverton Trust, Lord Kilmaine, it is likely that he was responsible for this early attempt to take control of the colleges.

In November 1958, on their way to Rhodesia, the Hunters arrived in Kenya to make contact with Capricorn there. My diary records: '6 November 1958: Hunters + 50 at home' – a welcoming party to introduce them to members of the Society and others involved with the proposed college. Early in January 1959, after the Hunters had completed the Rhodesian part of their trip, I went with them to Mombasa by train, and then upcountry to meet people who would be useful. The Hunters' sympathetic understanding of the realities of life in Africa can be caught in the following quotation from their report: 'We have already noted the emergence of an African "middle class". Both in the federation and, to a much greater extent, in Kenya these men – only more rarely women – are filling posts of minor responsibility both in industry and commerce and particularly in the extension services – health, education, agriculture, local administration, social welfare – of government. This group is making an essential contribution both to administration and to the economy. They have been subjected to a considerable strain in moving from an indigenous culture and language into a Westernized system of thought, administration and technique. This strain has been increased by their isolation both from the bulk of their own society and from Europeans; by their difficulty in finding a wife of equal education and similar way of life, and by political and racial tensions in which they are unavoidably caught up. After their initial vocational training, during which they are in a homogeneous group and in constant and usually friendly contact with Europeans, they are often moved out to work where they have few friends of their own calibre, little or no access to books or cultural activity, only a formal contact with Europeans and often wholly unsuitable accommodation. A college which could offer these men a real sense that they were in fact colleagues in the task of building an economy and a society, which could give them a chance of discussion with their European counterparts on a basis of equality, which could give them a broader view of society, a longer view of history and fresh ideas and enthusiasm for their work – such a college would, in our view, provide an immensely valuable service.'[22]

Working in my office was a young man, David Mutiso, the first African from Kenya to qualify as an architect, who had written asking to join my practice before he left Sheffield University. He was naturally one of our number, working side by side, but I was aware of the difficulties he faced outside the office in finding a place to live and in finding friends who could span two cultures as he did. He would hum Mozart at the drawing board, but when a reporter interviewed him about his background, he insisted that his father was a peasant, not a farmer.

In the Rhodesian section of their report, the Hunters recorded 'their anxiety at the continuing barriers between the races'. They nevertheless felt that the proposed college might help to ameliorate the worsening conditions even if only in some small degree. The Hunters suggested that students should pay part of their fees because 'most will be in well-paid jobs'. In fact Africans in Southern Rhodesia were poorly paid and conditions in Kenya not much better. Employers (and whites generally) in central Africa resolutely refused to face up to the changes that were occurring in Africa, and were unwilling to subsidize staff education unless they could see an immediate benefit. Although businessmen in Kenya could hardly be described as liberal, they were realists and could see what the future held. Some employers and government departments were prepared to release staff and pay fees for a course that might not improve productivity, and indeed was more likely to encourage staff to examine the justice of their conditions.

In June 1959 the Beit Trust agreed to provide £12,000 and the Dulverton Trust £6600 for the 'Rhodesian experiment' to cover running costs (but not buildings) over three years.[23] At the same joint meeting of the trusts, the Dulverton trustees agreed in principle to provide funds for the construction of college buildings in Kenya – from which it appears they were more sanguine about the enterprise there.

In April 1959 I wrote to Lewis in London about the enthusiasm Dulverton had for the project and the way he kept things moving. 'You will know that Lord Dulverton arrived here on Friday morning – I met him at the airport and took him to the Norfolk [Hotel] where he met Martin Capon and Derek Erskine (the latter representing the Outward Bound Trust) so that we could discuss his programme. We were delighted to learn that he had come out specifically to investigate the colleges of citizenship situation. He is enormously keen ... [and] has met a number of us here for long talks about the project ... and has virtually promised us about £20,000, either lump sum, or over three years, whichever is convenient to us and without any conditions. We have also made clear to him that we have great hopes of ICA [US International Cooperation Administration, now the US Agency for International Development] producing a substantial sum of money for capital development with all its implications that this is not entirely a Dulverton baby, although ... without his personal help the project would come to naught. ... Our policy with Dulverton was to let him force the pace and talk to whomever he wished about it. On Saturday he came to my house for lunch with Martin [Capon] and Musa Amalemba, then went to see Wadley (former director of education in Kenya and now a member of the management committee), saying he would probably telephone me when he came back from Gilgil, which might be on Wednesday or Thursday. Three-quarters of an hour after leaving me, having seen Wadley, he came back and we had a long talk in the forest across the valley. He then left [saying] that he would probably get in touch with me later in the week. At a quarter to ten that night he rang up again and said could we have another talk about it, so I went down to the Norfolk and we discussed the matter in detail until 12 and he now has virtually no more worries about it and has pretty well committed himself.'[24]

Opposite our house and across a stream was the Karura Forest, a possible site for the college if government released it for educational purposes. While we walked in the forest I tried hard to persuade Dulverton to support the college and believe that we walked up and down until he agreed. Dulverton described himself as 'a forester' so perhaps the environment made him amenable to my arguments.

My report to Lewis continued: 'I feel he has been greatly impressed by the amount of enthusiasm and work that has been put into the project and that all the worries that he had in London, which, as he said, were largely through ignorance about conditions here and of the people involved, have now been resolved. *Please* do nothing about this until he makes the next move. I feel it is most important not to interfere with this honeymoon by pressing them in London, or in any other way snooping around until he gets back to confirm the decisions he has made out here. I believe that it would also be *unwise* to pass around the information I have given you on his keenness or commitment any wider than is absolutely necessary, and *certainly* don't let any members of his trust know what he is thinking until he has an opportunity of doing this himself. Dulverton has also undertaken to enlist the services of Sir Donald MacGillivray and P. J. Rogers [chairman of the East African Tobacco Company Ltd and known to Dulverton, whose father had been chairman of the Imperial Tobacco Company] as serving members on the committee to strengthen it from the public relations point of view.'

Donald MacGillivray was a retired colonial governor – tall, bronzed, elegant and courteous – who farmed at Gilgil in the Rift Valley; P. J. Rogers (later to become Sir Philip) was a member of Legislative Council, and one of the commercial men who thought Capricornists, as he liked to call us, were dangerous radicals. However, he was keen to be involved, even with a project initiated by Capricorn, when asked to do so by a Lord (Rogers famously kept an up-to-date edition of *Debrett's Peerage* by his desk). Both MacGillivray and Rogers were also involved in campaigns for multiracial secondary schools. I saw Dulverton again with Coutts and after he had spent ten days in Kenya took him to the airport, confident that we had the funds to build the college in Kenya. The Dulverton Trust granted £20,000 in June 1959 for buildings with a further £15,000 in July that year for the access road, a borehole and travel for the principal.[25]

In 1998 the Dulverton Trust contributed to research for a book written by three academics – Paul Fordham, the second principal of the Kenya college, John Fox who had been a tutor and Patrick Muzaale, who had been a student at the college.[26] It is a thorough analysis of how it affected the lives of the students, although the second chapter describing the genesis of the college shows how much Capricorn was misunderstood. The two expatriate authors, with a background in workers' education in England, arrived in Africa at a time when the political climate was light years away from the conditions in which the 1958 Education for Nationhood Conference had been held. Fordham joined the college in 1962, when Jomo Kenyatta was prime minister and there was universal suffrage in Kenya, and Fox arrived in 1966, three years after the country became a republic. They had scant sympathy for the problems of a country controlled by the Colonial Office and settler politicians. The following quotations indicate how inaccurate their knowledge was of Capricorn's intentions (emphasis added).

The Capricorn Society thought 'the "heady wine" of African nationalism as something which was undesirable in itself, and something that could be countered by reducing the social isolation of the various racial groups – *albeit in carefully controlled circumstances*. The 1958 conference *carefully* excluded the "light-hearted drinkers of the heady wine of African nationalism" and, of the 29 patrons of the Conference, only eight were African'. The chapter continued: 'It was perhaps unfair to castigate Capricorn's educational policies as no more than "multiracial tea parties"; but the first principal was certainly right in thinking that by 1960 it was no longer possible to *select students on the basis of racial origin*. ... Capricorn sought *an equal balance* between blacks, whites and Asians – when the population balance was most unequal.'

Although the authors were academics they reflected the distortions common in the 1960s, when Africans enjoyed independence and regarded the multiracial ideas of the previous decade as irrelevant and undemocratic. In the section on Dulverton's visit to Kenya, the authors describe the trust as having 'links with Kenya business interests' – unaware of the connection in London between Capricorn and the Dulverton Trust – isolating Capricorn from having raised the money. The authors continued: 'In order to move ahead as rapidly as possible, Lord Dulverton visited Nairobi in April 1959 and staged a coup within the management committee. A new board of governors was appointed (including only one Capricornist, Mrs Susan Wood) with the key figures of Sir Philip Rogers (later chairman) and Sir Donald MacGillivray ... wresting control from Capricorn and ensuring the support of local business interests.' The myth of the 'coup' comes from some triumphalist correspondence from Kilmaine. During the development of the college he wrote frequently to the governors over matters of detail, creating many problems for those on the spot. Dulverton Trust records show that two local trustees were appointed on the advice of Sir Leslie Farrer, the trust's solicitor, to safeguard money being transferred to Kenya. There is no indication in the record of 'wresting control from Capricorn'.[27]

In Southern Rhodesia, the situation was different from Kenya in many ways: after the comprehensive and ambitious brochure published in July 1958, the College of Rhodesian Citizenship Association had to pause until the Beit and Dulverton trusts funded the Hunter report. In March 1959 a meeting was held in Salisbury attended by Sir Alfred Beit and Dulverton, with trustees from each trust, together with Hunter and Basil Fletcher from the university.[28] Hunter made clear how important it was to appoint a principal before any start could be made, which was generally accepted. Beit confirmed that his trust would definitely not make any contribution towards permanent buildings, and called for a detailed scheme for a three-year experimental period. In June 1959, the two trusts jointly agreed to provide £18,600 (Dulverton one-third and Beit two-thirds) to the college in Southern Rhodesia for running costs over three years, but not for capital expenditure.

David resigned as president in late 1959, but continued to take a keen interest in the two colleges, complaining at their apparent independence from Capricorn, although he had specified that they should be so. In March 1960 Hunter felt that he had to respond to some of David's wilder statements. Mason has said that Hunter did not like David, and Kenneth Mew quotes a letter from Hunter to Fletcher saying as much.[29]

They were, of course, quite different sorts of men, and there is a sense of exasperation in Hunter's letter to David. 'I gather that you and many members of Capricorn have been much disturbed that our report has restated the "independence" of the colleges, and that even words like "disowning Capricorn" have been used. For the record, we have used always, in the report and in Africa, a phrase given us by Michael and Susan [Wood] — that the original initiative and inspiration was from Capricorn, but that the management of the colleges was independent. ... We deliberately made the report as factual and professional as possible, and I think the decisions of Beit and Dulverton to support them (and much other support) would have been much harder to get if we hadn't. You can't have the advantage of independence and also control things. You've chosen your committees, who are like-minded and you have to trust them to keep it right — they are full of good Capricorn members to watch that. ... I feel that what has happened is a fit of acute disappointment that Capricorn cannot at present get either badly needed finance for, or actual direction of, the colleges; but that was in the nature of the scheme as originally drawn up. If you do get the colleges going, and I believe they *will* go, you will have immense credit, and something which really will justify appeals *for the Society*: indeed, I'm sure you ought to be appealing *for the Society* now, as well as for the college. Lou and I have had the greatest help and kindness from many Capricorn people, here and in Africa, for which we are indeed grateful and have mentioned it particularly in the report. We should be very sorry indeed to lose that good feeling, and quite unjustifiably, because we have stuck pretty tight to the terms of the whole scheme. ... I hope you can put this right; and I'm sure, that if you play straight ahead through the management committees and council, you will get this thing going and in quite a big way.'[30]

Chapter 13
Ranche House College

On 21 July 1958 David Stirling completed and issued the 21-page brochure for the College of Citizenship, listing the many notable vice-presidents, convenors, trustees, sponsors and convenors of regional committees.[1] Jeannine Scott was to be the representative in London and David himself was chairman of the appeals committee and a trustee. An important section was the charter, which conveys the breadth of David's vision and his sense of language.

'Man's ability to achieve full stature as a human being in material and intellectual accomplishment depends much on the strength of his spirit; and the health and stature of a nation in its turn depends on how vigorous is the spirit of its people. The College of Rhodesian Citizenship exists primarily to serve and train the spirit of the individual, and thus play its part in the creation of a great nation. The college will seek to show that in our country people of different colour, religion and culture, and people from the countryside and from the towns can, by understanding their spiritual and material dependence on each other, achieve a sense of common national purpose. ... Only by encouraging the especial genius of each [race] will it become possible, through the influence of a shared patriotism, for the roots of our different heritages gradually to grow together to feed the tree of a greater national ideal. ... The college will teach that this concept of nationalism, compared with the narrow concepts of the last century, opens up a far greater range of freedom – a world free from the exclusiveness of race, tribe or culture, yet one which acknowledges the validity and distinctiveness of each as nourishing and not restricting factors in the wholeness of our country's being.'

The brochure also detailed the syllabus and development programme and noted that negotiations for a 50-acre site, about ten miles from Salisbury, were in hand. There was a budget and estimates of the cost of the expert consultant who would be required in stage two, although David had already taken the major decisions. Characteristically, he added 'the expert must accept absolutely the validity of the idea behind the college as presented in the charter.'

Kenneth Mew, the principal of the college from 1964 to 1982, was a passionate supporter of the project but was dispassionate in analysing its origins. In a thesis written in 1977, he wrote: 'Stirling's abounding optimism still enabled him to start the introduction to the college brochure with the words: "the Federation of Rhodesia and Nyasaland gives high promise of bringing happiness and prosperity to its peoples." Could this really be taken seriously? It was the year [1958] that the African National Congress had become established in Southern Rhodesia; the year that Prime Minister Garfield Todd was "forced out of office" for his "liberal" views. Within months severe repressive legislation had been introduced, and a state of emergency existed [in Southern Rhodesia and Nyasaland]. ... The brochure claimed that "the college will fail in its purpose" unless a high proportion of the students "become convinced salesmen of partnership and Rhodesian nationhood". Partnership had been suspect by Africans since pre-federation days; by 1952, African opposition to the federation had consolidated, and between 1956 and 1958, [the federation] was doomed.'[2]

Mew continued: 'At this stage the [Capricorn Africa] Society's influence [over the college] can hardly be over estimated. In every aspect of planning ... the Society had something specific to say. In a letter to Capricorn London in June 1958, Stirling stressed that the selection of the principal was of vital importance, "but his function will be to give service to the charter and not merely impose his own personality. ... If a candidate for the college principalship does not believe in this charter he will not get the job. If a principal, after appointment, does not do credit to the charter then he can be replaced." This was clearly a point upon which Stirling felt very strongly.' The first principal, J. M. Gibbs, thought that 'such a rigid agenda could not be reconciled with the notion of a college encouraging free enquiry and thought'.[3]

The grant from the two trusts for running costs over three years meant that the College of Rhodesian Citizenship Association could continue to negotiate over leasing part of the land owned by the Methodist mission at Epworth. This had the apparent advantage of being excluded from the restrictive land apportionment act, so that people of all races could meet there without breaking the law, but only while it remained owned by the mission.

The site had been offered through the influence of Fred Rea, a

Capricorn member and Salima veteran, who was keen to have the college at Epworth. There were delays because the lease could not be finalized until the association had legal articles, and then in August it was decided that the matter of the site should not be settled until the college had a principal. To create an impression of action, a public event was organized at Epworth with Robin Plunket and Lawrence Vambe going to the site to dig the first sod. Plunket, saying that he came from Ireland, carried the shovel while Vambe smoked and enquired when the Irish became civilized.[4]

Worries over the short lease and difficulties over water supply led to Epworth being abandoned. Although this meant delay in finding a permanent home, it was fortunate as the college depended heavily on volunteer and part-time staff, which would have been difficult at a distance from the city. Guy Hunter had written to the management committee urging that a less remote site than Epworth would be preferable, and setting out minimum requirements for the college buildings.[5] Gibbs and Leo Takawira thought 'volunteers and participants would flock to a self-build people's college,' but agreed that it would probably have been closed down by the Smith government.[6]

Basil Fletcher, vice-principal of the university, agreed to be chairman of the management committee, although he was concerned about the 'political' nature of the Capricorn connection. Fletcher, an able administrator with considerable experience in adult education, hoped for close involvement with the college but this became difficult when political tensions in the country affected academic life.[7] Edwin Townsend-Coles, who was teaching in the university Institute of Adult Education, offered the college help but firmly resisted making the college part of the university, fearing that when Southern Rhodesia took over responsibility for university education from the federation the college would lose its independence and possibly its very existence.[8] An unofficial link between the university and the college was maintained through Townsend-Coles's appointment as chairman of the college executive committee.

Fletcher, Rea and Plunket formed a selection panel that appointed John Michael Gibbs as the first principal. Born in the country, he had been to Oxford, had taught at St Paul's School in London and at the University of Cape Town. Gibbs started work on 1 January 1960 and in March wrote, bravely under the circumstances: 'For the time being the college is in two rooms of my home, 131 North Avenue. It is a humble beginning, but one which, given support and encouragement, can develop until it makes a really effective contribution to the growth of understanding in this country.'[9]

In his first newsletter, dated July 1960, Gibbs stressed: 'The [Capricorn Africa] Society made it clear that any college would be completely independent.' However, he wrote to Jeannine Scott about a proposed course at Umtali: 'It would be the first of many joint enterprises, with the college laying on the programme, and Capricorn doing most of the recruiting and all the hospitality.'[10] The college may have been legally autonomous, but in the early years Capricorn members on the management committee provided valuable support to the principal while also giving the Society a badly needed sense of purpose. Gibbs has written: 'the relationship between the college and Capricorn was one of mutual respect, good friendship and quite a lot of shared endeavour.'[11] The executive committee of the Society regularly debated the college's progress and problems; in April 1963, it was reported that current courses were run on 'sub-economic lines',[12] to which the Society responded with bursaries for three students. After the Southern Rhodesian branch of the Society was dissolved, Herbert and Victoria Chitepo, Plunket, Rea, Stanlake Samkange, Ndabaningi Sithole, Leo Takawira and other Capricorn members, or lapsed members, remained as governors or supporters of the college.

During 1960 Gibbs travelled to Northern Rhodesia with Takawira, Amon Jirira and Sithole to attend a conference and meet potential students and sponsors. Back in Salisbury he held courses in whatever accommodation could be borrowed or rented. The decision of the Beit trustees that they would not initially fund buildings proved to be a serious handicap. Running courses of any kind in two rooms in the principal's house and some offices in the Wonder Shopping Centre, Kingsway (now Julius Nyerere Way), was challenging.

Gibbs has written that the Wonder Shopping Centre 'was a truly cosmopolitan corner of Salisbury, full of surprise and paradox, owned by ... a supporter of the segregationist Dominion Party! Downstairs were teeming shops and blaring music coming from a multiracial cafe. Upstairs the college of citizenship had offices and a lecture room. Other offices were tenanted ... by Stanlake Samkange, later professor of African history at Harvard but at that time public relations for Rothmans and purveyor of free cigarettes and wonderful light relief, Josiah Chinamano, wisest of friends and colleagues, a doctor, an African herbalist with a mind-boggling collection of resources, and a couple of people whose front activity was selling insurance. Lectures were held either in the upstairs lecture room or on a few occasions ... in the concourse downstairs. ... I have vivid memories of some of these occasions, for example Herbert Chitepo lecturing to a rapt audience while a police informer struggled to make notes. It was the nearest we got to a people's college/WEA experience, and I often looked back on our time there from the respectability of Ranche House!'[13]

John Michael Gibbs, 2001

In December Gibbs wrote to the Beit and Dulverton trustees, drawing their attention to the dangers of continuing without premises and quoting a letter from Hunter to Lord Kilmaine in which he warned that starting without buildings would result in 'a loss of effect' and 'destroy its prospects'. Gibbs added he believed that that was what was happening. In addition to these difficulties, the principal had to spend much of his time negotiating with the authorities and trying to make the public aware of the college while political tensions in Africa were rising. The year 1960 had opened with Harold Macmillan's 'wind of change' speech in Cape Town; in April there were riots in Durban; in June the Belgian Congo became independent; in November Nigerians gained their independence and in January 1961 there was the Sharpeville massacre in South Africa. In February 1961 the principal reported to the executive committee that attendance at a shopkeepers' course was affected by the Salisbury riots, and that access to university buildings was barred. Late 1958, when the Hunters wrote their report, seemed very far away.

In November 1960 the chief justice of the federation, Sir Robert Tredgold resigned in protest at a repressive law and order bill, and had to leave his official residence, Ranche House, in Salisbury. Tredgold, a Capricorn supporter, encouraged the college to lease the house. In an early pioneer part of town there was ample space for additional buildings in five acres of wooded land. The house itself, built in 1895, stands on a low hill (a *kopje*) with a long flight of steps up from the parking area by the road. It is a classic single-storey colonial mansion under a corrugated iron roof, surrounded on three sides by a wide veranda with dressed stone columns, and a pediment over the entrance. After extended, Kafkaesque,[14] negotiations with government and the city council, a 30-year lease was agreed at a rent that was modest for a site close to the centre of Salisbury, although there were onerous maintenance clauses on the building and a restriction on 'becoming involved either directly or indirectly in party political activities in the future'.

Valuable, and free, legal advice was given to the college by Pat Lewis, Hardwicke Holderness's partner. After an amendment was passed to the Land Apportionment Act the Beit Trust agreed to provide one-third of £40,000 for development costs and £1000 annually for running expenses. In December 1961 Gibbs, who had been to Europe and East Africa to study similar institutions, reported with enthusiasm: 'The Beit Trust have offered a portion of the capital and income required for the Ranche House, with further generous grants offered by the British South Africa Company, Rhodesian Selection Trust and Anglo-American Corporation, and with the grant offered last year by Sir Stephen Courtauld, we are now in sight of achieving stage one of the building plan.'[15]

Gibbs continued: 'we have the added difficulty of persuading people that there is value in a residential college whose purpose is not to give direct help to people aiming to complete their formal education or to get paper qualifications. It was therefore immensely encouraging to find on my tour that we are pioneering here something that is becoming established elsewhere in Africa and is highly developed in Germany, Denmark and Britain. Kivukoni College in Dar es Salaam, started this year, is awakening a group of Tanganyikan students to the hard economic and administrative challenges of "Freedom".' Townsend-Coles, who sat in on a course there, has said 'that Kivukoni was a government-led college teaching people to adhere to a particular political ideology [and] woe betide any student who deviated from the official line'.[16]

Julius Nyerere's achievement in spreading his concept of 'African socialism' over Tanganyika, as that large country was then, demonstrates Kivukoni's success. Gibbs continued: 'The College of Social Studies in Kenya, inspired originally like ours by the Capricorn Africa Society ... has already gained popular support among

Africans. ... In Scandinavia attendance at one of the people's high schools is considered a normal complement to the formal education given in school, and the [folk] high schools have played an inestimable part in giving people a true sense of values, independence of mind and a resistance to mass attitudes and cultural inertia.'

With the capital sum a dormitory, lecture hall, dining room and staff housing were built. Gibbs was fortunate to find a sympathetic architect, Erhard Lorenz who, being Danish, was familiar with the folk high school tradition, in which aesthetics plays an important part, and was enthusiastic about local crafts. Ranche House College moved into its permanent home on 7 May 1962. During the previous year the committee discussed a name for the college and met with the same concerns as we did in Kenya. Gibbs wrote to Jonathan Lewis in London: 'It was perfectly clear from what the African members on the board said that although they have considerable hopes of what the college will achieve, they feel that the word "citizenship", which as you know is highly emotive in these parts, should not be included in the title.'[17]

There was also some sensitivity over the settler style and name 'Ranche House', which was thought to be less relevant to local people than self-help buildings out of town might have been, but in the end that was the name adopted. In independent Zimbabwe the notepaper is now headed 'COLLEGES OF CITIZENSHIP ASSOCIATION — RANCHE HOUSE COLLEGE' and the current principal confirms that David's 1959 charter continues to be valid and relevant.

When Gibbs was the principal the objective was to encourage the spirit of the individual in a non-racial context while providing vocational or academic teaching. The 1962 brochure listed the main headings of the courses offered as 'The principles and purpose of government, including the nature of democracy; economic factors in national development, including industrial relations and the human factor; human relationships, including personal, social and community problems in a changing society and lastly, clear thinking, speaking and writing, including discovering the difference between fact and opinion.'[18] At the time the ruling party in government and the majority of the white population in the country regarded discussing these ideas in a mixed race group as dangerously subversive particularly when students were sharing unsegregated accommodation.

In the first year at Ranche House, there was a variety of courses, including those on community development and on adult education run by the university and held at the college. For the principal there was an enormous amount of work to be done on the grounds and the new buildings, as well as organizing courses, volunteers and students, with limited staff, academic or domestic. He had been guiding the college on lines that were becoming increasingly unpopular in the country; Takawira and other friends had been arrested and for Gibbs himself there was the threat of conscription into the army to fight a war he was unable to support. In April 1963 there was a crisis when the incessant pressure led to a breakdown in Gibbs's health (he has said that he snapped),[19] which forced him to take his accumulated leave and go to South Africa with his family.

The US Agency for International Development came to the rescue, seconding Colonel H. G. Pardey for five months to hold the fort, although his experience of education was limited. During this fraught period, the locally appointed economics tutor, Edward Ndoro, was a key figure in keeping courses going. Before he left, Pardey, whose field was economic development, sent a report to the executive committee setting out his views on the future role of the college. He wrote that the majority of Africans in Rhodesia had rejected the multiracial approach, believing it to be a device to delay their advance, while the white minority had abandoned any semblance of a non-racial outlook, adding that the gap between the races had widened to such an extent that 'it was not now possible to present a unified idea of nationhood'.[20] He suggested that what he called the 'non-functional' values offered by the college would be of interest to the African majority only when they had 'political emancipation' so that the only practical purpose for the college was to provide 'functional knowledge'.

Pardey's approach was different from the Capricorn-inspired programme initiated by Gibbs, but by the end of 1963 Kenya, Uganda and Tanganyika were independent African republics, Northern Rhodesia and Nyasaland about to join the club, and the atmosphere in Southern Rhodesia hardening, so his proposals had to be considered in the political context of the time.

In August Gibbs returned from his leave, intending to continue as principal, but it was clear that his health made this impossible and he resigned, leaving the country to return to teaching in England. When he left he hoped that there would soon be more African staff and perhaps a principal, but it was more than 20 years before Miss Ramushu was appointed. The Anglo-American Corporation seconded a training officer from Kitwe, Hilary Currey, to act as principal until Kenneth Mew was appointed in January

1964. Mew was a Methodist lay preacher, nearly 50, described by Peter Garlake as hyperactive with a quick, alert mind and inspirational in the pulpit.[21] After war service he worked for ICI in South Africa and Northern Rhodesia before moving to Salisbury, where he joined Capricorn and became a powerful writer of letters to the editor and speaker on the need for greater understanding between the races. Throughout his 18 years as principal of the college he continued to criticize the right-wing policies of the government in speeches and articles in the press. After his appointment he enrolled as a part-time student in the university faculty of adult education, which included writing a thesis using Ranche House College as a case study.[22] In his thesis Mew was vague on the impact the colonel's report made on the college executive committee with its strong Capricorn membership. He refers to an executive meeting of the Society at the time of the report, which recorded that there was a tendency for the college to function as a centre for 'technical courses attractive to Africans' and that 'African-European contacts were not as strong as had been hoped'.[23] In 1964 the student body was 85 per cent African, 12 per cent European and 3 per cent Asian with generally similar ratios in the following year.

While Pardey was in charge a memo noted that the programme had changed 'from enrichment with training to training with enrichment'.[24] The debate over vocational or liberal adult education programmes is a classic, occurring in many staff common rooms and was also an issue in Kenya. At Ranche House the recognition that adult education was about giving people skills they had previously been denied was made easier because by this time David was in London setting up television stations in developing countries as another form of adult education. A policy document was formulated that accepted that the courses would be functional, recognizing, and hoping, that in a residential college 'partnership' would rub off on the students as they shared accommodation and facilities. For African students it was their only chance of learning skills and being able to indulge in open discussion of the wider issues of the day.

In 1965 Mew went to Britain, Germany, Denmark and Sweden hoping to persuade donors to support Ranche House. He visited similar colleges – following in Gibbs's footsteps – but at a gallop, going to 19 different institutions and seeing 28 trusts and individuals in the month he was away.[25] Financially, the trip was not a success: Ian Smith's government was about to declare UDI, which he did in November 1965, so most organizations refused to offer help for any institution in Southern Rhodesia, however worthy. Although running costs continued to be difficult to find, the college prospered in capital terms because after UDI local sources of funds — Anglo-American, RST, the Beit Trust, and Sir Stephen Courtauld — being unable to remit cash overseas were more generous locally. Between 1963 and 1970 a language laboratory was built and equipped, with a library and a nondenominational chapel. Friends of Gibbs's father, lately Dean of Chester, started a fund to buy building materials for the chapel, which was built by Ephraim Mukasa, a trainee minister at Rea's mission at Epworth. While Mew was principal there was a short voluntary service in the chapel every morning (it was full of desks and typewriters in February 2000).

Kenneth Mew, 1995 (photo: K. Mew)

The college was always hampered by financial stringency: it was some years before students were sponsored by their employers, and in 1966 the annual grant from the government of £500 a year was withdrawn, although one further payment was made the following year.

In some ways the need for extreme economy was a blessing, as it sometimes is: the life of the college was enriched by a number of devoted volunteers from the university, government offices and commerce who taught there, sometimes for years. During 1966, 14 people from different professions gave two or three evenings a week to the college without payment, teaching languages and O or A level subjects. Mew recorded with justifiable pride that Ranche House was the only educational institution in Rhodesia where British Voluntary Service Overseas members were on the staff — from 1963 to 1976 five VSO members brought enthusiasm and optimism, as they did in so many places in Africa and elsewhere. The other consequence of financial stringency was that the permanent staff, working for long hours on low pay, had to be dedicated to stay, and stay many of them did. Mew wrote that four of the senior staff who joined in 1967 or earlier, were still there in 1977, when he wrote his thesis.

The political situation deepened the dilemma over the syllabus, as it was realized that education for citizenship was futile for Africans with no opportunity of practising it, nor was it relevant for those whose main concern was trying to make a living in a hostile climate. In 1966 white Rhodesian Front politicians, hostile to any multiracial activity or any possible breach in the land apportionment act, attempted to persuade government to close down the college. Two sympathetic officials warned of the danger, which was averted, but the incident illustrates the difficulties under which the principal and staff worked. The college newsletter had to be passed by the censor, as government tightened controls over the media and all publications in the country.[26]

The 1966 programme listed courses in shorthand, typing and book-keeping, librarianship, training for bank staff, languages for cadet district commissioners, art, child welfare, trade unions, business, and GCE, A and O level subjects. The reluctant acceptance that the political situation in Southern Rhodesia militated against David's vision ensured that the college survived through the often-violent changes in the country. It continued to provide essential training to thousands of Rhodesians while the federation collapsed, independence was unilaterally declared by the white minority and a civil war was fought and won by the majority.

From 1972 the schedule of courses indicates the vocational nature of the curriculum. 'Residential courses from a few days to three months duration for businessmen, trade union leaders, nursing sisters, church leaders, teachers, school matrons, and missionaries (for intensive language study).'[27] Non-residential full-time courses included dressmaking, shorthand and typing with some intensive language training for army and police officers. There were also part-time day and evening classes in Shona and English, O level English and A level history, geography, English, mathematics and accountancy. The college became a centre for meetings, workshops and seminars, especially for multiracial activities. The intention was to give Africans a chance to make up what they had missed through lack of opportunities when they were younger.

In spite of many difficulties, external and internal, the numbers of students passing through the college is impressive: 400, including 230 residential students, in 1963 rose to 2300 (1061 residential) in 1968. By 1976 the total was 4680, with only 409 residential students, which meant the numbers sharing accommodation and learning to understand one another was declining. In 1977 Mew recorded that over 2000 Africans and about the same number of Europeans used the college every year, and wrote: 'At no time were any attempts made to "mix" courses or to manipulate groups to provide racial diversity.'

Mew concluded that Ranche House justified the hopes of the founders and ended his thesis with the following statement. 'One of the paramount objectives of adult education is to reduce the tensions caused by change, and although in the social and political context in which [the college] functioned it may be more accurate to say that the tensions were the consequence of lack of change, it neither reduces nor simplifies the task. ... [I have] tried to assess the extent to which it succeeded in a primary objective of improving race relations. [There was] a continuous link between the Capricorn Society and the college based on a fundamental belief in the nature of man. [It] was, therefore, essentially religious in character, and it is suggested that ... the acceptance of the college [by Africans] related to the religious nature of the African nationalist movement. It is, perhaps, the only explanation for the fact that [it] survived, and continues to grow in almost all measurable ways, despite obvious inadequacies in its organization and weaknesses in administration.' Mew hoped that bringing individuals together for practical, and very useful, courses would lead to greater understanding. It may have done, but analysing the realities and restrictions of everyday life in a tutorial on political philosophy would have been more effective. It would also have had the college closed down.

In his thesis Mew paid tribute to the governors, nine of whom served for ten years or more. By 1965 the African nationalists on the board in the early days, Chinamano, Shamuyarira and Sithole, were in gaol or exile and there was a majority of European governors, some of whom had been Capricorn members. Many, both African and European, were people of influence, and it was through their contacts that the college became the venue for significant meetings, some unofficial and some between government bodies, during the period of illegal independence from 1965 to 1979. Ranche House was the one place in the country where government and guerrilla leaders could meet on neutral ground without publicity although it was also a magnet for visiting press. It is a tribute to Mew that both sides continued to believe that their confidential discussions at the college would remain so. Mew has written that the visitors' book lists every senior diplomat in Salisbury; every visiting official from the UK Foreign Office, with visits by members of the Smith government and African nationalist leaders including Robert Mugabe, Chinamano, Sithole, Abel Muzorewa, Mike Mawema and Joshua Nkomo, a few of whom were frequent visitors.[28]

The media included *The Times*, *Telegraph*, *Express*, *Observer*, *US News*, *Newsweek*, *New York Times*, *Wall Street Journal*, *Le Soir*, *Libre Belgique*, *Die Welt*, CBS, Radio France, BBC, Reuters, FBC Finland, and others. There were visits from the universities of Cape Town, Witwatersrand, Berlin, Uppsala, LSE, Oxford, Yale, Dundee, Leicester, Israel, Botswana, Australian National, Malawi, St Paul's Minnesota and Cornell. Many trade union leaders of international organizations such as ICFTU (for whom the college ran some courses), paid visits. The AFL-CIO of the USA held a conference at Ranche House and the heads of local unions were frequent callers. Mew added that for many months the British Council and Canadian CIDA had their headquarters at the college.

The fact that the college could continue throughout the period of white domination and subsequent turmoil was in large part due to Mew's pragmatism. He loudly and often expressed his concern for the oppressed majority but he also recognized that minorities must have a future in the country. He could be critical of emerging African governments as well as white domination in South Africa and Southern Rhodesia. At the time of the 1972 Pearce Commission, which was based at the college and to which he gave evidence, he said. 'One would accept external criticisms more readily if they came from countries with stable governments, progressive economies, and at least freedom of speech and political beliefs,'[29] adding that stability and democracy were not characteristics of the new Africa. Some of the conversations in his office at the college, or in the principal's house, helped to bring about the eventual accord between the Smith government and the African nationalists. It is an aspect of the college that David could not have foreseen when he proposed adult education as the way forward, but he would have been proud of its contribution to peace as well as to education. The *Rhodesia Herald*, not known for its liberal opinions, published an article by John Kelly, which said: 'Ranche House College is a crossroads of non-racialism, an open gate for anyone to change his life. ... It has an overriding idealism, which makes it different from other adult education centres in Rhodesia. ... People discover the value of better human relationships.'[30]

Mew left in 1982, having served for 18 years. There were two principals over the next four years until the appointment in 1986 of Kate Ramushu, who has continued until the present time.

Writing to the author in November 1998, she confirmed that the college ethos has changed little since its formation 40 years earlier. 'As you are aware, the country has experienced changes since the Capricorn Africa Society period. Pre- and post-independence activities have also brought about a shift in some programme areas, necessitated mainly by the political, economic and social environment Ranche House College operates in. However, the original aims behind the founding of the institution remain our guiding principle. These are summarized under the charter of the Colleges of Citizenship Association (1959), which states that "The College of Citizenship exists primarily to serve and train the spirit of the individual and thus enable it to play its part in the creation of a great nation." The college does not receive any financial support from the government. Fees paid by students comprise the bulk of the income, while donors occasionally come in to support specific projects, which have a time frame in terms of funding. ... Most of our students (about 90 per cent) are black Zimbabweans ... seeking skills training in various areas such as the secretarial field, tourism, business studies, systems analysis, computer programming and clothing technology. The remaining 20 per cent is comprised of students from the southern Africa region, white Zimbabweans and staff of some overseas embassies in Zimbabwe studying languages such as English, Portuguese, Shona and Ndebele.'[31]

Gibbs, Mew and the original governors would recognize the same institution they started many years ago from that letter and the accompanying mission statement. From the beginning David had difficulties with the functional programme as it developed, but he would have understood that his concept of the importance of adult education in creating a nation survives.

Chapter 14
The College of Social Studies

By early May 1959 the college in Kenya had a board of governors charged with taking over development from the management committee of the Kenya College of Citizenship Association. All the first governors were very much part of the establishment except for two, Susan Wood and John Porter. The establishment figures were the first chairman, R. E. Anderson, OBE, a Nairobi accountant; the Honourable Kirpal Singh Sagoo, MLC (member of Legislative Council), large and genial with an immaculate white turban and a long straggly beard, a stalwart of the United Kenya Club and father to the Sikh community; Sir Donald MacGillivray, GCMG, MBE; W J. D. Wadley, CMG, a retired Kenya government director of education and the Honourable P. J. Rogers, CBE, MLC.

The first meeting appointed an African governor, the Honourable Musa Amalemba, MLC, stout, modest, quiet and always smiling. Amalemba, like the African Capricorn members came from western Kenya, and was by no means a radical in politics, so after independence he was sidelined to doing good works. A second African was appointed to the board in 1960: the Honourable Jeremiah Nyagah, MLC, a teacher who had been to Makerere University and had a diploma from Oxford. Nyagah remained a governor for many years, and was later a senior minister in the government of independent Kenya.

Of the two who were not Honourables (members of Legislative Council) or been decorated, it was Susan Wood who fought hardest to maintain Capricorn's idea of a multiracial citizenship college, and to press for action in the face of lethargy as the months went by and the political climate changed. The other members of the board, from various perspectives, were wary of Capricorn and what they thought it meant, so there was much time wasted in resisting what the establishment believed to be a campaign by Capricorn to take over the college, in spite of the Society's oft declared intention that it would be independent.

Relations started well, Wadley wrote to Martin Capon, enclosing the first minutes of the board of governors with expressions of appreciation for all that had been done.[1] The minutes he forwarded record: 'it was agreed that the time had come for the Association formally to ask the board of governors to take over the management of the first college. It was noted that it was of vital importance that the most friendly relations should exist between the board and the association, and that the association should increase interest in the project and raise funds locally, but that applications for funds overseas would be made by the board which would consult the management committee of the association for its advice and support.'[2]

It was generally accepted in the debates about the wording of the charter that Dulverton had agreed to support the college on the basis of Guy Hunter's report. In the summary of his conclusions Hunter wrote: 'There is a real need for multiracial adult education. In particular, the African in responsible work must feel accepted as a colleague; the Asian needs more and deeper contact with Western thought; the European needs to recognize the quality of emerging African and Asian society. A multiracial college would be acceptable both in east and central Africa, though some objections would be raised in the federation.'

In July 1959 the Association of the College of Citizenship Corporation of Kenya (which became the legal owner of the college) published its formal memorandum. In none of these documents did the dreaded word 'Capricorn' appear, while the theme of common citizenship among people of different races appears in all, and yet the establishment figures, egged on by Lord Kilmaine from the Dulverton Trust office in London, continued to see a conspiracy by Capricorn to overthrow the board and take control of the college. It is true that we were suspicious of the motives of businessmen who had consistently opposed our attempts to break down the barriers between the races and we were concerned about the lack of progress.

The governors had been doing something, however, even if it was not what Capricorn expected: in the files there is a memo marked SECRET from Rogers, which reads. 'Honorarium for chairman — 700 gns. But probably preferable part of this (say £12 a month) as transport allowance — tax. Period of honorarium would be until the principal is in the saddle, which might be as much as a year, or even more.'[3] Fortunately, Capricorn members knew nothing of this, as we all worked voluntarily and would not have been amused by the proposal that the chairman of East African Tobacco, who had a chauffeur-driven company car, should be paid what he delicately called an honorarium, arranged to minimize his income tax (the college principal's salary was to be £2250). It appears from the minutes that this wheeze was approved.

The second half of 1959 and all of 1960 were difficult times for Capricorn in Kenya as our African members drifted away, so we were especially sensitive to any suggestion that a positive achievement was being taken away from us. In an unsigned memo from Michael Wood to Capon he tried to salvage a line of authority over the board from the 1958 conference, which indubitably was a Capricorn event. This document, although it did not specifically mention the Society, created a reaction in the establishment.[4] Kilmaine wrote to Wadley: 'I am glad to know that you find Capon personally reasonable, but note the difficulties you anticipate with certain other members of the old committee. I may say that every sort of attempt has been made by members of the Capricorn Society in this country to persuade Lord Dulverton ... to modify in favour of the Society the terms he made about the control of the college when he was in Kenya. Lord Dulverton has resisted all these attacks with the utmost firmness, and I know would wish you to do the same in resisting local pressure out there. I think you will inevitably, in the end, have to face some sort of showdown, but we know we can rely on you to do some "plain-speaking" when the time comes!'[5]

The plain speaking being used in London and Nairobi tended to stoke the fire and achieve little. Capricorn's main worry, as the months passed, was to make some progress over appointing a principal, finding a site and building the college. However, Wadley and Kilmaine continued to excite one another, and it seems that I was causing trouble. Rogers wrote to MacGillivray: 'I shall give credit to Capricorn for what they have done, but insist on the complete independence of the Association. I realize that this will make me unpopular with the hard-core Capricorners, but I think it has to be done so that the situation may be clarified and the public know that the project is to be carried through independently of Capricorn. I was all the more convinced of the need for a showdown by the conduct last Friday of Mrs Wood and Hughes who both attacked me most violently on this very question of the charter. There is no doubt that Capricorn want to keep a firm hold on this thing — a view which is confirmed by Lord Kilmaine.'[6]

Wadley took a little longer to describe the attack, writing to

Kilmaine in August: 'The situation *vis-à-vis* Capricorn, which I had previously told you was somewhat uneasy, came to a head at the last meeting of the management committee when Richard Hughes, the local Capricorn chairman, attacked me violently over the board's attitude in regard to the charter saying that he felt they (that is Capricorn, I presume) had been betrayed. I managed to preserve reasonable calm at the time, but it was clear to me that the time had come for a showdown and I therefore wrote to Capon, the chairman, saying that I could not possibly accept Hughes's arguments.'[7]

Kilmaine then started to use threats: 'We are very much concerned at the continuing hostile attitude of the Capricorn Society as described by you, and particularly by the attack made upon you by Mr Hughes. We also hope that you will be able to tell us that the Capricornists are prepared to drop all insistence of the incorporation of the full charter in the constitution of the college, all attempts to criticize and impede the governors in their work, and all insistence on behaving as if the Capricorn Society had a priorital right in the college. If you're not shortly able to give us these assurances and that the governors are going to have complete freedom of action ... the Dulverton trustees will have no hesitation in withdrawing all their proffered financial support to the governing body as now constituted, and will offer it instead to the reconstituted governing body purged of members connected with the Capricorn Society, the association and any other body in any way connected with the Capricorn Africa Society. The trustees are prepared to take this action and to inform the Capricorn Society of the reasons for it at any time that you may notify us that the situation is such that no other course is possible to ensure the early inauguration of the College with the complete freedom and independence which you consider essential. They are not prepared any longer to tolerate the efforts of the Capricorn Society to sabotage the project. If the Society is not prepared loyally to carry out the agreed scheme, then the trustees and those upon whose loyalty they can rely, will go forward with it without the Capricorn Society. If, in the meantime, you feel that at any time the judicious revelation of your knowledge that this is the trustees' intention would help to bring the Capricornists to heel, you are at liberty to repeat it at your discretion.'[8]

The situation was getting out of hand, though whether Kilmaine was writing on instructions from the Dulverton trustees is doubtful, as they met only once a quarter. In Wadley's absence,

Anderson replied in reasonable tones, hoping to cool things down: 'I am most grateful for your letter of 14 August. With regard to the Capricorn Society, I am not unduly pessimistic. I am of the opinion that the clearing of the air, to which I referred to in my letter of 8 August has had its effect, and I hope and think that we shall be able to steer our way safely through these early stages without resorting to the disruption of the present board which would be unfortunate. ... It is worth while, I think, going to considerable trouble over this for we need as much goodwill as possible and do not want to run the risk of alienating those who, whatever their faults may be, are genuinely behind the college.'[9]

This correspondence crossed with a letter from Wood, writing as president of the Capricorn Africa Society, to Dulverton, which must have been painful to write but should have settled the matter: 'I want to make one point absolutely clear and that is that I shall circulate the membership of the Capricorn Africa Society to say that in future no reference to Capricorn must be made in connection with the colleges. I told you that I would do this when I spoke to you on the telephone from London and I assure you that I will keep my word. Naturally as individuals we will do everything we can to get support for the venture through the Association but from the point of view of the Society itself we will fade out and I am sure the project will be enormously successful.'[10]

The dispute between the governors and Capricorn rumbled on for some time with a secret letter from Rogers, writing from London, to Wadley about Susan Wood and her 'attitude', adding: 'Lord Dulverton and I are firmly of the view that Capricorn should be kept completely out of it and I think we are all agreed on this point although it would, of course, have to be diplomatically handled.'[11] This letter followed a meeting at the Dulverton Trust, which had been called because Hunter was disturbed at the slow progress.

In September 1959 I wrote to him, with a copy to Jonathan Lewis: 'Your frustration echoes my own precisely. I have been waiting to hear from Wadley what their intentions are for some months now, particularly since your successful [meeting] with Dulverton, Rogers & Co. I have to tread so delicately to avoid scaring them into thinking that the beastly Capricorn Society is trying to take over. However, I'm going to have another try, as the Aga Khan is now out here and I have been discussing with Michael Curtis, his personal adviser, how one could get him interested in it and [Curtis] has asked for a brief memo on the scheme to present to the Aga Khan before we discuss it. When one thinks that within less than 12 months of the Education for Nationhood Conference you and Lou had been all over east and central Africa, written your report, [we had] got £20,000 out of Dulverton and were all set to go, and compares that pace with the last six months, in which nothing constructive appears to have been done at all by the governors ... then one really despairs.'[12]

The same day I wrote to Wadley stressing the need for urgent action and asking innocently about the advertisement for the principal, which in fact had not yet been published: 'I am eagerly awaiting news of whether you have considered it possible for Guy Hunter to come out to Kenya to get the colleges started in advance of the principal. ... The situation in Kenya seems to be building up with such intensity and speed that I feel that every day lost is serious and will make it more difficult to get the college started in the right atmosphere when it does open.'[13] Eventually, in November 1959, the advertisement appeared in English papers, resulting in 257 applications being sent to Hunter at the Royal Commonwealth Society. A strong candidate was Ronald Wraithe, who had taught at Makerere College in Uganda, and whose book *East African Citizen* had been bought and circulated widely in Kenya by Capricorn.[14] He turned the job down and Harold Wiltshire was warmly recommended by Hunter. Wiltshire, seconded from the extra-mural department of Nottingham University, had considerable experience of adult education with the anti-colonial prejudices of a left-wing academic. Another six vital months passed before the new principal could make an exploratory visit to Nairobi.

By March 1960 Susan Wood was writing to Lewis in London, venting her frustration and expressing some naive hopes about the new principal, Wiltshire. 'At our last board meeting with MacGillivray I made a special plea for getting on with the job with maximum energy, and that courses should be run at intervals from January 1960 onwards. At the time he seemed wholeheartedly to agree with this. ... Richard was present and we were able to discuss plans for the building in a certain amount of detail. It is tragic that Wiltshire will not be here until May. We shall try to fill the gap by suggesting to Richard that Capricorn runs some courses meanwhile. David has just been through and his account of the Rhodesian college has emphasized to me once more how much we need Wiltshire at once to take control, expedite the thing and see it through. Between you and me I am greatly afraid that with the additional members they are trying to put on the board that the college runs a pretty good risk of not being in the Capricorn image unless Wiltshire can be made a built-in Capricorn man.'[15]

In May 1960 Wiltshire arrived in Nairobi for a fortnight and spoke at a small conference. His official programme, prepared by Rogers's office, made no mention of any meeting with Capricorn members, although there was some free time allowed, during part of which he had dinner at the Woods' house, where we met him. I cannot remember whether he then expressed any of the views he later put into his report. I thought he was a typical Englishman – pipe-smoking, white hair, horn-rimmed glasses, the slight stoop of an academic and a wine buff. I discovered later that he was also a male chauvinist, which did not help his relationship with Susan Wood, whom Wiltshire regarded, quite wrongly, as a white Lady Bountiful dispensing tea and sympathy to the blacks. He later described Capricorn's educational policies as no more than 'multiracial tea parties', which was one thing we never held. Wiltshire appeared to get on well with me, perhaps because he had seen my buildings illustrated in the magazine *Architectural Review*. He wrote to me from Nottingham congratulating me and asking if he could have the same large windows in the principal's house at the college that he had seen in ours.[16]

On his return to Nottingham Wiltshire submitted a report to the Dulverton Trust that established the future direction of the college. 'The Capricorn association must I am afraid be expunged as quickly and completely as possible. I had not realized how strong the objection was, not only among European businessmen (who tend to regard Capricorn supporters as impractical visionaries) but also among African leaders (who would certainly boycott the college if it remained, or seemed to remain, under Capricorn auspices). I discussed this whole matter very fully and frankly with some leading members of the Capricorn Africa Society in Kenya, and I think that they did in the end agree that their own purpose of fostering interracial understanding and cooperation might in practice be better served by an independent academic institution than by a college working under Capricorn direction and preaching Capricorn doctrines. The words "multiracial" and "citizenship" should also disappear from the title and description of the college. I am persuaded that to African ears "college of citizenship" must sound very much like college of obedience or college of good behaviour; any institution with such a name, sponsored and financed by Europeans, must suggest an attempt to impose upon Africans those concepts of citizenship which are convenient to the

European minority. The term multiracial, too, must in this context imply a last ditch attempt to retain some shreds of privilege for European (and Asian) minorities – unless it means non-racial.'[17] He added, disingenuously, because his experience of local conditions was so limited: 'But if it means non-racial it means something so obvious that it need not be stated, [namely] that in considering entry to an academic institution race is as irrelevant as stature.'

After some debate the name College of Social Studies was agreed by the governors as being accurate and non-political. Wiltshire's report continued: 'I cannot state too strongly my conviction of the importance of securing the confidence and support of African leaders. Without this the college cannot have any future; with it, it may. All the associations of the college were from this point of view unfavourable and it was a great disappointment (though not wholly a surprise) when Dr Kiano [MLC, a senior Kikuyu academic and minister for commerce and industry in the Kenya government] ... wrote to say that that he would not be able to give his support to the project. Towards the end of my stay I had a long talk with Dr Kiano and I found [him] much concerned about the Capricorn and citizenship associations and generally doubtful of the academic bona fides of the college. At this stage of political events it must in any case be difficult for any African leader to give political support to any such project, but I did, I think, convince them that I should not be concerned with the college if it were to do anything other than a straight job of teaching in the social studies. I think that there is now a reasonable chance that there will be at any rate no African opposition to the college and that it may be given time to prove itself and gain African support.'

Hunter, writing to the Capricorn London office about the report said: 'Very good of you to send me Wiltshire's report. I know it must have struck you a painful blow. It is, all the same, a first rate document isn't it? Clear, frank, practical; I feel there's a really good man on this now & I can die in peace.'[18] The overriding factor, aside from Wiltshire's background and antipathy to a 'settler-dominated' country, was that the political situation had altered out of all recognition in the two years since the Education for Nationhood Conference. In January and February 1960 Kenya politicians of all races and degrees of radicalism had been to a conference at Lancaster House in London to establish a timetable to independence much swifter than the most optimistic African politicians expected.

I can find no record of any reaction in the Kenya branch of Capricorn to Wiltshire's report; at the time the Woods were moving to their farm at Ol Molog in Tanganyika where Susan was occupied being a farmer, while those of us in the 'realist tendency' probably, and reluctantly, accepted it as true. Kenneth Mew, in his thesis on the Rhodesian college, thought that Wiltshire exaggerated the danger of a Capricorn association with the college, writing that the Society was of little consequence by that time.[19]

Kilmaine added to the febrile suspicions about Capricorn in July 1960 by announcing at a meeting at the Dulverton Trust, attended by Wiltshire and Rogers, that he had received a report from Fletcher of a meeting in Salisbury, addressed by David Stirling, who was alleged to have said that the members of the College of Kenya Citizenship Association had decided to disassociate themselves from the governors and to embark on setting up a rival college. After this exciting news was flashed to Nairobi, Anderson discussed it with Wood, then president of the Society, and wrote to reassure Kilmaine: 'Michael Wood ... is completely shocked at the statement reported to have been made by David Stirling in Salisbury. He cannot credit such a statement, and gives his assurance that the Capricorn Society in East Africa would never set up a rival college to ours.'[20] If David really had made a wild statement about Kenya, it would not have been the first time he was guilty of exaggeration, and he was becoming fractious and anxious about the lack of progress in Kenya.

The contrast between the awkward situation in Kenya and the easy relationship between Capricorn and Ranche House College is marked. In Kenya we had businessmen and middle of the road politicians as governors with a principal from an English adult education background, while in Salisbury the governors were African nationalists, local academics and Capricorn members. Equally relevant was the fact that the first, indeed all, the principals in Rhodesia were recruited locally and were sympathetic to the Capricorn philosophy, even if they thought that it did not go far enough.

Early in 1960 a site at Kikuyu, about 20 miles from Nairobi, on land owned by the Church of Scotland mission was leased to the college through Susan Wood's contacts. It was thought ideal: not too far from the city, but not close enough for students to wander off in the evening. The continued success of Ranche House College, a few minutes walk from the centre of Salisbury (Harare) has proved this idea irrelevant. The governors were rather alarmed when they learnt that the mission authorities had inserted in the lease bans on the public consumption of alcohol and on European style ballroom dancing. The large area of land at Kikuyu granted to the mission early in the century was an educational centre with the two leading schools in Kenya for girls and for boys — the African Girl's High School, of which Susan Wood was a governor, and the Alliance High School. I knew and admired the heads of both schools, Mary Bruce and Carey Francis, and designed numerous buildings for both schools, including a small chapel for the girls' school which was later illustrated in a book on churches.[21] In March the governors appointed me to be the architect for the college. Dulverton came to Kenya in July that year and was at a meeting of the governors when I presented the tenders, recommending the lowest, which the board accepted. After furnishing and settling in, the college opened in June 1961, with 24 students.

The building materials were few and simple: white painted exposed concrete blocks with corrugated asbestos roofs generally and a twisted hyperbolic timber roof over the dining hall. A courtyard was enclosed on three sides by the two-storey bedroom block, dining hall and teaching wing. The entrance gates were the only extravagance: made of welded steel rods they were three-dimensional and triangular in plan, with a cast aluminium plaque bearing the letters CSS suspended within the structure. At an altitude of nearly 7000 feet (2000 metres) the air was crisp and fresh and the springy Kikuyu grass in the courtyard, seen through the gates, was always green.

Wiltshire liked the college building, writing later: 'An important part of our teaching was done for us, tacitly, by the building in which we worked and the organization of life within it. Our building was neither costly nor elaborate. But it was elegant, beautifully sited, well equipped and new; everyone who worked in it (and I include, of course, the domestic staff) was proud of it so that it was well cared for, orderly and ran like clockwork. Students unconsciously respond to such an environment. As a result, the prophesies of old Kenya hands were confounded. We had been told that our white paint would be dirtied, our light furniture broken, our modern cutlery pocketed, our open library pillaged, and that we could not expect punctuality or strict adherence to the timetable. None of these things happened: in over a year nothing was spoilt, one ill-made chair was broken, and unpunctuality was most unusual, work was handed in on time, we lost one spoon and two books. It was to a very great extent the influence of the building and of a plan of study and domestic routine which were set out in detail and adhered to without fuss.'[22]

Wiltshire had taken over as principal on 1 October 1960 and began to form the college in his own image, writing later: 'I was wholly free to plan the work of the college as I thought fit and to decide what should be taught, how it should be taught and who should teach it.'[23] He decided that the methods that he used at Nottingham were generally suitable to the new situation, although he recognized that the teaching of social sciences had to be related

Architect's sketch of the College of Social Studies, Kikuyu, Kenya

to the adult experiences of the students, which, for newly enfranchised Kenyans would be different, if only in degree, to his students in the English Midlands. He wrote: 'Any people undergoing a process of economic, political and social change must learn to understand and control it as well as to suffer it.'[24]

The subjects listed in the brochure were: economics — resources, material and human; processes and institutions; wages and prices; relations between worker, employer and government and problems of growth in an underdeveloped economy. Government — development and present patterns of government; administration and social services; nature and institutions of democracy; functions of political parties; government and the law. Social psychology — stresses of social change; groups and individual behaviour; formation of public opinion; nature of prejudice; intergroup relations; problems of racial and tribal relations in a mixed community; the making of a nation. And as part of other courses, communication — uses and abuses of language, clear expression; logic, argument, rhetoric and propaganda.

Wiltshire continued: 'The students raised other issues such as land use, party organization, and communism — which were also incorporated. We had always to try to base our teaching on real East African problems and to help our students analyse these with the tools of the economist, the political theorist or the sociologist. ... We were trying to help men and women ... to see problems more clearly, realize their interconnections and think straight about them. We could not say "we will consider the economics of this but we will not consider its political aspects or its social implications." We had no choice but to do all three together.'

Wiltshire believed that it was not possible or desirable to select students on the basis of racial origin — a subject that continued to be a matter of dispute with the governors. In the month the college opened the governors recorded: 'It was unanimously agreed that every endeavour should be made to have not less than two Europeans and/or Asians on each course.'[25] After some months Rogers, the chairman, wrote to the principal: 'The governors have said at meeting after meeting that we must establish the fact that the college is for all races. Furthermore, I have repeatedly offered my help to find some Europeans, and indeed, have firmly promised some from my own company. Despite this, nothing has happened and I'm wondering whether, in fact, you disagreed with the policy of the governors?'[26] To which Wiltshire blandly replied: 'Now, about European students. It is all very fine for the governors to talk about the desirability of having European students in the college but, as I have said at meetings, there is very little that I can do about it. We shall not get them as individual applicants; there are very few Europeans, they are outnumbered 99 to 1 by Africans and Asians, and those that there are tend to feel that they have no need of further education.'[27] This last was a statement that he had no way of knowing or testing.

The next year Rogers tried again with the new principal, Fordham: 'Since the beginning the governors have been most anxious to have some Europeans on our courses. It is my view that it would be advisable to have two on a course at a time, for if you have only one he might feel lonely!'[28] He received a firm answer, particularly to the risible suggestion that a single European student might not be able to cope alone.

When I went on a three-week course in 1963 — the only European student ever to attend what we had envisaged as a multiracial college — it would have been a complete negation of the purpose of being there had there been another white student. It would have meant either that we ignored each other, or the two of us would have formed an exclusive unit, or we would have been expected to do so by the other students, who would have kept aloof. I thoroughly enjoyed being a student there, for one thing it gave me a rare insight into how a building I had designed actually worked, and the course was fascinating. The Ford Foundation Nairobi office had made available a tutor who specialized in what they called 'T groups', in which the students and the tutor played roles in coping with situations concerned with employment, race and other sensitive issues. There were no holds barred as we all felt strongly about the subjects, personally or in our allotted role as employer, settler or worker. As the only white face, I was not necessarily chosen to play the role of employer or settler, but was treated by both tutors and students as one of the crowd.

Fordham, also from Nottingham University, was seconded from Makerere University in Kampala as the principal after Wiltshire left in 1962. He remained until the college became the University of Nairobi Institute of Adult Studies of which he was the director until 1968. In *A Chance to Change*, Fordham and his fellow authors describe how being a student at the college changed the lives of 2000 who had been on the short courses and 140 students who had taken the year-long course.[29] The record of career paths of the students showed how valuable the institution had been to many Africans and Asians, and the book included quotations giving a vivid idea of what the college meant to them. The British staff found there was a major difference in approach between students in England and in Kenya, which was basically the difference between two types of adult education. One is the liberal tradition, which encourages the student to develop as an individual, and the other is vocational training, which prepares the student for a better job or further education.

The difference was expressed with almost brutal frankness in *A Chance to Change*: 'The students who came to the new college were motivated by a desire for personal advancement rather than desire for social or political change. Whether they were sponsored by industry or government, or had simply applied on their own account, they could no longer be thought of as "non-vocational" or interested mainly in social or political purposes. Of course, as adults living in those changing times, they were extremely interested in discussing social, political or economic issues of the day. But nobody could have been under any illusion that they were doing so for some disinterested concern for social progress. What they wanted was to get on in the world, and to take advantage of the new opportunities then opening up.' Edwin Townsend-Coles, writing about Ranche House, said: 'In a world where unemployment was a stark reality, who can blame those who wanted help in getting qualifications?'[30]

As a student at the college, chatting in the bedroom corridor or lounging in the courtyard, I was struck by my fellow students' passion to have a better job and make money, and even more by their bitter envy of their successful compatriots who drove past in large cars. They appeared to hold no parallel feelings about Europeans and their large cars. This burning desire for advancement, together with a number of outstandingly able people coming to the college without formal academic education, led to a decision to run courses of one academic year giving the successful student access to Nairobi University. Staff from the British liberal tradition in adult education saw this as a retrograde step but recognized that it met the needs of the students and the country, for there was a serious shortage of graduates in the new Kenya.

The introduction of the long course, allied to Wiltshire's innocence about Africa and his background in the university tradition, led him to an error of judgement in deciding that the future of the college would be secure under the aegis of Nairobi University. In the event, the essential independence of the college was compromised when it was merged with the University Institute of Adult Studies in 1965. In 1971 the buildings became part of the university's correspondence course unit and the college itself was closed down on the grounds that there was no need to encourage mature entry to the university because there were said to be plenty of school leavers available. This decision was doubly tragic: it ignored the plight of talented people who had missed the opportunity of further education who depended on adult education to make up time, and it rejected the vital concept that education was more than gaining a degree leading to a good job. The genesis of the premature end to the college lay in the decision to run the long course leading to university entrance. It was argued that adult education must reflect its context, and the majority of the students wanted education in order to advance themselves, but it was a long way from the high hopes of the 1958 conference.

Writing in retrospect, Wiltshire believed that the college could: 'help Kenya in the twentieth century, as adult education helped Britain in the nineteenth, to pass through a difficult period of social change ... not to produce specialists, but citizens who are better informed about the issues of the day, better able to play their part in dealing with them. ... What [the college offered] was in fact a short period of intensive intellectual training. The problems with which we were dealing often roused strong feelings and touched on deep convictions in students and tutor alike. It was our job to see that these feelings and convictions were made explicit so that they could be brought into the arena of rational discussion. In addition to the existing political and communal passions a respect for facts and a passion for truth were needed. No one can experience this respect and passion without undergoing an educational experience which is moral as well as intellectual.'[31]

Although the college was not what we in Capricorn had envisaged in 1958 — it was not multiracial for one thing — for the years it was in being, it changed many lives for the better, and radically transformed the future for the few who went on to further education. The college was part of the nation-building process of the new Kenya and if there had been some European and more Asian students it would have made little difference to how Kenya developed. Whatever the college was called, and whatever their colour, students were encouraged by rigorous teaching to face up to the realities of being citizens of a fast changing and developing country. Its short life compared with the continued growth and success of Ranche House in a far more hostile political environment is poignant. Perhaps, after all the argument, the Kenya college might have survived had there been more Capricorn members on the board of governors, as there were in Rhodesia.

Chapter 15
The London Connection

From the early days, when Dudley Clarke had been persuaded to set up an African intelligence room, David Stirling had a base in London. After Jeannine Scott offered to help in 1954 her house, 43A Cheval Place, became David's London office and a centre for Capricorn members and friends. When Jonathan Lewis was appointed in 1955 it was elevated to being the London branch of the Capricorn Africa Society to continue the unremitting search for funds to keep the branches in Africa operational, if not solvent. In the years after Salima the pace of change in Capricorn countries accelerated and local branches of the Society, adapting to new situations, became increasingly independent of David's control. In London, Sir John Slessor, Jeannine Scott, Henry Crookenden, Charles March and Lewis, while continuing to support the branches in Africa, also began to develop their own agenda. To benefit from charitable status, the Capricorn Africa Trust was set up in 1956 with specifically non-political objectives, including 'Among African peoples: (a) to promote the relief of poverty and suffering, (b) to conduct research and enquiry into cultural, human and racial relations and (c) to promote education in and dissemination of such information.'[1] In the broadest sense, the aims of the Capricorn Africa Society were obviously political, however often the Society said otherwise, which made fund-raising for the Society difficult.

Shortly after Salima, Jeannine Scott organized a lunch with Crookenden and Norbert Okare, a Capricorn member from Kenya, for Trevor Huddleston, then back from South Africa, in an attempt to forge some links with the Fabian Society's Africa Bureau, which he supported. Capricorn thought that the bureau was too much in thrall to the African nationalist cause, while the bureau considered Capricorn too close to the settlers. Both organizations were competing for funds from the same sources, which made the idea of a truce attractive, but Huddleston could not see the point of a halfway house like Capricorn and nothing came of it. Jeannine Scott reported the event to David, writing: 'He is clearly very ignorant at present about Capricorn and our aims. There may have even been certain confusion with MRA. ... He has, however, been in touch with Alan Paton and I think Alan suggested he should sign the contract, subject to accepting the multiple vote only as a temporary expedient and not a long term proposal. This he has said he is not willing to do.'[2]

In the 1960s when I designed buildings for Huddleston in Tanzania, where he was Bishop of Masasi, the three East African countries were independent and Capricorn only a memory, so we talked more of the future than the recent past as he drove me round his diocese in his old Land Rover. In 1998 at his memorial service in Westminster Abbey I was struck by parallels between Huddleston and David: in 1943 Huddleston, when he was 30, was sent to South Africa and within a few years was obsessed by the inequalities and waste of the apartheid regime there; David, when he was a year older, went to Southern Rhodesia in 1946 and also soon realized that racial prejudice was economically wasteful and could not be defended or tolerated. Both spent many years fighting for their beliefs and, although David was not a priest as Huddleston was, he was motivated by the faith of his Catholic upbringing.

There is a limit to these comparisons – although David never married, he was not celibate, he certainly enjoyed the good things of life and was a famous gambler, while Huddleston was committed to a life of poverty, chastity and obedience. And while David, by background and inclination was a conservative, Huddleston described himself as a socialist. Both men, tall and striking and with great personal charm, were leaders who could inspire men and women with their enthusiasm, and they were both great fun to be with, whether driving round southern Tanzania, or arguing about franchise proposals over a good dinner in Nairobi. David would have endorsed this sentence from Huddleston's *Naught for Your Comfort*, written in the year before Salima: 'Any doctrine based on racial or colour prejudice and enforced by the state is ... an affront to human dignity and *ipso facto* an insult to God himself.'[3]

In 1956 the Cheval Place team set up the Council for Aid to African Students with Mary Trevelyan, the redoubtable overseas student adviser at London University. In October that year she organized the first meeting of a group of foreign students at the university, the Goats' Club, specifying that there should be no more than six members from any one country. Every week during term time students from many parts of the world met to hear and question a distinguished speaker (whose identity was secret until the meeting) often moving on to the nearest pub to continue arguing and getting to know one another.

In the 1950s there was a small, but growing, number of African students in London who found accommodation difficult or impossible. Landladies were unwilling to have 'darkies' in the house, and some felt the same about Jews, Irish, Welsh or vegetarians,[4] however well educated, and for many students the cost of living in London was more than they could afford. Before they left Africa, some had been encouraged to call at the Capricorn office in Cheval Place if they needed help or a friend in a strange city. The students needed somewhere to live and the Capricorn trustees needed to justify their charitable status. The solution was for Capricorn to provide homes for the students. That bold and compassionate initiative, started over 40 years ago, continues today with overseas students living in houses now owned and managed by the Zebra Housing Association. But it has always been more than merely accommodation; the concept was to provide somewhere that would make the students feel at home while they stayed in Britain. At that time overseas students could come to Britain, without needing a permit, to be educated at a university almost free. When they arrived off the boat, or at Victoria station, they were met by Jesuits, evangelists or communists, all offering help and advice, but with strings attached. The colleges took little interest in the students as visitors to the country and there were few organizations without an axe to grind looking after their welfare.

Crookenden, chairman of the Capricorn Africa Trust, with March, Lewis and Jeannine Scott, set about raising funds to buy or lease a house in London. In 1958 the Dulverton Trust made a grant of £7500 towards the purchase of the freehold of a house in Kensington,[5] the balance (£5000) being lent by Jeannine Scott and Lewis who set up a registered charity, Zebra House Limited, as the owner. No 3 Marloes Road was a typical Victorian terrace house with a bay window and steps up to the front door over an area giving light to the basement. A walled garden was reached down steps from the ground floor. The warden, with a room on the first floor, was very much part of the household, sharing the students' bathroom and kitchen. In 1959 Zebra House opened with 14 single students, most of whom came from Africa. The impressive and carefully balanced list of sponsors included the Archbishop of Canterbury, the Mayor of Kensington, Viscount Chandos, Patrick Gordon-

Walker (recent Tory and Labour colonial secretaries) and Laurens van der Post. Miss Wilkinson was the first warden, followed by one of Lewis's many friends, Richard Waller, who was succeeded in the summer of 1961 by Peter Comyns.

Comyns, like David, went to the Roman Catholic boys' school, Ampleforth, and served in the Scots Guards, being wounded in Germany. When the war was over he joined ICI as a trainee and

The Zebra House football team (photo: Peter Comyns)

then moved to the stockbrokers James Capel as an investment analyst where he stayed for 18 years, using his knowledge to make some money for himself. He shared a flat with other well-off men in a smart street in London, and at an age when his contemporaries were starting families, he took up the new sport of water skiing, joined the SAS territorials as a parachutist for a few years and developed an interest in the wider world, which led him to Mary Trevelyan's Goats Club. Comyns was soon involved in helping running the Goats, which gave him a lasting interest in overseas students, especially from Africa.

In 1962 Mary Trevelyan founded International Students House in an elegant crescent of Nash houses overlooking Regents Park, with funds from the Dulverton Trust and the newly formed Overseas Students' Welfare Expansion Programme (OSWEP). The experience and the fun of being with young students from around the world encouraged Comyns to offer to be the warden of Zebra

House on a voluntary basis. Although Comyns was, and remains, a key member of Zebra, he was not a wholehearted believer in the multiracialism of the Capricorn Contract, which he considered a delaying tactic. As a loner without family he was an ideal candidate to look after the young students from Africa, though he was often short and brusque in dealing with them. His natural frugality kept the house going without having to charge rents beyond the means of the students, who were not worried about fresh paint or new stair carpets. Zebra House was a happy community with the students organizing football matches, visits around the country and excellent Christmas parties.

At the time Comyns became warden of Zebra House, No 7 Marloes Road came on the market. Six Capricorn supporters lent £7,500 between them to buy the freehold with a mortgage for the balance. Oliver Carruthers, who had been a temporary Capricorn executive officer in Northern Rhodesia before serving in the colonial service there, was back in London with an inheritance from his mother's estate. He took over the freehold for £14,000 and leased it back to Zebra at a peppercorn rent for 30 years. Within a year No 1 was available and the trustees were able to buy the freehold with the money received for No 7. Grants for internal alterations to link the adjacent properties with connecting doors came from the local authority and OSWEP, through the British Council, which supported Zebra for many years with a representative on the executive committee.

Lewis reported in a newsletter: 'Zebra House: warden Peter Comyns is at present on the continent with six Zebras who are seeing France, Germany, Italy and Austria for the first time. The community at present is as follows: 6 Kenya, 2 Southern Rhodesia, 1 Malaya, 1 Tanganyika, 1 Ghana, 1 Ceylon, 1 Uganda, 2 Sierra Leone, 1 German, 1 Ivory Coast, 2 Nigeria.'[6] Over the years the majority of the students in Zebra House were single and many were from Africa as word was passed round that a friendly welcome and an inexpensive room were to be found in Marloes Road. Occasionally, students would leave without paying their rent and sometimes it was paid late – in 1971 Lewis reported receiving a letter from Nigeria with a cheque for four weeks rent at £6.6*s*.10*d* outstanding since 1963.

The reputation of Zebra House spread far and wide so that during the vacations many of the rooms were taken up by African students from universities in the Soviet Union who wanted a break from communist ideology. Comyns remained as voluntary warden until Zebra House was sold in 1999 when the cost of renovation after 40 years of hard wear, together with increasingly strict health and safety requirements, made it uneconomic if rents were to be kept reasonable.

In the late 1950s some companies in Britain, including BP, Shell, BOAC (as it was then), BAT and ICI, were hearing from their overseas managers that some students returning from education in Britain had become anti-British and sometimes communist sympathizers. Clearly something was wrong with the way they had been treated in spite of receiving good degrees on subsidized fees. In 1961 the companies discreetly set up the Overseas Students' Trust (OST) with an annual income of £50,000. The intention was to make small grants, without too much bureaucracy, to organizations or individuals working with overseas students, but not for buildings or to the students themselves. After a year the first director left and was replaced by Martin Kenyon, a lively enthusiast who continued to run the trust until his retirement in 1992, when the trust was wound up. Kenyon's interest in Africa was first stimulated in 1959 when his family introduced him to Huddleston through whom Kenyon met young African students and became increasingly absorbed with their problems. When he was appointed director of OST, an early contact was Mary Trevelyan, which led to a long personal involvement with the Goats Club and International Students House as well as the provision of financial assistance from OST. News of money for student work soon spread, which brought Lewis to Kenyon's flat/office, near Zebra House, asking for grants to help Zebra. This produced help for wardens' salaries and contributions for other expenses. Kenyon soon became, and has remained, an enthusiastic Zebra trustee and member of management committees for Zebra hostels.

In 1961 Theo Bull, a Capricorn member from Northern Rhodesia with Beit family money behind him, bought the freehold of three houses in Primrose Hill: Nos 8 and 9 Chalcot Square and the house that backed on to them, No 30 Chalcot Crescent, which he then leased to Zebra for 25 years at a peppercorn rent. Bull has written recently: 'I have tried with varying degrees of success, to run my life on the basis of the triple motto "make money, do good and have fun". The system was for the rich guy to buy the freehold of one or more properties, then lease it for 25 years for a nominal rent to a charity which got a government grant to convert and do it up and then let the accommodation so created to overseas students. The benefits to the students and the charity are obvious. In a socially rising area the capital gain on the property over 25 years could be phenomenal. Chalcot Square has proved it. Early in Holy Week of 1961 Jonathan [Lewis] and I drove around looking for likely properties. I think Jonathan was driving either Daisy or Ben, his much loved Rollses. I got James Lemkin [Capricorn supporter and lawyer] to bid at the auction and we got the houses for about £9000 each.'[7]

Many students from Africa were married with children by the time they came to study in Britain and without reasonable accommodation it was impossible for them to bring their families with them for the three or four years they would be away from home. The disadvantages of leaving them were many, even if the marriage survived the long separation. Left behind, the wife (it was almost always men who were studying) would have had little understanding of the new way of life that her husband took for granted, so it was important for the wife to share her husband's experiences abroad. Bull and the Zebra trustees decided that the new houses would be for married students, who became a priority for the future. Zebra House Limited leased the houses from Bull's property company and obtained grants from OSWEP and the local authority for converting the houses into flats. Living in the square was Jon Barnsley, a young architect with little work, who was asked to undertake the conversion. He passed the job to his new assistant Alan Hewett who continued to work for Zebra on their alteration jobs almost to the end of the century. Hewett has said that a characteristic of Zebra jobs was that there were too many people involved and too little money.[8] In 1983 a major fund-raising drive produced sufficient to purchase the two freeholds in Impala House, as it was called, from Bull at less than the current market price, but, as he anticipated, for a great deal more than he had paid.

The 1962 Zebra Newsletter recorded that the flats in Impala House were complete and occupied by families from Kenya, the Sudan, Nigeria, Southern Rhodesia, India and Uganda, and that negotiations for buying the houses next door had begun.[9] In 1963 Zebra House Limited bought the freeholds of No 8 Chalcot Square and 32 and 34 in the crescent with a local authority mortgage and improvement grants, making a unit of five large houses connected by an open garden area, equipped with climbing frames and swings for the children. During the 1980s loans and a mortgage were raised to buy the outstanding freeholds of Zebra House and Impala House at figures below market price in each case.

When the Belgians precipitately withdrew from the Congo in

1960 (recently Zaire and now the Democratic Republic of Congo) a large part of Africa was left, and remains, in turmoil. The risk of the surrounding colonial countries, unsteadily moving towards independence, being destabilized made it important for the British government to have inside knowledge of the rapidly changing situation in the Congo. The 10th Lord Vernon, later to be chairman of the Zebra Trust, had his London home near Cheval Place and had worked for MI5 before joining the Colonial Office in the Kenya Department.[10] As a friend of Jeannine Scott and Lewis at 43A, he thought Capricorn would be an ideal cover for sending men into the Congo to report on the position, so another charity was established in Cheval Place, 'Capricorn Lecturers', with Crookenden, March and Lewis as trustees. The overt purpose was 'appointment of teaching staff (English language) in Congo'.[11] Carefully vetted young men were sent to Leopoldville and Elizabethville (now Kinshasa and Lubumbashi), and in 1965 a married couple was still in the capital. The cost of the operation was listed as £500 a year though there are no records of where the money came from or of the reports the teachers sent back to London, except for their comments on the manifold difficulties over food, transport and occasional danger from gunfire.

The close links between Cheval Place and International Students House (ISH) was maintained not only through the involvement of Comyns and Kenyon in the Goats' Club but also because Lewis was a friend of Lord Dulverton's younger brother, Patrick Wills, an important supporter of Mary Trevelyan's work. Wills says he now cannot remember if the tennis they played was real or lawn. Some years later, as Lewis became more and more difficult, they fell out, which meant that Wills and the family trust gave up Zebra and concentrated support for overseas students on ISH, of which he is still vice president. The need was so great that there was never a sense of competition between the Zebra and ISH, the former concentrating on students from Africa in the early days while the latter welcomed students from all over the world.

Throughout 1963 the Cheval Place team wrestled with the problem of the relationship between the Capricorn Trust and Zebra House Limited. Equally difficult was how to break the news to the dwindling band of the faithful in Africa that the London team had decided that Capricorn, as an organization in London, was over. In January Lewis drafted a letter to Robin and Jennifer Plunket setting out the case for hauling up a new flag, as he put it. He began: 'It is with the greatest trepidation that I send you and Sue/Michael

[Wood] the enclosed. ... No one has a greater admiration for your continued battling under the Capricorn flag in Africa, but the unhappy fact is that if this trust is to move into the next round and continue its work this end, the name will remain a great handicap to us. I only hope that our acceptance of this is not going to be a disappointment.'[12] He drafted a similar but longer letter to Laurens van der Post and David.

The files do not show whether these letters were actually sent and the issue was still being debated at the end of the year when Crookenden circulated a paper on future proposals. This, among other things, said: 'the word "Capricorn" is now more of a hindrance to work of this kind than a help, particularly with Africans, and it would seem that whatever policy now emerges this word should be dropped and the Capricorn Africa Society in the UK closed down.'[13] Although this was irrefutable it was difficult to accept for those who had worked long and hard in London and in Africa for the Capricorn ideal, whether as volunteers or, like Lewis, as staff. It was to be three more years before the Zebra Trust deed was signed and the title 'Capricorn' was finally dropped. By that time the branches in Africa had all been dissolved. In 1974 the trustees finally laid the Society to rest by presenting all the files and papers to the Centre for South African Studies at York University where they have been kept as an archive ever since. Each piece of paper, important or not, was microfilmed, copies of which have been invaluable in the research for this book.

The BBC week's good cause before Christmas 1962 was given by the Bishop of Coventry to raise funds for the Zebra Trust. Stimulated by the bishop's enthusiasm and inspired by the success of Zebra and Impala Houses in London, a house for overseas students was opened in Coventry. Continuing to be concerned about students outside London, in 1968 a large house in Miles Road, Bristol, was bought with substantial help from Carruthers, who insisted that it be owned by the Zebra Trust to avoid adding to the growing number of companies under the Zebra umbrella.

An OSWEP grant helped to make seven flats and ground floor accommodation for the warden. Zebra House, Bristol, as it was known, was managed by a local committee with Nigel Boosey as chairman. It was a valuable asset for students at the university, but the small number of units eventually made it uneconomic under National Housing Corporation guidelines for maintenance and administration. Finally, and with regret, in 1995 the trust decided that the house should be sold. The proceeds from the sale were invested by the trust although it was some years before a tentative policy was developed on how the income was to be spent.

Lewis and the Cheval Place team did not allow themselves to be distracted by ventures out of London. When a rambling old hotel in Harrington Gardens, ten minutes walk from Marloes Road, came on the market in 1964 Lewis and John Sutcliffe, who had spent a year in Kenya[14] and was chairman of Zebra House,

Jerome House, Kensington, London (R. Radović)

promptly put down the deposit and thought how the balance was to be found. They called the new hostel Jerome House, after the saint shown as a man of learning seated in his study in Africa, often plus grateful lion.

The somewhat seedy atmosphere in some ways helped to make the house more of a home, particularly for the large number of children who had the run of the long corridors and badly lit staircases. Jerome was substantially larger than the other hostels with room for a resident warden, 118 students and wives plus 34 children. A breakdown of the residents listed 34 different countries of origin from Australia to Zambia with students taking advanced courses in a variety of subjects including 11 in medicine.

The first warden was Basil Hare-Duke, a former officer in the Sudan political service so the house had a majority of Sudanese among the residents in the early days. An item from an American college magazine gives the special flavour of the house: 'The cheapest place to stay in London is at a place called Jerome House. ... This fantastic huge house will surpass anything you've imagined in your wildest dreams. It costs about 75¢ a night to stay in this Dickens-like abode. Hundreds of international intellectuals from places like Afghanistan, Tanganyika, India, Pakistan and even France and England call Jerome House home. You'll be able to get into some mighty interesting conversations there.'[15] Later Lewis employed his wife, Zivka, as warden, where she remained until her death at the end of 1973.

Zebra House council made a decision that there were too many hostels under one management so Jerome Housing Fellowship was set up to own the new property.[16] Some years later this decision created problems when trusts with divergent objects had to be amalgamated with difficulty and expensive legal advice. According to the files Jerome Housing Fellowship also owned a house near the Crystal Palace, in Church Road, Upper Norwood; although the records show that it was bought and converted, nothing further can be found about the property. Lewis was an enthusiastic buyer of houses that looked cheap with possibilities for conversion.

Within four years of the first Dulverton grant Zebra, through various companies and trusts, owned a total of eight houses in central London full of single or married Commonwealth students. Over the following 20 years Zebra grew in size and complexity, as more property was bought with Capricorn members guaranteeing mortgages, or giving long leases at nominal rents.[17] Each hostel was set up in a different way depending on how the property had come into the Zebra net, so that by 1976 there were five different property-owning companies and trusts based in the Cheval Place office. Lewis's cheerful and irreverent style sometimes clashed with the lengthy bureaucratic procedures of local authority bodies from whom he was seeking grants. It was often opportunistic and sometimes daring, almost reckless, but it worked, and many hundreds of students from overseas went back to their home countries with an understanding and a fondness for Great Britain because they had been housed and looked after by the Zebras. It was an extraordinary achievement for a small group of enthusiasts who believed that the money could be found somehow or somewhere to meet the commitments they made.

The letters coming to Cheval Place from students whose lives had been changed were a constant source of encouragement and some were quoted in Lewis's newsletters. Typical was a letter from an Indian Ph.D. student who had been at the University of London. 'But for you our stay here could so easily have turned into an ordeal affecting the very quality of my work. For the first two months here I floundered around quite out of my depth, looking for suitable accommodation. Although one should not speak disparagingly of one's hosts, I must tell you that I had expected more of the English. Since infancy, we from the Commonwealth grow up with the idea that England is the Mecca for the final polish to education. ... And yet our Mecca provides us with no facilities to live and work in reasonable comfort. It was such a relief when I found Jerome House. It was marvellous to find a students' hostel with convenient access to the university libraries and museums, actually catering for postgraduate married students with children. I realize that I was one of the lucky few to have found accommodation geared to my needs and would be able to accomplish the task I had come halfway round the world for, free from extraneous worries. I shall always consider the Zebra tie you gave me a cherished privilege and wear it with pride.'[18]

Some time in 1965 Lewis drew up a list of the charitable foundations 'fostered' in Cheval Place, with notes on their purpose and achievements. It is a formidable list, including the hostels, Congo lecturers and some set up to aid the well-being of African peoples, both at home and abroad. There were distinguished office bearers with Lewis listed as secretary, founder member, or chairman of each. The full list was: Capricorn Africa Trust; Zebra House Council; Coventry Overseas Students Trust; Jerome Housing Fellowship; Malaysia Housing Society; Royal College of Surgeons Faculty of Anaesthetists (Mary Kinross Charitable Trust, which was negotiating for houses in Chalcot Square); Council for Aid to African Students; Capricorn Lecturers; Chalcot Trust; Verdri (Bull's property owning company) and the Zebra Trust for the 'promotion of all charitable activities listed above and all future projects'.

In June 1967 both Comyns and Carruthers were worried about the problems of having a number of separate trusts, governing councils and property-owning companies, most made up of the same individuals trying to remember which property was being discussed at which meeting. Carruthers, as chairman of the management committee of Jerome Housing Fellowship, wrote in a paper that: 'There are at present certain difficulties in the constitutional structure of Jerome House, which I think also apply to many of the institutions in which the Zebra Trust has an interest. ... The more one says one is responsible for them, the more it should be said that the Zebra Trust should own them.'[19]

Comyns made a similar point: 'It is no secret that a management reorganization is required at Jerome House and the proposal is that the composition of the Zebra House Council and the Jerome Housing Fellowship should be identical.'[20] Restructuring charitable bodies meant involving solicitors, accountants, the charity commissioners, time and money, so it is not surprising that these and similar sensible proposals were discussed over the years but not acted upon until the National Housing Corporation (NHC) forced consolidation some 30 years later.

A group of London merchants with interests in the Far East asked Zebra in 1969 to manage a hostel they wished to establish for students from Malaysia. Three adjacent houses in Upper Montague Street, Mayfair, made 22 flats for married students, to be called Sentosa House – 'peace and happiness' in Malay. Because this was a scheme they supported, the city merchants raised the finance on the telephone in a morning, which showed it could be done. Five years later two houses were bought in Richmond Avenue, Islington, which added 16 units to Sentosa. After some years Zebra took over ownership and control, and later Sentosa was incorporated into the Zebra Housing Association, confirming that Zebra served students from around the world.

For over ten years Lewis had directed the development of Zebra in his own unique way: exciting and often risky but successful, as new communities of students were taken into the family and made at home. Throughout that time he was supported, encouraged and controlled by three crucial individuals: Jeannine Scott, his wife Zivka and Crookenden. In 1969 Jeannine married Admiral Josef Bartosik, a man whose naval background and precise manner were very different to Lewis, to whom she had been close for many years, which led to a lack of mutual understanding between the two men. Jeannine (now Bartosik) continued as deputy director of the Zebra Trust although she was often abroad and her priority was her husband rather than Lewis and the Zebra office.

Crookenden's charm and his good sense, expressed in carefully argued and elegantly written papers, were key ingredients in the success of the early years of Zebra activity in London, and his death in April 1972 was a serious blow to the organization and to Jeannine Bartosik and Lewis. Lewis wrote in the newsletter that summer. 'Henry Crookenden since 1956 has been a rock-like support to our organization and everyone in it. His wide-minded toleration and wise counsel were of inestimable value to us all and many times it was he who smoothed over the inevitable difficulties in running an organization like this, relieved tensions and solved problems.'[21]

Then, 18 months later, Lewis's wife Zivka died over Christmas, choking on a piece of meat while Lewis himself was away with a girlfriend known as Bluebell. The loss to Jerome House, where Zivka was the popular warden, to Zebra and to Lewis himself (made worse by guilt) had an enormous effect on the atmosphere of the Cheval Place office. A letter written some years later recorded her importance to Zebra and to Lewis himself. 'Zivka, of course, was his sheet anchor. She was also the sheet anchor of the Zebras for many years ... she made all the curtains for all the communities – 886 pairs! The success of the communities is a living tribute to her prodigious dedication and, above all, the wonderful spirit that she engendered and perpetuated. ... These two created the foundations out of which Zebra has burgeoned.'[22]

For most of 1974 Lewis acted as the temporary warden of Jerome House, a job that kept him occupied but was a harrowing experience as he was constantly reminded of Zivka.[23] Lewis now found himself almost alone and his enthusiasm and drive became erratic and unreliable. He had always been fond of what he called a jar of the Irish (whiskey) but now his drinking was becoming excessive and an increasing worry to his friends and colleagues. Comyns used to buy sherry in bulk for bottling and blames himself for providing Lewis with copious amounts of economical sherry, which he drank throughout the day. Beside the alcoholism, he had spells in hospital for other problems, and his personal finances were complicated, making him increasingly ineffective as the key figure in the Zebra organization. Correspondence in the files for the next few years includes anguished letters to Vernon or Sutcliffe, as chairmen of the trust, describing Lewis drunk and incapable in the office, alternating with sparkling letters from Lewis himself, full of ideas expressed with his old charm and wit.

By 1974 OSWEP grants were becoming difficult or impossible to obtain and the UK economy was at a low point so that there was little chance of large donations or even continued payment of individual subscriptions. The trustees also had to consider how Zebra was to be managed, without wanting to put Lewis out to grass, although they had to force him to go on a cure for alcoholism. One solution was to register with the newly created National Housing Corporation (NHC), which they hoped would provide finance for hostel improvements and introduce some discipline and order into Zebra affairs. Lewis appears to have made little protest about the proposal to register the Zebra companies with the NHC although he, like the trustees, probably had little idea how great the loss of independence would be. At the end of a Zebra Trust meeting on 25 September 1974, with Vernon in the chair, under any other business, the minutes record: 'The chairman asked the secretariat to go ahead as soon as possible ... and register the Zebra Trust with the Housing Corporation in order that we are eligible for the new sources of statutory finance.'[24] Thus was the decision taken that was to change the culture and operation of Zebra forever and was to cause much heartache and argument over the increasing burden of bureaucracy and control.

In July 1975 the trustees were urging the secretariat to do everything possible to get the four Zebra entities registered social landlords under the corporation. The minutes recorded: 'the Trust and its communities would have access to substantial sums of money not only for management and maintenance of the houses and central office, and for debts incurred through increased running costs (for example as a result of inflation), but also for approved development schemes, i.e. expansion.'[25] The trustees' enthusiasm for new funding is palpable but they had not yet realized that the new status would mean changes in the way the organization and each hostel were run, as NHC officials could make inspections and report on management shortcomings and were in a position to require compliance to their many regulations under the law. At a meeting of the Zebra Trust executive committee in July 1976, the consultant on the NHC negotiations reported that all four Zebra entities had been registered and could start applying for grants.

Although it is clear that the Cheval Place team did not anticipate the amount of control they would find imposed on their activities, it seems equally clear that NHC officials had not fully realized the haphazard manner in which the Zebra hostels were run. There were to be many years of adverse reports from the corporation, mutual misunderstanding and complaints of unnecessary interference and bureaucracy before a working relationship was established, and it is questionable whether that situation has been reached even now at the time of writing. In retrospect, NHC officials showed considerable patience over two decades of dealing with what they regarded as slapdash amateurs in the housing business.

During the negotiations with the NHC, in September 1975, the consultant wrote to Sutcliffe and Vernon in some despair: 'Rory [McNeile, a member of the executive committee], relaxed and amiable throughout, suggested more than once that members of the [Zebra Trust] committee should simply tell the Housing Corporation that they didn't understand and it was all very difficult. I think that he forgets that, although no use has been made of the statutory funds available, Jerome, Malaysia and the Trust itself have been formally constituted as housing associations for some time. If the ZT were to appear too puzzled and incompetent one result might be a DOE [Department of the Environment] decision to put a representative on the committee and even to appoint staff. The new act authorizes them to take action of this kind.'[26]

In 1977 Jeannine Bartosik retired as deputy director of the trust and Zebra had to move from the cosy, and rent-free, domesticity of Cheval Place to a ground floor room in Jerome House, where they were at least close to the action, but it was a wrench after more than 20 years, and the move added to the feeling that the old order was changing, as it was. As the 'band of brothers'[27] broke up and it was realized that their casual but effective way of working was unacceptable to the NHC it was not long before a counterattack was mounted.

After a meeting in April 1978, described by a trustee as an 'instructive, though not particularly pleasant, confrontation with Housing [Corporation] bureaucracy',[28] Comyns circulated a paper to the trustees, 'A Personal Statement Recommending Withdrawal from the Housing Corporation'. He wrote: 'In recent weeks we have become more aware of the kind of management reorganization and control that the Housing Corporation requires of us. ... Our present central advisory office under Jonathan Lewis would be replaced by a housing manager/director who, nominally appointed by the trustees, would effectively be the mouthpiece of the corporation. Our rents would be adjusted by direction to meet the higher administration costs, and this would undoubtedly mean increases. New rules have recently been instituted which are likely to put revenue deficit grants out of reach to us as the overseas student category does not enjoy the priority of the average indigenous homeless family, and our required rent levels would be required to exceed "fair rents". ... The Zebra Trust and its trustees have, from the beginning, been a body of like-minded people interested in the welfare of overseas students and prepared to give up their time to carry out this objective. It has been successful and overall its financial position is strong. The objectives of the Housing Corporation are impersonal, politically motivated and not related in any way to the aspiration and needs of overseas students as such, and its motivation is generally hostile to voluntary effort. I believe that we can and should negotiate our independence, and that the future of the Zebra Trust with anything like its present form and objectives can only be safeguarded by withdrawal.'[29]

Some 20 years later many of the same thoughts were being expressed in the Zebra Housing Association board of management, particularly the point that Zebra exists to help overseas students, which means discrimination against local homeless families, the concern of the Housing Corporation. A year after Comyns's powerful paper, Lewis wrote a despairing memo on 'The Zebra Trust's sterile and very expensive negotiations with the Housing Corp, 1974–1979'[30] in which he recorded his frustration over the delays and obfuscation in dealing with bureaucrats. He quoted the legal adviser of the Charity Commission as describing the NHC people as 'obdurate, autocratic or plain ignorant, I'm not sure which', to which Lewis had replied 'all three'. His frustration was fuelled by the urgency of finding funds for repairs to Charles Hayward House, which was in a seriously bad state, adding in characteristic style: 'Mr Dalyell, MP, said in the House last night "where else can we look for help when our leak starts roofing". Well, our leak is roofing full flood.'

In 1983 Comyns called for new and younger members of the boards of Zebra Housing Association (ZHA – the title of the amalgamated companies) and Zebra Trust to replace those who would retire before the end of the decade. Some 20 years later, although a few younger members have joined, most of the same names are still contributing to Zebra meetings. In 1984 pressure from the NHC for better management encouraged the trustees to appoint a professional administrator, and after advertising in the *Daily Telegraph*, Michael Dodwell was appointed. He set about organizing the office and raising funds from the NHC while Lewis continued as secretary or trustee of the numerous charities that had grown round Zebra. Grants were obtained to complete renovation work at Jerome and Zebra Houses, and applications were put in for improvements at Impala, Sentosa and more at Jerome, where the size and age of the property meant a constant fight to keep the building in good, or even acceptable, repair. Funds for work to the outside of Jerome were provided by the Greater London Council after which the trustees commended Dodwell's skill in extracting funds from public bodies for necessary work on the ageing hostels. Some years later, after he had retired, the accountant discovered that he was also skilful at extracting funds from Zebra accounts for his own purposes and, after police investigation, avoided being tried for embezzlement by dying of a heart attack.

After I joined the board of ZHA and the Zebra Trust in 1987, we were confronted with a fiercely critical report from NHC inspectors, which I and others hoped, vainly as it turned out, would stimulate a more efficient administration of the five hostels that made up our portfolio. At the time I did not realize that it was not the first adverse report, or that it was not to be the last. I was soon involved in discussions about the viability of Jerome House and looking over buildings to buy after selling Harrington Gardens. A property developer solved the problem by offering to take over Jerome in exchange for an old hotel, which he would completely refurbish to our requirements with the addition of a very large sum of money, provided he had the old Jerome with vacant possession when the new building was ready.

Glendower Place, near South Kensington underground station, seemed to be ideal and the possibility of cash for another hostel was also attractive. The new Jerome would be somewhat smaller than the old, which many thought was too big to manage in any case. I was involved with the development of the design and the progress of the work including selecting the furniture, but not with the arrangements for rehousing or moving the families from Harrington Gardens. When, after nearly two years, the new Jerome House was ready in 1991 a small number of students refused to move, even when offered cash, which meant that when the due date arrived the developer claimed that the contract was void without vacant possession. This lost Zebra a large proportion of the expected cash, cost a great deal in legal fees and cast a blight over what was otherwise a success. The new hostel is popular with student families and, unlike most of the other buildings, was to require little expensive maintenance for some years.

Between 1960 and 1993, when the separate housing trusts were finally merged into ZHA, three names occur and recur as chairman or vice-chairman: John Vernon, John Sutcliffe and John Senior.

They had all lived in or been closely involved with Africa, a tradition that was continued in 1993 when Denis Acheson, born in Northern Rhodesia and a Salima veteran, was made chairman of the ZHA and the Zebra Trust. He retired in 1997 and was replaced by Gordon Stevens, the first chairman without any connection with Africa, whose managerial experience, it was hoped, would smooth the relationship with NHC officialdom. The Zebra Trust maintained its independence when the housing organizations were merged in the Zebra Housing Association, although the tradition of having the same chairman for the trust and the association continued despite the trust now having different priorities, as it no longer owns any student accommodation.

Zebra has always given the students more than merely accommodation: from the beginning there were picnics, visits to supporters' houses in the country and help for the wives and children, many of whom had little English or experience of living in a strange, and often cold, city. Jocelyn Carruthers and Veldes Raison organized an informal group of supporters, which included Jeannine Bartosik and my wife, Anne, to help students' wives with English, knitting and the mysteries of a supermarket, which made the Zebra hostels into real communities rather than blocks of flats. Now that fees for overseas students at British universities are so high, and many African countries have difficulties over foreign exchange, the students staying in the Zebra hostels are from South America, the Far East, America and Europe, who are richer than African students and need less practical help. The students themselves, both men and women, continue to provide exotic catering and decorations for the Christmas parties.

The Zebra Trust added the proceeds from selling the Bristol house to its investments and, no longer responsible for housing students, cast around for another role and use for its investment income. One decision was to give grants to secondary schools in Africa. The problem is how to select which schools should be helped from the tens of thousands without adequate accommodation, desks or textbooks. Individual trustees pooled their experience — Comyns teaches at schools in Tanzania and southern Africa, Jennifer Plunket still lives in Zimbabwe, I know of schools in Kenya that need help, and there are other links to deserving cases — the problem is that they are all deserving. After much debate £600 was granted to a few schools in east and central Africa where there was someone who could oversee its expenditure. Letters of thanks with school reports are coming in, which augur well for being able to increase the amounts and scope of the help in the future. The amount being spent at present is within the income from the trust's investments, so there is room for expansion, given that the need in Africa is boundless.

In spite of the apparent difference of emphasis, there is symmetry between the work of Capricorn in Africa and Zebra in Britain. The leading figures in both came from a similar privileged background, with a tradition of caring for those less fortunate than themselves, which in Africa sometimes included an element of long-term self-interest. Although there are now few students from Africa staying in Zebra hostels, the trust's present initiative is giving back to Africa's children the fruits of the early donations of Jeannine Bartosik's 'band of brothers' who live in England but whose hearts remain in Africa. Providing homes in England to thousands of students from around the world and helping struggling schools in Africa are proud legacies.

Chapter 16
The End in Africa

The beginning of the end of Capricorn in Africa can be dated as early as the second half of 1956 when we failed to build on the initiative, enthusiasm and media interest generated by the success of the Salima convention and the publication of the contract. The moment was lost at Salima itself when time for the debate on the Society's post-convention programme was taken up by the ceremonial signing of the contract and the loyal address to the Queen — an early example of presentation over substance. We dispersed full of goodwill, for Salima had been a unique and extraordinary event, but with no plans for the future. The items on the agenda that morning (in only an hour and five minutes) were 'the campaign to launch the Contract — public meetings, house-to-house canvassing, the relationship of the Society to political parties ... and the short and long-term future of the Capricorn Society and its financial position'. The crucial issue was the relationship to political parties: our failure to establish a policy, or even some guidelines, on this essential matter was fatal to any chance of success.

A month after Salima President Nasser of Egypt nationalized the Suez Canal Company controlled by Britain and France, in response to their refusal to fund the Aswan High Dam. The canal was a vital waterway between Europe and the east, and particularly the oil wells of the Arabian peninsula. At the end of October Israel invaded Egypt as part of a secret plan with Britain and France who then occupied the Canal Zone to 'keep the peace'. The United Nations Security Council, supported by the USSR and USA, strongly disapproved of the operation and threats of Soviet armed intervention added to the danger inherent in the misguided British and French enterprise. The invading troops withdrew at the end of the year, leaving Nasser in control of the canal with his reputation for standing up to the imperialists greatly enhanced. The affair signalled the unrivalled influence of America in world affairs and that Britain and France were no longer imperial powers. Africans in colonies throughout the continent took heart: if the United States was against colonialism then freedom would come sooner rather than later.

In Nairobi and Salisbury we were isolated from international opinion on colonialism and knew little of the debates in the United Nations. We were aware of anti-colonial rhetoric from Cairo, which we dismissed as communist inspired. We believed that West Africa, without white settlers, where there had been contact with European traders and missionaries for hundreds of years and where ancient city-states flourished, was fundamentally different from east and central Africa. To the outside world Africa between the Sahara and the Transvaal appeared as a homogeneous continent inhabited by black people with the occasional and tiresome addition of a few white settlers. This view was also adopted by African politicians so that when, in 1957, the Gold Coast became independent Ghana under Kwame Nkrumah's leadership, they saw no reason why the same freedom should not be given to the people of east and central Africa. Nkrumah invited African politicians to the All Africa People's Conference in Accra in February 1959, a meeting that fired the enthusiasm of African leaders in colonial territories for early independence. The Colonial Office recognized the inevitable, setting up constitutional conferences at Lancaster House in London at which moves to self-government with a universal franchise were mapped out for the countries of east and central Africa except, tragically, the self-governing colony of Southern Rhodesia.

In late 1959 we held a weekend conference at our house in Nairobi to debate future policy in Kenya. The three Africans, four Asians and eleven Europeans present concluded that writing letters and articles for the local press would be useful, a disappointing result after much eating and drinking and friendly talk. In November that year Michael Wood called a general council meeting in the London office at which he said the Society had to decide whether the aim was to be a mass movement or a small thinking group.[1] The treasurer, Charles March, rightly pointed out that Capricorn could not afford a mass membership and anyway it could only be achieved in Africa behind a political machine. Characteristically, Laurens van der Post disagreed with the idea of a small intellectual group, though he offered no solution to how any alternative could be achieved. On the agenda was Wood's statement that he could not continue to carry the burden of being president without help, perhaps from an African who could take on the presidency in the following October. Wood travelled widely and was highly intelligent and sensitive, but the idea that an African of any influence in his community would take on the presidency of Capricorn in 1960 was irrational.

Africa continued to change around us at a terrifying pace.[2] In November 1959 there was serious rioting at Stanleyville in the Belgian Congo, close enough for white fears to harden as fleeing settlers arrived in Kenya and the Copper Belt with tales of rape and pillage. In February 1960 the prime minister, Harold Macmillan, made his prophetic speech in Cape Town, which should have made the settlers feel the impending chill had they been less insular. In his reminiscences dictated to Alan Hoe, David Stirling said he had been warned about the speech and arranged a meeting with Macmillan through Iain Macleod, the colonial secretary, and Alec Douglas-Home, then foreign secretary, in an attempt to persuade the prime minister to change his mind.[3] David said that in spite of some hours of talk he got nowhere and the speech when delivered was substantially unchanged. Comparing Macmillan's speech with many of David's statements it is difficult to see why he was concerned because David himself could have written most of it.

The Prime Minister said, 'Fifteen years ago this movement spread through Asia. Many countries there of different races and civilizations pressed their claim to an independent national life. Today the same thing is happening in Africa, and the most striking of all the impressions I have formed ... is of the strength of this African national consciousness. ... The wind of change is blowing through this continent, and whether we like it or not this growth of national consciousness is a political fact. We must accept it as fact and our national policies must take account of it.' Macmillan continued: 'We reject the idea of any inherent superiority of one race over another. Our policy, therefore, is non-racial. It offers a future in which Africans, Europeans and Asians ... will play their full part as citizens in the countries where they live, and in which feelings of race will be submerged in loyalty to the new nations.' Tom Hopkinson, who was editor of the South African magazine *Drum* at the time, wrote that Macmillan's speech did not sound remarkable to him until he listened to the angry and confused reply of the South African prime minister, Dr Verwoerd.[4]

In March there was the Sharpeville massacre in which South African police fired into an unarmed crowd killing 69 African men, women and children and wounding 180. Although it would be more than 30 years before South Africa achieved universal suffrage, Macmillan's speech and the killings and riots raised the political temperature in east and central Africa. This was followed by Belgium's abdication from the Congo in June 1960, creating a huge, unstable, independent state sharing borders with nine countries in east and central Africa. Over 40 years later the Congo continues to be unstable and a danger to its neighbours. In July 1960 there were riots in Salisbury, expressing African frustrations, which in turn led to greater repression by the Southern Rhodesian government. By November Lawrence Vambe, one of the most influential and thoughtful of African supporters, concluded that he had lost faith in Capricorn.[5] The London office was becoming concerned that they were collecting funds to support a multiracial society in Africa with hardly any African members.

Guy Hunter, whose sympathy for our ideas was not in doubt, wrote to Jeannine Scott and Jonathan Lewis offering some thoughts on the future. 'Dear J and J, ... Re Capricorn – have been having thoughts. I think you must face that a rearguard action for political partnership is no good. This tide and torrent and hurricane sweeping over Africa will never stay until there is majority rule by Africans in every country from the Mediterranean coast to the N[orthern] frontier of Southern Rhodesia. [Harold] Wiltshire[6] is right in saying that Africans [are] convinced (& they're right really, to be honest) that "partnership, multiracialism, citizenship" are all in a way disguises for continued European political privilege. But *But BUT* all the good Africans know they need European economic help. Could there not now be a major new thought for Capricorn, *vis*: "how can the Europeans help you Africans to make an economic success of Kenya, NR, Nyasaland, Tanganyika when you take over power?" If, as David has so often said, the real object is to combine European know-how with African freedom then why not stop arguing about the freedom and say "Alright we accept you are going to be the government, now let's sit down & work out just what you need & what guarantees of stability and fair dealing you must give to get it." You could go a long way on that, both with Africans and the city – though not with [right-wing Kenya settlers]! Guy.'[7]

The debate about future policy, including the question of whether Capricorn had a future at all, was most acute in Kenya, where nearly all the executive committee thought that to continue as the Capricorn Africa Society was doing our beliefs more harm than good. In September 1959, as branch chairman, I put forward a proposal, known as the infiltration option, to the AGM: 'In the belief that the Society's strength in Kenya lies in its ideas and its individual members rather than its name, it is proposed that wherever possible the aims of the Society should be achieved by influencing individuals and institutions and if possible changing existing organizations rather than creating new ones. To avoid jeopardizing the activities of individual members in their various fields it is proposed that no further publicity should be sought for Capricorn in Kenya and no publicity outside Kenya without consultation with the chairmen of the branches. The ideas for which Capricorn stands must be put before the public on every possible occasion as valid ideas in their own right.'[8]

Alone in the Kenya branch, Michael and Susan Wood strenuously argued that we must keep faith with Capricorn and carry on in spite of the realities of the political situation. From Ol Molog Susan Wood wrote four powerful pages arguing that 'Capricorn is a live organization today. We must do nothing to shorten or injure that life. If we let the Capricorn name go too much I believe that we shall be depriving future generations of a source of inspiration.'[9] Her optimism could partly be explained by being isolated on the slopes of Kilimanjaro, far from the realities of Nairobi politics, and by her feelings for David, who personified the movement in her eyes. Because her emotions were involved, the debate became increasingly awkward – Wood wrote me an undated note: 'As I have said to Eric [Wilkinson] no difference of opinion on this will make any difference to our friendships as far as I am concerned.'[10]

When John and Cecilia Sutcliffe, newly married in 1959 and with family money, moved into their London house round the corner from Cheval Place, they soon met Jeannine Scott and Lewis and were absorbed into the Capricorn network. Seeking adventure, they agreed in March 1960 to go to Kenya for a year to help Wood with Capricorn and the flying doctor project. Lewis also hoped for information on the true state of affairs in Kenya. The Sutcliffes flew to Khartoum and travelled in Nile paddle steamers, old Land Rovers and trains to Nairobi, where they stayed in the Woods' house. When they met other members of the Society in Kenya they thought we were fairly disillusioned and worried about the future of Capricorn. During the year the Sutcliffes spent in Kenya they too became increasingly disenchanted about the Society as they realized the level of poverty among urban Africans and the little being done to help. On their return to England in March 1961, Sutcliffe became a key member of the Capricorn and Zebra trusts.[11]

In theory, Capricorn was governed by decisions made at general council meetings with delegates from all the branches. In preparation for the next council it was decided that Lewis should make a tour of Capricorn's branches in Africa 'to gain first-hand impressions of the situation and to explain to the branches the functions and activities of the London branch'.[12] Lewis was keen to get back to Africa and wanted to find out the real position in the field after reading Sutcliffe's letters from Nairobi. In July 1960 he set off on a long tour through east and central Africa, writing a comprehensive and damning report on his return. He spent eight weeks in Kenya and Southern Rhodesia, with four days in Nyasaland, listening to a wide variety of opinions and meeting people, many of whom were Capricorn members, and some whom were not. His sympathy for their dilemma and his natural charm meant that people talked to him frankly, as a friend.

Lewis's report, dispassionate, frank and clearly written as one would expect from an ex-colonial service officer, is a crucial document in understanding the decline of the branches in Africa by 1960. The first paragraph records his compassion for his friends and colleagues in Africa when he refers to 'untiring and indomitable efforts ... to overcome almost insuperable obstacles ... by those who for ten years have fought to make the Society's ideals and philosophy live. It would be altogether impertinent for me to dismiss without recognition the activities which have been initiated out of genuine concern to match words with action.' Succeeding paragraphs show his determination to record the truth, however painful it was for him: 'Membership has fallen away catastrophically since Salima and now numbers on paper 262 all told in Africa. The Society can no longer be regarded as a serious force – or indeed as a force at all. The leadership is divided, African support is minimum, I found no evidence to suggest that the Society is taken seriously by any African. The Society appears to suffer universally the handicap of a bad name for various reasons – the belief that it has not practised what it has been preaching; a vague suspicion that it has not always been very scrupulous over finance; and the image of a European led/dominated organization – a last ditch movement. ... A deep division of opinion in the Kenya branch executive has existed since 1959. On the one hand are those who consider the branch should be much more active in promotion of specific projects directly as Capricorn and only as such, and on the other are those who consider the branch should remain primarily a thinking group, achieving its end by infiltration into other groups ... comments made by members, ex-members and informed observers: "Plenty of ill-will and no role for CAS in modern black Africa. Kenya branch has ceased to exist, just a loose, but loyal, old friends' association. CAS got members by its philosophy, not its welfare work. May lose many rounds, will win final. CAS must not abdicate — even politically".'

'Central African Branch: no proper records have been maintained in the office in Salisbury. Only 3 out of the 18 local associations replied to our questionnaire asking for details of membership and activities — a measure of how alive the movement is. ... The branch's main activities in the past year have been the organization of three successful and well-attended study conferences. The local association in Melsetter has continued to provide a valuable meeting ground by organizing discussion groups. No other local association appears now to be in existence. ... The Salisbury office is similarly depressingly lifeless Capricorn-wise — except when the chairman is in from Epworth — and the executive officer [Leo Takawira] completely taken up with politics/NDP affairs. The office has been little more than a political HQ for NDP whose leaders use the amenities and the telephone freely — as do others who have nothing but abuse for the Society and are doing their utmost to discredit us. The treasurer resigned December 1959, and from that date ... the ledger, cashbook and petty cash books were not maintained. Most people seem to agree that the Society's organization has collapsed completely, and this has been due in no small part to the vacuum after Salima conference.'

Lewis reported in a letter to Jeannine Scott that he had met a prominent Rhodesian Capricorn member, Nathan Shamuyarira, who told him that the mood of the Africans in Salisbury was determined, united and bitter over the detention of National Democratic Party members and that there would be serious trouble if they were given long sentences. He said that Shamuyarira wanted Capricorn to organize a round table conference to discuss the franchise and a bill of rights to avoid the Africans resorting to violence, adding that he still thought that Capricorn had an important role to play in Southern Rhodesia.[13]

His report summed up by asking 'whether our present costly structure of offices, paid staff, etc. is achieving anything worthwhile, whether the Society is, to quote the Revd Rea's words, "Doing the job relevant to the situation". ... London office has always regarded itself an outpost of the movement in Africa. ... But what is the London unit backing up? UK Capricorn members subscribe their £1 in the hope that they are helping to overcome racial difficulties in Africa. ... It is clear to me that they would not be very happy subsidizing the present offices, particularly when being used as a political HQ. ... In the light of this report the maintenance of the London office on its present basis cannot be justified. ... A people who are largely ill-paid, ill-fed, ill-housed and ill-clothed, with no security whatsoever in sickness or old age, are not interested in the trumpetings of multiracial societies which sound all too like the orchestration of hypocrisy.' Lewis's concern for the under-privileged is shown in his report by the trouble he took to list organizations in Africa that needed help, however modest, with details of the amounts needed. His understanding of real needs was one of the driving forces that created hostels for African students in London.

In August Susan Wood wrote an impassioned air-letter to Jeannine Scott in August: 'You will have Richard with you by now ... I feel at the moment that he has gone off on a wrong tack – perhaps he lacks the resilience born of faith. While leaving no stone unturned to reach an agreed policy I think there comes a time when one has to stand firmly for what one sees as right. I take this decision so seriously that I believe that if we desert action and the expression of our faith and philosophy in deeds as well as words we shall fail to work out our (CAS's) destiny and purpose in the history of Africa. Enormous things are at stake and to my mind we fail in our trust and betray our vision if we do not fight the battle at every level and with every faculty in our power. The political level is but one of the levels in which human relations can be influenced, and not even this battle is entirely lost, but endless opportunities for creating the oneness of the human race as we see it are before us.'[14]

I was in London in September 1960 when Lewis showed me the draft of his report, with which I had to agree, although parts were painful. On 3 October he wrote to Sutcliffe in Nairobi: 'Report: Charles March hundred per cent behind us. ... Hughes powerful piece herewith'[15] (my paper for the general council written in the London office). Although the essence of the Lewis report did not come as a surprise to some of us, his frank dissection – analysis is too weak a word – of Capricorn in Africa was devastating for Michael and Susan Wood. In London van der Post and David were unable to accept the reality of its conclusions while Jeannine Scott was torn between her fondness for Lewis and her emotional ties to David and the Woods.

The period between Lewis's visit to Kenya and the general

council meeting called for January 1961 was difficult for all of us, and especially Susan Wood, who wrote to Jeannine Scott. 'Oh how I long for a talk with you, and David and Joe [Oldham]. I feel completely flummoxed by Jonathan [Lewis]'s view of CAS future which to my mind is identical with Richard's. Mike and I cannot keep going by ourselves, and that is all that there is left now here as far as I can see. John [Sutcliffe] I think now feels the same as Jonathan. I long to know what you think. ... I shall strive to find a way whereby Mike and I can cause the Capricorn idea to survive here the present winter of unbelief. ... But I am grief stricken at our failure to carry the main Capricorn members with us. This is our failure and our private grief.'[16]

Lewis's weekly correspondent in Nairobi was Sutcliffe, who had a difficult row to hoe: he worked closely with Susan Wood on the Zebra Club and with Wood on the flying doctor service, and for some months he and Cecilia lived in the Woods' house in Nairobi. He was sympathetic to the Lewis report and to my views on the realities of the situation in Kenya, as their correspondence makes clear (Lewis to Sutcliffe). 'Weekend: a stern business. The line-up is just as we envisaged with David/Laurens/Jeannine clearly pained by my report and forming a block in favour of carrying on at all costs. "Just the moment Capricorn needed more than ever" sort of stuff, "must not lose faith" etc. Very perplexing.'[17]

Sutcliffe replied to Lewis that 'Cecilia thought your report could not have been bettered. ... It states the facts in an unbiased, unemotional way and neither of us can believe that its conclusions would be unacceptable – they're inescapable – and I only wish that those who feel that there are other and better alternative courses of action could come and see what you and I have seen going on here. The experience is humiliating and when one knows how much difference £1 will make to people coping with the real nub of the human problems of Africa I would wish that we could recover the £100s spent, and relive our six months here effectively in the ways of your report rather than any Capricorn charter which means nothing – just nothing, unless translated into "brass tacks". Just as Salima meant nothing after it had taken place because it was not translated in the field of effective action. "There is a tide in the affairs of men, which taken at the flood (1956), leads on, etc.". We failed to take the current when it served – must we lose our venture by refusing to be practical and effective even at this 23rd hour?'[18]

The following week Sutcliffe wrote again: 'Sue regards your

report, as she is entitled to do, as being totally deviationist, which I suppose it is. And with "Capricorn has work to do" reports flowing in from the south, Kenya appears to be utterly out of step due to general closing down forced by divisions in the ranks. Michael [Wood] writes to Rea "delighted to hear you are going ahead. I am equally determined to this end and we must just get rid of those people who feel we have no further work to do".'[19]

The general council meeting was held on 21 and 22 January 1961 at St Julian's, the Woods' old house, near Nairobi. In preparation for the crucial meeting Lewis issued a comprehensive file including his own report and statements by the president, two recommendations from the Kenya branch written by Eric Wilkinson and myself, three letters from the central Africa branch, the treasurer's report with the accounts and strong recommendations by the trustees of the Capricorn Africa Trust in London. In my paper I proposed that the branches in Africa be wound up and that individual members join the Society in London, whose objectives would be to maintain interest in rational political, social and economic developments in Africa and to raise money for projects that were in line with Capricorn's concerns.[20] I thought it would keep Capricorn alive and active while recognizing that its political ambitions in Africa were not acceptable to African (or world) opinion.

Wilkinson, writing with greater insight into African political ambitions, was blunter. 'I have known for two years that the branch was on the wrong lines and recently since Lancaster House [1960 Kenya constitutional conference] and the Congo, I have been certain that we should stop spending money on the efforts that have been approved by the executive – particularly such things as social evenings, advice bureau and the co-op farm idea. Firstly we must understand that Kenya is a mono-racial country and any hope that we might have built a multiracial nation are dead. We might have been successful had we moved faster in the period 1946–50. We didn't and we now pay the price for our folly. The real liberals were far too few and even today liberalism is frankly only based on fear and is not deep down in the hearts of the vast majority [of Europeans and Asians].'[21] He added that the African found nothing in common with most Europeans, who can only hope to be accepted as individuals. Susan Wood was to prove him right some years later when she started Kazuri, a ceramic workshop to provide work for unemployed young women and single mothers living in destitution on the outskirts of Nairobi. As an individual she is accepted and loved by the women who are part of a successful business making colourful beads and pottery.

Among the papers for the general council was a letter from Fred Rea, chairman of the central Africa branch, about the recent national convention of all races in which Capricorn had played a part. He added that a number of delegates had expressed their strong conviction that, on no account, must Capricorn regard its work as over.[22] In answer to his request for views on Capricorn's future, only one reply was attached. Bob Menzies had written from Northern Rhodesia: 'So far as the Copper Belt is concerned ... one has only two effective weapons: the church and politics. ... Thus I must repeat, with infinite regret, that for now Capricorn could do nothing here. Let us use it overseas.'[23] Also from Northern Rhodesia, Charles Fisher wrote a brief note to Lewis suggesting there should be a strong organization in London and local branches should wither unless they grew naturally.[24]

The treasurer, March, reported that the London office cost about £700 per annum more than Capricorn's income, an expense that had to be reduced, adding that there were still overdrafts in Salisbury and London.[25] He believed that there was a measure of respect and sympathy in London for Capricorn, tinged with regret that Salima bore no tangible fruit. A paper submitted by members of the London committee said that many UK members 'may well still believe that the active membership in Africa includes an important African element, and that the branches hold regular meetings and are engaged in various worthwhile activities in which the three races combine (the UK members ought not to be left much longer in ignorance of the true state of affairs).'

'During the present phase in the political development of the territories, any association with whites which is political, or regarded as such, must be harmful to any African, and the loss of Capricorn's African membership is not surprising. Any idea of continuing the Society as a forum for ideas, a kind of Fabian Society, is foredoomed to failure since any such enterprise must inevitably become impregnated with politics (as the Fabian Society was).'[26] The statement ended with two questions for the general council: should the London office continue, and was there any prospect of renewed multiracial activity in the African branches? The London chairman, Sir John Slessor, bluntly stated that Capricorn had no future in Africa as a popular, constructive and interracial organization, and should fade out and the London office be closed.[27]

The London office had a vigorous staff and a lively membership, with access to the corridors of power, though not to large sources of finance. Although this had developed through personal friendships, shared backgrounds and family connections, to be effective it had to be underpinned by the reality of Capricorn's membership from all races in Africa, which the London office realized no longer existed.

A paper from the London office signed by Henry Crookenden, March, Lewis, Jeannine Scott and Slessor proposed that the Capricorn Africa Trust stop supporting the London office.[28] Van der Post disagreed profoundly, writing: 'the whole [Lewis] report is a trivial, petty and completely negative approach to the problems we face. ... The Society has not ceased to be a multiracial group although its African membership has, to a certain extent, gone undercover and disappeared from obvious view. ... I know a great many of the people mentioned in Jonathan's report and from what I know of them I am certain that it is they who failed Capricorn and not Capricorn who failed them. They are merely projecting their own inadequacy and sense of guilt on to the Society.'[29] He continued that Capricorn's membership might not be as multiracial as it used to be, but its purposes were multiracial, so the work of the Society should continue. Van der Post's often-erratic political opinions, based on a sentimental and self-referential view of the African people, was an important influence on Susan Wood and Jeannine Scott in their reactions to reality.

Because many of the documents prepared for the general council were not dated, it is impossible to know if Wood and his wife had read them before drafting the president's submission, which covered the history of Capricorn from 1949 to the current impasse. He wrote: there is 'a difference of opinion within the Society as to whether it should remain as a small intellectual pressure group, or ... once again enlist membership for its activities'.[30] He added that what happened to Capricorn in Kenya would drastically affect the work and effectiveness of the Society in London and in the federation. This seemed unlikely – the London office was busy providing accommodation for overseas students, while in Southern Rhodesia no rational observer of the white politicians there could hold out any hope of a Capricorn-type solution. The president correctly described as schizophrenia the attempt to handle a political idea without getting involved in politics, though he offered no solution to the dilemma.

He continued the presidential tradition of irrational optimism, writing: 'In Kenya a new constitution presents the country with the possibility of making the first halting steps towards nationhood. It is not a perfect constitution from the Capricorn point of view, but it is a feasible start, and one for which Capricorn is to some degree responsible. It will be contended that the day of multiracialism is over and that it is now unacceptable to African and European alike, and that Capricorn has failed to get the spirit of the contract embodied in the constitution. ... The final constitution of Kenya is not written; there is still time and there is still a vast opportunity to affect affairs and make the Capricorn philosophy win the day. ... The task which Capricorn has set itself – that of promoting the active belief in the unity and dignity of the human race, cannot be achieved or lost in one encounter. It may well take several decades; it may take several lifetimes. Present setbacks, the difficulties of lack of finance and lack of personnel, are not reasons for lessening our efforts to this end. Kenya is at a critical time in her history when the views of the Society are more desperately needed than ever before. Can we deny or turn our back on this need? "No man lights a candle and puts it under a bushel, but on a candlestick; and it giveth light unto all that are in darkness." These words were spoken centuries ago to a handful of men and women no more numerous than the leading members of Capricorn, and often facing just the same kinds of problems which we face. They are still true today, and they are followed by an inescapable demand "Let your light so shine".'

This paper by the president accurately reflects the confusion and misunderstandings that caused so much heartache in the Kenya branch. The idealists, with strong religious faith, believed that precept one of the Contract, that all men are equal in dignity before God, was of primary importance. In opposition were the pragmatists, who accepted precept one but thought the precepts on the franchise, land and education were essential issues for a diverse electorate. Wood's quotation from the New Testament, comparing the handful of idealist members of Capricorn with Christ's Apostles made the ensuing debate particularly awkward. Some of the pragmatists, myself included, had little or no religious belief and did not relish arguing politics with the Disciples. Susan Wood recently suggested that her husband fought harder than he should have because she was losing something important to her.[31] During the meeting Moody Awori, the only African present, took her aside and told her that it was over, that we had become a handicap to men like himself who had no influence while they were attached to a European organization.[32] This she was unable to accept, even from a loyal friend and supporter.

Wood circulated influential letters from the heavyweights in London – David and van der Post. Extracts from David's letter showed, unsurprisingly, that he was firmly in the idealist camp and that he had lost touch with African opinion (and reality). 'I have yet to talk to an African on the question of the Society's future who is not convinced that Capricorn has a most valuable part to play in the period subsequent to the transfer of political power. ... Africa demands a new political philosophy and Capricorn has for long been on the road to the point of its emergence. The final and valid definition of this philosophy still eludes us and as you know I am convinced that its full revelation may only come in the new circumstances, which will prevail after political power has passed from the European to the African. ... Few people, in fact not even many members of the Society, understand the central objective of our work remains and must always remain the bringing to book of the reality of the oneness of the human race. All history has been an infinitely gradual progress towards realization of this proposition and at this moment in time, Capricorn – non-swanks – is one of history's agents. To those of us who understand and grasp this fact it is quite unthinkable to consider giving in to those who don't.'[33] Reading these papers after half a lifetime forcibly reminds me of the frustration and irritation Wilkinson and I, supported by other members of the Kenya executive committee, felt at the lack of logic and failure to recognize unpalatable reality shown by some of our friends and colleagues.

Lewis had prevailed upon Sutcliffe to act as secretary to the general council meeting, which he did splendidly, producing 31 pages of almost verbatim report in addition to the formal minutes.[34] The meeting began with Rea from Southern Rhodesia summarizing recent events in the central Africa branch and adding: 'we must not do that counsel of despair – try to justify our existence by welfare work' although that was exactly what they were doing. The discussion was diffuse and slightly bad tempered, as debates often are when participants do not keep to the point. Wilkinson said very firmly that Kenya was going to be a mono-racial society, which Wood disputed. Awori agreed with Wilkinson and said that the African would welcome the European in the background with himself in the spotlight. At one point Wood hopefully asked if an African government, facing hard economic facts, could afford to squeeze out the Asians if it was to be a responsible government.

Wilkinson responded that it had been done elsewhere and it would be done again. In 1972 Uganda was to prove him right.

Although Susan Wood was the most emotionally involved of those present, she said nothing during the meeting – Sutcliffe remembers her wincing when Wilkinson or I spoke, although I opened my statement with fulsome, and genuinely felt, praise for the work that the Woods had done for Capricorn over many years. I said Capricorn in Kenya was beset by fundamental questions: was the current political situation something we could welcome? If Kenya was to become an African, not a multiracial country, was that a policy of which Capricorn approved? We had once been too advanced for the Europeans but now found ourselves accused of being in the last ditch, of offering to work with Africans only to keep a toe in play. I said I found the situation was disconcerting, and continued: 'Capricorn set itself up and many joined, and I joined, because it tried to create, codify and get accepted a political philosophy under which we might live in this part of Africa. As far as Kenya is concerned it was not achieved. If this is what the majority of us joined for, it is not surprising we are at a loss. If, on the other hand, one joined for running clubs, doing welfare activities and for reasons of personal friendship, they are all that remain.'

Although the council later agreed that the Society's primary purpose was to promote a political philosophy and that it should not promote welfare projects to justify its existence, Wood reacted strongly to my speech, saying to me. 'You have produced a situation, which you set out to do, in which there is no need for the Capricorn Society in Kenya.'[35] All I could reply was to ask 'Is that what you really think?' to which he replied 'Yes'. This was a bad moment in the two days of discussion. It is little comfort that events proved the pragmatists right – indeed events have shown that in some respects we were over-optimistic about the future.

Wilkinson reported on work being done on testamentary legislation for Africans (at that time it was not legally possible for an African to make a will), on a draft bill of rights and on our satisfactory financial position, speaking as the branch treasurer. Referring to the Kenya Party, he said that we had done a great deal of work on the political front, including a submission to the Colonial Office but few of our proposals had been adopted. Awori reported on the club and the citizens' advice bureau, the latter regarded only as an employment exchange. He continued: 'Today Capricorn as an active body has no role to play, at least in the Kenya I know.'

On the second day the general council faced a formal agenda with resolutions and the usual attempt to understand the balance sheet and statement of income and expenditure. Then we came to the crucial Lewis report, which the president diminished by saying, 'Jonathan had arrived in a fog and had left in one, and was in a very depressed mood.' I countered this, saying: 'In making this report, Jonathan was being unkinder to himself than to anyone, because he believed totally in Capricorn and believed the work he did on small pay was backed up in Africa. ... His report had to be ruthless, accurate and honest.'

Resolutions were passed directing the London office to continue and the central Africa branch to employ fresh staff and continue the good work. Then I proposed that the council recommend the Kenya branch be wound up, and Wilkinson moved that individual members in Kenya should join an overseas group, based in London. In moving the first resolution, Sutcliffe's tireless report recorded that I said: 'as Dr Oldham wrote recently in a letter to Jonathan Lewis – "the prejudice against the Society and the lack of African support seem decisive handicaps." Put bluntly, the name and organization we have all tried to serve for so long is a liability to the idea. The concern of those who support this resolution is that the Capricorn idea can be preserved out of harm's way in the neutral territory of London, and in Rhodesia where the opportunity of creating the type of society we all want is still open and must not be lost. We have heard Moody Awori, one of our oldest and staunchest African supporters, when he said with great regret, that although Capricorn in Kenya today has no role to play, he's convinced that our ideas will rise again from within the African ranks. But we must frankly recognize that a renaissance is unlikely while the Africans think the ideas come from Capricorn, a name they connect with European control, and with dragging our feet in the mad rush towards the Africanization of Kenya. To pass this resolution would be a courageous recognition of unpalatable facts. Capricorn has always been courageous and straightforward, and we must continue to be so in our disappointment and eclipse by the historical situation in Kenya today.' Wilkinson made a moving and powerful statement, in which he recognized the paradox: 'the movement should close down in Kenya if it is to go on.' The meeting decided both these proposals should go to a postal vote, which rejected them.

At the end of February 1961 I received the results of the postal vote[36] and in March called an executive meeting of the Kenya branch, at the end of which I resigned from the committee, as did the other members.[37] I continued to support the ideals set out by Capricorn and did what I could to carry them out, particularly over education. After five years of effort and enthusiasm for Capricorn I turned to other things beside my growing architectural practice. I started dinghy sailing (and have not yet stopped) and, more seriously, became involved in the preservation of Lamu, an ancient Islamic town on the coast of Kenya, and with environmental politics. I helped set up, and later chair, the international Environment Liaison Centre to coordinate non-governmental activity with the newly formed Environmental Programme, based in Nairobi. Wood agreed to chair the forthcoming AGM, at which Joyce Raw intended to propose winding up the branch, in spite of the failure of our motion in the postal vote. The AGM put off the final closure and the branch limped on, with Susan Wood as chairman, although she was living at Ol Molog. Wood's term of office as president of Capricorn came to an end and there were no candidates to replace him, so the office lapsed. In Southern Rhodesia the branch continued with Kalahari Kate, the mobile unit, and gave valuable help to Ranche House College. The historian Ian Hancock summed it up: 'In the 1950s Capricorn set out to change the world; by the 1960s it was reduced to performing good works of increasingly small dimensions.'[38]

The London office continued to be perplexed about the situation of the branches in Africa. In June 1962 Lewis wrote to Theo Bull in Northern Rhodesia: 'The whole question of the Society's position I must say we find totally baffling. The general feeling seems over here that the Society has shot its bolt and we would be best advised to concentrate on the trust [in London]. Let's face it, our major endeavours are hostels here and youth in Africa – all under the trust. The Society ... is based on a political programme – community knit together by a common patriotism, vigorous development of country's resources, interracial communities, etc. which is certainly still fine stuff but not on as things are. Sir John [Slessor], our chairman, described [our situation in Africa] as OBE (overtaken by events), whereas the scope of the trust is infinite.'[39] Bull agreed, referring to the current difficulty over finding a president: 'I do totally share your view re the Capricorn front. Presidency to lapse, the Society itself to lapse – anyway this end. All our endeavours are now practical endeavours under the auspices of the two trusts (Capricorn and Zebra).'[40]

The Capricorn office in London was the first to bite the bullet –

in March 1963 Lewis announced the intention to close in a letter to Rea in Salisbury.[41] He wrote that the name had become a very real handicap to their provision of student accommodation, and also to Wood in his medical work, which must have been particularly painful for Wood to accept. By then the plan to close was supported by David, van der Post, Wood, Crookenden, March, Jeannine Scott and others. The Capricorn Trust's resources and energies, in the active form of Jeannine Scott and Lewis, were passed to the Zebra Trust, which continued to provide accommodation for overseas students and help in Africa.

Two years after the general council, a few months before Kenya became an independent republic, Susan Wood sent me a moving letter, which I was very glad to have. 'My dear Richard, I wanted to write and tell you myself that we had decided to fold up the Kenya branch of Capricorn. ... I suppose I felt at the time that we argued about it all that good things depended for their success on the strength of our efforts. Now I see that good things can fail as easily as anything else. So I can live with the failure, and accept that we cannot do any more along that line at present. I am so sorry that I have been so slow in coming to what was obvious to you, and I only hope that damage was not caused to any good we might have done. Forgive me please for fighting too long when I should have given in, and for any sadness I caused you as a result. We can be so proud of much that Capricorn achieved, and after all there's still so much to do in thousands of ways. I am busy being a farmer and I love it! Much love, Sue.'[42]

When their farm was taken over by the Tanganyika government in 1977 the Woods moved back to Nairobi, and after the reconstructive surgery building was cancelled we met rarely, but always as friends. Wood's belief in Capricorn was an extension of his religious convictions, writing to Jeannine Scott shortly after the Kenya branch had closed: 'The cross of Capricorn seems to get no lighter as the years go by but I want you to know that I would never deny Capricorn. ... Sue and I in our small way are perhaps more tied to Capricorn and its expression in Africa than to anything else. We need you so badly as so many stalwarts are baling out from Africa and the path ahead looks stony.'[43]

Rea bravely carried on in Salisbury. In May 1962 he wrote to Lewis describing their annual general meeting with justifiable pride: 'We had 24 at the AGM, ten of them were African and one coloured. I know you like to be reassured that we are still multiracial. I called for a debate on whether we should continue and there was a unanimous yes. So we are still breathing.'[44] He thought that Capricorn still had a role to play in Southern Rhodesia, and the branch kept going in spite of reduced numbers of African members. In June 1965 Ken Mew, branch chairman and principal of Ranche House College, told the members that the branch was to be dissolved.[45] In November white-ruled Southern Rhodesia unilaterally declared independence, which was the beginning of the end for white dominance, although the end took a long and bloody time coming. During UDI Rea wrote to me from Salisbury to say that life was normal for the time being, adding that he could not bring himself even to think of cooperating with outside forces applying sanctions to ruin the economy and bring down the Smith regime in ruins.

The break-up of Capricorn in Africa illuminates many of the fundamental difficulties we faced from the beginning and raises questions on the operation of the Society in the decade when it was active on the continent. In the debate on colonialism phrases like 'holding the line' or 'last ditch' became terms of abuse, but for earlier generations had a heroic resonance. Capricorn was often castigated for being a 'last ditch' group of Europeans, and indeed they were defending an ideal in the face of overwhelming odds – and they lost.

Epilogue

The failure of Capricorn's campaign and indeed the general collapse of colonialism in Africa raises some hard questions. Why, at a time when it was still possible, did none of the countries involved accept what we believed essential: a common roll with qualified multiple voting? Southern Rhodesia did have a common roll but it was a mockery for Africans. The substantial Colonial Office files on Capricorn show that the Society was taken seriously in Whitehall, in part due to David Stirling's easy access to the establishment and his fluent advocacy. But in the face of determined settler opposition to a genuine common roll, and equally determined demands for universal franchise by African politicians, Whitehall prevaricated until universal franchise was the only option available.

Why was Capricorn so unpopular and why did we fail to persuade politicians and the public in Africa to accept our programme of a common citizenship and loyalty to the country rather than to tribe or race? Going through the documents recording the opinions of those whom we thought were more or less on the same side makes depressing reading. Our attitude of being liberal and virtuous must have been irritating to politicians and civil servants struggling with insoluble realities, and there were suggestions that Capricorn was linked to Moral Rearmament. The powerful personality and self confidence that persuaded men and women to follow David could also repel some who should have been allies. His determination to campaign in five countries, disparate in every respect except being African and under British control, distracted effort from Southern Rhodesia where some progress might have been made before the country descended into civil war.

Were we too gentlemanly or exclusive? Capricorn in England and in Africa did have a preponderance of well educated men and women of all races, people who regarded the realities of politics — the need to follow mass opinion — with some distaste, so there was little possibility of creating a popular campaign that might influence events. When the Sutcliffes went to Kenya in 1960 they were given no information about the Kenya branch of the Society or introductions to anyone there except the Woods.[1] This underlines one of the causes of our failure – the Society effectively consisted of a select group of close friends of the same social background, who corresponded in affectionate terms and stayed with one another frequently, without thought that a functioning movement needs troops on the ground who need to be involved and to feel involved. These issues, plus the cerebral nature of our political programme, meant that Capricorn could never be a mass movement. In politics, power depends on numbers and we could command few enough members, let alone voters, to be of interest to the politicians who were responsible for changing the future.

Was there any chance of success? The answer has to be no, for reasons that Capricorn members in Africa ignored or misunderstood. Most European and Asian colonists could remember before the war when the number of African men and women with a university degree, or experience of the outside world, was insignificant, and in the 1950s they noticed little change. But beyond their experience the world was turning against them. Our calls for logical franchise proposals were seen as continuing colonialism, which had been unacceptable to majority world opinion since 1945. David, who was familiar with men of influence in the United States and Britain, might have understood how history was moving had he not been so convinced of the rightness of his crusade that he was blind to the inexorable forces ranged against it. By the late 1950s David should have recognized the realities of political advance in West Africa and that it would be inevitable in the east.[2] Susan Wood has suggested that 'David hated losing and did not want to be associated with failure – perhaps that was one reason why he resigned when he did.'[3] Nevertheless, at the end of his life David believed that Capricorn was the most important thing he had done.

During the decade when the Society was active in Africa, it was the obduracy of the majority of Europeans that prevented and delayed change. Most white settlers believed that the region depended on their continuing leadership, which to the other races meant European domination. If any progress was to be made towards an integrated and democratic society, then Europeans had to change their attitudes and policies, but most saw no compelling reason to do so. In Capricorn we tried to persuade them otherwise, but we were insufficiently revolutionary to make any difference, and in any case many of our European members believed that their leadership, even in a multiracial context, was essential for the foreseeable future. It might seem facile to describe Capricorn as a small European group trying ineffectively to resist the tide of African nationalism, but the truth is found in the records with their paucity of comment or contribution from Asian or African members. There were some valuable and enthusiastic supporters from those communities but it cannot be pretended that they were other than followers and rather few at that.

David concentrated on the idea of the moment and was always prepared to go into action, confident that his lead would be followed. Reading the files for this book has shown that David was often hasty and sometimes wrong, but while I worked with him from 1956 to 1966, in Capricorn and on his television projects, I believed in him and enjoyed it. I believed in him not because he was a legendary war hero but because I responded to his enthusiasm and idealism. On the other hand, Laurens van der Post was also a celebrated figure but to me was unconvincing in spite of the warmth of his rhetoric about Africa. Fitzroy Maclean wrote in David's obituary that he had 'the ultimate quality of a leader, the gift of capturing the imagination and confidence of those he led to the extent of carrying them with him on enterprises that by any rational standards seemed certain to fail, and convincing them that under his leadership they were, against all probability, bound to succeed'.[4] He was writing about war, but David was equally effective in convincing his followers in peacetime. His optimism, which most of us adopted, kept the Society going for some years after Salima, and much good was done in the creation of the two colleges.

Why did the Society continue after it should have been clear that we had failed in our primary objective? Because Capricorn began, and remained, in thrall to David's powerful idealism – even at second-hand through Michael and Susan Wood after David resigned as president. We remained Sancho Panzas after the Don had left the field and, besides, we enjoyed the battle. David personified Capricorn when it was active in Africa – he led it and inspired its members at each phase of his personal journey from paternalism to majority rule. Because he had an extraordinary quality of leadership we were prepared and delighted to follow him and in some cases to adore him. As the historian Terence Ranger put it, there is 'a great pathos in reading about all those idealistic and romantic men, and especially women, who devoted themselves to the enchanter'.[5]

As David thought about the difficulties Capricorn had faced in changing opinion in widely dispersed and mostly illiterate populations he concluded that television could be a potent source of influence and education, and might also solve his financial problems. In 1961 he set up Television International Enterprises Limited (TIE) with his friend Colin Campbell and limited financial backing. Their base in the early days was a small room in the Cheval Place office where he was surrounded, indeed hemmed in, by Capricorn. Alan Hoe quotes David as remembering: 'We had one small room which Colin and I took turns to use. The other had to sit at the top of the stairs. Consequently we never, but never, allowed visitors.'[6] He failed to secure the television contract for Southern Rhodesia, probably because the government, not unreasonably from their perspective, thought he would use it to further his radical politics. One of David's early ventures was the Kenya Broadcasting Corporation for which I was asked to design and supervise the new television centre in Nairobi. In typical David style the date for the formal opening in October 1962 was settled in advance of commissioning the architect, so the studios, control rooms and offices had to be, and were, designed and built in 11 months. Later, David asked me to design the television and radio centre in Mauritius and to look at a possible site in Aden, where I later learnt he needed a base for incursions into the Yemen. In all, TIE set up 12 independent television stations,[7] including the most successful, Hong Kong.

After he resigned as president of Capricorn in September 1958 David had more than two decades of constant activity before he began to slow down – activity with the same bounding ambition and breadth of vision as his attempt to redraw the map of British Africa while changing the deep-rooted convictions of the inhabitants. Once he decided that television was the answer then his small company was going to overwhelm the Commonwealth and beyond. Recognizing in 1962 that the invasion of the Yemen by Egyptian forces would increase Soviet influence in the region and threaten Aden, David organized the supply of men and *matériel* for the Yemeni resistance.[8] After the Suez fiasco the British government could offer only support behind the scenes, which allowed the operation to be pilloried in the press as mercenaries and gunrunners. David's enthusiasm for cloak and dagger affairs helped to fuel suspicions about the operation – found in the bar of a Nairobi hotel he would urge that no one be told that he was in town, an impossible demand.

As he travelled round Africa and the Middle East David developed a network of friends and contacts who supplied him with intelligence and gossip, from which he realized that many of the newly independent countries in Africa were liable to coups and revolution. Unable to see a problem, however intractable, without wanting to take action to solve it David set up Watchguard with SAS veterans to supply protection to vulnerable presidents and train their bodyguards. Nearer to home he started Truemid, an organization to prevent the disruption to British life that he anticipated from the actions of radical and militant trade unions. Then he had solutions to the UK education system and much else that he thought was not as good as it could be. In the prevailing liberal climate of the time he was often attacked as a right-wing extremist remembering his days of glory in the Western Desert, although while I knew him he never mentioned the SAS or his time in Colditz prison.

Michael Wood continued to be the driving force in the African Medical and Research Foundation he had founded in the Capricorn years.[9] In 1984, shortly before he was due to retire from AMREF, Wood and his friend David Campbell set up the Food and Agricultural Research Mission, known as FARM-Africa. Believing 'that food is the best medicine'[10] Wood hoped that by supporting a range of demonstration projects in east and southern Africa their organization could make a difference to the lives of the millions in Africa who depended on the land. FARM-Africa, like AMREF, is now a powerful organization with a London headquarters and many successful projects in Africa. Both are testaments to Michael Wood's vision and his determination to improve life in the continent where he lived and died.

It is no comfort to the survivors of Capricorn's campaign to watch the chaos and corruption that characterizes so many governments in Africa after two generations of independence and universal franchise. There is no doubt that the speed with which European governments laid down their colonial responsibilities – often faster than African nationalist politicians expected or wanted – increased the possibility of unstable government. Presidents and ministers who feel insecure need to surround themselves with people they can trust leading to nepotism, already intrinsic in African culture where the extended family unit is all-important. Insecurity also encourages corruption as those in power require wealth to impress and suborn supporters, and believe they must save against an uncertain future, while ensuring that they remain in power forever. As I write, the unfolding tragedy of Zimbabwe is an extreme example, exacerbated in the eyes of the world press by the murder of white farmers and the ruthless expropriation of their productive land. This has tended to overshadow the larger disaster suffered by the African people of the country, particularly those who wish to change the situation and return the country to the prosperity it enjoyed only a few years ago. An opposition supporter expressed the fears of all who passionately want Africa to succeed when he said, 'If a country like this, highly educated, with resources, can't function, what hope is there for the rest of Africa?'[11]

Where there has been a change of government, constitutional or otherwise, the incoming ministry soon makes up for the opportunities for wealth denied them out of power. In countries with minerals in demand by the West, the situation is inflamed by international companies willing to pay large commissions, otherwise known as bribes, and shore up unstable regimes. Ironically for supporters of Capricorn's common loyalty and code of citizenship, some contemporary commentators have concluded that the failure of African states is because there is no concept of citizenship, no sense of responsibility for one's fellows beyond the family unit and tribe.[12] Arbitrary frontiers established by European powers at the end of the nineteenth century, dividing ethnic groups while forcing others to live together under one government, have not helped, though African governments are adamant that their boundaries are sacrosanct.

Capricorn in London had its excitements as Jonathan Lewis bought property and set up trusts or companies, but there was always a bedrock of reality – the hostels and the students were real and the good that was done was manifest. To contrast the positive achievements of the London team with the lack of success in Africa ignores the time and the context. In spite of David's boundless enthusiasm and the devotion of those who followed him, international opinion and the tenor of the times ensured that the Capricorn concept would fail in Africa, which is why, on the first page of this book, I used the word 'doomed' to describe our enterprise. In spite of the larger failure in Africa, we were not irrelevant. Capricorn acted as conscience and goad to liberal European and Asian politicians in Kenya in the years between Salima and independence, and friendships across racial barriers established in citizenship committees endured. Capricorn supporters in Southern Rhodesia did much quiet good in spite of conditions that became increasingly difficult as the country moved to the settlers' illegal declaration of independence and then civil war. And we can be proud of Ranche House and Kalahari Kate in Zimbabwe, the Zebra hostels in England and Zebra Trust's growing support for secondary schools in Africa.

Appendix 1: Zebra Trust and Zebra Housing Association Hostels

Zebra House	1958	3, Marloes Road, London, W8	2 flats, 35 rooms
	1961	7, Marloes Road	
	1962	1, Marloes Road	
	1998	Closed and property sold	
Impala House	1961	8 and 9, Chalcot Square and 30 Chalcot Crescent, London, NW1	28 flats, 11 rooms
	1963	7, Chalcot Square and 32 and 34, Chalcot Crescent, London, NW1	
Jerome House	1964	19–25, Harrington Gardens, London, SW7	22 flats, 58 rooms
	1989	Closed and exchanged for	
	1991	8–13, Glendower Place, London, SW7	29 flats, 8 rooms
Coundon House	1964	Southbank Road, Coventry	46 rooms
	1976	Closed	
Zebra House (B)	1964	9, Miles Road, Bristol 8	7 flats
	1996	Closed and property sold	
Sentosa House	1967	15–19, Upper Montague Street, London, W1	17 flats, 20 rooms
	1973	125 and 127, Richmond Avenue, London, N1	
Charles Hayward House	1972	33–34, Leinster Gardens, London, W2	5 flats, 14 rooms
	1980	Closed	

Appendix 2: Dates of Independence in Africa

Date	*Country (colonial name)*	*Colonial power*
1941	Ethiopia (Abyssinia)	Italy (since 1936)
1956	Sudan	UK
1957	Ghana (Gold Coast)	UK
1958	Guinea (French West Africa)	France
1960	Cameroon (French Cameroon)	France
1960	Central African Republic (French Equatorial Africa)	France
1960	Chad (French Equatorial Africa)	France
1960	Republic of Congo (French Equatorial Africa)	France
1960	Benin (Dahomy)	France
1960	Gabon (French Equatorial Africa)	France
1960	Ivory Coast (French West Africa)	France
1960	Madagascar	France
1960	Mali (French Sudan)	France
1960	Mauritania (French West Africa)	France
1960	Niger (French West Africa)	France
1960	Nigeria	UK
1960	Senegal (French West Africa)	France
1960	Somalia (Somaliland)	Italy and UK/UNO
1960	Togo (French West Africa)	France
1960	Burkina Faso (Upper Volta)	France
1960	Zaire (Belgian Congo)	Belgium
1961	Sierra Leone	UK
1961	Tanzania (Tanganyika)	UK/UNO
1962	Burundi (Ruanda)	Belgium/UNO
1962	Rwanda (Ruanda)	Belgium/UNO
1962	Uganda	UK
1963	Kenya	UK
1963	Zanzibar	UK
1964	Malawi (Nyasaland)	UK

1964	Zambia (Northern Rhodesia)	UK
1965	The Gambia	UK
1966	Botswana (Bechuanaland)	UK
1966	Lesotho (Basutoland)	UK
1967	Swaziland	UK
1968	Equatorial Guinea (Spanish Guinea)	Spain
1968	Mauritius	UK
1974	Guinea-Bissau (Portuguese Guinea)	Portugal
1975	Angola	Portugal
1975	Cape Verde	Portugal
1975	Comoros (French Overseas Territory)	France
1975	Mozambique	Portugal
1975	Sao Tomé e Principe	Portugal
1976	Seychelles	UK
1977	Djibouti (French Somaliland)	France
1980	Zimbabwe (Southern Rhodesia)	UK (UDI 1965–79)
1990	Namibia (South West Africa)	South Africa
1993	Eritrea (Ethiopian Province)	Ethiopia
1994	South Africa	(Apartheid)

Notes

Introduction

1. Illustrated London News, 23 June 1956.
2. Letter from N. Boosey to J. H. G. Senior, 27 December 1986, Mrs J. Bartosik archive.
3. See Chapter 15.

Chapter 1: David Stirling Goes to Africa

1. Cowles, 1958.
2. Hoe, 1992.
3. Ibid.
4. Interview with author, 31 August 1999.
5. File 12, UoY archive.
6. Army Records, PRO, Kew.
7. Hoe, 1992.
8. Letter from A. Stokes to A. Hoe, 6 May 1991, Alan Hoe archive.
9. Alan Hoe interview with author, 31 August 1999.
10. Letter from D. Stirling to Sir Ernest Oppenheimer, 28 August 1950, file CA9/1/1/5, ZNA, Harare.
11. Alport, 1952.
12. See Chapter 5.
13. Clements, 1999.
14. Hailey, 1957.
15. Holderness, 1985.
16. Hailey, 1957.
17. Clements, 1999.
18. Ibid.
19. *Indians in Kenya.* Cmd 1922, 1923, from Hailey, 1957.
20. Clements, 1999.
21. Statement of the Conclusions of HM Government on Closer Union in East Africa, 1930.
22. Hailey, 1957.
23. Hansard, 19 January 1946.
24. File CO 822/1365, PRO, Kew.
25. File CO 967/39, PRO, Kew.
26. Ibid.
27. *Life Magazine*, 10 October 1942, quoted by Hailey, 1957.
28. Hailey, 1957.
29. Huxley, 1935, p.183.
30. Mason, 1984.
31. Telegram to the Kabaka of Uganda, file DO35/4705, PRO, Kew.

Chapter 2: Two Pyramids

1. Report by Viscount Montgomery of Alamein, 1947, file CO 967/39, PRO, Kew.

2. CRO memo dated 2 January 1948, file DO 35/2380, PRO, Kew.
3. Letter from H. Holderness to author, 16 April 2000.
4. Hancock, 1978.
5. See Chapter 10.
6. Holderness, 1985.
7. Hoe, 1992.
8. Interview with L. Vambe, 9 February 2000.
9. Holderness, 1985.
10. Undated 'Notes for N H: Suggested Conditioning Factors to Keep in Mind', Ian Hancock archive.
11. Stirling and Wilson, 1950.
12. Garlake, 1973.
13. Caton-Thompson, 1931, quoted in Garlake, 1973.
14. Mason, 1958.
15. Brookes, 1925.
16. Interview with H. Holderness, 21 March 2000.
17. K. Ward, 'The Movement for Capricorn: A First Appreciation', 8 July 1950, file CA9/13/1/1, ZNA, Harare.
18. H. R. Hughes, 'Tropical Building by 1950', author's archive.
19. Hancock, 1978.
20. Letter from B. O'Connell to D. H. Fowler, 5 August 1952, file CA9/1/1/3, ZNA, Harare.
21. See Chapter 5.
22. Letter from D. Stirling to B. O'Connell, 5 January 1951, file CA9/6/1/12, ZNA, Harare.
23. Letter from D. Stirling to O. Woods, 16 May 1951, file CA9/6/1/12, ZNA, Harare.
24. Letter from D. Stirling to N. H. Wilson, 8 November 1951, file CA9/1/1/4, ZNA, Harare.
25. Record of proceedings of inaugural meeting of CAS, 9 April 1951, Ian Hancock archive.
26. Letter from D. Stirling to P. Allsbrook of Kier & Cawdor Ltd, 1 January 1951, file 8, UoY archive.
27. Undated paper, Ian Hancock archive.
28. Hancock, 1978.
29. See the debate on 'infiltration' in Chapter 16.
30. Minutes of CAS meeting, 28 February 1952, file 8, UoY archive.
31. Interview with author, 12 May 1998.
32. Lewis et al., 1951.
33. See Chapter 11.
34. Ian Hancock archive.
35. File CA9/5/1/16, ZNA, Harare.
36. Undated note by K. Ward, file CA/9/13/1/6, ZNA, Harare.
37. Meeting of European elected members, Nairobi, November 1951, file CA9/6/1/ 12, ZNA, Harare.
38. Letter from K. Ward to D. Stirling, 25 November 1951, file 8, UoY archive.

Chapter 3: The Declarations

1. Letter from Archbishop of Canterbury to D. Stirling, 17 October 1951, file 9, UoY archive.
2. 'Capricorn Africa: The Society's Formula for the Political Application of its Race Relations Policy', 1952, file 65, UoY archive.

3. Memo by D. Stirling, 11 March 1952, file CA9/5/1/13, ZNA, Harare.
4. Letter from D. Stirling to Prime Minister of Southern Rhodesia, 26 February 1952, file 8, UoY archive.
5. Letter from J. Baines to D. Stirling, 2 April 1952, file 8, UoY archive.
6. File 8, UoY archive.
7. Ibid.
8. Prain, 1981.
9. Note dated 16 November 1960, file 35, UoY archive.
10. Letter from D. Stirling to Miss J. Scott, 6 June 1955, Mrs J. Bartosik archive.
11. Notes on meeting, 8 February 1952, file 65, UoY archive.
12. Letter from D. Stirling to A. Lennox-Boyd, 13 March 1952, file CA9/1/1/4, ZNA, Harare.
13. Letter from A. Lennox-Boyd to D. Stirling, 3 April 1952, file 65, UoY archive.
14. Letter from A. Lennox-Boyd to D. Stirling, January 1952, file CA9/13/1/2, ZNA, Harare.
15. Letter from D. Stirling to J. Baines, 11 February 1952, file 8, UoY archive.
16. Undated paper in file 8, UoY archive.
17. *Manchester Guardian,* 24 March 1952, file 68, UoY archive.
18. Letter from Sir E. Twining to D. Stirling, December 1951, file 8, UoY archive.
19. From paper by Alistair Ross entitled 'The Capricorn Africa Society in Tanganyika, 1949 to 1958'.
20. Author of *Permanent Way,* vols I and II, 1949 and 1957.
21. Letter from W. Havelock to D. Stirling, 23 September 1952, file 8, UoY archive.
22. Letter from D. Stirling to W. Havelock, 31 October 1952, file 8, UoY archive.
23. Letter from M. Blundell to D. Stirling, 23 September 1952, file 8, UoY archive.
24. See Chapter 12.
25. Letter from D. Stirling to R. Anderson, 28 November 1952, file 8, UoY archive.
26. Letter from R. Darwin to D. Stirling, 29 October 1952, file 65, UoY archive.
27. P. Mackay archive.
28. Letter from D. Stirling to A. Stokes, 22 March 1954, file 12, UoY archive.
29. File 81, UoY archive.
30. P. Mackay archive.
31. File 68, UoY archive.
32. *Daily Herald*, London, 8 December 1952.
33. *Daily Telegraph*, London, 8 December 1952.
34. *News Chronicle*, London, 9 December 1952.
35. *Economist*, London, 13 December 1952.
36. *Catholic Worker*, January 1953.
37. *Truth*, 12 December 1952.
38. *Tanganyika Standard*, Dar es Salaam, 8 December 1952.
39. *Rhodesia Herald,* Salisbury, 8 December 1952.
40. *Bulawayo Chronicle*, Bulawayo, 9 December 1952.
41. *New York Times*, New York, 4 January 1953.
42. *Christian Science Monitor*, Boston, 30 December 1952.
43. *Birmingham Post and Mail*, December 1952, file 81, UoY archive.
44. Perham, 1956.
45. Lugard, 1893.

46. Letter from D. Stirling to W. Havelock, 11 December 1952, file 65, UoY archive.
47. Letter from T. McNaulty to D. Stirling, 31 December 1952, file 65, UoY archive.
48. From Alan Hoe, *David Stirling*, Little Brown & Company, 1992.
49. Letter from D. Clarke to D. Stirling, 4 September 1953, Jeannine Bartosik archive.
50. Hailey, 1957.
51. See Chapter 13.
52. Tredgold, 1968.
53. Hancock, n.d.
54. Holderness, 1985.
55. Letter from H. Holderness to author, 31 March 2001.
56. Letter from D. Stirling to J. Amery and others, 11 June 1953, file 9, UoY archive.

Chapter 4: Transformation and Growth

1. van der Post, 1968.
2. van der Post, 1952.
3. *African Affairs*, July 1952, quoted in Jones, 2001.
4. Hoe, 1992.
5. CAS Minutes, 11 June 1952, Salisbury, file 65, UoY archive.
6. Mrs J. Bartosik archive.
7. Letter from Elspeth Holderness to the author, 6 March 2001.
8. Mason, 1984.
9. Interview with the author, 15 April 1998.
10. Vambe, 1972 and Vambe, 1976.
11. Quoted in interview with P. Mackay, 5 February 2000.
12. See Chapter 9.
13. Hancock, n.d., I. Hancock archive.
14. Ibid.
15. Letter from D. Stirling to Jeannine Scott, 23 September 1954, Mrs J. Bartosik archive.
16. Leakey, 1954.
17. Wood, 1964.
18. See Chapters 12 and 14.
19. Letter from D. Stirling to O. Lyttleton, 27 October 1953, file 10, UoY archive.
20. Paper from file CO/822/1742, PRO, Kew.
21. McLeave, 1961.
22. Wood, 1978.
23. Interview, 27 January 2000.
24. Letters from D. Stirling to M. Wood, 5 and 20 October 1953, file 9, UoY archive.
25. Letter from D. Stirling to M. Wood, 26 October 1953, file 9, UoY archive.
26. See Chapter 8.
27. *Architectural Review*, London, July 1960.
28. See Chapter 11.
29. See Chapter 14.
30. Greaves, 1969.
31. See Chapter 10.
32. Wraithe, 1959.
33. Johnston, 1971.

34. Hoe, 1992.
35. Ibid.
36. Letter from D. Stirling to M. Hill, 27 August 1953, file 44, UoY archive.
37. Letter from D. Stirling to CAS, Salisbury, undated 1953, file 44, UoY archive.
38. *East Africa and Rhodesia*, London, 13 and 27 August 1953; *New Commonwealth*, London, 14 September 1953; *AA Journal*, July/August 1953; *Daily Mail*, 28 July 1953.
39. Author of *Africans and British Rule* series, including *Lugard: The Years of Adventure, 1858–1889*, Collins, London, 1956 and *Lugard: The Years of Authority, 1898–1945*, Collins, London, 1960.

Chapter 5: New Hope in Africa

1. Letter from D. Stirling to M. Wood, 15 October 1953, file 10, UoY archive.
2. Letter from D. Stirling to R. Stratford, 15 October 1953, file 10, UoY archive.
3. *Capricorn Africa*, London, 1953, P. Mackay archive.
4. Paper by D. Stirling, September 1953, file DO35/4705, PRO, Kew.
5. CRO memos dated 17 and 24 October 1953, file DO35/4705, PRO, Kew.
6. CRO memo dated 9 November 1953, file DO35/4705, PRO, Kew.
7. From Intelligence Digest, No 179 of October 1953, file DO35/4705, PRO, Kew.
8. Letter from Gorrell Barns to Sir E. Twining and other governors, 21 December 1953, file DO35/4705, PRO, Kew.
9. Letter from G. H. Baxter, CRO to the High Commissioner, Salisbury, 29 January 1954, file DO35/4705, PRO, Kew.
10. Letter from I. M. R. Maclennan, High Commissioner in Salisbury, to G. H. Baxter, CRO, 6 February 1954, file DO35/4705, PRO, Kew.
11. Letter from British consul, New York, to the colonial attaché at the British embassy in Washington, 18 December 1953, file DO 35/4705, PRO, Kew.
12. Letter from D. Stirling to A. Stokes, 6 December 1953, file 12, UoY archive.
13. *Rhodesia Herald*, and others, 26 February 1954.
14. *East Africa and Rhodesia*, London, 18 February 1954.
15. *Rhodesia Herald*, Salisbury and *Star*, Johannesburg, 27 February 1954.
16. *Tanganyika Standard*, Dar es Salaam, 27 March 1954.
17. *Observer*, London, 1 April 1954.
18. *Truth*, London, 2 April 1954.
19. *East African Standard*, Nairobi, 30 April 1954.
20. *African Weekly*, Salisbury, 3 March 1954.
21. Letters from N. H. Wilson to the *Rhodesia Herald*, 27 February 1954 and 13 March 1954; *Bulawayo Chronicle*, 5 March 1954; *African Weekly*, 17 March 1954.
22. *Rhodesia Herald*, 16 March 1954.
23. *East Africa and Rhodesia*, 12 March 1954.
24. Letter from D. Stirling to A. Stokes, 28 September 1953, file 51, UoY archive.
25. Interview with L. Vambe, 4 August 1999.
26. Letter from D. Stirling to M. Wood, 8 April 1954, file 12, UoY archive.
27. Letter from D. Stirling to Sir Philip Mitchell, 22 July 1954, file 12, UoY archive.
28. Frost, 1992, p. 256.
29. Letter from D. Stirling to A. Stokes, 6 May 1954, file 12, UoY archive.
30. Minutes, 13–14 August 1954, file CA13/7/1/1, Zimbabwe National archives, Harare.
31. Interview with L. Vambe, 28 January 2000.

32. Letter from D. Stirling to Jeannine Scott, 25 March 1954, Mrs J. Bartosik archive.
33. Oldham, 1930.
34. Clements, 1999, p. 202.
35. Perham, 1960, pp. 658 and 675.
36. Cmd. 3234.
37. See Chapter 13.
38. Clements, 1999, p. 449.
39. Lines by Dr J. Oldham, Mrs J. Bartosik archive.
40. Clements, 1999, p. 236.
41. Ibid., p. 449.
42. Letter from D. Stirling to J. Baines, 22 April 1954, file 12, UoY archive.
43. Members were Philip Mason, Professor Mackenzie, Professor Adams, Marjery Perham, Walter Elliot, Arthur Creech-Jones, Sandy Fraser and others.
44. Letter from D. Stirling to Betty Couldrey, 26 July 1954, file 12, UoY archive.
45. Letter from D. Stirling to Betty Couldrey, 20 July 1954, file 12, UoY archive.
46. Letter from D. Stirling to J. H. Oldham, 21 September 1954, file 12, UoY archive.
47. Interview with L. Vambe, 4 August 1999.
48. Paper dated 10 November 1954, Mrs J. Bartosik archive.
49. Oldham, 1955.
50. File CO 822/450, 1955, PRO, Kew.
51. File CO 822/450, 1955, PRO, Kew.
52. Letter from Sir E. Baring to O. Lyttleton, 27 July 1954, file CO 822/450, PRO, Kew.
53. See Chapter 11.
54. *East Africa Royal Commission 1953–1955 Report*, Cmd 9475.
55. Ibid., Chapter 25.
56. See Chapter 8.
57. See Chapter 7.

Chapter 6: Outposts and Officers

1. Letter from D. Stirling to Jeannine Scott, 9 February 1955, Mrs J. Bartosik archive.
2. Letter from D. Stirling to Jeannine Scott, 26 October 1954, Mrs J. Bartosik archive.
3. Letter from D. Stirling to Jeannine Scott, 6 June 1955, Mrs J. Bartosik archive.
4. See Chapter 15.
5. CAS Minute Book, 5 September 1955, I. Hancock archive.
6. CAS Minute Book, 22 June 1955, I. Hancock archive.
7. Dulverton Trust Minute No 234, 1956.
8. Dulverton Trust Minute No 269, 1957.
9. CAS Minute Book, 23 April 1956, I. Hancock archive.
10. Hancock, n.d., I. Hancock archive.
11. Interview with L. Vambe, 4 August 1999.
12. Northern Rhodesia Tour Report, 14 June–9 July 1955 by C. Chipunza, P. Mackay archive.
13. Interview with P. Mackay, 29 January 2000.
14. File 124, UoY archive.
15. Letter from D. Stirling to Jeannine Scott, 9 February 1955, Mrs J. Bartosik archive.
16. *CAS Handbook for Speakers*, 1955, Question C 6.

17. Ibid., Question E 14.
18. Ibid., Question H 1.
19. Interview with the Duke of Richmond and Gordon, 19 February 1999.
20. See Chapter 8.
21. Hancock, n.d., I. Hancock archive.
22. Fisher, 1992, p. 183.
23. Letter from Dr Monica Fisher to the author, 20 April 1998.
24. Lamb, 1999.
25. Interview with R. Menzies, 19 March 1998.
26. R. Menzies, MSS memoir, p. 388.
27. Letter from R. Menzies to author, 1 July 1998.
28. R. Menzies, MSS memoir, p. 390.
29. Executive officers' activities report for 1955, P. Mackay archive.
30. See Chapter 15.
31. Letter from T. Bull to D. Acheson, 31 March 1994, author's archive.
32. Letter from D. Stirling to T. Tyrell, undated in 1955, file 10, UoY archive.
33. Letter from D. Stirling to R. Johnston, 2 November 1955, file 11, UoY archive.
34. See Chapter 11.
35. *Africa South*, March/June 1958.
36. Letter from K. Ward to P. Mackay, 21 October 1955, P. Mackay archive.
37. Letter from D. Stirling to R. Johnston, 6 May 1955, file 13, UoY archive.
38. See Chapter 8.
39. File CO 822/450, PRO, Kew.
40. Letter from D. Stirling to J. T. Lewis, 21 November 1955, file 48, UoY archive.
41. *East Africa and Rhodesia*, London, 31 May 1956.

Chapter 7: An Essential Difference

1. See Chapter 8.
2. Letter from D. Stirling to J. Lewis, 17 November 1955, file 48, UoY archive.
3. *Handbook for Speakers*, Question E 14, Capricorn Africa Society, 1955.
4. In conversation with the author, 10 October 1998.
5. Mason, 1984.
6. Capricorn Weekly Summary, 25 January 1958, file 4, UoY archive.
7. *Concord*, October 1956, and file CA9/5/1/12, ZNA, Harare.
8. Sir Thomas Chegwidden, 'Some Thoughts on the Electoral System', P. Mackay archive.
9. 'Voting and the Franchise', 1955, P. Mackay archive.
10. Note by P. Mackay, P. Mackay archive.
11. Papers from president's office, Salisbury, 27 December 1955, P. Mackay archive.
12. Report of the Commissioner appointed to Enquire into Methods for the Selection of African Representatives to the Legislative Council, 1955, Government of Kenya.
13. Coutts Report on African Electoral Systems, 1955, file CO822/929, PRO, Kew.
14. W Gorrell Barnes to SoS, CO, 17 September 1955, file CO822/929, PRO, Kew.
15. *The Times*, London, 29 December 1955.
16. Minutes of Nairobi Hughes committee, 30 April 1956, author's archive.
17. Quoted in Hoe, 1992.

18. 'The Salima Convention', *Kenya Weekly News*, Nakuru, 15 June 1956.
19. *Sunday Mail*, Salisbury, 17 June 1956.
20. *Illustrated London News*, 23 June 1956.
21. Letter from R. Hughes to J. Lewis, 10 August 1959, file 55, UoY archive.
22. See Chapter 16.

Chapter 8: Salima

1. *Kenya Weekly News*, Nakuru, 15 June 1956.
2. CRO minute dated 30 September 1953, file DO 35/4705, PRO, Kew.
3. CRO minute dated May 1954, file DO 35/4705, PRO, Kew.
4. CAS executive committee minutes, 26 March 1956, I. Hancock archive.
5. Letter from P. Mackay to D. Stirling, 19 March 1956, file CA9/1/1/1, ZNA, Harare.
6. Interview with J. Skinner, 22 July 1999.
7. Wood, 1964, pp. 95–8.
8. Kenya Weekly News, Nakuru, 29 June 1956.
9. Gibbs, 1961.
10. *Kenya Weekly News*, Nakuru, 29 June 1956.
11. A. Ross, 'Capricorn in Tanganyika, 1949–1958', 1975, I. Hancock archive.
12. Statement dated 5 June 1956, I. Hancock archive.
13. From the author's archive.
14. From the author's archive.
15. Letter from L. van der Post to A. Hoe, 29 September 1991, A. Hoe archive.
16. Jones, 2001, p. 255.
17. From the author's archive.
18. H. Crookenden, *National and English Review*, August 1956, London.
19. See Chapter 12.
20. *Kenya Weekly News*, Nakuru, 29 June 1956.
21. Mason, 1958.
22. Mason, 1984.
23. See Chapters 12–14.
24. See Chapter 9.
25. Hickman memo No 1, file CA/9/1/1/2, ZNA, Harare.
26. *Sunday Mail*, Salisbury, 17 June 1956.
27. Author of *Cry the Beloved Country*, 1948 and *Too Late the Phalarope*, 1953.
28. *Bantu Mirror*, Salisbury, 18 August 1956.
29. *Manchester Guardian*, June 1956.
30. *The Rhodesian*, Salisbury, 18 June 1956.
31. *Tablet*, London, 1956.
32. *Illustrated London News*, 23 June 1956.
33. *East African Standard*, Nairobi, 5 July 1956.
34. Ibid.
35. Ibid., 20 July 1956.
36. Huxley, 1935.
37. *Time and Tide*, London, June 1956.
38. See Chapter 16.

Chapter 9: Against the Odds in a Self-Governing Colony

1. Hickman memo No 1, file CA/9/1/1/2, ZNA, Harare.
2. Holderness, 1985.
3. Interview with P. Garlake in Harare, 7 February 2000.
4. Hickman memo No 1, file CA/9/1/1/2, ZNA, Harare.
5. File CA/13/7/1/1, ZNA, Harare.

6. File CA/13/7/1/1, ZNA, Harare.
7. Letter D. Stirling to Col A. S. Hickman, file CA/9/1/1/2, ZNA, Harare.
8. Letter D. Stirling to P. J. S. Mackay, P. Mackay archive.
9. Hickman memo No 1, file CA/9/1/1/2, ZNA, Harare.
10. Ibid.
11. Minutes of SR Executive, 7 January 1957, file CA/13/7/1/1, ZNA, Harare.
12. Letter from K. M. Stevens to Dr Dewe, Que Que, 8 January 1957, file CA/9/1/1/1, ZNA, Harare.
13. Hickman memo No 2, 22 January 1957, file CA/9/5/1/11, ZNA, Harare.
14. Letter from Dr Dewe to G. Savory, 5 February 1957, file CA/9/1/1/1, ZNA, Harare.
15. Letter from D. Hamilton to J. Lewis, 22 October 1957, file 56, UoY archive.
16. *Mail on Sunday*, London, 14 December 1986.
17. Letter from G. Savory to M. Wood, February 1957, file CA/9/1/1/1, ZNA, Harare.
18. Letter from A. Pilavachi to D. Hamilton, n.d., file CA9/1/1/1, ZNA, Harare.
19. Letter from J. R. Olivey to H. Amherst, October 1958, I. Hancock archive.
20. File CA9/6/1/5, ZNA, Harare.
21. Joint meeting of the Royal African Society and Royal Empire Society, 7 March 1957.
22. Mrs J. Bartosik archive.
23. See Chapter 12.
24. Letter from D. Stirling to H. Crookenden, 23 December 1957, file 48, UoY archive.
25. Unsigned letter on 'David Stirling' notepaper, 3 December 1957, file 48, UoY archive.
26. Letter from Jeannine Scott to the Countess of Dalhousie, 13 December 1957, Mrs J. Bartosik archive.
27. Letter from D. Stirling to H. Crookenden, 23 December 1957, file 48, UoY archive.
28. *Equinox*, Capricorn Africa Society, Salisbury, June 1958, I. Hancock archive.
29. Letter from P. Mason to the author, 2 September 1998.
30. Interview, 15 May 1998.
31. Letter from M. Wood to J. Lewis, 30 December 1958, file 47, UoY archive.
32. Letter from J. Lewis to M. Wood, 20 January 1959, file 47, UoY archive.
33. Letter from M. Wood to J. Lewis, 23 January 1959, file 47, UoY archive.
34. Letter from H. Amherst to Revd F. Rea, 26 April 1959, I. Hancock archive.
35. Minutes of central Africa branch AGM, 21 February 1959, file 48, UoY archive.
36. Annual report from executive officer, 27 February 1960, file 62, UoY archive.
37. *Rhodesian Herald*, 15 September 1958.
38. Report on conference held 5–6 September 1959, file 32, UoY archive.
39. Letter M. Wood to J. Lewis, 21 January 1960, file 47, UoY archive.
40. Letter from R. Hughes to J. Lewis, 2 February 1960, file 55, UoY archive.
41. Author's archive.
42. Press release, 21 January 1960, file 62, UoY archive.
43. Minutes of Southern Rhodesia branch AGM, 27 February 1960, file 36, UoY archive.
44. Letter from L. Takawira to J. Lewis, 4 March 1960, file 36, UoY archive.
45. See Chapter 13.
46. Report by L. Takawira, April 1960, I. Hancock archive.
47. CAS Newsletter, June 1960, file 43, UoY archive.

48. Letter from D. Stirling to L. Vambe, 13 July 1960, file 43, UoY archive.
49. Executive officer's report, 12 August 1960, I. Hancock archive.
50. Interview with P. Mackay, 5 February 2000 and letter from L. Takawira to D. Stirling, 18 November 1960, file 43, UoY archive.
51. Letter to the author, 1 August 1901
52. See Chapter 13.
53. See Chapter 16.
54. Chairman's report to AGM, 6 May 1961, I. Hancock archive.
55. See Chapter 16.
56. Executive committee minutes, 10 October 1963, I. Hancock archive.
57. Letter L. Takawira to Jennifer Plunket, 10 April 1970, Lady Plunket archive.
58. Press statement, 10 March 1964, I. Hancock archive.
59. See Chapter 13.
60. Fothergill, 1984, pp. 136–48.

Chapter 10: Action in East Africa

1. *East African Standard*, Nairobi, 16 July 1956.
2. Memorandum by M. Wood, 28 February 1957, author's archive.
3. See Chapter 15.
4. Frost, 1978.
5. *Kenya Weekly News*, Nakuru, 8 February 1957.
6. Letter from Sir Evelyn Baring to the SoS, 27 September 1957, file CO822/1802, PRO, Kew.
7. Wood, 1964.
8. Quoted in Chapter 5.
9. Letter from P. Marrian to D. Stirling, 28 October 1956, file 55, UoY archive.
10. *Rhodesia Herald*, Salisbury, 23 October 1956.
11. Letter E. Wilkinson to J. Lewis, 18 June 1957, file 50, UoY archive.
12. Letter from Susan Wood to E. Wilkinson, 1 July 1957, file 50, UoY archive.
13. Letter from R. Dick-Read to J. Lewis, undated (October) 1957, file 50, UoY archive.
14. Letter from R. Dick-Read to J. Lewis, undated (December) 1957, file 50, UoY archive.
15. Robert Dick-Read, *Sanamu*, Rupert Hart-Davis, London, 1964.
16. *Kenya Weekly News*, Nakuru, 26 July 1957.
17. Ibid.
18. Letter from A. Lennox-Boyd to Sir Evelyn Baring, 20 May 1957, file CO822/1802, PRO, Kew.
19. Quoted in *Kenya Weekly News*, Nakuru, 22 November 1957.
20. See Chapter 11.
21. Interview, 11 June 1999.
22. Clements, 1999.
23. Oldham, 1955, pp. 75, 76.
24. File CO/822/1750, PRO, Kew.
25. Karmali, 2002.
26. Author of *Race Against Time*, 1978 and *Enigmatic Proconsul*, 1978.
27. See Chapter 6.
28. Letter from A. W. Horner, Ministry of Education, Kenya, to Ford Foundation, NY, 1 October 1958, file CO822/1750, PRO, Kew.
29. Letter from W. A. C. Mathieson, Ministry of Education, to CO, 25 October 1958, file CO822/1750, PRO, Kew.
30. Letter from CO to R. W. Powers, US embassy, London, 29 October 1958, file CO822/1750, PRO, Kew.

31. Memo from Ministry of Education, Kenya, 18 November 1958, file CO822/1750, PRO, Kew.
32. Minute from Ministry of Education, Kenya, November 1958, file CO822/1750, PRO, Kew.
33. Letter from W. A. C. Mathieson, Ministry of Education, to CO, 3 January 1959, file CO822/1750, PRO, Kew.
34. Letter from W. A. C. Mathieson, Ministry of Education, to R. Hughes, copy to CO, 26 January 1959, file CO822/1750, PRO, Kew.
35. Letter from W. A. C. Mathieson to CO, February 1959, file CO822/1750, PRO, Kew.
36. Letter from W. A. C. Mathieson to CO, 6 October 1959, file CO822/1750, PRO, Kew.
37. Letter from M. Wood to Lord March, 31 March 1959, file 11, UoY archive.
38. Letter from Lord March to M. Wood, 15 April 1959, file 11, UoY archive.
39. Kultermann, 1963; *Architectural Review*, July 1960.
40. Wraithe, 1959.
41. Statement and letter from P. Mason to Susan Wood, 18 February 1959, Mrs J. Bartosik archive.
42. Letter from R. Hughes to J. Lewis, 19 February 1959, file 55, UoY archive.
43. See Chapter 11.
44. See Chapter 14.
45. See Chapter 16.

Chapter 11: Playing at Politics

1. File CO813/065, PRO, Kew.
2. Letter from Sir E. Twining to CO, February 1957, file CO813/065, PRO, Kew.
3. Letter from Sir E. Twining to SoS, November 1957, file CO822/1368, PRO, Kew.
4. Tanganyika Intelligence Summary, November 1957, file CO 822/1368, PRO, Kew.
5. Letter from D. Bryceson to D. Stirling, 18 August 1956, file 11, UoY archive.
6. Letter from D. Stirling to D. Bryceson, 1 February 1957, file 11, UoY archive.
7. Johnston, 1971.
8. Note dated February 1959, file CO 822/1370, PRO, Kew.
9. File CO 822/1338, PRO, Kew.
10. Letter from M. Wood to Lord March, 27 June 1959, file 11, UoY archive.
11. Report dated 6–31 July 1956, file CO822/844, PRO, Kew.
12. Memo by P. Mackay, 7 February 1956, file CA9/5/1/4, ZNA, Harare.
13. Author's archive.
14. Letter from D. Bryceson to J. Lewis, 11 April 1957, file 11, UoY archive.
15. Letter from P. Marrian to D. Stirling, 28 October 1956, file 42, UoY archive.
16. *Kenya Weekly News*, Nakuru, 5 October 1956.
17. CO minute by J. L. F. Buist, file CO/822/1422, PRO, Kew.
18. Special Branch report for 1–31 August 1956, file CO822/844, PRO, Kew.
19. File CO/822/844, PRO, Kew.
20. Minutes, 29 October 1956, author's archive.
21. Karmali, 2002.
22. File CO/822/1466, PRO, Kew.
23. Douglas-Home, 1978.
24. Blundell, 1964.
25. Circular letter from R. Hughes, 17 July 1957, author's archive.

26. File CO/822/2107, PRO, Kew.
27. Letter to SoS for the Colonies, 16 October 1957, author's archive.
28. CO minute dated 29 November 1957, file CO/822/1532, PRO, Kew.
29. Letter from M. Blundell to Joyce Raw, 19 November 1957, author's archive.
30. CO brief dated 17 February 1958, file CO/822/2107, PRO, Kew.
31. File CO/822/1309, PRO, Kew.
32. Letter from R. Hughes to J. Lewis, 16 January 1959, file 55, UoY archive.
33. Letter from R. Hughes to J. Lewis, 19 February 1959, file 55, UoY archive.
34. Memo 17 February 1959, file CO/822/1349, PRO, Kew.
35. Letter from R. Hughes to D. Stirling, 18 March 1959, author's archive.
36. Letter from Susan Wood to D. Stirling, copied to M. Wood, R. Hughes and E. Wilkinson, 28 March 1959, author's archive.
37. Blundell, 1964.
38. Letter from S. V. Cooke to R. Hughes, 3 April 1959, author's archive.
39. Letter from R. Hughes to J. Lewis, 7 April 1959, file 55, UoY archive.
40. Letter from F. H. Sprott to M. Blundell, 10 April 1959, author's archive.
41. Letter from M. Blundell to R. Hughes, 21 April 1959, author's archive.
42. Letter from R. Hughes to A. Jamindar, 17 August 1959, author's archive.
43. Letter from acting governor to CO, 24 December 1957, file CO/822/1426, PRO, Kew.
44. Licence to convene a meeting, 8 October 1959, author's archive.
45. Wood, 1960.
46. Letter from Elizabeth Couldrey to R. Hughes, 15 March 1999, author's archive.
47. Letter from Susan Wood to Jeannine Scott, 1 August 1959, file 55, UoY archive.
48. Minute dated 18 February 1959, file CO/822/1338, PRO, Kew.
49. Minute dated 18 November 1959, file CO/822/1345, PRO, Kew.
50. Letter from C. Janson to R. Hughes, 23 May 1959, author's archive.
51. Letter from Susan Wood and R. Hughes to D. Stirling, 2 June 1959, author's archive.
52. Letter from D. Stirling to R. Hughes, 29 April 1959, author's archive.
53. Paper by D. Stirling, dated 28 April 1959, Mrs J. Bartosik archive.
54. Letter from D. Stirling to R. Hughes, 22 May 1959, author's archive.
55. Letter from Jeannine Scott to Susan Wood, 28 May 1959, file 55, UoY archive.
56. Letter from D. Stirling to Susan Wood and R. Hughes, 12 June 1959, author's archive.
57. See Chapter 16.
58. Letter from Susan Wood to R. Hughes, 25 September 1959, author's archive.
59. Letter from D. Stirling to Lord March, 2 June 1960, file 52, UoY archive.
60. Letter from R. Hughes to C. Janson, 2 February 1960, file 55, UoY archive.
61. Kenya Police Special Branch report, 4 December 1960, file CO/822/2026, PRO, Kew.
62. Quoted in Huxley, 1985.
63. Brief for SoS, 6 April 1961, file CO/822/2228, PRO, Kew.
64. CO memo, 31 October 1961, file CO/822/2228, PRO, Kew.
65. Hunter, 1962.

Chapter 12: Education for Nationhood

1. See Chapter 14.
2. See Chapter 13.

3. 'Education for Citizenship in Africa', Colonial No 216.
4. Clements, 1999, p. 234.
5. Letter from E. Townsend-Coles to author, 13 April 1901.
6. Minutes SR branch executive committee, 12 September 1957, file CA9/5/1/13, ZNA, Harare.
7. H. Amherst, 'First thoughts on Capricorn Residential Schools', 30 July 1957, I. Hancock archive.
8. Letter from R. Dick-Read to J. Lewis, undated (*c.*23 September 1957), file 50, UoY archive.
9. D. Stirling, 'Proposals for the Future', 5 October 1957, I. Hancock archive.
10. Note dated 4 December 1957, Mrs J. Bartosik archive.
11. SR branch executive committee minutes, 18 January 1958, I. Hancock archive.
12. Study group reports, 8–12 April 1958, author's archive.
13. Dulverton Trust minute 303, 20 January 1958.
14. Letter from P. Fordham to author, 2 March 1999.
15. *The Times*, London, 3 July 1958.
16. *Kenya Weekly News*, Nakuru, 19 September 1958.
17. The College of Rhodesian Citizenship, Salisbury, 1958, I. Hancock archive.
18. *East African Standard*, Nairobi, 12 September 1958.
19. Hunter, 1962.
20. Dulverton Trust minute 355, 1958.
21. Letter April 1960, quoted in P. Wangoola thesis, 1980, P. Fordham archive.
22. 'Adult Education in the Federation of Rhodesia and Nyasaland and Kenya: Proposals for Colleges of Citizenship Report' by Mr and Mrs Guy Hunter, April 1959, author's archive.
23. Dulverton Trust minute 392, 1959.
24. Letter from R. Hughes to J. Lewis, 7 April 1959, file 101, UoY archive.
25. Dulverton Trust minutes 392 and 434, 1959.
26. Fordham et al., 1998.
27. Dulverton Trust minute 434, 1959.
28. Notes of meeting, 19 March 1959, file 25, UoY archive.
29. See Chapter 13.
30. Letter from G. Hunter to D. Stirling, 21 March 1960, file 101, UoY archive.

Chapter 13: Ranche House College

1. I. Hancock archive.
2. Kenneth Mew, 'Residential Adult Education: A Rhodesian Case Study', Institute of Adult Education, University of Rhodesia, September 1977, the Lady Plunket archive.
3. Letter from J. M. Gibbs to the author, 20 March 1901.
4. Interview with the Lady Plunket, 21 May 1998.
5. Memo from G. Hunter, 30 December 1958, file 25, UoY archive.
6. Letter from J. M. Gibbs to the author, 4 April 2001.
7. Conversation with J. M. Gibbs, 6 March 1901.
8. Letter from E. Townsend-Coles to the author, 13 April 2001.
9. Article in *Equinox*, 10 March 1960, by J. M. Gibbs.
10. Letter from J. M. Gibbs to Jeannine Scott, 8 May 1961, file 29, UoY archive.
11. Letter from J. M. Gibbs to the author, 20 March 2001.
12. Minutes of executive committee of CAS, 1 April 1963, ZNA, Harare.
13. Letter from J. M. Gibbs to the author, 22 March 2001.
14. Letter from J. M. Gibbs to the author, 22 March 2001.

15. Newsletter, 4 December 1961, quoted by K. Mew.
16. Letter from E. Townsend-Coles to the author, 13 April 2001.
17. Letter from J. M. Gibbs to J. Lewis, 11 June 1961, file 25, UoY archive.
18. Ranche House College brochure, 1962, J. M. Gibbs archive.
19. Letter from J. M. Gibbs to the author, 22 March 2001.
20. Memorandum to RHC executive committee, H. G. Pardey, October 1963, quoted by K. Mew.
21. Interview with P. Garlake in Harare, 7 February 2000.
22. Kenneth Mew, 'Residential Adult Education: A Rhodesian Case Study', Institute of Adult Education, University of Rhodesia, September 1977, the Lady Plunket archive.
23. Minutes of CAS executive committee, 10 October 1963, ZNA, Harare.
24. Monograph, RHC, *c.*June 1962, quoted by K. Mew.
25. Fothergill, 1984, p. 98.
26. Kenneth Mew, 'Residential Adult Education: A Rhodesian Case Study', Institute of Adult Education, University of Rhodesia, September 1977, the Lady Plunket archive.
27. Ibid.
28. E-mail from K. Mew to the author, 15 June 2001.
29. Fothergill, 1984, p. 105.
30. *Rhodesia Herald*, 21 March 1972, quoted by K. Mew.
31. Letter from Miss K. Ramushu to author, 9 November 1998.

Chapter 14: The College of Social Studies

1. Letter from W. J. D. Wadley to M. Capon, 19 May 1959, P. Fordham archive.
2. Minutes of the first board of governors, 7 May 1959, P. Fordham archive.
3. Memo dated 16 April 1959, file 101, UoY archive.
4. Memo, unsigned, June 1959, P. Fordham archive.
5. Letter from Lord Kilmaine to W. J. D. Wadley, 25 June 1959, P. Fordham archive.
6. Letter from P. J. Rogers to Sir Donald MacGillivray, 4 July 1959, P. Fordham archive.
7. Letter from W. J. D. Wadley to Lord Kilmaine, 5 August 1959, P. Fordham archive.
8. Letter from Lord Kilmaine to W. J. D. Wadley, 14 August 1959, P. Fordham archive.
9. Letter from R. E. Anderson to Lord Kilmaine, 22 August 1959, P. Fordham archive.
10. Letter from M. Wood to Lord Dulverton, 11 August 1959, P. Fordham archive.
11. Letter from P. J. Rogers to W. J. D. Wadley, undated, 1959, P. Fordham archive.
12. Letter from R. Hughes to Guy Hunter, 24 September 1959, author's archive.
13. Letter from R. Hughes to W. J. D. Wadley, 24 September 1959, author's archive.
14. Hunter, 1959.
15. Letter from Susan Wood to J. Lewis, 11 March 1960, file 101, UoY archive.
16. Letter from H. Wiltshire to R. Hughes, 8 July 1960, author's archive.
17. Report by H. Wiltshire, 14 May 1960, P. Fordham archive.
18. Letter from G. Hunter to J. Lewis and Jeannine Bartosik, May 1960, file 37, UoY archive.
19. Ken Mew, 'Residential Adult Education: A Rhodesian Case Study', Institute of

Adult Education, University of Rhodesia, September 1977, Lady Plunket archive.
20. Letter from R. E. Anderson to Lord Kilmaine, 10 August 1960, P. Fordham archive.
21. Maguire and Murray, 1965; *Church Buildings Today*, (London), January 1962.
22. Harold Wiltshire, 'Adult Education in Kenya: A Fresh Start by 1963', P. Fordham archive; Fordham et al., 1998.
23. Ibid.
24. Quoted in Fordham et al., 1998.
25. Minutes of directors, College of Social Studies, 26 June 1961, P. Fordham archive.
26. Letter from P. J. Rogers to H. Wiltshire, 14 November 1961, P. Fordham archive.
27. Letter from H. Wiltshire to Sir Philip Rogers (copy undated), P. Fordham archive.
28. Letter from Sir Philip Rogers to P. Fordham, 30 July 1962, P. Fordham archive.
29. Fordham et al., 1998, p. 24.
30. E. Townsend-Coles letter to the author, 13 April 2001.
31. Harold Wiltshire, 'Adult Education in Kenya: A Fresh Start', 1963, reprinted in *The Spirit and the Form*, 1976, University of Nottingham.

Chapter 15: The London Connection

1. J. Sutcliffe archive.
2. Letter from Jeannine Scott to D. Stirling, 22 August 1956, file 63, UoY archive.
3. Huddleston, 1956.
4. *Guardian*, 3 November 1966.
5. Dulverton Trust minute, November 1958, file 240.
6. Zebra newsletter, September 1962, author's archive.
7. Attached to a letter from T. Bull to D. Acheson, 26 May 1994, author's archive.
8. Conversation with the author, 5 October 2000.
9. J. Sutcliffe archive.
10. Obituary, *The Times*, 23 August 1900.
11. Charitable foundations fostered in Cheval Place, May 1965, J. Sutcliffe archive.
12. Draft letter from J. Lewis, January 1963, file 63, UoY archive.
13. 'Past History, Present Situation and Future Prospects', 2 December 1963, J. Sutcliffe archive.
14. See Chapter 16.
15. Zebra Newsletter, Summer 1972, J. Sutcliffe archive.
16. Minutes of Zebra House Council, May 1964, J. Sutcliffe archive.
17. See Appendix 1 for list of Zebra Trust and Housing Association Hostels.
18. Zebra Newsletter, Summer 1971, J. Sutcliffe archive.
19. Paper by O. Carruthers, 28 June 1967, J. Sutcliffe archive.
20. Paper from 3 Marloes Road, London, W8, by P. Comyns, June 1967, J. Sutcliffe archive.
21. The Zebra Trust Summer Newsletter, 1972, J. Sutcliffe archive.
22. Letter from Sheila Fullom to Sir Eric Norris, 20 August 1980, J. Sutcliffe archive.
23. Letter from J. Lewis to J. Sutcliffe, 22 July 1974, J. Sutcliffe archive.

24. Minutes of Zebra Trust executive committee, 25 September 1974, J. Sutcliffe archive.
25. Minutes of Zebra Trust executive committee, 23 July 1975, J. Sutcliffe archive.
26. Letter from Stella Goldman to J. Sutcliffe, copy to Lord Vernon, 23 September 1975, J. Sutcliffe archive.
27. Jeannine Bartosik's phrase.
28. Letter from P. de V. Carey to J. Lewis, 12 April 1978, J. Sutcliffe archive.
29. Paper to trustees from P. Comyns, 24 July 1978, J. Sutcliffe archive.
30. Paper by J. Lewis on negotiations with the Housing Corporation, 1974–79, 4 July 1979, J. Sutcliffe archive.

Chapter 16: The End in Africa

1. Minutes of council meeting in London, 13 November 1959, author's archive.
2. See Appendix 2 for dates of independence in Africa.
3. Hoe, 1992.
4. Hopkinson, 1962.
5. Letter from L. Vambe to D. Stirling, undated, file 29, UoY archive.
6. First principal of the College of Social Studies.
7. Letter from G. Hunter to Jeannine Scott and J. Lewis, May 1960, file 37, UoY archive.
8. Annual general meeting, 'Future Policy of the Kenya Branch', 11 September 1959, author's archive.
9. Letter from Susan Wood to chairman and executive committee, Kenya branch, 13 September 1959, file 55, UoY archive.
10. Letter from M. Wood to R. Hughes, *c.*June 1960, author's archive.
11. See Chapter 15.
12. Terms of reference: Report to General Council by J. Lewis, October 1960, author's archive.
13. Letter from J. Lewis to Jeannine Scott, 3 August 1960, file 37, UoY archive.
14. Letter from Susan Wood to Jeannine Scott, 30 August 1960, file 57, UoY archive.
15. Letter from J. Lewis to J. Sutcliffe, 3 October 1960, file 57, UoY archive.
16. Letter from Susan Wood to Jeannine Scott, 28 September 1960, Mrs J. Bartosik archive.
17. Letter from J. Lewis to J. Sutcliffe, early October 1960, file 57, UoY archive.
18. Letter from J. Sutcliffe to J. Lewis, 15 October 1960, file 57, UoY archive.
19. Letter from J. Sutcliffe to J. Lewis, 5 December 1960, file 57, UoY archive.
20. Memorandum on future policy by chairman of Kenya branch, 4 October 1960, author's archive.
21. Letter from E. Wilkinson to J. Lewis, 27 September 1960, author's archive.
22. Letter from F. Rea to Capricorn friends, 15 November 1960, author's archive.
23. Letter from R. Menzies to F. Rea, undated, author's archive.
24. Letter from C. Fisher to J. Lewis, undated, author's archive.
25. Central treasurer's report to general council, January 1961, author's archive.
26. London branch recommendations by Crookenden, Lewis, March, Jeannine Scott, Slessor, author's archive.
27. Supplementary note on future of London office, by Sir John Slessor, 11 January 1961, author's archive.
28. London branch recommendations, undated, author's archive.
29. Dissenting report of trustee L. van der Post, undated, author's archive.

30. Memorandum to general council of Capricorn by M. Wood, November 1960, author's archive.
31. Interview with Lady Wood, 27 January 2000.
32. Interview with J. Sutcliffe, 23 March 1998.
33. Letter from D. Stirling to M. Wood, 19 January 1961, author's archive.
34. Report of general council meeting, 21 January 1961, author's archive.
35. Minutes of general council meeting, 22 January 1961, author's archive.
36. Voting result general council, 24 February 1961, signed J. H. V. Sutcliffe, author's archive.
37. Minutes of Kenya branch executive committee, 3 March 1961, author's archive.
38. Hancock, 1978.
39. Letter from J. Lewis to T. Bull, 21 June 1962, file 100, UoY archive.
40. Letter from T. Bull to J. Lewis, 11 July 1962, file 100, UoY archive.
41. Letter from J. Lewis to F. Rea, file 64, UoY archive.
42. Letter from Susan Wood to R. Hughes, 2 May 1963, author's archive.
43. Letter from M. Wood to Jeannine Scott, 19 June 1963, Mrs J. Bartosik archive.
44. Letter from F. Rea to J. Lewis, 20 May 1962, file 35, UoY archive.
45. Letter from K. Mew to CAS members, 25 June 1965, I. Hancock archive.

Epilogue

1. Interview with J. Sutcliffe, 23 March 1998.
2. Letter from P. Mason to the author, 2 September 1998.
3. Interview with Susan Wood, 15 May 1998.
4. *Guardian*, 6 November 1990.
5. Letter from T. Ranger to the author, 10 August 2001.
6. Hoe, 1992.
7. Ibid., Chapter 18.
8. See Chapter 4.
9. Wood, 1987.
10. Ibid, Chapter 20.
11. Quoted in *The Times Magazine*, 30 March 2002.
12. Bayart et al., 1999.

References

Alport, C. J. M. (1952) *Hope in Africa*, London: Herbert Jenkins Ltd.

Bayart, J.-F., S. Ellis and B. Hibout (1999) *The Criminalisation of the State in Africa*, Oxford: James Currey.

Blundell, Michael (1964) *So Rough a Wind*, London: Weidenfeld & Nicholson.

Brookes, E. (1927) *History of Native Policy in South Africa*, Pretoria: J. L. van Shaik.

Caton-Thompson, G. (1931) *The Zimbabwe Culture*, Westport, USA: Greenwood Press (1970).

Clements, Keith (1999) *Faith on the Frontier*, Edinburgh: T & T Clark.

Cowles, Virginia (1958) *The Phantom Major*, London: Collins.

Dick-Read, Robert (1964) *Sanamu*, London: Rupert Hart-Davis.

Douglas-Home, Charles (1978) *Evelyn Baring: The Last Proconsul*, London: Collins.

East Africa Royal Commission 1953–1955 Report (1955) London: HMSO.

Fisher, Monica (1992) *Nswana: The Heir*, Ndola: Mission Press.

Fordham, P., J. Fox and P. Muzaale (1998) *A Chance to Change*, Leicester: NIACE with Intermedia.

Fothergill, Rowland (1984) *Laboratory for Peace*, Bulawayo: Louis Bolze.

Frost, Richard (1978) *Race Against Time*, London: Rex Collings Ltd.

Frost, Richard (1992) *Enigmatic Proconsul*, London: The Radcliffe Press.

Garlake, Peter (1973) *Great Zimbabwe*, London: Thames & Hudson.

Gibbs, Peter (1961) *Avalanche in Central Africa*, London: Arthur Barker Ltd.

Greaves, L. B. (1969) *Carey Francis of Kenya*, London: Rex Collings.

Hailey, Lord (1957) *An African Survey*, Oxford: Oxford University Press.

Hancock, I. R. (1978) 'The Capricorn Africa Society in Southern Rhodesia', *Rhodesian History*, vol. IX.

Hancock, I. (n.d.) *White Liberals, Moderates and Radicals in Rhodesia, 1953–1980*, London and Sydney: Croom Helm.

Hill, Mervyn (1949 and 1957) *Permanent Way*, vols I and II, Nairobi: EA Railways & Harbours.

Hoe, Alan (1992) *David Stirling*, London: Little Brown & Company.

Holderness, Hardwicke (1985) *Lost Chance*, Harare: Zimbabwe Publishing House.

Hopkinson, Tom (1962) *In the Fiery Continent*, Victor Gollancz Ltd.

Huddleston, Trevor (1956) *Naught for Your Comfort*, London: Collins.

Hunter, G. (1962) *New Societies of Tropical Africa*, London: Oxford University Press.

Huxley, Elspeth (1935) *White Man's Country*, vol. II, London: Chatto & Windus.

Huxley, Elspeth (1985) *Out in the Midday Sun*, London: Chatto & Windus.

Johnston, Erika (1971) *The Other Side of Kilimanjaro*, London: Johnson Publications Ltd.

Jones, J. D. F. (2001) *Storyteller*, London: John Murray.

Karmali, Joan (2002) *A School in Kenya: Hospital Hill 1949–1973*, Worcestershire: Square One.

Kultermann, Udo (1963) *New Architecture in Africa*, London: Thames & Hudson.
Lamb, Christina (1999) *The Africa House*, London: Viking.
Leakey, L. S. B. (1954) *Defeating Mau Mau*, London: Methuen & Company.
Lewis, W. A., Michael Scott, Martin Wright and Colin Legum (1951) *Attitude to Africa*, London: Penguin Books.
Lugard, F. D. (1893) *The Rise of our East African Empire*, London: Frank Cass & Co. Ltd (1968).
McLeave, Hugh (1961) *McIndoe: Plastic Surgeon*, London: Frederick Muller Ltd.
Maguire, R. and K. Murray (1965) *Modern Churches of the World*, London: Studio Vista and New York: E. P. Dutton.
Mason, Philip (1958) *The Birth of a Dilemma*, London: Oxford University Press.
Mason, Philip (1984) *A Thread of Silk*, London: Duckworth.
Oldham, J. H. (1930) *White and Black in Africa*, London: Longmans Green & Company.
Oldham, J. H. (1955) *New Hope in Africa*, London: Longmans Green & Company.
Paton, Alan (1948) *Cry the Beloved Country*, London: Penguin (1989).
Paton, Alan (1953) *Too Late the Phalarope*, London: Penguin.
Perham, Margery (1956) *Lugard: The Years of Adventure, 1858–1889*, London: Collins.
Perham, Margery (1960) *Lugard: The Years of Authority, 1898–1945*, London: Collins.
Prain, Ronald (1981) *Reflections on an Era*, Surrey: Metal Bulletin Books Ltd.
Stirling, David and N. H. Wilson (1950) *A Native Policy for Africa*, Salisbury: Capricorn Africa Society.
Tredgold, R. C. (1968) *The Rhodesia That Was My Life*, London: Allen & Unwin.
Vambe, Lawrence (1972) *An Ill-Fated People*, London: Heinemann.
Vambe, Lawrence (1976) *From Rhodesia to Zimbabwe*, London: Heinemann.
van der Post, L. (1952) *Venture to the Interior*, London: Hogarth Press.
van der Post, L. (1968) *A Walk with a White Bushman*, London: Chatto & Windus.
Wood, Michael (1978) *Go an Extra Mile*, London: Collins.
Wood, Michael (1987) *Different Drums*, London: Century Hutchinson.
Wood, Susan (1960) *Kenya: The Tensions of Progress*, Oxford: Oxford University Press.
Wood, Susan (1964) *A Fly in Amber*, London: Collins-Harvill.
Wraithe, R. (1959) *East African Citizen*, Oxford: Oxford University Press.

Index